Praise for David Horowitz

"A clear and ruthless thinker. What he says has an indignant sanity about it."

TIME

—

"An enormously important figure among American conservatives."

WEEKLY STANDARD

—

"Other writers of the New Left figured larger in the awareness of the general public, but no one in those days figured larger among the leftists themselves."

VILLAGE VOICE

—

"An independent, rigorous, outspoken political analyst."

PUBLISHERS WEEKLY

—

"Who is the Most Valuable Player of the Right? I could name many candidates, but I now present David Horowitz, who has heart, guts, brains, and a beautiful pen."

NATIONAL REVIEW

—

"He has done so much, and in so many different ways, that one might be justified in suspecting that 'David Horowitz' is actually more than one person."

NORMAN PODHORETZ

"An indefatigable pugilist in the culture wars."

—

"Folks sometimes say they find Horowitz irritating, but it's probably the feeling of irritation people get when the person about whom they're complaining is right most of the time."

—

"His prose is splendidly savage and invigoratingly rude. David Horowitz has a message to deliver, and if he offends someone in the process, that's just too bad."

—

"A vigorous writer and relentless polemicist."

—

"How about making David Horowitz head of the Republican National Committee for a year or so?"

—

"He has been exceptionally courageous and paid a price for it."

LEFT ILLUSIONS

LEFT

ILLUSIONS

An Intellectual Odyssey

DAVID HOROWITZ

edited, with an introduction by, Jamie Glazov

SPENCE PUBLISHING COMPANY • DALLAS
2003

Published in the United States by
Spence Publishing Company
111 Cole Street
Dallas, Texas 75207

Library of Congress Control Number: 2003111270

ISBN 1-890626-51-1

Printed in the United States of America

Contents

III

SECOND THOUGHTS

IV

REFLECTIONS ON RACE

V

THE GRAMSCIAN MOMENT

VI

PROGRESSIVE WITCH-HUNTS

Preface

F SCOTT FITZGERALD ONCE OBSERVED that American lives have
no second acts. The odyssey of David Horowitz refutes Fitzgerald's claim. Born into a communist family, Horowitz became one of the founders and intellectual leaders of the New Left in
the 1960s. Then, as the result of a tragedy that was both personal and
political, he became profoundly disillusioned with the radical movement and its social vision. In the 1980s he began a second career as a
conservative intellectual, establishing an educational center in Los
Angeles, writing a series of books, and launching several magazines
that played an influential role in the culture wars the 1960s had spawned.

Horowitz's first career as a left-wing intellectual is perhaps best
summarized by a hostile critic who once shared his political allegiances.
In a 1986 *Village Voice* article the writer Paul Berman wrote the first
public attack on Horowitz' political turn, which also provided a testament to Horowitz's shaping influence on 1960s radicalism. "Other writers of the New Left figured larger in the awareness of the general public,"
wrote Berman, "but no one in those days figured larger among the leftists themselves."[1] Two decades later, Jay Nordlinger, the managing editor of the conservative *National Review*, delivered this encomium: "Who
is the Most Valuable Player of the Right? I could name many candidates but I now present David Horowitz, the ex-radical leftist who has
the heart, guts, brains and a beautiful pen."[2]

But it is the words of cultural critic Camille Paglia which most fully articulate the unique position Horowitz has come to occupy in his post-conversion years. In the midst of one of the numerous controversies in which Horowitz had become embroiled, Paglia wrote: "I respect the astute and rigorously unsentimental David Horowitz as one of America's most original and courageous political analysts. He has the true 1960s spirit—audacious and irreverent, yet passionately engaged and committed to social change. . . . As a scholar who regularly surveys archival material, I think that, a century from now, cultural historians will find David Horowitz's spiritual and political odyssey paradigmatic for our time."[3]

It is because David Horowitz has led such a controversial and complex—and influential—career that an effort to provide an intellectual guide to his work is warranted. The pieces in the present volume have been selected to give an overview of his writings and thus to provide the first map of his intellectual development. The selections range from excerpts from his first book, published forty years ago, to his most recent writings on the war on terror. The pieces include political polemics, journalistic reportage, and reflective articles, along with select chapters from most of his books. They cover a broad range of issues, including the origins of the New Left, the Cold War, the fall of communism, the nature of political radicalism, race relations, the war on terror, the intellectual culture wars, and modern conservatism. Twenty-eight of the selections have not been published in book form before or are contained in texts that are generally unavailable. A bibliography of Horowitz's writings is provided at the end.

JAMIE GLAZOV

The Life and Work of David Horowitz

DAVID HOROWITZ WAS BORN IN FOREST HILLS, NEW YORK, on January 10, 1939. It was the year of the Nazi-Soviet non-aggression pact, which shattered the illusions of many communists and other members of the "progressive" left. Until then they had thought of themselves as "premature anti-fascists," but most were able to rationalize even this pact with the devil as a pragmatic "necessity." After all, they had already rationalized Stalin's purges, show-trials, and collectivization policies that had led to the deaths of millions in the 1930s, whose only crime was to present obstacles on the path to the socialist future.

For some, however, the Nazi-Soviet pact proved a disillusioning event that inspired them to abandon their progressive faith. The fact that they were able to have second thoughts and break with the authority of the Communist Party revealed that powerful as the utopian spell might be, a person of strong character could resist it. Perhaps the hand of fate is detectable in the coincidence that David Horowitz was born in that year.

Horowitz's parents had met in the Communist Party in the early 1930s. They were enthusiasts of what their son has described in his autobiography, *Radical Son,* as a "political romance," thinking of themselves as "secret agents" of the Soviet future.[1] Phil and Blanche Horowitz were humble schoolteachers who probably never broke a law, but did hope and work for a Soviet victory in the Cold War. For many Party members, like the Rosenberg spies, their identity as secret agents was, in fact, "a fantasy waiting to happen."[2]

Horowitz's early years were spent in a communist enclave in Queens called Sunnyside Gardens. As a child, he attended the Sunnyside Progressive School, a pre-kindergarten program the Party had set up and, as an adolescent, spent summers at a Party-run children's camp called "Wo-Chi-Ca," which was short for "Workers' Children's Camp."

In 1956, when Horowitz was seventeen, the Soviet leader Nikita Khrushchev delivered a secret speech about the crimes of Stalin to the Soviet Communist Party. The "Khrushchev Report," as it was subsequently called, was leaked by western intelligence agents to the public, causing a crisis in the international progressive movement. Many abandoned Soviet communism and resigned from the Party, while others decided to form a "new left," with which they hoped to rescue socialism from its stalinist fate. Paradoxically, instead of inspiring doubts about the socialist project, the Khrushchev revelations prompted New Leftists to be even more confirmed in their political faith. They no longer had to defend the indefensible and this allowed a sentiment to grow among them that "real" socialism was achievable, and that a new radical movement was about to be born.

Horowitz was a college freshman at Columbia University when these events took place. A young man who did not have to make political choices, he devoted himself to literary studies without drawing any hard conclusions from the Khrushchev-inspired political debate. In 1959 he graduated from Columbia, married his college sweetheart, and moved to California where he began graduate studies in English literature at the University of California at Berkeley. Meeting up with other "red diaper" babies on the Berkeley campus, he began to reignite the passions of his youth and actively joined in the effort to create a new left.

While becoming more and more immersed in radical politics, Horowitz continued his studies for a master's degree in English literature. He was an editor of a new magazine the activists created called *Root and Branch*, which was one of three publications that would help launch the 1960s left.[3] In 1962, he became one of the organizers of the first campus demonstration against the Vietnam War, and in that year he published *Student*, the first book to express the political vision of the emerging New Left.[4]

In this book, the young author portrayed the university as the symbol of an oppressive corporate culture, foreshadowing the New Left critiques and campus eruptions to come. In dedicating his book to Supreme Court Justice Hugo Black and stressing his commitment to democratic politics, he also crystallized a difference between the fledgling New Left and the old communist vanguard. Horowitz criticized the Soviet invasion of Hungary and equated it with America's intervention in Cuba, and he broke with economic determinism and the idea that socialism had to follow a centralized plan.[5] These deviations from the communist line prompted an attack on the new book from the reviewer in the *People's World*, the Party's west-coast organ.

Horowitz's intellectual work in these years reveals some of the roots of his ultimate rejection of socialism. His 1965 book *Shakespeare: An Existential View*,[6] for example, expresses some profoundly anti-utopian ideas. The book is divided into two parts, the first of which is called "Imagining the Real," a phrase taken from one of his philosophical models at the time, Martin Buber, a non-marxist socialist.

In this essay, Horowitz follows the hegelian idea that human existence is defined not just by what actually *is*, but also by what is potentially real. But following Shakespeare, "Imagining the Real" also explores the tension between this romance of the possible and the skeptical outlook, which constantly reminds us of the brute facts of an existence from which we cannot escape.

Even in its praise of hegelian romanticism, Horowitz's argument implies a very different kind of humanism than that which can be connected to marxism. For he endorses the view that values are created by human will, and therefore that consciousness also determines being: "Everywhere, value attends commitment. Where men do not address their condition in the fullness of its claim, their experience fails to cross the threshold of significance. For value can exist effectively only where there are men committed to it. It is the commitment of men to the possible, to what is loftier than their attainment, beyond what the present has achieved, that permits the realization of the potential whose seed is already there."[7]

Horowitz's argument in this text is particularly incompatible with his leftist outlook. Whereas marxism asserts that material conditions determine values and ideas, Horowitz argues for the existence of a spiritual dimension in which consciousness determines being and not the other way around. This amounts to a rejection of marxist materialism, even though at the time and in the flush of enthusiasm created by the notion of a "new" left, Horowitz was not aware of the implications of his ideas.

After publishing *Student*, Horowitz left California, taking his young family (the couple had a son in 1961) to England and then Sweden. Spending almost a year in Sweden, he wrote *The Free World Colossus*, a "revisionist" history of the Cold War. It was one of the first expressions of the New Left's view of an American "empire," and like all his leftist books was translated into several languages.[8] In America, *The Free World Colossus* became a handbook for the growing anti-Vietnam War movement, providing a litany of America's "misdeeds" abroad—the coups in Iran and Guatemala, the Bay of Pigs and Vietnam—that became a staple of left-wing indictments thereafter.[9]

Horowitz spent the years 1964-1968 in London, where he worked for the philosopher Bertrand Russell's "Peace Foundation" and came under the influence and tutelage of the marxist biographer of Stalin and Trotsky, Isaac Deutscher. In this environment, Horowitz's writing career as a New Left marxist flourished. He edited two books, *Containment and Revolution* and *Corporations and the Cold War* and, inspired by Deutscher, wrote *Empire & Revolution: A Radical Interpretation of Contemporary History*.[10] This work was a reinterpretation of marxism that offered a New Left perspective on imperialism, communism, and the Cold War. Heavily influenced by Deutscher and Trotsky, it represented Horowitz's effort to rescue socialism from its stalinist past and to reformulate a marxist theory that would account for Stalinism and yet still keep the prospect of a revolutionary future alive.

Returning to America in 1968, Horowitz became an editor at *Ramparts* magazine, the largest publication of the New Left. He also published a collection of his writings titled *The Fate of Midas and Other Essays*, which spanned a period of almost ten years in his intellectual development.[11] The essays attempted to integrate Keynesian economic theory with traditional marxist analysis, develop Marx's theory of social class, and assess the impact of the "corporate ruling class" on American foreign policy and intellectual life. The collection also featured personal appreciations of both Isaac Deutscher and Bertrand Russell and critiques of the Weather Underground and SDS.

These three books placed Horowitz at the intellectual center of the New Left, but a careful reading of *The Fate of Midas* reveals that he already stood outside radical orthodoxy in significant ways. Writing about Deutscher, Horowitz referred to "The Message of the Non-Jewish Jew,"[12] an essay in which Deutscher describes rejecting his orthodox upbringing and how he became a heretic to communism as well. Horowitz would eventually reprise his mentor's alienation. As Deutscher had become a heretic to communism, Horowitz would become a dangerous heretic to the New Left.

By 1969 the great hopes of the 1960s left had disintegrated in futile acts of violence and extremist rhetorical postures. Horowitz was gradually coming to realize that social engineers could not reshape human nature. But his loyalty to the cause prevented him from recognizing the implications of his thoughts. He now reflects,

> I pretty well realized even at that time that you couldn't sit everybody down and re-educate them, make them good parents and good citizens. This meant that you couldn't really remake the world as the left intended without totalitarian coercion. But it was much more difficult to accept the consequences of that realization. For a long time, I simply could not face the possibility that there was no socialist future, that I was not going to be a social redeemer, and that we didn't have the answers to humanity's problems—in short, that I wasn't part of an historic movement that would change the world.
>
> The difficulty of coming to terms with one's own insignificance —which is a consequence of this realization—is why so many leftists can never leave the faith and are leading the same lives they did thirty and forty years ago. To give up the progressive fantasy would be too great a blow to their *amour propre* and beyond that, their *raison d'etre*. When I look at my former comrades today, it is as though all that has happened to them and all they have wit-

nessed have had no effect on their expectations or illusions or real life choices. It's really quite sad.[13]

In the early 1970s, while Horowitz was editor of *Ramparts*, he was introduced to Huey Newton, the leader of the Black Panther Party for Self-Defense. The Panthers were a group of radical blacks that had made a point of carrying weapons in public and had been anointed the "vanguard of the revolution" by SDS leaders like Tom Hayden. They were supported and defended by the entire New Left. Now Newton announced that it was "time to put away the gun" and turn to community activities. Soon Horowitz found himself raising funds to purchase a church in Oakland's inner city, which he turned into a "learning center" for 150 Panther children. In 1974 he recruited his *Ramparts* bookkeeper, Betty Van Patter, to maintain the accounts of the tax-exempt foundation he had created to manage the school. In December 1974, the Panthers murdered Betty. This event had a traumatic impact on Horowitz, changing him and his politics forever.

The discovery of Betty Van Patter's bludgeoned body adrift in San Francisco Bay, threw Horowitz into a state of despair that was to last nearly a decade. The police knew who Betty's murderers were, but local prosecutors were unable to bring an indictment, and the federal government seemed decidedly uninterested in the killing of a white woman by radical blacks. The press, too, lacked any interest. This was the opposite of what progressives themselves constantly claimed: that "racist" law enforcement and a willing press were constantly witch-hunting militant blacks.

Pursuing his own inquiry into the murder, Horowitz was forced to confront three stark facts: his New Left outlook was unable to explain the events that had overtaken him; his lifelong friends and associates in the left were now a threat to his safety, since they would instinctively defend the Panther vanguard; and no one among them really cared about the murder of an innocent woman (even though they were people who made a point of their "social conscience") because the murderers were their political friends.[14]

To the mind of the left, even questioning the Panthers' role in Betty's fate reflected disloyalty to the cause, since such curiosity could lead to devastating criticism of the Panthers and by extension themselves. It would have been the same as implicating the socialist vanguard in the murder of innocents during the heyday of the communist regimes.

Thus, the death of Betty Van Patter forced Horowitz to look at the Panthers and the left in a way he had never allowed himself before. He realized that it was the enemies of the left who had been correct in their assessment of the Panthers (just as they had been correct in their assessment of the Soviet Union), while the left had been wrong. The Panthers were not victims of police repression because they were political militants. They were common criminals who were dangerous to others. It was the "revolution" that had conferred on them the aura of a political romance, which protected them from the consequences of their deeds.

As Horowitz considered how insignificant Betty's life was in the eyes of his comrades, he recognized a familiar historical reality being played out in the events of his own. Real human flesh and blood had been sacrificed on the altar of utopian ideals. A collusive silence had followed.

Having been forced to face the sordid reality of a political movement to which he had dedicated himself, Horowitz began to ask whether there was something rooted in marxism or in the socialist idea that had led to socialism's worldly horror. In so doing, the repentant revolutionary made a leap that others could not. He faced the possibility that his entire life until then had been based on a lie. He was willing, further, to connect what had happened to him to the crimes his parents' generation of the left had defended, and thus to accept the fact that there was no "new" left, and that his generation of radicals had repeated their parents' guilt: "It had been forty years since Stalin's purges. The victims were dead, their memories erased. They were unpersons without public defenders, expunged even from the consciousness of the living. Those who knew the truth had to keep their silence, even as I had to keep mine. If we actually succeeded in making a revolution in America, and if the Panthers or similar radical vanguards prevailed, how would our fate be different from theirs? Our injustice, albeit mercifully smaller in scale, was as brutal and final as Stalin's. As progressives we had no law to govern us, other than that of the gang."[15]

Everything Horowitz had previously believed, everything he had built his political life on, now crumbled before him. Like Whittaker Chambers, a figure of the previous generation, he began to experience a conversion. In a vignette that Horowitz wrote for the *New York Times Magazine* (which they predictably failed to print[16]) he recounted the stages of his metamorphosis: "Being at the center of a heroic myth inspired passions that informed my youthful passage and guided me to the middle of my adult life. But then I was confronted by a reality so inescapable and harsh that it shattered the romance for good. A friend— the mother of three children—was brutally murdered by my political comrades, members of the very vanguard that had been appointed to redeem us all. Worse, since individuals may err, the deed was covered up by the vanguard itself who hoped, in so doing, to preserve the faith."[17]

Abandoning this romance took a heavy toll on the writer, who had no choice but to shed the sides of his personality that demanded a belief in the utopian future. "Like all radicals," he wrote, "I lived in some fundamental way in a castle in the air. Now, I had hit the ground hard, and had no idea of how to get up or go on."[18]

Unlike his former comrades, who now shunned him, he refused not only to turn a blind eye to Betty's murder, but also to the mass murders that socialist ideals had spawned around the world. He perceived that just as his progressive friends were indifferent to Betty's death, so too the left as a whole had failed to reckon with the horrifying toll taken by communist-led and New Left-backed revolutions in Cambodia, Vietnam, and elsewhere. Radicals still considered themselves socialists, but simultaneously exonerated themselves from complicity in socialism's crimes.

In pursuing answers to Betty's death, Horowitz discovered that the Panthers had murdered more than a dozen people in the course of conducting extortion, prostitution, and drug rackets in the Oakland ghetto. And yet, to his growing bewilderment, the Panthers continued to enjoy the support of the American left, the Democratic Party, Bay Area trade unions, and even the Oakland business establishment. They were praised by prominent writers such as Murray Kempton and Garry Wills in the *New York Times* and by politicians like then-Governor Jerry Brown of

California, who was a political confidant of Elaine Brown (no relation), the Panther leader who had ordered Betty's death.

To Horowitz's surprise, the mainstream press also protected the killers; local media refused to cover the story. Horowitz began to realize that the establishment that shaped the culture and determined the parameters of political discourse was sympathetic to the left rather to than the ruling class interests that marxism had postulated.

Notwithstanding the media blackout and the silence of the Panthers' supporters, the details of their crimes have surfaced over the years principally as a result of Horowitz's efforts. The first notice of what had happened was a courageous article in *New Times* magazine by a left-wing journalist named Kate Coleman, whom Horowitz had approached and provided with information.[19] In a 1986 piece in the *Village Voice*, Horowitz himself identified the Panthers as Betty's killers,[20] and in *Radical Son*, which appeared in 1997, Horowitz gave a detailed account of his Panther experience and Betty's death.

These efforts had an impact even on some of the Panther survivors. In his last televised interview on *60 Minutes*, Eldridge Cleaver, the former Black Panther "minister of information," admitted the brutal ruthlessness of his comrades and himself. "If people had listened to Huey Newton and me in the 1960s, there would have been a holocaust in this country," he said. Years later, former Panther chairman Bobby Seale also made a public confession about Panther criminality and specifically acknowledged that the Panthers had murdered Betty Van Patter.[21]

But for the most part, progressive keepers of the historical record were determined to take their secrets to the grave. SDS leader and later California State Senator Tom Hayden and *Los Angeles Times* journalist Robert Scheer, who worked with the Panthers and promoted their agendas have never written a word about Panther crimes in the thirty years since. Former SDS president Todd Gitlin's history of the 1960s fails to acknowledge Panther criminality or mention Betty Van Patter, or the murders of police officers for which the Panthers and other leftist groups were responsible.[22] Like other New Left historians, when Gitlin deals with the Panthers, he presents them as abused victims who sometimes

were driven to indefensible (but unspecified) acts because of their persecution. In Kenneth O'Reilly's *Racial Matters: The FBI's Secret File on
Black America, 1960-1972,* the Panthers do no wrong and are the targets
of legal genocide.[23] Other academic works follow this pattern familiar
from progressive silences of the past.

In his essay "Still No Regrets," Horowitz writes, "A library of memoirs by aging new leftists and 'progressive' academics recall the rebel-
lions of the 1960s. But hardly a page in any of them has the basic honesty
—or sheer decency—to say, 'Yes, we supported these murderers and
those spies, and the agents of that evil empire,' or to say so without an
alibi. I'd like to hear even one of these advocates of 'social justice' make
this simple acknowledgement: 'We greatly exaggerated the sins of
America and underestimated its decencies and virtues, and we're
sorry.'"[24]

In accepting responsibility for what the left did, Horowitz is almost alone among its public intellectuals. Only a handful of others,
including Peter Collier, Eugene Genovese, and Ronald Radosh have
taken his path.

The journey from left to right, of course, had been made before.
But Horowitz's conversion took on a somewhat different and more acute
character than those of the ex-communists who had traveled to the
right before him. Unlike the contributors to *The God That Failed,*[25]
most of whom remained socialists, Horowitz made a comprehensive
break with the radical *Weltanschauung.* This was because Horowitz's
"conversion" was actually his second. The first was his break from communism after Khrushchev's revelations, while the second was from the
socialist idea itself.

His comrades who remained on the left continued to believe that
the idea could succeed by transcending the failures of "actually existing
socialism." This was the disposition shared by the writers of *The God
That Failed.* For them, Stalinism was a socialist aberration. For Horowitz,
the roots of Stalinism—of totalitarianism—lay in socialism itself.

Thus, in his momentous personal journey, Horowitz moved from
Communist[26] to New Leftist to a conservative position in which he
rejected the utopian idea. His odyssey would cause him to see the left
from a unique perspective, enabling him to make an important contri-

bution to its historiography in the works he subsequently wrote. In particular, Horowitz played a seminal role in rescuing the history of the New Left from the distortions of leftist historians who had come to dominate the academic profession.

After Betty's murder, Horowitz ceased his radical activism and his political writing for most of the following decade.[27] Silence about politics became his refuge, as he painstakingly reassessed his life and outlook. He was already involved in a project with Peter Collier to complete a multi-generation biography of the Rockefeller family. In 1975, *The Rockefellers: An American Dynasty* appeared to widespread acclaim, including a front-page rave in the *New York Times Book Review*. It became a bestseller and its success led to a series of other books—*The Kennedys: An American Drama* (1984), *The Fords: An American Epic* (1987), and *The Roosevelts: An American Saga* (1994).[28] These works earned Collier and Horowitz praise from the *Los Angeles Times* as "the premier chroniclers of American dynastic tragedy."

During this period, Horowitz also wrote *The First Frontier, The Indian Wars & America's Origins: 1607-1776* (1978),[29] a book which remained somewhat within the parameters of the leftist outlook, while attempting to establish the idea that a nation's character, as defined in its early history, shaped its destiny.

While he was at work on this book, events in Southeast Asia were writing a final chapter to the narrative that had defined his own generation. After the communist victory in Vietnam in 1975, the North Vietnamese began executing tens of thousands of South Vietnamese and setting up "re-education camps." The general repression prompted an exodus of two million refugees, unprecedented in the history of Vietnam. Hundreds of thousands of South Vietnamese boat people perished in the Gulf of Thailand and in the South China Sea in their attempt to escape the communist new order that the efforts of the New Left had helped to bring about.

In Cambodia, the victory of the communists led to the slaughter of some three million Cambodian peasants.[30] More peasants were killed in Indochina in the first three years of communist rule than had been killed on both sides during the thirteen years of the anti-communist war. Horowitz later reflected on the cause of these events:

Every testimony by North Vietnamese generals in the postwar years has affirmed that they knew they could not defeat the United States on the battlefield, and that they counted on the division of our people at home to win the war for them. The Vietcong forces we were fighting in South Vietnam were destroyed in 1968. In other words, most of the war and most of the casualties in the war occurred because the dictatorship of North Vietnam counted on the fact Americans would give up the battle rather than pay the price necessary to win it. This is what happened. The blood of hundreds of thousands of Vietnamese, and tens of thousands of Americans, is on the hands of the anti-war activists who prolonged the struggle and gave victory to the Communists.[31]

As the Indochinese tragedy unfolded, Horowitz was struck by how the left was unable to hold itself accountable for the result it had willed—a communist victory—and how it could not have cared less about the new suffering of the Vietnamese in whose name it had once purported to speak. He became increasingly convinced, as his friend and colleague Peter Collier had tried to persuade him, that "the element of malice played a larger role in the motives of the left than I had been willing to accept."[32] If the left really wanted a better world, why was it so indifferent to the terrible consequences of its own ideas and practices?

The more I thought about the moral posturing of the Left . . . the more I saw that its genius lay not in reforms but in framing indictments. Resentment and retribution were the radical passions. In *The Eighteenth Brumaire*, Marx had invoked a dictum of Goethe's devil: "Everything that exists deserves to perish." It was the progressive *credo*. To the left, neither honored traditions nor present institutions reflected human nature or desire; the past was only a dead weight to be removed from their path. When the left called for "liberation," what it really wanted was to erase the human slate and begin again in the year zero of creation. Marxism was indeed a form of idolatry, as Berdyaev had written, and the Creator/Destroyer that the left worshipped was itself.[33]

Horowitz's reference to Nicholas Berdyaev was indicative of the course that his own anti-radical philosophy had taken. After the Russian Revolution of 1905, Berdyaev wrote that communism was a form of idolatry in which the radical vanguard worshipped themselves as gods. Like the inhabitants of Babel, the communists proposed to build a tower to heaven. Berdyaev warned that, in perpetrating this dangerous spiritual crime, communists had unleashed demons they would be unable to control. In the attempt to build heaven on earth, marxists would inevitably create a hell. Berdyaev's prophetic vision of marxism became a central component in Horowitz's new outlook.

In 1979, Horowitz wrote a column for the *Nation* titled, "A Radical's Disenchantment." It was the first public statement by a prominent New Leftist that the New Left had anything to answer for. "A Radical's Disenchantment" described his disillusion with the left, referring to many of the horrors that socialism had produced. Horowitz also confronted the silence with which the left had met these horrors, ending the piece with questions he had been asking himself: "Can the left take a really hard look at itself—the consequences of its failures, the credibility of its critiques, the viability of its goals? Can it begin to shed the arrogant cloak of self-righteousness that elevates it above its own history and makes it impervious to the lessons of experience?"[34]

He already knew, however, the answer was no. In November 1984, Horowitz turned another corner. He cast his first Republican ballot for Ronald Reagan. On March 17, 1985, he and Collier wrote a front-page story for the Sunday magazine of the *Washington Post*, "Lefties for Reagan," and explained their vote.[35] As they certainly expected, the article inspired vitriolic responses from their former comrades and forced them to re-enter the political arena to respond.

Dissecting the left's hypocrisy now became a Horowitz *métier*. "I guess you could say," he reflected recently, "that it was the ferocity of my loyalty to the principles of socialism that translated into the ferocity of my attack on the left for betraying those principles."[36] A former believer in the left's political romance, Horowitz could attack the progressive myth with the familiarity of an insider. He and Collier delivered their first stunning blow in *Destructive Generation: Second Thoughts*

About the Sixties,[37] a 1989 book in which they analyzed the legacy of the New Left and its corrosive effects on American culture.

Destructive Generation represented the first dissent from the celebration of the 1960s that had been issuing forth in volume after volume from the left itself. For a long time *Destructive Generation* remained the only critical work on the radicalism of the decade. In a summary indictment, the authors charged that the left had steadfastly refused to make a balance sheet of what it had done. Progressives who prided themselves on their "social conscience," showed no concern with the destructive consequences of their acts on ordinary people like the Vietnamese and Cambodian peasants who had been slaughtered in the wake of America's forced withdrawal.

In the course of identifying the left's historical amnesia, the authors themselves became victims of a kind of amnesia socially constructed by the left. The book's publication marked their eclipse in the literary culture, which their adversaries and their allies now dominated. Once their political turn became clear, the celebrated pair were marginalized. As Horowitz recalls, "after *Destructive Generation*, we were finished in the literary culture. Christopher Lehmann-Haupt, the chief reviewer at the *New York Times*, who had called *The Fords* 'an irresistible epic' turned on us and described us as 'extremists' because we had voted for George Bush. [Years later, the same reviewer wrote a laudatory *Times* obituary for the communist intellectual Herbert Aptheker, without mentioning his role in the Party or his book defending the Soviet invasion of Hungary.] Our books, once prominently reviewed everywhere, were now equally ignored. With a few notable exceptions, we became pariahs and unpersons in mainstream intellectual circles."[38] It reminded him of Bertolt Brecht's cynical comment that no matter how bad communism might be, he would remain a communist so that his works would be produced after he was dead.

Horowitz's next work was an autobiography, *Radical Son*, published in 1997, and immediately recognized as the most important literary memoir by anyone from the 1960s generation. *Radical Son* has earned a place among the best in the genre of ex-revolutionary literature, a company that includes Chambers' *Witness*, Arthur Koestler's *Darkness at Noon*, and George Orwell's *Animal Farm*. The author's achievement prompted George Gilder to call his book "the first great American autobiography of his generation."

In this memoir the author was able to provide an account of his life, the details of which were already being distorted by his enemies, and to describe the intellectual process of his political conversion. Like Whittaker Chambers' classic, *Witness*, Horowitz's memoir is eloquent and riveting, and provides a cogent moral and intellectual context for his change of heart. *Radical Son* even goes beyond *Witness* in one important respect: it engages in a fearless examination of self, which is almost unprecedented in political memoir. A by-product of his candor is that Horowitz is able to illuminate the connection between human neuroses and the marxist dream.

By going further than any previous narrative in demonstrating how deeply the marxist fairy tale is entwined with the character and psychology of its believers, Horowitz reveals the seductive power of the progressive faith. He shows how the socialist lie reaches into every corner of its believer's soul. He makes clear why the break from radicalism can be a personally devastating decision.

Horowitz's fall from utopian grace was much darker and much steeper than that of many who went before him. This was because, unlike many of those who embarked on the journey from left to right, he made a *complete* break with his past. As already noted, while the writers in *The God That Failed* broke with communism, they did so only in the narrow political context of moving from Stalinism to "democratic socialism." Chambers was different again; he had a sense of the religious dimension of the utopian dream, but even he did not articulate a comprehensive break with the radical *Weltanschauung* in the way Horowitz did, or produce a conservative response to radical themes. Norman Podhoretz, who was never as far to the left as Horowitz, has commented on this aspect of Horowitz's work: "He differs from some of the other 'second-thoughts' generation in having pulled no punches and in having broken more decisively than some of them with left-wing pieties—whether liberal or socialist. None of the older bunch ever became really pro-American or pro-capitalist in becoming anti-communist. We older types (Irving Kristol and I, for example) did, and so have David and some others."[39]

Horowitz's next book was *The Politics of Bad Faith*,[40] a collection of six essays published in 1998 that provided what he called "an intellectual companion piece" to *Radical Son*. The book builds on *Radical Son*'s attempt to understand the psychological roots of radicalism and to deconstruct marxism's historical vision and false logic.

A central theme of the book is the refusal of radicals to accept the implications of the collapse of communism for the future of the socialism. "For radicals, it is not socialism, but only the language of socialism that is finally dead. To be reborn, the left had only to rename itself in terms that did not carry the memories of insurmountable defeat, to appropriate a past that could still be victorious."[41] Thus leftists now call themselves "progressives," "post-modernists," and even "liberals."

The second chapter, "The Fate of the Marxist Idea," is arguably the most powerful essay Horowitz has written.[42] An autobiographical segment, it takes the form of letters to two former radical friends. The first, titled "Unnecessary Losses," is to Carol Pasternak Kaplan, a friend since childhood who refused to attend his father's memorial service because Horowitz had abandoned the cause. As Horowitz notes, "In the community of the left—it is perfectly normal to erase the intimacies of a lifetime over political differences."[43]

Horowitz illuminates the way in which devotion to the political *idea* ties radicals together rather than love for "the people" or any other human connection. He does this by describing his haunting ordeal in attending his father's memorial:

> The memories of the people who had gathered in my mother's living room were practically the only traces of my father still left on this earth. But when they finally began to speak, what they said was this: *Your father was a man who tried his best to make the world a better place...* And that was all they said. People who had known my father since before I was born, who had been his comrades and intimate friends, could not remember a particular fact about him, could not really remember *him*. All that was memorable to them in the actual life my father had lived—all that was real—were the elements that conformed to their progressive Idea.[44]

The way these friends were in some profound way never really connected to his father beyond their shared political agendas, was exactly the way Carol was never connected to him. After a lifelong friendship, he had ceased to exist for her because he was no longer connected to her through belief in the progressive idea.

The second letter, which was to the English socialist Ralph Miliband, entitled "The Road To Nowhere," examined the Soviet experience, the refuted positions of the New Left, and the bad faith arguments through which the New Left proposed to rescue its blighted dreams: "Wherever the revolutionary left has triumphed, its triumph has meant economic backwardness and social poverty, cultural deprivation and the loss of political freedom for all those unfortunate peoples under its yoke. This is the real legacy of the left of which you and I were a part. We called ourselves progressives; but we were the true reactionaries of the modern world."[45]

The third essay, "The Religious Roots of Radicalism," analyzes the messianic dimensions of socialism going back to the Kabbalistic doctrine of *tikkun olam* and the "false messiah," Shabbtai Zvi. The author illuminates how the left's social melodrama is a secular version of traditional Judeo-Christian eschatology. In the secular utopian vision there is also a Fall from an ideal communal state, a journey through a vale of suffering and tears, and a road to redemption. But because it is secular and depends on human agencies, the socialist redemption invariably leads to social disaster.

In a fourth essay, "The Meaning of Left and Right," Horowitz attempts to provide a paradigm for reinterpreting the history of the last two hundred years in light of the failure of all socialist dreams. He argues that the negative result of two hundred years of socialist efforts means that from its beginnings the modern revolutionary left cannot be regarded as a "progressive" force, but one that is destructive and reactionary. Consequently, the categories of historical interpretation need to be revised: "The divisive crusades of the left and its failed 'experiments' must be seen now for what they are: bloody exercises in civil nihilism; violent pursuits of empty hopes; revolutionary *actes gratuites* that were doomed to fail from the start."[46]

The fifth essay, "A Radical Holocaust," examines how the post-communist left has revived the marxist paradigm applying it to sexual orientation, gender, and race. Horowitz calls this maneuver "kitsch marxism" and in this chapter reveals how the left has revived the destructive force of the original paradigm as well. Along with his co-author Peter Collier, Horowitz wrote one of the early articles on AIDS (reprinted in this volume as "Political Origins of An Epidemic" [47]). In the piece, written for *California Magazine*, they reported the manipulation of the crisis by radical groups in San Francisco in the service of ulterior political agendas.

In "A Radical Holocaust," Horowitz shows how the theory of "gay liberation" prompted leaders of the gay community to oppose traditional public health methods for combating disease and in the process produced a public health disaster: "I think that the AIDS catastrophe is a metaphor for all the catastrophes that utopians have created. It's about the delusion that thinking can make it so, that an abstract idea can be imposed on reality, that the laws of nature can be defied with impunity. The story of the AIDS epidemic reveals how powerful the leftist idea remains and how far reaching is its impact." [48]

The Politics of Bad Faith remains the only book written after the fall of the Berlin Wall that systematically confronts the arguments of the left with the history that refutes them. Not surprisingly, the left has ignored it. "The failure of the left to respond to this book," Horowitz comments wryly, "is just one more evidence of its bad faith." [49]

Horowitz's next book, *Hating Whitey and Other Progressive Causes*, appeared the following year and quickly turned into the most controversial work the author had written, putting him into a national spotlight. [50] Embarrassed by the defeat of Soviet communism, leftists changed their language and tactics, putting class hatred on the back burner and turning to racial combat instead. *Hating Whitey* took its name from a trait Horowitz had discerned in African-American radicals and leftists in general — a loudly professed prejudice against white people as the new "class enemy." [51] The new radical mindset demonized white males specifically and saw them as an ersatz ruling class (or —more accurately—caste) responsible for every social disparity between racial groups and genders.

Hating Whitey deals with the racial component in kitsch marxism. The author shows how leftists propose themselves as opponents of racism, when in fact their agenda is not about racism at all, but about subverting the *status quo* social order. In the absence of real racists in university admissions offices, the left created a myth—"institutional racism"—that is alleged to explain all disparities in university admissions. The creation of this myth is essential to keep alive "the discredited marxist idea that an alien power separates the citizens of democratic societies into rulers and ruled, the dominant race and the races that are oppressed."[52] Behind the doctrine that all blacks are victims lies the agenda of sustaining the marxist paradigm and its social war.

Just as the racial struggle represents the continuation of the marxist battle by other means, so does the gender war. Horowitz has analyzed this phenomenon in a short essay, "V-Day, 2001" (which is included in this volume), that discusses demonstrations sponsored by Jane Fonda in 2001.[53] It was an effort by feminists across the country to transform Valentine's Day, a millennia-old celebration of romance and friendship, into "Violence Against Women Day," a mass indictment of men. Horowitz shows that, like all radical faiths, the V-Day religion is rooted in resentment and hate. "Those who are saved are saved only because others are damned." Adding race, gender, and sexual orientation to "the struggle," kitsch marxism is able to identify even more social "enemies" and to ascribe more inequalities to the society under attack.

In an article not included in this volume, "Up From Multiculturalism," Horowitz analyzed another post-communist radical doctrine. Like socialism, "multi-culturalism [is] an invention of well-fed intellectuals. It did not well up from the immigrant communities and ethnic 'ghettoes' of America as an expression of cultural aspirations or communal needs. Instead it was manufactured by veterans of the Sixties left, who had established a new political base in the faculties of the universities." In the new multicultural version of the radical vision, racial and ethnic status replace class status as a political trump card. Horowitz points out that emphasizing ethnic identity over class solidarity situates the multicultural left squarely in the tradition of classic European fascism. Intellectually, as he writes in his essay, the postmodern left "owes more to Mussolini than to Marx."[54]

In a pair of recent books, Horowitz has turned his writing talents to providing advice to conservatives on political tactics. In *The Art of Political War and Other Radical Pursuits* (2000)[55] and *How To Beat the Democrats and Other Subversive Ideas* (2002), Horowitz proposes to take the techniques of political combat he learned on the left and apply them to the task of defeating the left. These books have been commended by White House political strategist Karl Rove, who called the first "the perfect guide to winning on the political battlefield," and by House Majority leader Tom DeLay, who recommended the second to "every Republican who wants to win."

The Art of Political War and Other Radical Pursuits reformulates Clausewitz's famous dictum and describes politics as "war continued by other means." According to Horowitz, conservatives often fail to understand that there is a political war at all, or disapprove of the fact that there may be one. The conservative paradigm is based on individualism, compromise, and partial solutions, and regards politics as a management issue, an effort to impose limits on what government may do. This puts conservatives at a disadvantage in political combat with the left, whose paradigm of oppression inspires missionary zeal and is perfectly suited to aggressive tactics and no-holds-barred combat.

Horowitz advises conservatives that at the center of America's imaginative life is a romance of the underdog. A party that presents itself as a champion of the vulnerable has a tactical advantage in the political struggle. He recommends that conservatives turn the tables on the left, framing "liberals" and "progressives" as oppressors of minorities and the poor. This is not only a tactically indicated move but is substantively grounded as well. Since Democrats and political leftists have for fifty years controlled the councils of every major city in America, including their schools, they are responsible for everything that is wrong with inner cities that public policy can affect. This target is ripe for conservatives to attack.

In the spring of 2001, Horowitz put his own tactical advice into action by attempting to take out ads in college newspapers across the country calling the campaign to pay slave reparations to black Americans who had never been slaves a "racist idea" that was bad for African Americans themselves because its principle effect was to alienate them from other Americans. Forty college newspapers refused to print the ad, generating a furor over free speech. Donald Downs, a liberal political scientist at the University of Wisconsin summed up the reaction: "The Horowitz controversy has laid bare the cultural and intellectual splits that rivet the contemporary university."[56] Horowitz later described these events in his next book, *Uncivil Wars: The Controversy over Reparations for Slavery* (2001). While making the case against reparations, *Uncivil Wars* also drew a vivid portrait of the state of American universities in the era of "political correctness."

Horowitz has been strikingly successful in exposing the left's agenda, and describing its control of the commanding heights of American culture. In this context, it is crucial to point out that the left's prominence in the literary culture has affected almost everything Horowitz does—the amount of time he has had to devote to building his own platform as a public intellectual; the way this has forced him to conceive his later books as hybrid collections usually with a long thematic essay to shape the volume; and the way he has had to define himself as a writer under attack.

One exacerbating factor in these attacks was that they were often launched from the institutional heights of the mainstream culture, which made them difficult to respond to since Horowitz now lacked access to a platform in that culture. Thus an ignorant but damaging aside by Gary Wills in a *Time* magazine cover story on the Sixties to the effect that Collier and Horowitz were "marginal" figures in the decade could not be answered. An irresponsible slander by *Time* columnist Jack White, who called Horowitz a "bigot," was allowed to stand, despite the embarrassment of *Time*'s managing editor, who was familiar with Horowitz's work and to whom Horowitz appealed.[57] A malicious insinuation by Jacob Weisberg that Horowitz was a closet McCarthyite in the *New York Times Magazine*[58] could not be replied to, and so forth.

Another factor to deal with was the vitriol of the hard left, along with its contempt for indisputable facts. When Horowitz dissected some writing by MIT Professor Noam Chomsky,[59] Chomsky responded in an online venue, "I haven't read Horowitz. I didn't used to read him when he was a stalinist and I don't read him today." Chomsky's claim was false on all counts. First, he knew that Horowitz's "Stalinism" was an accident of birth and that as an adult Horowitz had been an outspoken and visible *anti*-stalinist. Second, Chomsky had not only read Horowitz's work as a leftist but had admired it. Horowitz's *Ramparts* article, "Sinews of Power,"[60] is even cited in Chomsky's book *Problems of Knowledge and Freedom*.[61] Third, after Horowitz published "A Radical's Disenchantment," his farewell to the left, Chomsky sent him two nasty letters, consisting of twelve single-spaced typewritten pages, because Horowitz had referred to Chomsky in the body of the article.[62] Evidently the professor had read it.

Pretending Horowitz didn't exist was not unique to Chomsky among leftists and took many forms. Eric Alterman, a commentator for MSNBC and a columnist for the the *Nation*, wrote a scathing review of *The Politics of Bad Faith*,[63] but failed to discuss a single idea in the text. Instead, he passed on to readers Paul Berman's unhinged claim that Horowitz was a "demented lunatic," a charge made in the course of a bitter attack in the pages of *Dissent*.[64] These attitudes towards Horowitz's political deviance paralleled those that had caused Soviet dissidents, such as Andrei Sakharov, to be force-fed drugs in psychiatric hospitals. Alterman and Berman, of course, did not have the power to put Horowitz in an asylum—but it is clear from their own words that they wished they did. "When Horowitz finally dies," Alterman wrote in the same review, "I suspect we will be confronted with a posthumous volume of memoirs titled 'The End of History.'" The operative word here is *finally*. Leftists like Alterman evidently regret that Horowitz is still with us.

Just as the Soviet regime consistently rewrote its own history and erased inconvenient individuals from its past, so the academic and literary left have diligently kept Horowitz's work out of sight. The politicization of the university by tenured leftists has created a situation which may be said to be extreme for a democracy. Despite Horowitz's significant role in the events of the decade and his position as a principal critic of its social movements, and despite the large academic industry devoted to the subject and the existence of several specialist archives in the field, he has not received a single inquiry about his views, recollections, expertise, or documents from any of the thousands of left-wing scholars and their students writing theses, articles, and books about this history. Nevertheless, several faculty devoted to these same historical pursuits have boycotted his campus appearances.

Similarly, non-conservative institutions in the literary culture—the *New York Review of Books*, the *New Republic*, the *New York Times*, and the *Washington Post*—have studiously ignored his work since he moved to the conservative camp. *The New York Review of Books* has not reviewed a Horowitz book since 1985, when *The Kennedys* was published; *The New Republic* stopped with *Destructive Generation* and *The New York Times* and *The Washington Post* with the publication of *Radical Son*. Two exceptions to this rule have been the *Los Angeles Times Book Review* and the online magazine *Salon.com*, which for several years featured Horowitz as a regular columnist, providing him with an opportunity to reach an audience beyond his conservative constituency, for which he has been publicly appreciative.

Some sectors of intellectual conservatism have also kept a distance from Horowitz, reflecting a discomfort with his political and literary style. Conservatives are cautious by philosophical predilection, favoring the interests over the passions. Horowitz's style, by contrast, tends to the aggressive, embracing conflicts conservatives are schooled to avoid. In books like *Hating Whitey* and *Uncivil Wars* he has pushed the rhetorical envelope in order to move the public debate. For this achievement, he has paid the price of remaining something of an intellectual outsider not only to the debate in "mainstream" American politics, but also in some quarters of conservatism. Norman Podhoretz, the former editor of *Commentary*, who published several pieces by Collier and Horowitz in the 1980s, observes that "some conservatives think he goes too far, and my guess is that some also believe his relentless campaign against the left focuses too much on the 'pure' form of it that has become less influential than its adulterated versions traveling under the name of liberalism. Then there's his polemical style, which still resembles the one invented by the left. Even though it has made the left its target, there are conservatives, I think, who feel uncomfortable with it."[65]

The historian Richard Pipes is puzzled by the failure of some conservative intellectuals to embrace Horowitz. "It may have to do with style and decorum. Conservatives do not like aggressive argumentation—they prefer to stand above the fray. For the same reason they ignore Rush Limbaugh for all his enormous success and influence. It is a weakness of the conservative movement, this fear of giving battle."[66]

Notwithstanding that some literary conservatives have kept him at arms length, it cannot be denied that Horowitz has enjoyed significant support in the conservative movement generally and even from the conservative media. While his later efforts may not always have received the attention they merit, *Radical Son* was a cover story in the *Weekly Standard*, Ramesh Ponnuru wrote an elegant and appreciative review in *First Things*, and the book received very favorable notices in *National Review* and other conservative organs.[67]

To overcome the many obstacles he has faced in the political culture, Horowitz has been forced to create his own institutional base to carry on his work. He has done this with the help of conservative foundations and forty thousand individual supporters who contribute funds to the Center for the Study of Popular Culture. Its online journal, FrontPageMagazine.com, is devoted to "News of the War at Home and Abroad" and receives over one and a half million unique visitors a month. Creation of the center has enabled him to speak at over two hundred colleges and universities in the last ten years, and to appear on well over a thousand radio talk shows and television programs in the same interval. At the same time, the work involved in orchestrating these activities and maintaining his engagement in contemporary ideological battles has forced him to focus his energies on the essay form, and has resulted—with the exception of *Uncivil Wars*—in the composite works of his later years.

Through these efforts, Horowitz has been able to play a significant role in the battle of ideas. Paul Hollander, himself the author of notable books on radical politics, including *Political Pilgrims* and *Anti-Americanism*, has made the following comment on this aspect of Horowitz's contribution:

> He played a very important part in the culture wars, and has been exceptionally courageous and paid a price for it by becoming the most detested ex-radical among his former comrades. Especially valuable has been his willingness to "dirty his hands" so to speak by debating and addressing often hostile debaters and audiences.

I know that many people think that he has embraced another ex-treme, that he has been too confrontational, etc. He exemplifies to some degree the dilemma of how to avoid becoming like one's adversaries: how do you avoid the designation of 'ideologue' if you fight ideologues? Or avoid politicizing your own self as you fight the politicization of things, which should not be political? Would he have been more effective if he had been perceived as more 'moderate?' Hard to know. I basically applaud virtually all the stands he has taken, including most recently on the repara-tions for slavery.[68]

Horowitz sums up the conservative reactions this way:

Employing the aggressive style of the left to combat the left is a self-conscious attempt to pay for my misspent youth, and to take away the moral ground from which the left launches its attacks. But the posture has undoubtedly rung alarm bells for many con-servative intellectuals aspiring to a style that is more "civilized" and detached. At the same time, I have had many gratifications in private communications from conservatives who have thanked me for saying what had been thought to be unsayable, thus enlarging the parameters of discourse for others. Moreover I could not have accomplished what I have, had not conservatives welcomed me into their ranks and generously supported my efforts.[69]

Horowitz's background in the left and his fifty years of activity in the field of civil rights have not prevented him from being scarred in these battles. The left's hatred for Horowitz's achievement in exposing and crystallizing the pathology of the radical romance has drawn the following appreciation from Norman Podhoretz:

David Horowitz is hated by the left because he is not only an apostate but has been even more relentless and aggressive in at-tacking his former political allies than some of us who preceded him in what I once called "breaking ranks" with that world. He has also taken the polemical and organizational techniques he learned in his days on the left, and figured out how to use them against the left, whose vulnerabilities he knows in his bones. (That he is such a good writer and speaker doesn't hurt, either.) In fact, he has done so much, and in so many different ways, that one might be justified in suspecting that 'David Horowitz' is actually more than one person.

In many respects, one can make an analogy between what Horowitz represents to the academic left in America and what the dissident intelligentsia in Russia represented to the Soviet regime. Horowitz exemplifies the irritating and threatening reminder to tyranny that human freedom and the triumph of the human spirit can ultimately never be suffocated or suppressed. Henry Mark Holzer, a libertarian lawyer who was Ayn Rand's attorney and has represented Soviet dissidents fleeing communism for freedom in the West, has given expression to sentiments shared by many of Horowitz's supporters among conservatives:

> I don't say loosely that someone is a hero. But in my view, David Horowitz fits the definition of that term. He is a man who has stood up, and for a long time stood up alone, for his values. And his confessions are invaluable. We didn't have Alger Hiss providing us with a book about why he turned to treason. But Horowitz has expressed how and why many Americans betrayed their own country in the face of evil. In this sense, he has provided a great service. And this service is enhanced by the fact that he shows how this form of treason operated on the psychological level. I am not sure that this has ever been done before.[70]

In referring to Horowitz's standing alone, Holzer is certainly correct. For many years Horowitz did stand alone, and withstood vicious attacks while doing so from his former leftist comrades. Yet despite the left's repeated efforts to muzzle him, and despite all of the character assassination and violent intimidation that has come with those efforts, Horowitz is still standing, and still fighting back.

JAMIE GLAZOV

Author's Note

BEFORE I WAS THIRTY, and when I was still a man of the left, I received two formal letters from scholarly archives requesting the rights to my papers. At the time, I had written three or four books and edited three or four others. One of the letters came from the Wisconsin Historical Society whose collections are devoted to social movements and political activism and are the largest in the nation. I can no longer remember the name of the other.

I didn't answer either letter. Perhaps it was the rebel in me, perhaps I wanted a greater challenge. I thought there was something not quite right in the interest these archives showed in the work of someone so young and unproven, who had made what seemed to me still so small a mark. In my eyes the letters diminished simultaneously the importance of history and the significance of a request that one day I might regard as an honor.

Another factor in my decision was a nagging suspicion that the archivists who had requested my work had done so for political rather than scholarly reasons. If my work was to receive recognition, I wanted the recognition to be for its intellectual merit, not because it appealed to the political enthusiasms of some radical archivist. I had enormous respect for the academic profession and acted on the presumption that university archives should generally be guided by scholarly rather than political considerations.

Evidently this was a mistake. Since then, the corpus of my work has grown many fold. It has received peer recognition and can reasonably be said to have influenced an intellectual and political generation. One study that attempts to quantify influence (a quixotic ambition at best) lists me among the one hundred leading public intellectuals.[1] Yet in the more than thirty years that have passed since those first academic requests, I have never received another.

Not a single university archivist or any scholar interested in the events or movements in which I have been prominently involved has ever contacted me about my papers or recollections, let alone my views either on the subjects and events with which I am personally familiar or those about which I have become an authority. It is not that there is any lack of historical interest in the political movements of the 1960s or the historiography of the left generally. On the contary, in those thirty years the left I was a part of has come to dominate university faculties in the field of history and the other social sciences. The presidents of the American Historical Association and the Organization of American Historians, the two leading professional societies, are routinely figures of the political left, often marxists and usually activists themselves.

During their tenure, they have transformed the liberal arts colleges of American universities into political institutions, to whose faculties only the like-minded are hired, and in whose classrooms only the "progressive" worldview is respected and taught. It is estimated that nationally there are more than two hundred university courses exclusively devoted to the history of the 1960s. Every third-tier functionary of the American Communist Party or left-wing activist who played a role in even minor events or movements of the period seems to have been visited by a doctoral candidate and had an oral history taken to record their historical "contribution." At the same time, virtually no such effort seems to have been made to preserve the memories and activities of the participants in the equally influential movement of the 1960s that began with the Goldwater campaign, but whose perspective was conservative and therefore unattractive to the guardians of the historical record.

In sum, this academic disinterest in my work is not a personal matter, but the expression of a political fact. It is a reflection of the ideological debasement of our institutions of knowledge by a movement whose hallmarks are narcissisitic self-absorption and intellectual intolerance, and whose attacks on tradition, objectivity, and intellectual standards are already the stuff of legend. The effect of these attitudes on academic archives is a systematic amnesia about the efforts, thoughts, and recollections of ex-radicals and conservative rivals like myself.

This is neither the place nor the occasion to examine the vast lacunae in our historical memory bank resulting from the political agendas of this lamentably ideological generation of academics. I draw attention to these facts because they may help to explain the creation of the present volume as an effort to establish some details of a record that might otherwise have been lost. I only wish I could do the same for the many other conservative intellectuals who do not have this opportunity, whose work suffers neglect because of the indiscreet choice they made in lending their intellectual talents to the service of freedom, instead of the destructive fantasies of the socialist cause, in the last half of the twentieth century.

DAVID HOROWITZ

Acknowledgments

I WANT TO THANK Elizabeth Ruiz, my executive assistant, for help in putting this manuscript together; Andy Jones for compiling the bibliography and filling in gaps in the footnotes; and Jamie Glazov without whom it would not have happened. I also want to thank my publishers, Tom Spence, Mitchell Muncy, and Bill Tierney for standing by me. Finally, my wonderful family, wife, stepson, children and grandchildren made the life beyond this work a pleasure beyond it as well.

DAVID HOROWITZ

I

BEGINNINGS

Prologue

THE AUTUMN AFTER MY MOTHER DIED, I visited the cemetery where I had buried her, alongside my father, in the Long Island earth. The soil on her grave was grown with grass and had begun to be almost indistinguishable from his, joining them again, a couple in death as they were in life. Picking some pebbles from the path beneath me, I placed them on their headstones, tokens of remembrance, according to the Jewish custom. My mother's headstone bore the inscription "Always," a song which had become her favorite in her last years in California, and which symbolized to me the steadfastness with which she had stood behind her family, especially me. My father's headstone, which I had put up five years earlier, was already beginning to weather. I had directed the mason to inscribe it with the words "Life Is Struggle," a favorite quotation from his mentor, Karl Marx. It was a struggle he had lost long before we finally laid him to rest.

This return to origins, if only symbolic, was a way of measuring the distance I had come. It often seemed as far as the poles themselves. By the time I was a parent myself, my own parents were already strangers, so remote in experience that I hardly looked to them for counsel. And yet, at times, it had not seemed that far at all. There was not a moment in my adult life—not even now that they had been returned

From *Radical Son: A Generational Odyssey* (1997).

to their primordial dust—that they failed to assume in my imagination the aspect of fifty years before, when I felt they could see through me as though I were glass and provide all the comfort I needed. It seemed to me a metaphor for life itself, which sets us free only to bring us relentlessly back to earth.

Feeling my parents' presence again, I tried to imagine myself as I had appeared to them when they were alive. But, try as I might, I could not put myself in their place. I could not imagine how they saw me, how they felt the personal agonies I endured, or how they understood the metamorphosis I underwent: the murder that had changed my life in midcourse; the breakup of the family I had loved so intensely and worked so hard to create; the pilgrimage I had made from the snug progressive ghettos they inhabited all their lives to an America they barely knew and ultimately rejected.

I thought about the way I had become a stranger to them politically, joining the other side in a cold war against a faith they had embraced as humanity's best hope. I was like Whittaker Chambers in their generation—a young man inspired by the high-minded passions of the left who had broken through to the dark underside of the radical cause. Like Chambers, I had encounters with totalitarian forces that involved betrayal and death, and even a Soviet spy. Like him, I had been demonized for my second thoughts by a culture sympathetic to the left and hostile to its adversaries. I, too, had to face the savage personal attacks by my former comrades that were designed to warn others to remain within the fold.

Like Chambers, I had become the most hated ex-radical of my generation. And like him, I had discovered that the enemies against whom I once battled so furiously were more fantastic than real. I also discovered that I was not alone. Second thoughts turned out to be a natural process that others, less publicly visible than myself, had also pursued. Eccentric as my life seemed—at times even to me—it was not isolated, but more like a piece of the epoch itself.

As a result of my experience, I have often thought of how different a life looks from the outside in, of the name that identifies me but describes someone else, of the external details that convey little of who I am, yet represent me. The problem is not unique to me, but the serpentines of my life have made its progress unusually difficult for others to follow. Even allies who applaud the present acts of my public self often have reservations about the private man whose experience they do not share and whose intentions they do not fully trust. As for the comrades I have left behind, who are still at odds with what I have become, it is as though I have ceased to exist. To them I can never be someone who felt what they felt, dreamed what they dreamed, suffered, and learned through pain. Seeing me as one of them would pose questions too humbling to face: What second thoughts might they have had too? What illusions would they have to give up now? Instead, they prefer the easier path of denial, and revile me as one who left them—worse still, as someone they fear to become.

I am now as prominent on the conservative side of the ideological divide as I once was in the ranks of the left. But the conservatives I have joined are unlike the enemies I once imagined. The name itself does not begin to identify who they are—or who I am. The collapse of communism and the progressive future reveals how the moral language of politics has been hijacked by radicals. The fallen angels of the progressive left—marxist and socialist—have been exposed as the reactionary ghosts of an oppressive past. It is the ideological adversaries of the left who float on the wave of a future that is free.

Among my new comrades-in-arms, many began with second thoughts, having started out as 1960s radicals like myself. Indeed, in the last few years, the nation as a whole has begun to draw back from the radical decade and its destructive agendas. What I had learned one way or another in the course of my journey, other Americans seem to have learned as well. Irving Kristol, who had second thoughts before me, has observed that every generation faces a barbarian threat in its own children, who need to be civilized. This is the perennial challenge: to teach our young the conditions of being human, of managing life's tasks in a world that is (and must remain) forever imperfect. The refusal to come to terms with this reality is the heart of the radical impulse and accounts for its destructiveness—and thus for much of the bloody history of our age. My own life, which has often been painful and many times off course, is ultimately not discrete—a story unto itself—but part of the narrative we all share.

Idols

I DID NOT RECEIVE INSTRUCTION in the marxist catechism from either of my parents, although when I asked questions about current events, the answers always came with a preface encompassing the progressive worldview. The view itself, however, was transmitted far more effectively through a kind of osmosis rather than directly by homily and lecture. My instruction was in the environment I moved in and the air I breathed: the headlines in the *Daily Worker* carefully folded under the *New York Times*; the titles of the political books arrayed on the shelves (*Stalingrad, Scottsboro Boy, The Plot Against the Peace*), and the adult concerns that surfaced in my parents' conversations with friends. It emanated from festivities like a benefit for Spanish Civil War vets, which would elicit simple explanations of the cause, and from the epithets my father hurled at the "ruling class" enemy—*son-of-a-bitch, hypocrite, bastard*—which, in a backhanded way, added up to a social creed.

To live up to my parents' ideals, I knew I had to take on responsibilities in the larger world. My school, PS 150, provided a microcosm. Surveying my classmates, I imagined I could see the inequalities of their future estates. I was only in the fifth grade, but the natural hierarchy of the schoolyard already weighed on my socialist conscience:

From *Radical Son: A Generational Odyssey* (1997).

the gifts of beauty and grace and physical prowess that seemed so un-
evenly distributed, the disparity that marked intelligence as we vied
for classroom grades. It seemed unjust that some, like me, should excel,
while others fell behind. I attributed my own success to the fact that
my parents were teachers and able to help me, and the failure of others
to the lack of such privilege. The remedies I devised for these injustices
were clichés of our progressive culture. Physical ability was an accident
of nature, emphasized too much in a society "distorted" by competition. In the world to come, athletics would be a pastime rather than a
contest, and everybody would be a winner. Likewise, beauty could be
seen as a social myth, exterior to the individual, its standards shaped
by the commercial market. In our future, the standard would be inner
qualities, and no one would be left out. I yearned for a *monde idéal*,
where the True, the Good, and the Beautiful would be one.

Ponderous though these thoughts might seem for a fifth-grader,
these ideas were indeed mine. Intelligence presented the thorniest problem, since it appeared to be inseparable from the self. But if one believed in the possibility of justice and the shaping power of social forces,
as I had been taught to do, unequal knowledge could be redressed by
the proper attention, opportunity, and hard work. In my developing
political imagination, the schoolyard was full of mute, inglorious
Miltons, deprived of their chances for achievement by a system that
neglected or stunted them because it was concerned about profit alone.
Socialism would provide the answer, leveling the playing field and bringing victory to all. As a result of the marxist ideas I had already absorbed, I was thus able by the age of eleven to dispose of the enduring
pathologies of our social condition.

At some deeper and more psychological level, however, I had also
embraced an idea that contradicted these earnest conclusions. There
was a way in which my own experience seemed to provide a paradigm
of justice: if you worked hard and did right, you were rewarded. My
parents' protectiveness added an even more powerful assumption:
conflicts could be referred to a wiser authority, and thereby resolved. It
is a paradox to me that, well into adulthood, I acted regularly on these
optimistic expectations in the areas that affected me personally. Rather

than be suspicious of others, or prepare for their injustices (as marxism should have led me to do), I was trusting to the point of recklessness. As a result, I was constantly blindsided by events, until pain and disappointment eventually confronted me with our common fate: there is no inevitable reward for our virtues and no authority to whom we can safely appeal.

Looking back, I see that there is a way in which my entire youth was a form of quarantine. There was the protective environment of our political community itself, a kind of hospital of the soul. We were embattled, surrounded by enemies, and this made the members of our tribe like family. There was instant recognition of others who shared our values and political commitments, and exaggerated estrangement from those who did not. I was a sociable youngster, good at athletics and quick to make friends, but I was always separated from the world of my peers by an invisible wall. Even before I became close to a playmate, I knew that unless his family shared our politics (and the risks that accompanied them), we would always be strangers. It was not just that a whole area of my life had to be kept secret, but also that, if the wall were ever breached, I knew the friendship would end.

I lived in two worlds. One was filled with the currency of the common culture: favorite radio programs like the *Lone Ranger*, *Captain Midnight*, and *Ozzie & Harriet*, and with the exciting new medium of television shows like the *Texaco Star Theater*, the *Honeymooners*, and Ed Sullivan's variety spectacular. On Saturdays we went to the Bliss Theater, where my imagination was fired by cinema idols like Marlon Brando and John Wayne. In the *Movietone News* there were shots of my sports heroes in action: Joe Louis, Glenn Davis, Doc Blanchard, and—towering over them all—the Yankee Clipper, Joe DiMaggio. But I had another, secret world that was lit by different stars, the likes of whom none of my friends outside our progressive circle had ever heard of. Among them were the folk singers Pete Seeger and Martha Schlamme, the writers Albert Maltz and Howard Fast, the communist leader Elizabeth Gurley Flynn (an enormous woman who came to Sunnyside and shook my hand), and the politician Vito Marcantonio, who stamped his foot and yelled into the microphone at a rally I attended. Above them all was the enduring hero of my political youth, Paul Robeson, the Negro singer whose sonorous bass was like a great bell that made your bones resonate with its sound.

When this physically grand person appeared at the progressive rallies I went to, a palpable reverence filled the air. As he entered the room, a hush stilled the audience, virtually all white, which rose as one and began to clap rhythmically, Soviet style, to pay homage to the great man. When the Robeson voice boomed "Go down, Moses" and summoned the Hebrew leader to tell old pharaoh to "Let my people go," it was as though he were issuing a summons to free us all. The sound of his voice filled every bosom in the room with a glow of satisfaction, as though his presence confirmed our truth.

In our political catechism, the suffering of the Negro people was always a central image. The crime against the Negro was like an American crucifixion, and we constantly used it to pierce the veil of American benevolence and reveal the inequality and oppression underneath. Both my parents stayed after school to conduct "extracurricular" Negro history and culture clubs for their students, my father at Seward Park on the Lower East Side, my mother at Girls' High in the Bedford-Stuyvesant section of Brooklyn. My mother's files contain a note of commendation she received when her club put on a play about the "underground railway" and Harriet Tubman. These hidden heroes of "the struggle" supplied the material of my fantasy life. When my father and I took our neighborhood walks, he would explain how the streets were named for real-estate magnates and businessmen, and how, after the revolution, they would be renamed. I sensed something off in his claim, since I knew that many street names were those of presidents and military figures. But I took up the idea anyway and began imagining the revolutionary names that would replace the old. I began my list with Harriet Tubman, Frederick Douglass, and Paul Robeson.

My only real contact with Negroes, however, was with our housekeeper, Henriether Smith, one of seventeen children from a Tennessee sharecropper's family. She lived with us and took care of us when my parents were at work. My parents tried to help her get ahead by correcting her spelling and sending her to night school, where she learned how to read and write. Henriether was a devout Jehovah's Witness, and she took me once to a religious rally at Yankee Stadium. On another occasion my grandfather Sam engaged her in an argument about God and, to my great distress, ridiculed her religious beliefs. But Henriether just laughed, confident that he was the one who would eventually regret it. Henriether was a reserved, kind person who never had an angry word for us. When I married, she gave me a diamond ring as a present.

My instruction in the history of the Negro struggle included reading such books from my parents' shelves as Howard Fast's *Freedom Road*, and an account of the Scottsboro Boys, who had been falsely convicted of raping two white women, and whose case the Party had taken up. Another was *We Charge Genocide*, which the Party had published through one of its fronts, the Civil Rights Congress, and which contained a petition to the United Nations condemning America's "genocide" against Negroes. Paul Robeson had written the introduction, and the text was illustrated with a famous photograph—which I could hardly bring myself to look at—of Negroes being lynched by smiling whites. It was part of the Party's effort to help the Soviet Union by suggesting that the United States was like Nazi Germany.

In the pages of the *Daily Worker* there were always reports of injustices to Negroes that only our progressive community seemed to care about. Often these were Negro males charged with felonies the Party claimed they did not commit. These cases were referred to by collective names like "The Martinsville Seven" or the "The Trenton Six." In all these cases the issue of guilt remained unclear, but the general condition of racial injustice was enough for us to draw the appropriate conclusions. Linking these cases to the Cold War was a favorite Party strategy. After the formation of NATO, Robeson told news reporters that Negroes wouldn't fight if the United States found itself at war with the Soviet Union. After Robeson's statement, there was a riot at a concert he gave in Peekskill, New York. Sugar Ray Robinson, the middleweight boxing champion and a hero of my other world, told the press he would punch Robeson in the mouth if he met him. The incident left me feeling embarrassed for Sugar Ray.

After the Russian Revolution of 1905, the philosopher Nicholas Berdyaev analyzed communism as a form of idolatry in a way that proved to be prophetic. Berdyaev traced the origins of what he called the marxist "heresy" back to the tower of Babel. In that story, people had tried to achieve their own redemption—without a transcendent God—by building a ladder to heaven. Communists had a similar ambition. They had projected onto fallible beings godlike powers that would enable them to overcome their human fate. In doing so, Berdyaev warned, the communists had created demons they would not be able to control.

Robeson's presence as a god in our midst seems prophetic to me now. In my radical generation, blacks would replace the proletariat in our imaginations as the Chosen People who were going to lead the rest of us to the Promised Land.

—

I first became aware of politics, in the ordinary sense, during the presidential election of 1948. My parents and their friends belonged to the Democratic Party and had voted for Roosevelt. It was what they called their "mass work"—going to where the people were, in order to lead them to something better. This had been the Party line since the days of the Popular Front, when under orders from Moscow the comrades abandoned their "ultra left" position and stopped calling Roosevelt a fascist. "Communism is twentieth-century Americanism," the Party leader Earl Browder had said, promoting the spirit of cooperation during the war against Hitler. But the postwar conflict over Eastern Europe had changed all that. William Z. Foster had replaced Browder, and had summoned progressives to an all-out resistance to "fascist America."

As the election of 1948 approached, the Democrats split into three factions. On the right, the Southern Dixiecrats were angry at Truman's support for civil rights, and formed a new party behind the candidacy of Governor Strom Thurmond. On the left, the communists were upset with the Truman Doctrine, which promised support for "free peoples" who were resisting Stalin's conquest of Eastern Europe. They regarded Truman as a "warmonger" and formed the Progressive Party to oppose him behind the candidacy of Henry Wallace. The fact that

Truman was a strong proponent of civil rights had been eclipsed in their eyes by his anti-communist policies. Their allegiance to the Soviet Union took precedence over their concern for anything else.

That spring, I marched with my parents in the May Day parade, which was organized by the Communist Party. In those days, the women wore dresses to political demonstrations and the men wore suits, carrying their jackets in the early summer heat. Our section marched behind a huge banner that said "New York City Teachers Union," and we chanted on cue:

> One, two, three, four,
> We don't want another war.
> Five, six, seven, eight,
> Win with Wallace in '48.

Along the sidewalks of Eighth Avenue, curious onlookers gathered behind gray police barriers with "NYPD" stenciled on them in black. Every now and then, I glanced warily at the crowds, encouraged when a few showed their support with applause. As our ranks approached Twenty-third Street, a group of teenagers in T-shirts and jeans were hanging over the barriers and chanting back:

> Down with the communists!
> Up with the Irish!

Forcing my eyes in their direction, I looked to see if there was anyone from my neighborhood among them. But there were only strange, jeering faces. My whole being wanted to shout, "We're doing this for *you*." But my voice died in my throat. The memory has remained with me as a symbol of the permanent alienation of progressives like myself who set themselves up as the people's redeemers.

—

Every morning, my father sat down at our dining room table, a cup of coffee and a stash of Uneeda biscuits within close reach, to read the

New York Times. It was his most observed ritual, but the meaning of his devotion was still a mystery to me. Weren't the *Daily Worker* and other progressive papers, like the *National Guardian*, sufficient to determine what was going on? Yet I attempted to follow his example, and struggled to read the *Times* myself, gaining a familiarity with the headlines that made me want to know more. During the election campaign of 1948, my fifth-grade teacher set up a debate over the presidential candidates. Our class was mainly Jewish and also liberal. I volunteered to speak for Wallace, whom the overwhelming majority supported, while Danny Wolfman agreed to represent the Republican, Tom Dewey, since no one else would. Nobody volunteered to speak for the Dixiecrat Strom Thurmond. The day before the debate, I sought out my parents, notepad in hand, and asked them to help me with my speech. They were in their bedroom, dressing for a political meeting. As they outlined for me the Progressive Party platform, its points seemed as simple and inevitable as the instructions they gave to be truthful and fair and to clean up after myself. *We don't want another war.* Who could argue with that? If only the people were allowed to know the truth.

Like my other political lessons, this one reflected the core sense our community had of its political mission: *The world is cursed by ignorance, and the task of progressives like us is to set everybody right.* It was not too different from the liberal view that inspired the social agenda of PS 150. And the Hollywood films my parents took me to, like *Gentleman's Agreement* and *Home of the Brave*, promoted the same ideas. My personal favorite was *The Boy with Green Hair*, starring Dean Stockwell and Pat O'Brien. It was about an orphanage kid, played by Stockwell, whose hair turns bright green overnight, making him a target of his adolescent peers. In a futile effort to escape his tormentors, Stockwell shaves his head. A kindly priest (O'Brien) comforts him and tells him that surface differences don't matter, except to the ignorant. Stockwell takes courage and decides to grow his hair back—green.

The moral of these progressive lessons seemed to be always the same: Evil is the failure to understand. And, of course, from our point of view, it was. We were badly misunderstood. Terrible hatred was directed at us because we were falsely perceived as spies, traitors, and defenders of tyranny, fifth-column supporters of the enemy. But we were really progressives, friends of Negroes and the poor, partisans of peace, and patriots of a future America in which there would truly be justice for all.

From the moment I was given the election talk in my parents' bedroom, their political cause became my passion. It occupied my fantasies in the way that winning the World Series or marrying Rita Hayworth occupied the daydreams of my peers. I can remember walking in solitude on the ocean beach in Hampton Bays in the summer of 1949. The sandpipers were running up from the foam and then following it down, as I walked along preoccupied with a speech I was preparing in my head to make to President Truman. It was a long speech, and I went over it again and again in order to memorize it. In the speech, I explained to the commander in chief the misunderstandings that had led to present world problems, beginning with the failure of officials like him to see that the Soviet Union was no threat, but a nation interested only in peace. Wall Street capitalists, ruled by the profit motive, were the only people who could have an interest in war and were responsible for the misunderstanding. After this discourse on international politics, I went over the progressive litany of racial and social injustices in America. It was an elaborate appeal, and I prepared it with a solemnity appropriate to the belief that at any moment I might be presented with an opportunity to confront Truman and persuade him of its merits.

I was just ten years old, but I thought of myself as someone who could lecture the president of the United States on the difference between right and wrong, and thus change the course of history. I was just starting out in life, yet was already suspended so high above everyone else. Was there anything I could do but fall?

Imagination and Perception

What a piece of work is a man! how noble in reason! how
infinite in faculty! in form and moving how express and admi-
rable! in action how like an angel! in apprehension how like a
god! the beauty of the world! the paragon of animals! And yet,
to me, what is this quintessence of dust?

Hamlet

THE TENSIONS between antithetic images of man, between "di-
vinity" and "dust" form a focal theme of the Shakespearean
world experience. In high Shakespearean comedy this conflict
of worldviews is modified by the lightness of its context. Here skepticism lacks the hysteria of despair which characterizes it in its tragic
setting, while its antithesis embodied in comedy as chivalric romance
is easily rendered ridiculous by being stretched to shallow extremes.

In a post-romantic age the notion that, to appear absurd, romanticism must first be made extreme, is not obvious. To explore the conflict
between skepticism and romance at the heart of the Shakespearean

---

From *Shakespeare: An Existential View* (1965). Although published in 1965, the original
draft was written in 1962 in a graduate program at the University of California,
Berkeley. This excerpt has been edited for this book.

perspective, it is necessary, therefore, to first examine the romantic attitude. The bearer of this attitude is an extravagant figure to begin with, and because he has an exalted vision of reality and its possibilities, he is always in danger of over-reaching himself, of fleeing barriers instead of vaulting them. But this is merely a peril for him and not a predestination. In its integrity, the romantic vision is more than fiction and answers to an experience that is authentic; there *are* rises in the human landscape that transcend the plain of mere physical action and decay. Love is such a transcendence and cannot be comprehended in the transactional terms of a prosaic world scheme.

For what is love but the binding of two strangers who step forth to disclose themselves, withholding nothing and risking all? What binds lovers? What presents them to one another with such exclusiveness, brooking such commitment? And what moves them to exclude from their experience the whole world, except as it comes to them through the other? The hyperboles of romantic language and action answer to the hyperbole of love itself.

Thus, the death of the lovers, which is a fundamental figure in the romantic world image, signs the fact that love is absolute in a world of relatives: lovers must die to the world in order to be born to each other. The literature of cheap romance resolves this tension by rejecting the world; authentic romance lives the tension and therefore is tragic. But only romance as a language can express this paradox of an impossibility that is embodied, the paradox of love.

An exalted mode of living is not special to romance in its amorous sense. One speaks (even if in a modern patronizing fashion) of the romance of many other spheres of human action as well. Romance, in the Shakespearean context, has indeed such breadth; it is the defining character of every human way that is "engaged," that has faith. From out of such faith (where "faith" must be understood as a binding in relation, and not simply as belief) meaning comes. For the one who is so bound, a certain structure of values is given, and this meaning not only supports but is the mode of his being. The breaking of the romantic's faith breaks *him*.

In this sense religion is quintessential romance. It is necessarily closed to attack from the outside, because its revelation and its faith (the relation from which all meaning springs) stream forth from a Being beyond the reality at hand. In romantic love, by contrast, revelation extends itself from a being whose outward form is apprehendable to all. The foundations of belief in romantic love do not involve factors beyond what seem to be accessible in the reality that all men know (although the term "know" and the reality that is tied to it are themselves of course problematic). Romantic love, therefore, is at once open to criticism, by a disengaged view, on the ground that it raises structures of extravagant faith on foundations of mere earth, that meanings which are absolute cannot be derived from phenomena which are relative and situated within a temporal world order. Such criticism in Shakespearean comedy can be witty and, at the same time, profound.

In *Much Ado About Nothing*, Beatrice is an exponent of this skepticism and is single-minded in her pursuit of the non-divine foundation of marriage, the immanent basis of its bond of absoluteness, and its essential absurdity in that light:

> *Leonato*: Well, niece, I hope to see you one day fitted with a husband.

> *Beatrice*: Not till God make men of some other metal than earth. Would it not grieve a woman to be overmaster'd with a piece of valiant dust?

But can one rest with such an extreme, if amusing, view of marriage (and man) any more than one can rest with only a single pole of Hamlet's dialectic? Indeed, the very fact that there is a *dialectic*, a double human potential, reveals something. It reveals that man is a dynamic being, a being in flux. It cannot be said with finality that he is *either* noble *or* bestial, that he *either* crowns the creation *or* merely settles on it as on inconsequential dust. One can only say that man is the being for whom such possibilities exist.

Moreover, man pursues these possibilities in a kind of freedom. One can say, therefore, something about the relation between the realization of human possibility and human consciousness, between the goals that men posit and the courses they pursue, between man's created image of the world and his actual steps along its ways.

To speak about these questions with relevance to the Shakespearean context and the polarities that dominate it, one must speak in terms of "romantic" and "satiric" visions of the world. For while romanticism can be regarded as an attempt to express in hyperbolic conception what is a hyperbolic experience, this is not its sole function. Like any ethical code, romanticism also answers to the task of lifting experience from the primitive level of its sources, to the creation of new forms of being. The primitive source of love is sexuality, desire. But desire is a consuming force and by its nature cannot be sated: it can destroy the very object it desires. The romantic code understands this and sets out to restrain primitive desire, or rather to redirect it. The quest of the romantic is not merely to attain, but to serve, the beloved, and is directed not merely towards the other, but towards the self—towards becoming worthy of love. It seeks not merely in the consummation of the relation, but in the relation itself.

He who sees in love only the sensual satisfaction of his lust, as a consequence of his perception (and the deed which springs from it) experiences only the sensual in his act. But everywhere, value attends commitment. Where men do not address their condition in the fullness of its claim, there experience fails to cross the threshold of significance. For value can exist effectively only where there are men committed to it. It is the commitment of men to the possible, to what is loftier than their attainment, beyond what the present has achieved, that permits the realization of the potential whose seed is already there. "In the realist, the miracle springs from faith, and not faith from the miracle" (Dostoevsky). "Whether we take . . . the Indo-Aryan rita . . . the primeval order of that which is right and just, or Israel's *tsedek*, in which truth and justice combine, or the Greek *dike*, the inexorable course of world events, and the 'measure' determined by it—everywhere transcendent Being has a side facing toward man which represents a shall-be; *everywhere man, if he wants to exist as man, must strive after a super-human model*" (Buber).

For all this, there is a Shakespearean language with its own emphasis: where men recognize the bonds of claim and responsibility that bind them to other men, where commitment to values stands above use and interest and the profit of self, where such commitment exists, the social and moral harmony of men is tuned, and the natural comes to fruition because its order has been preserved. But where the specialty of degree gives way to the specialty of interest, where the relations of men bow to the relations of commerce, where the bond of mercy is denied before the bond of trade, where the claims of humanity yield to the claims of self, there appetite is all that is left, and this appetite, "a universal wolf," makes everything its prey, until at last it "eats up itself." All the refinements and values of civilization, all the significances and meanings of morality, rise out of the brute base to refine and ennoble it, and when all these have been stripped off, there is "a bare, poor, forked animal," and no more. What lifts man beyond this? What stands to cover his nakedness? What to reform his desire? Is it no more than mere illusion? To this question, the voice of the satiric disengagement answers with an emphatic *yes.*

That *yes* can be sounded with an emphasis that ranges from the frenzied bitterness of a Timon to the melancholic petulance of a Jaques in *As You Like It.* It has its paradigmatic expression in the answer of Diogenes the Cynic to the world conqueror from Macedon who had stopped in his way to ask the philosopher what he desired of him, Alexander. Diogenes answered that he wanted only that Alexander step aside and cease to block his sunlight.

Thus Diogenes' view is as relentless in its pursuit of the base clay on which all human enterprise is founded, as is Beatrice's; in the end, the world king Alexander is but a man, a piece of "wayward marl"; his offer to Diogenes can be nothing more than the offer of a man, nothing more than a man can offer: advancement among his fellows. The vanity that makes Alexander king and would make Diogenes his servant. But if it is just about the material fulfillment of material desires, what richer gift than sunlight?

Even as Diogenes' view of the human condition takes into its account only the physical stuff that men are made of, so Beatrice sees only one truth: that man is a piece of valiant dust, not heroic, but a vainly strutting inconsequence. The already noted closeness of Beatrice's jibe to Hamlet's is in no way fortuitous, for the essential recognition of any philosophical skepticism as it poses for itself the question of human significance, the point from which it always begins, is the fact of human mortality, of man's decay in time.

What separates Beatrice's statement from Hamlet's is not merely its focus (which makes the issue light), but that in Hamlet's speech there is a dialectic of possibilities. For he is caught between the sight of human potential, a potential that may come to realization in supreme moments and supreme individuals, and the reality of man's condition, his corporeality and corruption, his domination by flesh and by time in the flesh, the inescapable decay that undermines and makes meaningless his project. The tragedy here is inexorable; its issue cannot be resolved, but only accepted and in readiness some way redeemed.

It is this redemption and its possibility that radical skepticism closes off. From a criticism that opposes itself to easy and therefore misleading solutions, a criticism that seeks to refine values and ideas, skepticism descends quickly into a position that negates the impulse to solution itself. This is the last illusion, an illusion that extends to itself no grace of possibility, and thus stifles in its own pride and dies.

———

The career of Don Quixote (albeit an "obsessed" romantic) illustrates how a critical realism that will not see what is unseen, misses the potential in reality to become something else. In this way it misses reality itself. Those who oppose the Don and his vision see only what man is (that is, what he has been). They do not see what might be. That is why the "madness" of Don Quixote is perception, and his quest heroic, while the "sanity" of those who surround him is in an important sense blind to reality, and in particular to the possibility of noble action.

Don Quixote's view is faithful to a nobility that might be, to a nobility that by his own action he makes exist, that he (to use a Sartrean construction) *exists*. Under the pressure of his vision, "nobility" is no longer potential. It *is*. By contrast, the view that mocks Don Quixote, being faithful only to the limited reality of what generally appears, exerts no pressure on "reality," but rests in this limit as its end.

It is not Don Quixote's fault if no one follows him. His view of the world is extravagant but not, in its essence, impossible. He is committed to what is noble in life, to every valued principle of social man: to truth, to honor, to justice, to the protection of the helpless against the strong, to the sense of the intense, rich experience of living—all of which is seized in the symbol of the Golden Age, which he is determined will come again.

It is precisely this perception of the world's heroic potential that gives Don Quixote the capacity to live heroically. Vision, faith in his vision, and the will to answer it, to act on it, give him his power. In all literature there is no figure more heroic than he, precisely because he is heroic with only this power, heroic, as it is given to every man to be— alone, in his integrity and grace.

Thus it is fitting that the great moment in Don Quixote's life, the climax of his career, is the moment of his defeat by the Knight of the White Moon. Committed to the chivalric code, which binds him to his word, he is required to submit to the conditions that his conqueror sets. And he submits to every condition set by the Knight of the White Moon (even giving up his knightly calling), every condition but one.

The Knight of the White Moon demands that he admit that Dulcinea del Toboso is not the most beautiful lady in the world, and worse—that she is not fairer than any woman. Here, at the door to this betrayal, Don Quixote sets the limits of his submission and defeat. Even though in refusing this point he will yield his life (a sacrifice that is not taken), he remains firm. His commitment to his lady, to the truth of his vision of her, a truth that has been the source of his strength and the inspiration for his service, stands above all other values. He cannot preserve his life and yield this vision. For to yield the vision is to die out of the world in which he has lived (and this is of course the meaning of his 'death' by 'sanity' at the end of the novel). To the Knight of the White Moon's command that he declare Dulcinea ugly, his truth and its beauty dead, the answer of the shamed and beaten knight, an absurd, bedraggled, ridiculous old man, is *no*.

Who is Dulcinea? By other eyes she is seen as a coarse, sweaty peasant girl, cruel to Don Quixote in their only confrontation, and oblivious to his service. What then stands between them, and what is asserted in his heroic gesture? It is the potential in every woman to be Dulcinea del Toboso to one man, to be most beautiful to him, and in her loveliness, to ennoble him, moving him to high service and to heroic actions. Dulcinea *is* his inspiration, hers is the spirit that moves in him; she is the symbol of his vision of the world, a world which under the impress of his passion has momentarily become this vision—the scene of authentic "golden" nobility by virtue of his golden deeds.

II

THE NEW LEFT

A Generation of Silence

"I HAVE PRAYED just one prayer in my life: Use me." These are the words of Spegel, the actor, in Ingmar Bergman's film *The Magician*. For my generation, that is no strange prayer, no unknown request; it has been on our lips, silently, for a long time. We have said very little, but we have experienced much. We have been made to live, as no other generation has, on the edge of the world's doom.

It is no exaggeration to say that we began our maturity with Hiroshima. For although many of us do not remember it as a once-present happening in our lives, with Hiroshima a new age began that was to shape and direct us, and so characterize the course of our futures. Even then, they were coming to us with their "Cold War," and we were being asked to recognize new enemies, to seek new struggles, to sacrifice new lives. My generation has been witness to more offers to sacrifice the world for freedom, for country, for God Himself, than we are likely to take without some revulsion and disgust. And every time we have heard the call to rally behind the "free world," to prepare ourselves for ultimate sacrifice for the "free world," don't you think

From the introduction to *Student* (1962). It was the first book of the New Left, and these chapters were in effect its first manifesto. I was twenty-one when I wrote it. This excerpt has been edited for this book.

we've thought of the dictators Rhee, Chiang, Trujillo and Salazar, Batista and Franco, Somoza, and the others? Don't you think we thought of Mississippi and Emmet Till?[1] And don't you think we've paled a little at the hypocrisy of it all? Does it help to think of the Russian crimes? Do you think we can think of Hungary and not remember Cuba?[2]

No sooner were we called on to support their "free world" crusade, than they began to witch-hunt in our ranks. I say "our ranks" because it was the intellectuals whose silence they sought, and among them were *our* instructors, *our* professors. I remember Einstein's letter to the *New York Times*. "Don't cooperate with any committees that investigate ideas," he said. When McCarthy was finally stopped, it was only because he abused his power. He violated certain proprieties among elites by attacking the military. He ought to have been stopped for being a threat to the very principles on which the nation was founded; he ought to have been stopped because the methods of his committee were effectively destroying every safeguard of free speech and free association that the Constitution affords to the individual, every protection for the innocent against unjust trial. But even the president of the United States, who disliked him, said nothing.

Every year of the last six of President Eisenhower's office, this nation has faced the responsibility of completing its task begun 175 years ago. Every year since the Supreme Court decision in 1954, President Eisenhower abstained from his moral duty to lead the nation in integrating the schools and fulfilling that task. No president in the history of the country could have accomplished more than he with less effort. President Eisenhower was, and still is, the most respected man in this country. The majority of the white citizens in the South regard him as a sincere and pious man. If he had appealed to them, as citizens of this nation, to learn to live as Americans *ought* to live, side by side, all colors, all creeds, he might have won a more meaningful and far-reaching victory for our country than he had been summoned in all his life to win.

The most powerful force defeating us in our lives as students is the irrelevance of knowledge in America today. By way of contrast, I like to think of an incident that happened to a friend of mine in Cuba in the summer of 1960. His tour attended the "graduation" of a thousand young men and women from a three-week training course. They had all volunteered to leave their homes and promising careers for three years to go to the mountains to teach the children there the simple elements of a basic education. For this purpose they had entered the training school and were now being graduated. Fidel Castro spoke to them. He warned them of the difficulties they would face there, their isolation from all to which they had been accustomed in their lives, and the natural resistance they would find among the peasants to this new venture. He urged patience among them and then thanked them for their sacrifice. You will go, he said, and help people lead better lives by helping them to knowledge and the fruits of your own learning.

What are we told in our own country? What can we be told? You will go into the world, and because you have your degree you will help yourselves to a better job, a better home, a better car?

Students refer to a school that is so large that any contact between professors and students is strictly accidental, so that the struggle for knowledge takes on the character of an assembly line from lecture to lecture, from exam to exam, as a "factory." The undergraduate population at the University of California is fifteen thousand students. There are probably more full-fledged departments at Cal (about eighty) than there are courses in some schools. Knowledge under this set-up becomes more and more a specialty, a technique, and less and less an integrated view of the world. The university becomes more and more a vocational institute for training personnel and less and less a marketplace of ideas.

Society is structured so that individuals work not for each other but for themselves. The scientist is bought by the industrialists to fulfill one purpose: to capture the market. For us this is no cliché. We know the way patents are bought and locked away. We have read the books on careers for college grads. I remember one in particular: "the most important product you'll ever have to sell is yourself," it said.

A man is not a product, nor is he an IBM record card.[3] He is a person with desires, fears, ambitions, and a great need to feel worthwhile, to fill some space in a community of men, to do some good for them. His plea is always to be used, to be useful to someone. The university ought to be a place where teachers and students can enter into the natural relation of those who have wisdom and experience and those who desire it. But the university at Berkeley is fast becoming an assembly line for high-grade technicians, what the poet Kenneth Rexroth calls the River Rouge of the Intellect.

Is it any wonder that the vacuum demands to be filled? Is it any wonder that the pure heroism of the southern students inspires here?

The truth is that man cannot live for himself alone, that sooner or later the emptiness of such life overcomes him and he seeks involvement with others. The community of men and their history has the power to complete us in a way in which we never would be otherwise completed; it involves us in a way in which we cannot escape being involved.

Some of those who spoke with their actions in May 1960, when students picketed the House Un-American Activities Committee[4] in San Francisco, were those who, in previous years, had succumbed to the compartmentalization and disorientation of social existence in the last decade. Most were not. Rather than a new mode of living, it was a new voice they found on the picket line, a way of acting together, a confidence in acting together that they had not had before. In the way itself there was a symbol. I remember my own impression at the time. So many people subjecting themselves to the discipline of non-violence, so many people who, unable to commit themselves to pacifism as a total philosophy, were nonetheless willing to commit themselves for a day, as the sign of a value they cherished as a future goal. And walking thus, I was made irrepressibly proud because we were separated from those who opposed us not only by our ends, but by our way, and from this, I thought there could come only good.

⁓ 5 ⁓

New Politics

WHAT ARE SOME OF THE DEMANDS of the New Left students, what are *their* aspirations? To begin with, the students would like to see a more meaningful commitment to the ideals embodied in the Constitution. They would like to see real freedom of speech, the right to be critical of American life without being subject to vilification, slander, loss of job, and exclusion from the community. They would like to see equality for all of America's citizens, and a respect for human life as evidenced by putting an end to capital punishment. They would like the foreign policy of their country to be more in consonance with the ideals set forth in the Declaration of Independence and the Constitution. These, roughly, are the demands of the large majority of those students who have become involved in campus political activity in the last few years.

The Communist Party, U.S.A., does not represent in its program or in its shared history with other communist parties, the bulk of these demands[1]:

I. *The concept of free speech as embodied in the Constitution.* Communists have never, in their theoretical writings, nor in their practice, concealed their contempt for "bourgeois" notions of free speech,

From the final chapter of *Student* (1962). This excerpt had been edited for this book.

free press, etc., that are guaranteed unconditionally in the Bill of
Rights, without regard for concrete so-called conditions:

> What to the proletarian, is liberty—the extermination of those
> bourgeois institutions and relations, which hold them in cap-
> tivity—is necessarily compulsion and restraint to the bour-
> geois, just as the old bourgeois liberty, generated non-liberty
> for the worker. The two notions of liberty are irreconcilable.
> Once the proletariat is in power, all attempts to re-establish
> bourgeois social relations will be attacks on proletarian lib-
> erty, and will, therefore be repulsed as fiercely as men repulse
> all attacks on their liberty. This is the meaning of the dicta-
> torship of the proletariat, and why with it there is censorship,
> ideological acerbity, and all the other devices developed by
> the bourgeois in the evolution of the coercive State which
> secures his freedom. [2]

2. *The right to be critical without being subject to vilification and
slander.* Everyone knows the abuse that was heaped on Boris
Pasternak by Party leaders in the Soviet Union who had not read
Dr. Zhivago. One has only to read some accounts of the inner
Party disputes of communists in this country, or their polemics
against socialists and other members of the left, to appreciate the
Party's lack of tolerance for any criticism leveled against it.

3. *Capital Punishment.* The students who have marched and stood
vigil at San Quentin are committed to the belief that it is wrong
for the state to hold power over human life, that punishments
must be corrective and not merely punitive. But the Soviet Union,
believing that morals can be legislated, has just instituted the death
penalty for embezzlement, fraud, and fomenting prison riots.

4. *Self-Determination of Peoples.* To those students who are part of
the current resurgence on the left, intervention in Hungary is as
insupportable as intervention in Cuba. The communists say the

Hungarian revolution began as a legitimate protest by the people in the unfortunate conditions created by the mistakes of the government. But the revolution fell into bad hands and was betrayed by being associated with fascist and capitalist elements. The United States says the Cuban revolution began as a legitimate protest by the people of unfortunate conditions created by the oppressive regime of Batista. But the revolution fell into bad hands and was betrayed by being associated with communists.

The students find neither of these views accurate, and neither sufficient to justify interventions in the affairs of a sovereign nation. What a nation does, internally, is its own responsibility. If a nation acts inhumanely towards its citizens, other nations may seek to influence it, but not to coerce it and dictate to it. Self-determination is merely the carrying over of the rights of the individual into the international sphere.

It is clear that these principles, which the students have distilled from their own heritage, would have a revolutionary effect in the world situation today if accepted by any of the large powers, including the United States. For behind these principles lies the philosophy that puts human beings in all their complexity first, that denies the existence of a single True Path in politics which everyone must follow, that establishes respect for others as the cardinal rule of all social actions.

If the students are radical in their critique of the market system, they are also radical in their critique of the marxist solutions. For traditional marxists, the social relations of men are determined by their relation to the means of production. The marxist believes that art, law, religion, ethics, politics, etc., reflect the character of the economic organization of society, its class or non-class structure, its competitive or cooperative nature. It is utopian, says the marxist, to expect to find good men in a bad world or selflessness in a society where only the selfish can economically survive. Therefore, changing the relations of men to one another is only possible by first changing the concrete conditions of their lives, which means the condition under which they earn their survival.

To the marxist, therefore, the social problems that move people to action and protest in capitalist society—unemployment, social inequality, juvenile delinquency, inadequate school and housing—are fully solvable only when the root economic conditions, which create these problems, are changed. In its vulgar formulation, this belief becomes the necessitarian doctrine that the only real problem in securing social justice is that of altering the economic substructure of society.

In the main, those students who believe in a fundamental restructuring of society cannot accept this determinism. The forty-year history of the Soviet Union has made such a doctrine utopian. Forty years is a long time to wait for a free press and an atmosphere of free intellectual discussion, and few excuses can be made for the fact that despite the revolution, there is a continuing struggle in the Soviet Communist Party itself, whose outcome does not always rest on votes. This does not reflect a fundamental change in men's relations to each other.

The shattering of faith in simple formulas of social change was a decisive event in the developing consciousness of the majority of those students who, had they come to college ten years ago, might have been members of the Young Communist League. This same generation today has questions which must be answered before it will join any group seeking social change through the restructuring of the economic organization of society.

In the first place, the long fight for civil liberties in this country has done much to convince these students of the necessity of these liberties in any society. The eloquence of Justice Black has converted many more people on the left to a mode of constitutionalism than it has converted to the right. In the second place, the students want to know about decentralization of economic power. They will not struggle just to create a new bureaucracy at the center of society, with control over all major economic power. They want to know about the distribution of power and its limits. They want to know about autonomy for certain institutions. Their own experience in state-owned institutions like the University of California has taught them the damage that can be done to the academic process and academic freedom by uninformed and irresponsible legislators.

They want to know how the market system is to be replaced. On what basis are goods to be produced and distributed? What will determine, for example, whether the radio station will play rock-and-roll or Beethoven, whether publishers will publish a book such as *Doctor Zhivago*?

In short, these students will not be led into the illusion that socialism will make the truth simple and non-controversial. They want to know beforehand the provisions that are being worked out to ensure that socialism will be politically democratic as well as economically efficient.

Hand-Me-Down Marxism

W HAT IS THE SOURCE OF SDS'S DESCENT into a politics at once so claustrophobic and incomprehensible as to virtually insure the isolation and defeat of those who adopt it? A politics so antagonistic to the imaginative, open spirit and creative action that has informed and powered the New Left since its emergence from the ashes of the Old a decade ago? The present vanguard seems to have forgotten that the New Left had to midwife its own birth precisely because the old party-line-toeing, Lenin/Stalin/Mao-quoting vanguard had finally encased itself in a sectarian, sterile solitude where it had only its own self-righteousness for company.

What we have here is hand-me-down marxism, where a political vocabulary developed in a different epoch is transposed whole and adopted as an all-embracing wisdom. This attempt to don the ideological garments of the Third World victims of imperialism may satisfy many egos and assuage much guilt, but it doesn't help to build radical constituencies in the United States. The self-styled marxist-leninist-

---

At the 1969 convention of SDS—the largest leftist student organization—the delegates split into two factions, chanting slogans in behalf of Communist dictator Mao Tsetung and Vietnamese dictator Ho Chi Minh. This was the antithesis of what a "new" left had meant to some of us who had helped to launch it in the early 1960s, and this article for the August 1969 issue of *Ramparts* was my response. It was reprinted in *The Fate of Midas* (1973). This excerpt has been edited for this book.

maoists of SDS would do well to remember that the New Left grew out of two bankruptcies—not just liberalism, but old-line marxism as well. The failure of marxist (or marxist-leninist, or marxist-trotskyist) vanguard parties to build revolutionary movements in the advanced capitalist countries is an historic fact that no revolutionary can afford to ignore. The "marxist-leninist" groups that exist in these countries have either isolated themselves as sterile sects or transformed themselves into reformist organizations like the Italian and French communist parties. An analysis of these failures will show that hand-me-down marxism and overseas mecca-watching played a significant role in each.

Can Maoism, the new vogue in SDS ideology, provide a reliable guide to the causes of the impasse in Western revolutionary marxism? There is little reason to think so. In order to pursue its ideological struggle with the Kremlin, the Chinese Communist Party has deliberately rewritten the history of its own movement to obscure the role of Stalin both in obstructing the Chinese Revolution and transforming the communist parties in Europe and elsewhere into reformist organizations. . . . A theory whose answers to key questions are based on the rewriting of history can hardly provide a sound guide to revolutionary practice. Sooner or later the manipulation of facts will lead to a gap that cannot be bridged by administrative measures and historical legerdemain. Perhaps the gap will not be as large as that which developed in the Stalin era and which discredited and disoriented a whole revolutionary generation in the West. However, the very existence of the gap will prove crippling to a party that tries to build a revolutionary program across it. Integrity is a basic weapon in the revolutionary arsenal just as the ability to grasp real social relationships and forces is its greatest strength. A revolutionary movement thrives on candor just as surely as a ruling class lives by deception.

These are not academic points. The "Weatherman" statement of the new SDS leadership is built around the strategic concept of "people's war" as laid down by China's Lin Piao. The concept envisages a united people's front of Third World liberation forces encircling the principal metropolis of imperialism, the United States. The concept is derived from China's own revolution, which was fought as a national war of liberation against the Japanese and progressed from its peasant base in the countryside to the towns.

The inadequacy of such a concept for a world characterized by uneven levels of development, in which nationalism and the nation-state are still vital historical factors, is obvious. One has only to look at the Sino-Soviet split (neither the history of the Soviet Union nor this split receive any mention in the fifteen-thousand-word global analysis of the "Weatherman" faction) to see how abstract and unrealistic such a conception can be.

No doubt, a consistent perspective in the maoist vein can still be constructed by ignoring the tensions between revolutionary policy and *raison d'etat*, and by assigning the Soviet Union to the imperialist camp (a ploy which makes a mirage both of the arms race between Russia and the U.S. and their military support for revolutionary struggles such as in Vietnam and Cuba). There are obviously more things on revolutionary earth than are dreamt of in maoist and Weatherman philosophy; these are things, moreover, which a revolutionary movement ignores at its peril.

The main consequence so far of SDS's newfound orientation is its essentially fifth-column mentality and its largely negative vision of revolution in its home environment. It is not surprising that Lin Piao and the Chinese should see the struggle against U.S. imperialism in negative terms (get off our backs), but the transposition of this attitude to the revolutionary vanguard inside the imperialist power renders it self-defeating, not to say absurd. Thus the Weatherman program in effect proposes approaching American workers with the argument that everything they possess is plundered from the Third World (a false proposition in any case: it is the imperialists who benefit and the workers who pay the costs of imperialism) and that a revolution should be made in this country so that they can give it back.

No revolution was ever built on a negative vision. Moreover, there is no reason even to attempt to organize an American revolution as a negative act, a program of social demolition. At a time when the industrial engine has reached a point in its development where it opens up a vista of material plenty and free time for all, America's imperialist system saddles its people and all mankind with militarism, war, pollution, deprivation, exploitation, racism, and repression. America now possesses the means to a humane, livable, democratic future for all its citizens, but only if they are ready to seize the means of production and overthrow the system which dominates their lives just as surely as it dominates the lives of those in the Third World who suffer under its aggression and rule. That is the revolutionary foundation and the internationalist bond as well. It is certainly true that the liberation of the Third World will hasten the liberation of the U.S. But it is no less true that the American revolution is the key to the liberation of mankind. This is the insight that was missing in Chicago; let us hope that it returns to sds before long.

Solzhenitsyn and the Radical Cause

ALTHOUGH ALMOST TWENTY YEARS HAVE ELAPSED since the famous Khrushchev Report on the crimes of Stalin, it is clear that many radicals still understand neither the significance of the events described nor their continuing impact on revolutionary politics. This is evident not only in the puzzled silence, which has been the response of large sections of the left to the exile of the Soviet writer Alexander Solzhenitsyn, but in the critiques of those who have defended him.

The politics of Solzhenitsyn are complex and do not fit any simple equation of the Cold War. Indeed, it may almost be doubted that they have any immediate reference to left-right politics as they exist in the West. In part, this is because of the censored intellectual and political environment in which Solzhenitsyn and his compatriots have been compelled to form their ideas. In part, it is because of the hybrid nature of Soviet society itself, which combines elements of a progressive marxism with the attitudes and practices of a Russian despotism that was overthrown but not uprooted in the course of the revolutionary struggle.

Solzhenitsyn's views, as expressed in his fifteen-thousand-word letter to the Soviet government, are often jarring and sometimes even

---

This essay first appeared in *Ramparts* in June 1974, my last year as a New Leftist. This is its first reprinting. It has been slightly edited for this volume.

bizarre. He both calls for a restoration of power to the soviets, for example, and complains that Lenin was not patriotic; he praises the Soviet Union's growth in military strength and power under communism, but complains about Soviet support for Cuba and Vietnam; and he offers the view that the Soviet people are not yet ready for democracy and may never be.

What has to be understood is that the strangeness and even repulsiveness of many of Solzhenitsyn's views are no more bizarre or repulsive than significant aspects of his life experience under fifty-five years of Soviet rule. It need hardly be said that much of what is noble in Solzhenitsyn's effort and struggle, his courage and service to an ideal, also draws its energy and character from the Soviet revolutionary experience and tradition. In sum, the paradoxical character of his thought, mixing elements that are both reactionary and progressive, humanistic and obscurantist, reflects in a painfully honest mirror the paradoxical and contradictory history of the Soviet Union since 1917.

Solzhenitsyn was born one year after the Bolshevik Revolution, and was a marxist and a communist until he was sent to Siberia in 1945. He was an officer of the Red Army and was even considered at one point as recruitment material for the NKVD secret police. It was in Siberia that his views underwent a sea change from marxism to a deeply religious and conservative view of human nature and society. The defense of Solzhenitsyn is not a defense of some White Guard remnant of the czarist era, as some leftists seem to be suggesting. It is the defense of a child of the revolution and a witness to its trials. Radicals have much to learn from his suffering, though it may not be precisely the same lessons that he himself has learned.

But the defense of Solzhenitsyn involves more than that. There are times when a principle becomes fundamental in itself, a ground beyond which there can be no retreat. The Soviet regime is fifty-seven years old and now governs the second most powerful state in the world. Political democracy was an integral part of the original Bolshevik program, and the democratic rights it guaranteed were suspended during the civil war as a temporary measure in the interests of the survival of the infant and invaded Soviet state. Yet they have never been restored.

At what point is one forced to recognize that the fulfillment of these rights has been permanently deferred by the present rulers of the Soviet Union, and that they will never be instituted without a struggle that will mean real changes in power? Is it not a pressing responsibility of the left to support this struggle? What could be of more vital concern to the international left than the directions that power will take in a state as important as the Soviet Union, and with as deep historical and ideological connections to the world socialist movement? And yet, there are radicals who regard the struggle for democratic rights in the Soviet Union as an unfortunate embarrassment and low on the priority scale of radical concerns.

The present importance of defending the principle of dissent *qua* principle and without regard for the political specifics of the individuals under attack is made clear by the witch-hunters themselves in the current wave of Soviet repression. They have suppressed the works of a committed communist and marxist like Roy Medvedev, with the same crude hand as they have Solzhenitsyn, who has renounced marxism. They have labeled both men "anti-Soviet."

When individuals as disparate in their views as Solzhenitsyn and Medvedev are lumped together in a repression, the issue is obviously not their analyses or programs or even allegiances, but the facts which they are attempting to bring to light. As Andrei Sakharov and nine other prominent dissenters declared in a statement protesting Solzhenitsyn's exile, "His treason consists of his disclosure, to the whole world, with shattering force, of the monstrous crimes committed in the USSR not very long ago." The Soviet government is afraid of the truth. Since it cannot refute the facts, its only feasible strategy is to outlaw all efforts to publish truths not sanctioned by the official apparatus. The "universal, obligatory force-feeding with lies" writes Solzhenitsyn in his appeal to the Soviet government, "is now the most agonizing aspect of existence in our country—worse than all out material miseries, worse than any lack of civil liberties." In such circumstances, the defense of the principles of freedom in the Soviet Union, of the right to speak and disseminate unauthorized versions of what is true and real, is an absolute necessity, a precondition of general political and moral progress, and not a mere luxury of intellectuals—as some misguided American radicals have claimed.

The glacier underlying the present structure of Soviet politics, the unresolved legacy of the Stalin era, makes it impossible for the Soviet leadership to tolerate historical candor and leads to such crudities as the exile of a world-famous writer and the incarceration in psychiatric hospitals of many of its leading scientists and intellectuals. It is this legacy and its continuing consequences that the historical works of Solzhenitsyn and Medvedev force into political consciousness; it is the issue of Stalinism's survival that the Soviet dissenters raise.

Many radicals in the West do not understand the urgency or importance of this struggle. Some seem to think of Stalin as an exemplar of revolutionary pragmatism who was not afraid to crack heads in a revolutionary cause. They acknowledge that he may have been responsible for some excesses, but regard these as inevitable in a class war, where any crimes he may have committed were more than likely balanced by the crimes of the oppressor he opposed. It seems evident that this is a view now widely held among the youth of the Soviet Union, who have not been able to read Medvedev's *Let History Judge*—the first attempt by a Soviet marxist to document the Stalin purges and analyze the Stalinist system—or Solzhenitsyn's *Gulag Archipelago.*

The hard fact that every serious revolutionary must confront is that Stalin killed the dream of the Bolshevik Party—the best, the most idealistic, the most revolutionary cadre in the Soviet Union, and other communist parties as well. In *Let History Judge,* Medvedev estimates that more than a million out of a total Communist Party membership of two and a half million disappeared in the purges of 1937-39:

> In short, the NKVD arrested and killed, within two years, more communists than had been lost in all the years of the underground struggle, the three revolutions, and the Civil War. The oldest members were special victims, as the composition of the [Party] Congresses shows. [At the 17th Congress in 1934] 80 percent of the delegates had joined the Party before 1920; the figure was only 19 percent at the 18th Congress [in 1939]. . . . These were not streams,

these were rivers of blood, the blood of honest Soviet people. The simple truth must be stated: not one of the tyrants and despots of the past persecuted and destroyed so many of his compatriots.

For Medvedev, Stalin's crimes against the Revolution's cadre make up the orienting axis of the analysis; for Solzhenitsyn it is Stalin's crimes against the nation. In the second half of 1937, when the Soviet Union was preparing for the coming war with Germany, the NKVD began its assault on the core of the country's military command. "Almost all the most outstanding Red Army commanders who had risen to prominence during the Civil War perished," writes Medvedev. According to one apparently conservative Soviet estimate by the Bolshevik A. I. Todorskii, whom Medvedev quotes, in the years just before the war with Hitler, those arrested included three of the five marshals, three of the four first-rank army commanders, all twelve of the second-rank army commanders, sixty of the sixty-seven corps commanders, 136 of 199 division commanders, and 221 of 397 brigade commanders; both first-rank fleet admirals, both second-rank fleet admirals, all six first-rank admirals, nine of the fifteen second-rank admirals, both first-rank army commissars, and thirty-four of the thirty-six brigade commissars. There were also huge losses among the field-grade and junior officers. "The shocking truth can be stated quite simply: never did the officer staff of any army suffer such great losses in any war as the Soviet Army suffered in this time of peace."

Many writers, Solzhenitsyn included, think that this wholesale destruction of the military leadership of the Red Army virtually invited Hitler's attack on the Soviet Union and was responsible for the terrible losses the Soviets sustained before turning the tide. Stalin's subsequent vindictiveness against the battered survivors of Soviet armies, especially those who had the misfortune to be taken prisoner, is in Solzhenitsyn's view, the gravest of his crimes. Solzhenitsyn himself fought with distinction for four years on three fronts, was decorated for bravery several times, and rose to the rank of captain, only to be arrested in East Prussia in the middle of a battle in 1945, and sent to Siberia for having criticized Stalin in a letter.

His own eight years in the Gulag Archipelago marked a turning point in Solzhenitsyn's life and consciousness. Apparently before that, his views were those of a rising member of Stalin's newest elite, a fact about which he is as searingly honest as he is about everything else: "I ate my officer's butter with pastry without giving it a thought as to why I had the right to do it, while rank and file soldiers did not." (In a bid for national support, after the purges of the officer cadre, Stalin had restored the ranks, orders, and ceremonial privileges enjoyed by the czarist army.) "This is what happens when you put epaulets on people's shoulders; they begin to feel like little gods."

One final response prevalent among radicals to the Solzhenitsyn exile (and the expulsions which have followed) needs to be dealt with. That is the response that dismisses all this as a media event with no more (and most likely even less) significance than that of persecuted writers in many countries around the world. Some go so far as to suggest that the interest is even concocted. The "mistakes of the past" cannot be resurrected as contemporary politics, writes one reader of *Ramparts* and leader of the old New Left, who should know better.[1] (How inadequate and even repulsive the expression "mistakes of the past" seems when applied to the Soviet tragedy and its crimes.) As though the political heart of a country could sustain such a succession of blows without feeling the consequences for generations, as though the very effort to silence Solzhenitsyn and Medvedev did not indicate in itself that this is a crucial contemporary issue in the Soviet Union.

To this day the Soviet people are not permitted to know the true extent and nature of the crimes that were committed in the Stalin years, and to this day the guilty go unpunished. "Given the widespread and unrestrained lawlessness that has reigned in our country for many years, and an eight-year campaign of slander and persecution against me," Solzhenitsyn declared in ignoring a court order before his exile, "I refuse to recognize the legality of your summons. Before asking that citizens obey the law, learn how to observe it yourselves. Free the innocent, and punish those guilty of mass murder."

The contemporary implication of the struggle in behalf of the Soviet Union's dissenters and political prisoners has been eloquently

summarized by the Soviet physicist Andrei Sakahrov, in the introduction to his new book, *Sakharov Speaks*:

> In the course of 56 years our country has undergone great shocks,
> sufferings and humiliations, the physical annihilation of millions
> of the best people (best both morally and intellectually), decades
> of official hypocrisy and demagoguery, of internal and external
> timeserving. The era of terror, when tortures and special [courts]
> threatened everyone, when they seized the most devoted segments
> of the regime simply for the general count and to create an atmos-
> phere of fright and submission—that era is now behind us. But
> we are still living in the spiritual atmosphere created by that era.
> Against those few who do not go along with the prevalent prac-
> tice of compromise, the government uses repressions as before.
> Together with judicial repressions, the most important and deci-
> sive role in maintaining this atmosphere of internal and external
> submission is played by the power of the state, which manipulates
> all the levers of economic and social control. This, more than
> anything else, keeps the body and soul of the majority of people in
> a state of dependence.

At stake in the struggle for the rights of Soviet dissenters and political prisoners is nothing less than the revival of politics in the Soviet
Union, and the birth of a true Soviet Left. In the dialogue between
Medvedev and Solzhenitsyn, we can already see the outline of the kind
of debates that might characterize a Soviet politics liberated from the
terror and lies of the Stalinist system and its less destructive but still
despotic successors. The present state of affairs is morally corrosive and
politically dangerous, as the growing conflict with China reveals. For
one of the especially corrosive effects of the suppression of politics in
the Soviet Union has been the growth of nationalism as a solidifying
social force. (Ironically, Solzhenitsyn, an almost religious nationalist,
provides a healthy dissent from the official Soviet chauvinism towards
China. He devotes the major portion of his appeal to the Soviet government to urging the avoidance of war with China—a possibility he
mistakenly attributes to a clash of marxist ideologies.)

Does the awful record documented in the *Gulag Archipelago* and *Let History Judge* mean that the critics of bolshevism were right and the Soviet experiment has failed? Do the crimes of Stalin negate any gains the revolution has made? When one peels away the layers of radical consciousness, this is the core reason why most leftists remain reluctant to speak out against the crimes and injustices that distort Soviet life and politics through to the present. In short, there is a fear of providing credibility to such views and damaging the revolutionary cause all over the world.

Yet, it should be evident that *this* is really the dead issue in the current debate, and if anything serves to keep it alive, it is the willingness of radicals to accept its terms. The Soviet regime is almost fifty-seven years old. Its gains in the material realm, and in science, public education, and health, have been vast[2]—a still-powerful beacon to those in the Third World who have not yet broken the chains of imperialism and capitalist underdevelopment, and who still suffer the "natural" torments of poverty, ignorance, hunger, and unnecessary disease.

No one, not even Solzhenitsyn, proposes turning back the clock to 1917 or even making significant changes in the system of social property in the Soviet Union. The Soviet experiment has survived. Its successes and its failures are monumental, but there is no practical scale in which they can be balanced against each other, or made to cancel each other out. The only live issue for the Soviet Union, and for radicals, is the future. Support for Soviet dissidents, and for every move to establish democratic rights in the Soviet Union and fulfill the promise of October, are acts not of despair about the Soviet past, but of hope for the Soviet future. And hope—for a better society and a better life for humanity—is what radicalism and revolution are about.

The Passion of the Jews

Do you have any Christian friends? The question was thrust at
me quite unexpectedly by a middle-aged Jewish doctor during an informal evening's discussion about the Middle East.
A man of forcefully liberal persuasions, the doctor had already revealed himself to be complexly aware of the moral and national issues
involved in the conflict, despite a visceral commitment to the Israeli
cause. In the course of the evening, he had also revealed that he had
been a conscientious objector before Pearl Harbor, after which he en-
listed without qualms, and to me it seemed that he retained a certain
nostalgic warmth toward "youthful" radicals like myself. The setting—
Berkeley's liberal hills—was also disarming, so that taken together the
combination of circumstance and speaker left me unprepared for the
"moment of truth" (what else could one call it?) that followed. For
when I responded affirmatively to his inquiry, that several close friends

From *Ramparts* (October 1974). This article appeared two months before Betty Van
Patter's murder and is the final piece in this book that I wrote as an unshaken leftist.
While I would agree even now with much that I wrote, the essay reflects the utopian
delusions of the left not only in its solutions to "the Jewish problem," but also in its
critiques of "imperialist" America and America's Israeli "client." I have footnoted a
few of the more egregioius statements in the original text, but not all. For my present
views, see "Why Israel Is the Victim," chapter 38 below. This article has been edited
for this book.

were indeed "Christian" (though they were no more religious than I), he paused dramatically and asked: *Would you trust them with your life?*

It was such a plummet into tribal depths that my reaction at first was to block the intent of the question itself. The very idea that in the year 1974, in middle-class America—in Berkeley yet—Jewishness might be considered an ultimate criterion of whom one could, under assault, count on as allies (for that was the implication) cried out for dismissal as absurd, paranoid, and morally repellant. One was ashamed even to hear it.

I thought of the Reform Jewish Temple to which the doctor and I belonged, and which I had joined when my children, growing up in integrated and ethnically conscious Berkeley, had shown the need for a cultural root. Its membership was drawn almost exclusively from the middle-class hill community, and in its majority would have regarded me as a barely tolerable heretic on the question of the State of Israel, as well as on many political and social issues likely to arise. In short, although their liberal commitments would provide some measure of support, it would be unwise to count on them as allies—Jewish or not—in any conflict which my own political commitments might entail.

But of course that was not what the liberal doctor meant at all. In the nightmare of his vision, the furies of destruction would come after me not as a radical, but as a Jew. That was the real danger for which one prepared. When *that* happened, I would know what it was to be alone among Jews. So, when I pushed the issue to its conclusion, replying *Yes, I would trust my life with my Christian friends* (for that is what one meant by friends), it was no surprise when he looked at me regretfully and said: *You are naïve.*

It would have been no use for me in attempting to refute this racial paranoia to invoke the remoteness of such a prospect from our immediate surroundings of material comfort, the influence of Jews in the local community, or the absence of overt anti-Semitism in the nation at large. For hadn't the German Jews—the inevitable reference point at such moments—been the most comfortably assimilated Jewish community in Europe before the War? The fact is that any paranoid fear of destruction that a Jew experiences in the contemporary world has its root in a reality that is both recent and unmistakable. Yet such fear has begun to grip wide sections of the Jewish community at a time when there is hardly a ripple of antagonism on the smooth surface of their assimilated existence in America. In a recent article on "Liberal Anti-Semitism" in the *Village Voice*, to cite one revealing instance among many, Ellen Willis—usually one of the coolest and most penetrating intellects of the New Left—complains about the inability of non-Jews to care about the survival of Israel and concludes: "Ultimately, I think, the Jews are 'close-minded' because they sense that they are alone, that they can depend on no one."

There are catastrophes in the life of nations so vast as to disrupt permanently the balance of their social and psychological existence; there are wounds a people can endure, which penetrate so deeply into their life structures, that though the surface may be repaired, the inner being can never be healed in the sense of being restored to its former self. The Nazi Holocaust was such a catastrophe and such a wound for the Jews. Through two thousand years of Christian persecutions and homeless exile, Jews became accustomed to suffering. In their trials, they managed not only to survive, but to survive *as a people* with a sense of mission born out of their suffering.

Israel—the dispersed nation—was to be a "light unto the nations," its very exile and suffering the source of a continual revelation of the moral principles that the nations, in their power, had lost. "You shall not oppress a stranger," was their commandment; "you know the heart of a stranger, for you were strangers in the land of Egypt."[1] A nation of the alien and oppressed, the Jews of the Diaspora possessed as their living heritage the sense of justice that is the immutable birthright of the victim and the Law of God above the law of nations, which Moses, the liberator, had received on leading them out of their slavery in Egypt. "Hear, O Israel, the Lord is our God, the Lord is One." One God, one humanity. The *Shema*, the credo of the Jews and the last words on the lips of Jewish martyrs throughout the centuries, implied the universal kinship of mankind.

But the Holocaust of the Second World War was a catastrophe of suffering beyond even the experience of Jewish history. All those centuries of persecution had not prepared the Jews for the disaster that befell them. The gas chambers in which six million perished—the entire Diaspora community of East and Central Europe—were built by a malice whose dimensions were beyond their imagination. That they would be persecuted, and many killed, they did not doubt; that they would be systematically eradicated, as so much vermin, they did not consider possible. It denied the very hope that sustained them, that one day the divine voice would be heard by all, that mankind and the nations would turn from their ways and bring on the messianic time when the lion would lie down with the lamb, all children and creatures of God—one family, one faith. Extermination foreclosed the hope of redemption.

Without a belief in the reality of the evil confronting them, the *inhumanity* which it portended, the Jews of Europe were slow to resist their destroyers. It was a fatal hesitation. Resistance might have saved many, but only a few resisted. As a result, in all the ghettos of Europe there are now only monuments of silence to the people whom God had chosen as His light.

Through the ashes the survivors came to realize, moreover, that it was not only the Nazis who willed this silence, but others less directly culpable. The Christian democracies of the West not only failed to come to the aid of the Jews in their agony, but afterwards closed their doors to the pitiful, tormented remnants whom the Nazis had not time to kill. The timeless resort of Diaspora Jewry, to flee persecution in one country and to seek refuge in exile in another, was shut off: Jews were not wanted in America, while the fleet of liberal England blockaded the Palestinian refuge. And that nightmare experience of credulity, betrayal, and destruction has worked a profound change in the structure of Jewish psychology, in the dimensions of Jewish hope, and in the dynamics of Jewish survival.

The most central expression of this change is the existence of the State of Israel, created as a Jewish state in 1948, and the most far-reaching result what one writer has called the *zionization* of the surviving Jewish communities. Before the war, the Jewish community was not only largely indifferent to zionism, but actively hostile to it. For zionism represented a sharp break with the tradition of the Covenant. Instead of a "light unto the nations," a people united across national boundaries, embodying in itself the unity of mankind, zionism sought to solve the "Jewish question" by making Israel "like the nations," a state bounded by a defined national territory. For the universalist message of the Torah, it substituted a narrow, national identification.

The betrayal of Judaic teaching implied by Jewish nationalism was resisted from the beginning. In the year following the original zionist congress, the Central Conference of American Rabbis declared that attempts to establish a Jewish state, "show a misunderstanding of Israel's mission which from the narrow political and national field has been expanded to the promotion among the whole human race of the broad and universalistic religions first proclaimed by the Jewish prophets. . . . We affirm that the object of Judaism is not political, nor national, but spiritual, and addresses itself to the continuous growth of peace, justice, and love in the human race, to a messianic time when all men will recognize that they form 'one great brotherhood' for the establishment of God's kingdom on earth."

To Zionists, like Theodore Herzl, founder of the movement, these were the sentiments of "amiable visionaries." To peg the improvement of the conditions "on the goodness of all mankind," he wrote, was utopian. "Universal brotherhood is not even a beautiful dream. Conflict is essential to man's highest efforts." The problem of the Jews was political, Herzl concluded, the result of their statelessness and inability to be assimilated in the nations where they dwelled. Forced into moneylending and trading during the Middle Ages, excluded from other spheres of business, the rich among the Jews were now concentrated in speculative activities and the stock exchange, the focus of hatred for the capitalistic system. Jewish intellectuals barred from academic positions and means of livelihood were becoming socialists and revolutionaries. Herzl: "Hence we . . . suffer acutely in the struggle between the classes, because we stand in the most exposed position in both the capitalist and the socialist camps. . . .When we sink, we become a revolutionary proletariat, the corporals of every revolutionary party; and when we rise, there rises also our terrifying financial power."

To Jews steeped in the prophetic tradition, this situation itself exemplified the central and universal character of the Jewish question and its place in the scheme of human redemption: the problem of the Jews would be solved only when a revolutionary transformation brought about the just order of the "messianic kingdom." This was the view of Marx and other Jewish revolutionaries and "idealists," who secularized the prophetic tradition of Israel in a program of social revolution. But the conservative Herzl sought a more pragmatic and immediate solution in ending the anomalous political character of the Jews' existence by establishing a Jewish state, like other states. If the cry of the anti-Semites was *Juden Raus* ("Jews Get Out"), wrote Herzl, who saw the slogan as the inner meaning of every anti-Semitic act, then why not get out, and gather in one's own territory, thereby solving the problem? By occupying their own territory, the Jews would become "normal," and thus could be finally admitted to the family of nations. In its own way, zionism is the supreme assimilating tendency in Judaism.

For years the argument continued between the zionists and the revolutionary socialists, who saw the solution to the Jewish problem as lying in the transformation of social existence in general. Nowhere was this debate carried on with more intensity than in the Diaspora communities of Eastern Europe in the 1920s and 1930s. And then the Nazis seemed to give the zionists a gruesome victory in the argument. It was this "victory" that won the Jewish majority to their cause.

The actual creation of Israel did not take place as the fulfillment of Jewish dreams, but—in the words of Isaac Deutscher—"an act of Jewish despair." Deutscher had himself been one of those Jewish radicals who before the War had argued in the East European communities the position of revolutionary internationalism. In an article on Israel, written in 1954, he confessed to having, "long since abandoned my anti-zionism, which was based on a confidence in the European labor movement, or, more broadly, in European society and civilization, which that society and civilization have not justified. *If, instead of arguing against zionism in the 1920s and 1930s I had urged European Jews to go to Palestine, I might have helped to save some of the lives that were later extinguished in Hitler's gas chambers.*"

For the remnants of European Jewry, continued Deutscher, "the Jewish State had become an historic necessity." And yet, that recognition did not make him a zionist. From a sinking ship, he argued, people jump onto a raft; the jumping is for them "an historic necessity" and the raft "the basis of their whole existence. But does it follow that the jumping should be made into a program, or that one should take the raft-state as the basis of a political orientation?" Such was Deutscher's thinking twenty years ago, and the interim events can only have served to intensify the doubts as to whether in the long run the zionists have indeed had the better of the argument. Not only has the existence of a Jewish state not solved the Jewish problem, but this abandonment of Jewish uniqueness, and assimilation to the law of nations, has had an ironic issue, raising the tragic potential of Jewish history to new levels.

For there can be no question that the most exposed Jewish community in the world today—the lightning rod of anti-Semitic antagonism and the fuse of communal peril—is Israel itself. An armed camp, surrounded on all sides by hostile and more numerous (if not yet more powerful) enemies with deep and seemingly irreconcilable grievances against her, Israel is poised on the brink of potential destruction (if not immediately, then in some not-too-distant future) and thus becomes an agonizing symbol of Jewish fate. This is the fact that creates the paranoia, not only of Israeli Jews, but of American Jews as well.

During the Yom Kippur War of October 1973 (regarded by most Jews as unprovoked, but which certainly was intended to halt the colonization of the Arab territories occupied in the 1967 war), Jews experienced "the deepest, most primitive fear of all," wrote the editor of *Commentary*. This fear, "rarely articulated, often repressed, but printed on the nerves of many who were astounded to discover that they even cared about Israel, let alone that they believed themselves to be personally implicated in its destiny [was that] if Israel were to be annihilated, the Jews of America would also disappear. . . . For if for the second time in this century, the world were to stand by while a major Jewish community was being destroyed, it would be hard to evade the suspicion that an irresistible will was at work to wipe every last Jew off the face of the earth, to make this planet entirely *Judenrein*."

Israel has thus become the focus of a riveting fear of destruction among Jews generally, and among American Jews in particular. The real jeopardy of Israel, surrounded by enemies and aided by uncertain friends, is what provides substance to the otherwise incomprehensible apprehensions of the liberal Berkeley doctor who, amid all his securities and comforts, considers the Day of Reckoning as a practical matter, and judges the trust I have in my fellow human beings to be naive. For now that the Yiddish-speaking communities of the Diaspora have been destroyed, Israel is not only a symbolic center, but the living focus, of Jewish cultural identity and spiritual life.

This is perhaps the most fateful aspect of the unsought conjunction of zionist mission and Nazi Holocaust: the confusion of a universalist ethical ideal with a particularist state. For the *galut* or exile of the people whom God had chosen for His witness symbolized, in Jewish tradition, the falling away of mankind from the path of the moral law. The return to Israel, or *aliyah* (literally, ascent), was coupled with the idea of redemption and specifically with a redemption brought about by communal effort. When the Jews of the Diaspora prayed "next year in Jerusalem" on the Day of Atonement or during the Passover service commemorating the exodus from Egypt, they did not mean a journey to the Middle East; they were praying for a universalist turning of the nations of mankind from their fallen ways, for the coming of the messianic kingdom on earth: the suffering of the Jews would end only when the suffering of humanity itself had ended.

For most Jews there was, of course, an element of confusion between the two ideas of return, since, like other communities, the Jewish community in its whole does not breathe the pure radiance of the divine spirit. (Even in the religious myth, the chosen-ness of the Jews does not raise them above the rest of mankind. Their very exile is a punishment for their own lapse from the moral ideal.) Otherwise, there would have been no spiritual wellspring for the original zionist mission. For the zionized majority, moreover, Jewish identity increasingly is no longer a spiritual but primarily an ethnic identification which involves a passionate but complex interest in the destiny of a particular nation-state. This ethnicization and nationalization of Jewish identity is taking place despite Israel's official effort to include a religious, and therefore universal, aspect to its legal definition of Jewishness.

Well, one might ask, what of it? Is that not the actual moral condition of mankind: national territorial identifications, which have a constant reference to larger ideals and aspirations, but remain firmly anchored in the morality of tribal loyalties and particularist interests? Such is indeed the case, and the Jews can hardly be faulted by the nations of mankind for adopting a morality common to them all. Nor can they legitimately be denied their claim (however misguided the hopes behind it) to self-determination and national "liberation," to a national state within whose territory they constitute a majority group. Such normality and such acceptance is precisely how the zionists would like to see the Jewish problem pragmatically solved. But in the end it is not solved. Because, in the end, the zionist solution comes up against the hard fact of Jewish destiny: Jews are not like the nations of mankind, and the Jewish state is not like other states. The problem of uniqueness, as every previous effort to assimilate has shown, cannot be overcome by the adoption of a particular aspect of normality, even one so seemingly fundamental as statehood.

One can begin with the fact of Israel's present peril—the threat that constitutes a permanent and recurring injury to the optimism and faith of even so privileged and powerful a community as American Jews. No other nation-state in the contemporary world has had to wage continuous war for its very existence as Israel has for a quarter century, and is likely to continue to for the foreseeable future. But that is just the symptom. What is the source?

In a way that can almost make one believe that there is a design to Jewish suffering, the exposed position of Israel in the international system today recapitalutes the exposed position of the people Israel in the international system of the nineteenth and early twentieth centuries. One of the primary reasons for the renewed anti-Semitic assaults of that period was the civil emancipation of the Jews following the French and American Revolutions. As the artificial barriers against them were lifted, Jews suddenly entered the social competition, to the dismay and increasing hostility of the classes and groups most threatened by their new privilege. Just as the Jews were among the last to enter civil society, becoming the scapegoats of its class turmoil, so they staked their claim to a nation-state at a pivotal juncture in its evolution, and came to occupy an exposed edge in its most fundamental conflicts.

Jewish nationalism took root at a time when the nation-state was no longer the embodiment of a liberating sovereignty, but was already transcending itself towards an imperial world system. At the time when it appeared as a solution to the Jewish problem, Jewish nationalism could find no land in which to establish itself that was not within the system of western imperialism. The Jews' collusion with empire arose both from necessity and from the logic of the bargain that zionism made with the oppressor: give us a land and we will get out. They were eventually given a permit to settle, but not a nation. By the time, fifty years later, when out of the nightmare of the Holocaust, they took up arms against the imperial power itself in their struggle for self-determination, the zionists were already face to face with the nationalist explosion their own settlement had caused.

If their future tragedy was woven like a fate into their historical situation, it was not unforeseen. In a book called *The Truth from the Land of Israel*, published in 1891, Ahad Ha'am, a leader of the Jewish "enlightenment," wrote of the effects of the "return" on the early Jewish settlers in Palestine: "They were slaves in the land of their exile and suddenly they find themselves in the midst of unlimited freedom, a wild kind of freedom, which can only be found in a country like Turkey [i.e. the Ottoman Empire]. This sudden change has produced in them a tendency to despotism, which always happens when 'a slave becomes a king.' They treat the Arabs with hostility and cruelty, trespassing on their territory unjustly, berating them shamefully without any valid reason and then boasting about it."

On the other hand, it probably could be said that while virtually every nation is built on an original conquest and subjection, often—as in the case of America—including the annihilation of the original inhabitants, few if any were accomplished with more effort at cooperation and more consciousness of guilt toward the native inhabitants than was the Jewish colonization of Palestine and the dispossession of its

Arab population. Moreover, because of their own numerical weakness, and the political and military dominance of the British in the whole Mandate area as well as in the encircling Arab states, the Jews had less control over the outcome than any comparable colonizers in history. They remained throughout, on the exposed edge of the historical conflict between imperialism and nationalism, facing on the one side the British oppressor and its client Arab regimes, and on the other, the rising tide of Arab and Palestinian nationalism.

Yet the fact remains that the dispossession and denial took place. Furthermore, it is far from over. Thus, while the state of Israel is the embodied national ideal of a people who for two thousand years were without a land and a state, Israel's leaders—in the interests of Jewish "survival"—continue to deny in principle the very existence of the people they have displaced and to thwart their claims to land and statehood. "It was not as though there was a Palestinian people in the Palestine considering itself a Palestinian people and we came and threw them out and took their country away from them," explained Israeli Prime Minister Golda Meir in 1969, "they did not exist."

There was a partial truth in this. The Arabs who lived in Palestine originally were not a self-consciously united people. But under the impact of their displacement and dispossession by the Jews, and in part inspired by Jewish nationalism, they began to develop a national self-consciousness and identity.[2] Yet because the rights of this people challenge the rights of Israel's, it has become a policy of the Israeli state to deny the national reality in whose creation they themselves have been so intimately involved. The Palestinians, in the view of Israel's Foreign Office, "are not a party to the conflict between Israel and the Arab states," and "have no role to play" in any peace settlement. Denied a legitimate voice, weak, disorganized, living in refugee camps and under Israeli military rule, the Palestinians have responded with acts of terror as a cruel, but therefore unambiguous, statement: *We exist.*

The outlines of Israel's present plight were partly foreseen by Ahad Ha'am in the days when the program of a bi-national state of Arabs and Jews in Palestine was still a prevailing idea among the zionists themselves (it was dropped only in 1942). "A Jewish state would be poison for our nation and drag it down into the dust." he wrote. "Our small state would never attain a political power worthy of the name, for it would be but a football between its neighbors, and but exist by diplomatic chicanery and constant submission to whoever was dominant at the time. Thus we should become a small and low people in spiritual servitude, looking with envy toward the mighty fist."

Israel has proved to be stronger than Ahad Ha'am guessed, but not strong enough to avoid the spiritual servitude he feared. Unable to stand independently, the Israelis had to seek out and curry favor with the powerful. Militarily and economically dependent on the United States—the chief imperial power of the age—Israel's leadership has not stopped short even at supporting America's genocidal war in Vietnam, under the argument of its own survival.[3] (Similarly, small subject nations in the Third World, like Ireland, Argentina, and Iran, colluded with the Nazis during World War II out of a narrow nationalist desire to gain leverage against Germany's imperial rivals.)

Set in an exploited and prized region of the world, surrounded by hostility, Israel has embraced the role of a fifth column ally of the imperial *status quo* and a determined opponent of radical Arab nationalism. This role had practical consequences of far-reaching significance during the invasion of Suez in 1956 by the French and British, and also in specific Israeli threats prior to the 1967 war—for example, to intervene in behalf of the Hashemite Kingdom of Jordan, if that regime should be toppled from the left.

In its role as an agent of western imperialism, Israel is very like the regimes in Saudi Arabia, Jordan and Iran, which exist parasitically on the stream of international oil.[4] By any reckoning, however, Israel is of far less importance to the West than any of these three, a fact which makes Israel's U.S. support sometimes tenuous and ultimately uncertain. Israel is also an "alien intruder." Taking a leaf from the anti-Semitic traditions of the Christian West, the Arab rulers have found that by scapegoating the Israeli Jews, they can obscure their own betrayal of the larger interests of the peoples of the Middle East. It is an effort made easy for them by Israel's continuing oppression of the Arabs of Palestine—not only in the denial of Palestinian self-determination and in the military occupation of the Arab territories, but in Israel itself.[5] For the subjection of Arabs in Israel is not only a contingent feature of Israeli society, but a principle of the Israeli state. The Jewish character of the Israeli state, a joint product of the zionist dream and the Nazi nightmare, is discriminatory *de jure* and not merely *de facto*. Under the Law of Return, designed to open the doors that the Christian nations had shut to refugee Jews and also to sustain the zionist hope for an ingathering of the dispersed nation, Jews—though not Arabs or any other non-Jews—are granted automatic citizenship status upon arrival in Israel. Israeli Jews, but not Israeli Arabs, are encouraged to procreate and increase their numbers. Similarly, significant tracts of Israeli land, and even whole villages, are reserved for exclusive Jewish ownership and settlement. There are other official and legal devices as well, which consign non-Jewish citizens of Israel to second-class status and emphasize the chosen quality of Israel's Jewish majority.[6]

At first these policies seem like a grotesque inversion of the principles of the Nazi persecutor and his Aryan myth, and for certain elements of the Israeli population—the religious fanatics and the irredentist right—they clearly are. There is more than an element of the mystique of blood and soil in the original zionist impulse, while the myth of the master race is a simple perversion of the Old Testament idea: without the ethical dimension of the Covenant, which binds God's elect to universalist principles and a special burden of suffering, all that remains of the notion of the Chosen People is a chauvinist arrogance and self-righteousness.

The basic ground of what can only be called the racist principles of the Israeli state is not ideology, however, but the pragmatism of survival in the context of a basic pessimism about the human condition (a pessimism confirmed by the isolation of Israel in the Arab Middle East). The *raison d'etre* of Israel is that it is the Jewish raft-state: ultimately Jews cannot depend on any other group for their survival; they must go it alone. If Jews lose control of Israel's government, Israel loses its *raison d'etre*. Therefore, the Arab population of Israel must be kept smaller, weaker, and subordinate to the Jewish population of Israel *as a principle of survival*. Since Israel is a tiny ghetto state (such is the ironic issue of Jewish nationalism in an age when the nation-state is no longer an adequate vehicle of sovereignty), systematic discrimination, however liberal and humane its forms, must be a constantly operative principle of Israeli politics.

What could be more alien to Judaism and the whole spirit of Jewish history than this result of zionism's efforts to promote Jewish survival by making the Jews like the nations? Yet because of the centrality of Israel in Jewish consciousness, this distortion of Jewish values has had wide repercussions in the Jewish community at large. Moreover, because of the dependent relationship of Israel to the United States and the pivotal role of American Jewry in maintaining that link in Israel's survival, this distortion has been injected into the attitudes of the American Jewish community with particular force.

One perverse but illuminating instance of this effect has been the campaign in behalf of Soviet Jewry, undoubtedly the major political effort of the Jewish organizations in America for the last decade. Boycotts have been maintained against Soviet cultural events; demonstrations have been staged at Soviet embassies; gold Stars of David inscribed "Let My People Go" have been sold as fundraising devices in temples across the nation; and a powerful political lobby, built in Washington, has only recently joined hands with the Pentagon opponents of détente to sponsor the so-called Jackson Amendment to the Administration's trade bill. This legislation would make the whole progress of new trade agreements with the Soviet Union contingent upon a relaxation of its repressive emigration policies so that discontented Soviet Jews could go to Israel.

Even though the propaganda to American Jews conceded that the immediate threat to the three million Soviet Jews was "spiritual destruction" through the denial of religious and cultural forms of expression, rather than a repetition of the Nazi Holocaust, it has nonetheless featured prominently the theme of deadly parallels. The Holocaust thus remains the pivot of the Jewish political imagination. In particular, the implication is always present and often articulated that American Jews are in danger of repeating their alleged crime of "silence" in the dreadful hour when European Jewry was extinguished. "What torments me most," concludes Elie Wiesel in *The Jews of Silence*, one of the major texts of the campaign, "is not the Jews of silence I met in Russia, but the silence of the Jews I live among today."

Several of the principle features of this campaign, which has been so central to the politics of the American Jewish community, illustrate the pitfalls of a zionized Judaism, of converting an ethical-ideal-as-ethnic-identity into an ethnic program parading as an ethical ideal. In the first place, the Jewish community is seeking, in the name of a universalist principle of human rights, to advance a particularlist interest—the emigration rights of Soviet Jews. Although the anti-Semitic nature of the Soviet persecution is undeniable, it is not the whole story by any means.

The religious and cultural persecution of the Jews in the Soviet Union is part of a more general persecution of religious and ethnic minorities. And these persecutions are related to the suppression of political and intellectual diversity and freedom, and to the struggle of Soviet dissidents—many of whom are Jewish—for a restoration of general civil and political rights. Thus the Jews of Russia are situated in the historic Jewish position of being able to advance the general social interest by the defense of their own—provided their struggle is based on a universalist hope and not on a parochial inwardness and pessimism. But instead of a campaign in behalf of religious, cultural, and political freedom in the Soviet Union, the campaign for Soviet Jewry is a narrow and parochially conceived struggle in behalf of one religious group. It is not a campaign for freedom in the Soviet Union after all. What is being demanded of the Soviet government is not that the Jews should be given freedom as Soviet citizens. What is meant by "Let My People Go" is literally that: let them have exit visas.

All this raises legitimate questions as to the nature of the motives behind this campaign. Is it the needs of Soviet Jews for self-expression that are paramount, or the needs of the State of Israel for Jewish immigrants? (Fifty percent of the total immigration to Israel in 1973 was made up of Soviet Jews.) The narrow nationalist objective of the campaign does more than raise questions, however. It detracts from the internal struggle in the Soviet Union. It creates a divided sense of responsibilities for Jewish dissidents and has had the more general effect of encouraging an exodus of non-Jewish dissidents as well.

This is a fact of special moment in the Soviet situation, since many of the failures of the Bolshevik Revolution are bound up with a phenomenon that might be called marxist zionism: the Stalinist program of Socialism in One Country, which made Russia the mecca of the world socialist revolution, and stimulated a profoundly chauvinist turn in its development by confusing the narrowly defined interests of a repressive state with the broad hopes of a movement for human emancipation.

The nationalization of the world socialist revolution was in a sense similar to the developments that took place in world Judaism. Stalin's slogan of "Socialism in One Country," which after Lenin's death became the policy of the Soviet state, was not so much a program of hope as an act of despair. The defeat of the revolutions in Germany and Europe, the western military intervention, and the Civil War—which destroyed the fabric of Russian society—worked a profound change in the revolutionary optimism that had inspired the Bolshevik mission. The diehard proponent of revolutionary optimism and defender of the original ideals and internationalist commitments of the Soviet revolution was the Jew, Trotsky. But he was exiled and murdered, and the pragmatism of national survival became orthodoxy under the Stalin regime. Out of the defeat of the hopes of world revolution—and a profound international pessimism—the Bolshevik Revolution turned inward and lost its original revolutionary élan.

The dissidents in Russia today, the forerunners perhaps of a revolutionary revival, are not charged by the Soviet government with democratic deviance or a lapse into liberal turpitude. For political and social democracy are goals of the socialist revolution, so deeply embedded into the socialist program that they cannot be formally abandoned by the Soviet state. The dissidents are charged with being *anti-Soviet,* unpatriotic, of colluding with the West in their efforts to express unorthodox and unapproved sentiments and viewpoints. The zionist-encouraged exodus of Soviet Jews and Soviet dissidents thus plays into the hands of the Soviet oligarchy, which wants to deny the legitimacy of every struggle for internal freedom in the Soviet Union, and convert it into an act of treason against the Soviet state.

In sum, the zionist campaign is a conservative rather than a radical force in the Soviet context. It tends to increase the historical negativism and conservatism of the Jewish community as well. By insisting on the unqualified anti-Semitic content of the Soviet situation—and by implication the failure of the socialist revolution to emancipate the Jews—it distorts the historical reality and denies the hope which can be based on its achievements.

—

It is true that the Russian Revolution failed to emancipate the Jews, as it failed to emancipate the other peoples of the Soviet Union. But it is not true that it made no difference at all, or that there were not large gains for the Soviet people generally or for the Jews in particular. It is not just that the Jews have been liberated from the Pale of the Settlement and make up one of the more privileged strata of present-day Soviet society, accounting for an even greater percentage of the scientific intelligentsia, for example, than in the United States. But even more indicative for their communal survival is the fact that Russia, the crucible of the most virulent anti-semitic outrages, the nation that gave the term "pogrom" to the world, saved two and a half million Jews from Hitler's gas chambers, when Stalin shifted virtually the entire Jewish population of Eastern Russia to the Soviet interior to keep them out of the reach of the advancing German armies.

This is one of those neglected facts that can alter a political and moral *gestalt*. For if this is not a historical basis for a more hopeful view of what might be gained by political struggle in behalf of universalist values, then what is? If the efforts of those Jews—Marx, Trotsky, Zinoviev, Kamenev, Rakek, Rosa Luxemburg, and so many others— who dedicated their lives to the socialist revolution and the ideal of human emancipation, did succeed in moving the historical process forward in a way that profoundly affected Jewish destiny as well, is that not an argument for such a "utopian" course of action, especially when the alternatives are so bleak? Is that not an indication that it was not the ideal that was wanting, but the effort in behalf of the ideal?

Like the zionist program to secure Israel's survival, the campaign for Soviet Jews also invokes the specific instrumentality of the American state. Here, too, the means can hardly be separated from the ends. No special insight is required to see that the freedom of Jews in Russia is of greater interest to Washington than the freedom of South Koreans, or Brazilians, or South African Blacks. Yet, far from creating suspicions as to the sincerity of the concern, this duplicity is eagerly embraced by the zionist establishment, which is also seeking to legitimize itself in America and resolve the problem of its own "dual nationality" via an anti-communist patriotism which is as disreputable as it is self-defeating. (Surely its pathetic symbol is the figure of the White House rabbi, Nixon's hapless last defender.)

Finally, there is the arrogance involved in so blatant an assertion of self-interest over the general welfare in forging an alliance with the military and jeopardizing the détente. Apparently the leaders of the campaign for Soviet Jewry feel well enough protected by the coincidence of this aggressively advanced self-interest with America's long-term anti-communist hysteria to take the risk.

Self-assertion, however, is not an attitude that can be confined to pre-determined areas where there is a convergence of patriotic prejudice and Jewish interest. Only recently, for example, a group of rabbis was urging in the media that Jewish couples eschew birth control and *not* limit their families. Although population growth was a serious social problem, the problem of Jewish survival came first. As an appeal, this managed to be both offensive and pointless, since raising the percentage of Jews in the population from its present 2.8 percent to 3 or even 5 percent would hardly enhance the prospect of Jewish survival.

A boldly self-centered attitude has become an increasingly prominent trait of the organized Jewish community in America. One hears a lot these days of the first half of Hillel's famous dictum, "If I am not for myself, who will be for me?" but not so much of the second half, "If I am only for myself, what am I?" This self-centeredness is regarded by the mainstream Jewish community as a form of self-defense. It is an attitude directly linked to the zionist achievement in Israel, and the source of its propagation among American Jews can frequently be traced to encounters with the *sabras* of the *kibbutzim*. For the constant theme of self-justification heard in Israel is that Jews have allowed themselves to be kicked around too long. Through the centuries, Jews have been humanity's Christians—passive victims turning the other cheek. In the name of universal justice, they have been committed to everyone's cause but their own. It is time for them to stand up for themselves and put their own interests first.

What is important in this message is only secondarily the distortion of Jewish history. For one fights realistic battles in the end, and the Jewish tradition is rich in heroes and martyrs who fought on the impossible terms presented to them: the mere fact that through all the persecutions, the Jews were not broken as a people attests to this fact. Moreover, if Israel could not survive a season without American military and economic support, as the Israelis are constantly reminding American Jews, what is the meaning of their "standing up for themselves" and what pride can they possibly have in paying the price of complicity in America's oppressive global policies and crimes? What is important in this nationalistic breast-beating is the distortion of basic values it entails. For the underlying assumption of the argument for Jewish nationalism is that Jews can expect no justice or aid from others, that the struggle for universal values is quixotic, and that they must and can go it alone on the basis of narrow self-interest.

The Israeli posture is defined by the present conditions of Israeli existence. But who is kicking the Jews in America around that they should be so pessimistic about potential friends and so intent on marshaling the clan for battle? It is not an oppressive ruling class that calls forth "Jewish power," but America's blacks and other subject minorities who are pressing against the fringes of Jewish middle-class privilege. The basic conservatism of this Jewish militancy, so strikingly parallel to the Israeli paradigm and so profoundly linked to its rationale, is illustrated by a bellwether editorial which appeared a few years ago in *Commentary* magazine, the sometime liberal publication of the American Jewish Congress, under the heading "What's Good for the Jews?"

Writing of the end of the "Golden Age of Jewish Security" which took place during the 1950s and early 1960s, when *everything* was good for the Jews," editor Norman Podhoretz warned that Jews would have to adopt a self-interested approach to social action. "Jews will either ask, *is it good for the Jews?* and act on the answers, or . . . wake up one day to find themselves diminished, degraded, discriminated against and alone." The tone of embattled isolation notwithstanding, the principle of self-interest advanced by Podhoretz and other liberal-conservative Jewish spokesmen, has less to do with survival than vested privilege.

For in the context in which the criterion of *what is good for the Jews* is advanced, it is really a defense of a *status quo* in which Jews have won positions of privilege and a measure of security, and which is now under challenge by other oppressed minorities. The Podhoretz editorial, for example, is specifically addressed to the problem of justifying Jewish opposition to affirmative action hiring which would increase the number of blacks and other minorities (but not Jews) in university and civil service positions.

It would be wrong to suggest that this trend has no opposition, even within the central organizations of the Jewish community. The Social Action Commission of Reform Judaism and the National Council of Jewish Women are on record, for example, as friends of the court in opposing the De Funis suit against affirmative admission quotas. Dr. Nahum Goldman, head of the World Jewish Congress, and other community leaders have expressed concern over the tendencies within the Jewish community to forget "timeless Jewish ideals" as the community becomes economically affluent and socially accepted. But the trend is there, and is even more pronounced among Jews lower down on the social ladder and therefore closer to the challenge of other minorities.

Wherever it exists, however, it is accompanied by a bad conscience. The bad conscience is so regular an aspect of the trend, moreover, that it invariably draws complaints from advocates of the new Jewish conservatism, like Podhoretz. Jews, they regret, seem to be more uncomfortable than others with the ethic of self-interest. If that is true, perhaps that is because it is such a betrayal of their tradition, and of all the suffering that has made up their history, of the fact that they have been strangers and know the heart of a stranger. Perhaps it is because no Jew is yet able to escape the sense of his or her own vulnerability, and therefore no Jew can fail to know subconsciously—even while the Jewish lobby is bending the foreign policy of the United States to the Jewish interest—that such power is illusory and that the more the Jewish interest is advanced as such, the more a backlash is inevitable. Ultimately, the ethic of tribal loyalty and group self-interest is not a pragmatic rule for survival but a sure path to destruction. A tiny minority like the Jews, with a two-thousand-year history as scapegoats and victims, will not survive without allies in a *bellum omnium contra omnes*. If the pessimism of the zionists and the conservatives were correct—and ultimately the Jews had no friends but Jews—there would be no hope at all.

The bad conscience of tribalist Jewry is accompanied by an enormous wave of self-pity and self-justifying paranoia. It is as though the intensity of the Jewish fear for Jewish survival in America were directly proportional to an inner sense within its own traditions that a tribal politics is morally indefensible. The bad feelings of those Jews who voted for Nixon are expunged in the thought that because of their votes Israel is safer. The uncharacteristic opposition of large sections of the Jewish middle class to the aspirations of a struggling minority is justified by the conviction that blacks are anti-Semitic and support the Arab cause. The peril of Israel thus becomes a necessary justifying basis for the conservative shift of America's Jews, much as the creation of Israel and the consequent nationalization of Judaism are organic elements of its cause.

This linkage is dramatized by a recent book on *The New Anti-Semitism* written by the director of the Anti-Defamation League of B'nai B'rith, which argues from the premise that criticism of Israel and Israel's supporters constitute a threat to Israel's security, a matter of deep moment to America's Jews, and concludes that criticism of Israel indicates an insensitivity towards Jews and indifference to their fate. This insensitivity provides the basis for what the authors define as the "new anti-Semitism." It is not exactly that these new anti-Semites don't like Jews, as one disconcerted Jewish reviewer for *The New Leader* put it; "it's that they don't like Jews enough." This same reviewer goes on to comment that "a good deal of what is presented here as anti-Semitism is not anti-Semitism at all" and warns that "unless the Anti-Defamation League is careful, it's going to give anti-Semitism a good name." That so bad a miscalculation could be made by such experienced authorities is an index of the ulterior function of the recent cries of anti-Semitic "persecution" in shaping a conservative politics in the Jewish community.

It is not surprising to find, therefore, that the principal "new anti-Semites" singled out by the authors are American blacks and the radical left—both new and old.[7] (There are also some representatives of the Protestant clergy who have had the temerity to criticize Israel's politics.[8]) According to the authors, the radical left, whose principal sin seems to be that some of its sects are hostile to both zionism and Israel, "today represents a danger to world Jewry at least equal to the danger on the right."

For a radical Jew, the greatest pain in this indictment and the situation it reflects is not caused by the attack on radicals, which is both traditional and expected. For the radical secularizers of the prophetic tradition in Judaism have always been a source of embarrassment to the social assimilators of the Jewish establishment and have always been attacked for it. But the alienation of the Jewish community from the sufferings and struggles of black people is a less expected and more deeply significant event. Like Israel's oppression of the Palestinian Arabs, it is a poignant sign of the falling away of the Jewish community from Judaic values, and a tragic alienation from its own history of suffering. For in a real sense, black people are the Jews of America, the obsessional victim of the white majority in much the same way that Jews have been the obsessional victims of Christian majorities in Europe.

Although subjected, until the postwar period, to significant forms of ethnic persecution and oppression, Jews in America have in fact been relatively protected from the more savage persecutions they experienced in their European exile. In part, this was the result of the absence of an established Christian Church and the exclusivist binding of religion and nationality that existed in European states, which sharply defined the Jews as an alien element. In part, it was because of the buffer of black suffering and oppression itself, as though one ritual victim was sufficient for the progenitors of racial violence.

Today Jews can look into the mirror of black America and see the paranoid nature of their own fears. For black apprehensions about survival are not nurtured amid the comforts of Yonkers and the Berkeley hills. American blacks, too, have an ancient homeland from which they were uprooted and dispersed, and they can witness, even now, the deaths of three thousand blacks a day in West Africa without a ruffling in the wind of world opinion, while in southern Africa their brothers and sisters are pressed under the heel of a white supremacist regime supported by the entire white democratic world. To gain a proper perspective on their own situation in America, Jews might consider a Jewish majority still living in poverty-ridden ghettos, brutalized and frequently murdered by racist police, their children psychologically beaten down in alien schools, while serious proposals are put to the National Academy of Sciences in behalf of theories of their genetic inferiority. For these are the real premises of black discussions of ethnic survival in America.

There is indeed an instructive parallel for Jews in these debates about survival that have taken place in the black community. Some of the proposals (usually the most widely noted) have been of a nationalist strain, often patterned explicitly on the zionist example. These seek a solution to the oppression of America's blacks in the possession of a national territory, either in Africa or the United States. But there is also a view, which corresponds to that of the internationalist radicals in the Jewish community, which sees that the very condition for a nationalist "liberation" do not exist for black Americans (as they do not really exist for Jews). This is in part because the land question (that is, the problem of where to settle) is insoluble, and in part because the nation-state is itself an anachronism in an age of modern technology and empire. True self-determination cannot be achieved on a territorial basis. But these practical considerations also combine with a broader vision of ethical responsibilities and goals to give rise to a new self-consciousness: America's blacks form a unique group, according to some black radicals, in that the condition of their self-emancipation is the emancipation of all groups from national and social oppression.

This is a view that was first expressed to me by Black Panther leader Huey Newton, whose slogan of "revolutionary intercommunalism" is an effort to give the concept a name. But while Newton and the Panthers are a black group insisting on the futility of the nation-state as a solution to the problems of national oppression, they recognize the historical necessity of "raft-states" for threatened peoples like the Palestinians and the Jews. A recent Panther position paper on the Middle East declares:

> Though . . .the ultimate survival of Jews and Palestinians, as of all peoples, depends on the revolutionary overthrow of world imperialism and capitalism, we call upon Jews and Arabs in the Middle East to recognize the national rights of their opponents: upon the Government of Israel to recognize the claims of the Palestinian people for independent national institutions, as originally provided by the UN, and of the Arab states and the Palestinian liberation movement to recognize the existence of the State of Israel, as the national sovereignty of the Jewish people. This is the moral basis from which a political solution to the immediate crisis in the Middle East can be found.

"Revolutionary intercommunalism" is the Panther catch phrase for the messianic kingdom dreamed of by Marx and the Jewish prophets. Because its goals are set explicitly beyond the nation-state, Newton and the Panthers have been sharply criticized by nationalist elements in the black community, just as their counterparts in the Jewish community have been historically charged with assimilationism.[9]

In a sense the charge is true. The Jewish radicals of Eastern Europe had sought to go beyond the boundaries of the parochial and back-ward-looking ghetto societies in which their aspirations were stifled by religious obscurantism and archaic attitudes. They identified with the tradition of Jews who had transcended Jewry, who were of Jewry but not in it—great Jewish heretics like Spinoza, Marx, and later Freud, who traversed the boundaries of many nations and traditions, freed themselves from communal dogmas, and were able to search the future for a new, more rational basis of human community and identity. The Jewish radicals sought out the progressive intellectual and political trends of the twentieth century and made the link between the ethical message of the Torah and the great secular struggle for social emancipation. "We knew the Talmud, we had been steeped in Hassidism," wrote Isaac Deutscher: "We had the eleventh and thirteenth and sixteenth centuries of Jewish history living next door to us and under our very roof; and we wanted to escape it and live in the twentieth century. To someone of my background, the fashionable longing of the Western Jew for a return to the sixteenth century, a return which is supposed to help him in recovering, or rediscovering, his Jewish cultural identity, seems unreal and Kafkaesque."

There is a deeper sense, however, in which the charge of assimilation hurled at the Jewish internationalists is not true, in which their Jewish identity is not negated by their mission, but brought to a new level of fulfillment. This Deutscher passage appears in an essay addressed to the question of "Who is a Jew?" In it he wrote of the "macabre truth" that "the greatest redefiner of Jewish identity" was Hitler: "Auschwitz was the terrible cradle of the new Jewish consciousness and of the new Jewish nation. We, who have rejected the religious tradition, now belong to the negative community of those who have, so many times in our history . . . been singled out for persecution and extermination."

Deutscher rejected the idea that a positive Jewish identity should be resurrected on the basis of race ("Are we now going to accept the idea that it is racial ties or 'bonds of blood' that make up the Jewish community? Would not that be another triumph for Hitler and his degenerate philosophy?"). He asked what then makes a Jew: "Religion? I am an atheist. Jewish nationalism? I am an internationalist. In neither sense am I, therefore, a Jew. I am, however, a Jew by force of my unconditional solidarity with the persecuted and oppressed."

Out of the negative community of those who have been singled out for persecution and extermination, there arises a community of those whose solidarity with the stranger, with the persecuted and exterminated, is unconditional. "A people," writes Martin Buber, "need not necessarily be the fusion of kindred stems. . . . But the concept 'people' always implies unity of fate." The Jews became a people in the course of their exodus from Egypt, when Moses led them out of slavery and gave them the teaching and the Law. Later, in the Diaspora, "the uniqueness of Judaism became apparent in a very special way. In other nations, the national powers in themselves vouch for the survival of the people. In Judaism, this guarantee is given by another power . . . the membership in a community of faith."

The revolutionary belongs to a community of faith.[10] It is a community that extends beyond the classes and the nations, and reaches across the boundaries that divide and oppress. Within every national group it forms the basis of a new human community and a new human identity. Today the revolutionary is isolated, obstructed by the divisions that form the cultural and political legacy of the past; the revolutionary is of the nations, but not in them. For the revolutionary's eye is on the future. Today there is black and Jew, American and Russian, Israeli and Arab. But within each nation—Russia, America, Israel, Egypt—there are the aliens, the persecuted, the unassimilated, the "Jews" who know the heart of the stranger and struggle for human freedom. Today they are separated; tomorrow they will be joined. Today the light of their faith shines in many national colors, but it is also expressed in the service that commemorates the Exodus and looks toward a future turning: *This year we are slaves; next year we shall be free men and women. This year in the lands of our exile; next year in Jerusalem.*

Telling It Like It Wasn't

T HE YEAR 1998—marking the twentieth anniversary of the "revolutionary" moment in the decade of the 1960s—was an occasion for nostalgia artists of the left to remember their glory days and the magic of a time that many of them have never left. It was a time, in their imaginations, of lost innocence, when assassination and repression brutally cut off their dreams. It was a failure of progressive hopes that has stranded them in a conservative landscape ever since.

A summary expression of these utopian regrets can be found in Steven Talbot's PBS documentary, "1968: The Year that Shaped a Generation." The film's narrative is shaped exclusively by 1960s radicals like Todd Gitlin and Tom Hayden, who are interviewed on camera. The choice of Gitlin and Hayden as authorities on the era is predictable. Talbot himself is a veteran of this movement that promoted itself as an avatar of "participatory democracy" but closes off debate over its own history in a way worthy of the Communist regimes it once admired. As the auteur of "The Year that Shaped a Generation," he protects this cinematic paean to his revolutionary youth from any adverse scrutiny by dissenters who were also there.

This critique first appeared on *Salon.com* and FrontPageMagazine.com on January 1, 1999. It was reprinted in *Hating Whitey & Other Progressive Causes* (1999). It has been edited for this book.

I myself am such a veteran who does not share Talbot's enthusiasm for 1968, or his view of it as a fable of Innocents at Home. One explanation may be that as someone ten years older than Talbot, I know firsthand the state of our "innocence" then. Yet Gitlin and Hayden are also pre-boomers, so that an age gap cannot really explain our different views of what took place. Naturally, I would prefer to recall the glory days of my youth in a golden light, just like Gitlin and Hayden. For me, however, the era has been irreparably tarnished by actions and attitudes that I vividly remember, but they in contrast prefer to forget.

In Talbot's film, the myth of innocence begins with President Lyndon Johnson's announcement in March 1968 that he would not run for re-election. Talbot was nineteen years old and draft-eligible: "We were all like Yossarian in Catch-22," he recalls in a commentary on the film he wrote for *Salon.com*. "We took this very personally. 'They' were trying to kill 'us.' But now Johnson had abdicated. We were free. It felt, quite simply, like a miracle." The miracle, of course, was the democratic system, on which the left had declared war, but which had responded to the people's will all the same. In 1968, radicals like Hayden, Gitlin, and Talbot were calling for a "liberation" that would put an end to that very system. For New Leftists like us the "system" was the enemy. But contrary to what we were saying, the system worked.

Looking back, we should all have defended the System, and worked within it, instead of what we did do, which was to try to tear it apart and bring it down. Gitlin and Hayden have hedgingly (and *sotto voce*) acknowledged this fact elsewhere, but without reassessing their past actions in this light. Talbot does not even notice the problem. Nor does he reflect on the contradiction between what he and his comrades advocated then, and what everyone recognizes to be the case now.

The "they" Talbot refers to in identifying our enemy, were assuredly not trying to kill us in 1968. (Even in its retrospective mode, the narcissism of the boomer generation is impressive.) The attention of Lyndon Johnson and Richard Nixon were actually not fixed on us at the time, but on the fate of Indochina. They had committed American forces to prevent the Communist conquest of South Vietnam and Cambodia and the bloodbath that we now know was in store for their inhabitants should the communists win the war. As a result of the communist victory (and our efforts that contributed to it), more people—more poor Indochinese peasants—were killed by the marxist victors in the first three years of the communist peace than had been killed on all sides in the thirteen years of the anti-Communist war. This fact has caused some of us veterans to re-consider our commitments and our innocence. But not Talbot or the other nostalgists he has invited to make his film.

For them, the moral innocence of the left remains intact to this day. According to them, their innocence was brutally ambushed when forces inherent in the system they hated conspired to murder the agents of their hope: Martin Luther King and Bobby Kennedy. And it was only those murders that caused them to become radicals at war with America in 1968.

"I experienced King's assassination as the murder of hope," writes Talbot, speaking for them all. In the film, Gitlin, whose history of the 1960s first announced this theme,[1] remembers his similar thoughts at the time: "America tried to redeem itself and now they've killed the man who was taking us to the mountaintop." This is a false memory, and there is something extremely distasteful in the fact that a participant like Gitlin is proposing it. For, as he well knows, in 1968 neither he, Tom Hayden, nor any serious New Left radical, thought of themselves as liberal reformers or was still a follower of Martin Luther King.

A key indicator of the self-conscious dissociation of radicals like Gitlin and Hayden from reformers like King is that neither of them, nor any other white student activist, SDS leader, or anti-war spokesman was in Memphis for the demonstrations King was organizing in 1968 at the time he was killed. In fact, no white spokesman of the New Left (at least no one who mattered) still regarded King as his leader in the year before King was assassinated. At the time, the black heroes of the New Left, like Stokely Carmichael, H. Rap Brown, Huey Newton, and the martyred Malcolm X, were prophets of separatism and violence. King had been unceremoniously toppled from the leadership of the civil rights movement two years before, without protest from his white radical supporters. The political agendas of the black radicals who pushed King aside were "black power" and revolutionary violence, both of which King explicitly rejected. Their dismissal of King's programs of nonviolence and integration resonated in the imaginations of the white student left, which fell in line behind their agendas.

Like other New Left leaders, Todd Gitlin was far from the idealistic liberal he impersonates in his book on the 1960s or in Talbot's film. Like practically everyone else in the New Left, Gitlin had (by his own admission) stopped voting in national elections as early as 1964 because, as the SDS slogan put it, "the revolution is in the streets."[2] To Gitlin and other New Leftists, the two parties were the Tweedledum and Tweedledee of the corporate ruling class. Activists who saw themselves as revolutionaries against a "sham" democracy dominated by multinational corporations were not going to invest hope in a leader like King, whose political agenda was integration into the system, and who refused to join their war on the Johnson administration and its imperialist adventures abroad or "tokenist" liberalism at home.[3]

In Talbot's film, Hayden, too, embraces a doctrine of original innocence, but with less blunt fabrication than Gitlin. Instead, he resorts to the kind of manipulation of the truth that is his recognized political signature. "At that point," Hayden says of the King assassination, "I had been so knocked out of my middle-class assumptions that I didn't know what would happen. Perhaps the country could be reformed and Robert Kennedy elected president. Perhaps we would be plunged into a civil war and I'd be imprisoned or killed."

Such is Hayden's myth. The reality is, Hayden had no such ambivalence and was telling other activists like myself that we would soon all be shot or in jail. Any "middle-class assumptions" held by Tom Hayden—or any prominent SDS activist—had already been chucked into the historical dustbin years before. Three out of four of the drafters of the famous 1962 Port Huron Statement were "red diaper babies," that is, marxists. The fourth was Hayden himself, who by his own account in his autobiography, *Reunion*, learned his politics in Berkeley in 1960 at the feet of children of the Old Left. (Hayden names leftwing veterans Michael Tigar and Richard Flacks, in particular, as his mentors.) By 1965, SDS president Carl Oglesby was proclaiming publicly, in a famous speech, that it was time to "name the System" that we all wanted to destroy. The name of the system was "corporate capitalism," and it was analyzed by SDS leaders in much the same terms as in party texts read by the communist cadres in Moscow, Havana, and Hanoi.

By 1968, Hayden was already calling the Black Panthers "America's Vietcong" and planning the riot he was going to stage at the Democratic convention in Chicago that August. This pivotal event is described conveniently, but inaccurately, as a "police riot" in Talbot's film, Gitlin's book, and Hayden's own memoir, which singularly fails to acknowledge his efforts to produce the eruption that ensued. Civil war in America was not something that was going to be imposed on the SDS revolutionaries from the outside or above, as Hayden disingenuously insinuates. Civil war was something that radicals—Hayden foremost among them—were trying to launch themselves. [4]

Talbot continues his mythologizing of the spring of 1968 and the period just prior to the Chicago Riot by romanticizing the political ambitions of Bobby Kennedy, and misremembering how the left reacted to them: "Out of the ashes of the riots in the wake of King's murder, new hope came in the form of Bobby Kennedy, who had undergone a profound transformation from Vietnam hawk and aide to Sen. Joe McCarthy to dove and spokesman for the dispossessed."

It is true, of course, that Bobby Kennedy made a feint in the direction of the anti-war crowd and more than one gesture on behalf of Cesar Chavez. It is also true that Hayden attended Kennedy's funeral and even wept a tear or two. But those tears had little to do with Hayden's political agendas at the time, which were more accurately summed up in Che Guevara's call to create "two, three, many Vietnams" inside America's borders (Hayden even recoined the slogan as "two, three, many Chicagos"). Hayden's tears for Kennedy were personal, and he paid a huge political price for them among his revolutionary comrades, who were not overly impressed by Kennedy's sudden political "transformation." After the funeral, SDS activists wondered out loud, and in print, whether Hayden had "sold out" by mourning a figure whom they saw not as the great white hope of the political struggle that consumed their lives, but as a Trojan horse for the other side.

With King dead in April and Kennedy in June, the stage was set for what Talbot calls "the inevitable showdown" in Chicago in August. And here he allows a glimmer of the truth to enter his narrative: "Both sides, rebels and rulers, were spoiling for a confrontation." But just as quickly, he reverts to the mythology that Hayden and his cohorts first created and that leftist historians have since perpetuated: "Chicago's Mayor Richard Daley made it possible. He denied permits for protesters at the Democratic Convention." This denial made confrontation inevitable.

In fact, the famous epigram from 1968—"Demand the Impossible"—which Talbot elsewhere cites, explains far more accurately why it was Hayden, not Daley, who set the agenda for Chicago, and why it was Hayden who was ultimately responsible for the riot that ensued. The police behaved badly, it is true—and they have been justly condemned for their reactions. But those reactions were entirely predictable. It was Daley who, only months before, had ordered his police to "shoot looters on sight" during the rioting after King's murder. In fact, the predictable reaction of the Chicago police was an essential part of Hayden's choice of Chicago as the site of the demonstration in the first place, and the reason why very few activists joined him.

In a year when any national action would have attracted a hundred thousand protestors, only about three thousand actually showed up for the Chicago rumble. That was because most of us realized there was going to be blood in the streets and did not see the point of it. Our ideology argued otherwise as well. The two-party system was a sham; the revolution was in the streets. Why demonstrate at a political convention? In retrospect, Hayden was both more cynical and shrewder than we were. By fomenting a riot that destroyed the presidential aspirations of Hubert Humphrey, he dealt a fatal blow to the anti-communist liberals in the Democratic Party and paved the way for a takeover of its apparatus by the forces of the political left—a trauma from which the party has yet to recover.

One reason the left has obscured these historical facts is that the nostalgists do not really want to take credit for electing Richard Nixon, which they surely did. As a matter of political discretion, they are also

willing to let their greatest *coup*—the capture of the Democratic Party—
go unmemorialized. Instead they prefer to ascribe the remarkable political realignment that followed the Chicago events to impersonal forces
that, apparently, had nothing to do with their own agendas and actions.
Talbot summarizes: "While 'the whole world [was] watching,' [Daley's]
police rioted, clubbing demonstrators, reporters and bystanders indis-
criminately. The Democratic Party self-destructed." Well, actually, it
was destroyed by the riot that Tom Hayden organized in Chicago.

When the fires of Watergate consumed the Nixon presidency in
1974, the left's newly won control of the Democratic Party produced
the exact result that Hayden and his comrades had worked so hard to
achieve. In 1974, a new class of Democrats was elected to Congress,
including anti-Vietnam activists like Ron Dellums, Pat Schroeder,
David Bonior, and Bella Abzug. Their politics were traditionally left,
as opposed to the anti-communist liberalism of the Daleys and the
Humphreys (Abzug had even been a Communist). Their first act was
to cut off economic aid and military supplies to the regimes in Cambodia and South Vietnam, precipitating the bloodbath that followed.
Though it is conveniently forgotten now, this cut-off occurred two
years after the United States signed a truce with Hanoi and American
troops had been withdrawn from Vietnam.

"Bring the Troops Home" may have been the slogan of the so-
called anti-war movement, but it was always a tactic, never the goal.
The goal was a "liberated" Vietnam. Within three months of losing
military aid, the anti-Communist regimes in Saigon and Phnom Penh
fell, and the communist genocide began. The mass slaughter in Cambodia and South Vietnam from 1975 to 1978 was the real achievement
of the New Left and could not have been accomplished without
Hayden's sabotage of the Humphrey presidential campaign and the
anti-communist Democrats.

While Talbot forgets this denouement, he does get the significance of the war itself: "The war in Vietnam and the draft were absolutely central. I remember a cover of *Ramparts* magazine that captured
how I felt: 'Alienation is when your country is at war and you hope the
other side wins.'" This is in fact a softened version of what we actually

felt. As the author of that cover line, let me correct Talbot's memory and add a detail. The *Ramparts* cover featured a picture of a Huck Finn-like seven-year-old (it was our art director Dugald Stermer's son) who was holding the Vietcong flag—the flag of America's enemy in Vietnam. The cover line said: "Alienation is when your country is at war and you want the other side to win." This represented what we actually believed—Hayden, Gitlin, Steve Talbot, and myself. What final lessons my former comrades draw from our service to the wrong side in the Cold War is not that important to me. I wish they would have the decency to remember the events the way they happened and take responsibility for what occurred.

I also wish they would have the good grace not to claim retrospectively that they had sympathies for the struggle *against* Communism, a struggle they opposed and whose true warriors and champions—however distasteful, embarrassing, and uncomfortable this must be for them—were Richard Nixon, Ronald Reagan, and the political right they hate and despise. Go over the fifty years of the Cold War against the Soviet empire and you will find that every political and military program to contain the spread of this cancer and ultimately to destroy it was fiercely resisted by those who called themselves "anti-anti-Communists" then, but who now invoke the anti-Communist "spirit of '68" in Eastern Europe as their own.

"Assassinations, repression and exhaustion extinguished the spirit of '68," Talbot concludes his story. "But like a subterranean fire, it resurfaces at historic moments." Citing the socialist writer Paul Berman, the originator of this myth, Talbot argues that "the members of '68... helped ignite the revolution of 1989 that brought liberal democracy to Eastern Europe and ended the Cold War."[5] The distortion of this memory is one thing for Berman, who at some point joined a miniscule faction of the left that was indeed anti-Communist, while still hating American capitalism almost as much. (How much? In Berman's case, enough to support the Black Panthers—"America's Vietcong"—in the 1970s and to praise the secret police chief of the Sandinista dictatorship in the 1980s as a "quintessential New Leftist.") But the attempt to hijack the anti-Communist cause for a left that supported Communism and abhorred its opponents, is particularly unappetizing in Talbot's case. Talbot made films into the 1980s celebrating Communist insurgents who were busily extending the Soviet sphere in Africa. America, bless its generous heart, has already forgiven Steve Talbot for the indiscretions of his past. So why lie about them now?

Of course, New Leftists were critical of the policies of the Soviet Union (as, at various times, were Khrushchev, Castro, and Ho Chi Minh). But their true, undying enemy was always democratic America— their hatred for which was never merely reactive (as is sometimes suggested), never truly innocent, and remains remarkably intact to this day. The worldview of this left was aptly summarized by the adoring biographer of the journalist I. F. Stone, who approvingly described Stone's belief that "in spite of the brutal collectivization campaign, the Nazi-Soviet Pact, the latest quashing of the Czech democracy and the Stalinist takeover of Eastern Europe . . . Communism was a progressive force, lined up on the correct side of historical events."

Berman, Gitlin, and now Talbot have mounted a preposterous last ditch effort to save leftists from the embarrassments of their deeds by attempting to appropriate moral credit for helping to end a system that the left had aided and abetted throughout its career It may be, as Berman and Talbot claim, that East European anti-Communists drew inspiration from anti-government protests in the West. But this was a reflection of their admiration for a democratic system that embraced dissent and promoted freedom, not the anti-western agendas of the New Left protesters. Even in its best moments, the western left still disparaged the threat from the communist enemy as a paranoid fantasy of the Cold War right.

The unseemly attempt to retrieve an honorable past from such dishonorable commitments might be more convincing were any of these memorialists (including Berman) able to identify a single demonstration of theirs against Communist oppression in Vietnam, or the genocide in Cambodia, or the rape of Afghanistan, or the dictatorships in Cuba and Nicaragua. Did one veteran leader of the New Left once publicly call on the Soviets to tear down the Berlin Wall, as Ronald Reagan did? Support for the anti-Communist freedom fighters in Afghanistan and Africa and Central America during the 1980s came largely from Goldwater and Reagan activists on the right, like Jeanne Kirkpatrick, Elliott Abrams, and Oliver North, whom progressives—for this very reason—passionately despise.

It would have been nice if the thirtieth anniversary of the events of 1968 had been used to end the cold war over its memories and start restoring a sense of the tragic to both sides. But to do that, the nostalgists of the left would first have to be persuaded to give up their futile attempts to rewrite what happened, and start telling it like it was.

III

SECOND THOUGHTS

Questions

M Y REFLECTIONS AFTER BETTY'S MURDER did not stop with
the Panthers.[1] I understood better now who they were, yet
was puzzled by the way they seemed to operate with impunity. This was a reality that was a far cry from the image of the persecuted vanguard we had created (and were able to establish widely in
the press). Law enforcement seemed unable to stop them and at times
was even paralyzed in its efforts to do so. If one thought about it without ideological blinders, the authorities we accused of harassing them
were surprisingly forbearing and on occasion even showed exceptional
consideration. Although Newton had murdered an Oakland policeman, the chief of the Oakland force had warned him when his life was
in jeopardy, even though the danger was created by his own criminal
acts.[2] And this was not the only instance I knew of. During Bobby
Seale's campaign for mayor, one of his bodyguards, jittery from lack of
sleep, in the early morning hours had inadvertently shot and killed a
crippled newsboy.[3] This presented the authorities and the press alike
an opportunity to destroy the campaign and do the Panthers serious
damage. But the bodyguard was prosecuted quietly, while Seale went
on with his campaign—which included regular denunciations of the
"fascist" power structure and its brutal repression of Panthers like him.

From *Radical Son: A Generational Odyssey* (1997).

While I was pondering these ironies, the police made a raid on the Twenty-ninth Street house that had been the original site of the school.[4] They found more than a thousand weapons, including M-15 and M-16 semiautomatic rifles, Thompson submachine guns, M-60 fully automatic machine guns, and even M-79 grenade launchers. Charles Garry, the Party lawyer, called a press conference to claim that Twenty-ninth Street was a "dormitory" for teachers at the Learning Center, and that the police had planted the weapons as part of their ongoing political repression of the Panthers. Garry's strategy was successful (the press was more than ready to believe him), and no one was prosecuted. The house may well have been a dormitory, but it was also (as Elaine herself boasted nearly twenty years later in her autobiography[5]) a Panther arsenal, just as the police had claimed. (Elaine even catalogued the weapons, her list corresponding to what the police had actually said at the time.) Meanwhile, Elaine appeared on college campuses with other leftists, making speeches about American fascism and denouncing the FBI's "Cointelpro" program to infiltrate and neutralize the Panthers solely because of their political beliefs.

If there was such a program, where were its agents? Why hadn't they saved Betty? Why hadn't they prosecuted Elaine or the Squad?[6] Where was the press, the supposed "tool" of the power structure? Why hadn't they turned the glare of publicity on this radical stronghold and its dirty secrets? I couldn't answer these questions, and they wouldn't go away In the absence of a serious investigation, and in the silence that surrounded Betty's murder, Elaine was able to complete her campaign for city council and win 40 percent of the Oakland vote. A year later, the electoral machine she put together from the Party apparatus was made available to Lionel Wilson, and provided the margin by which he was elected Oakland's first black mayor, as the press and the authorities continued their silence.

I later learned that jurisdictional disputes were part of the reason the police were prevented from conducting an adequate investigation of Betty's death. The victim had lived in Berkeley, but her body washed ashore in Foster City, across the Bay. Oakland, where the Panthers operated, was not even involved in the case. This confusion hampered the investigative effort. The high level of scrutiny the police could expect from a liberal press, the threat of legal suits from radical lawyers, and the charges of persecution that would accompany any serious probe, completed the constraints. Years later, I joined a downtown athletic club where one of my workout buddies turned out to be the former head of homicide for Oakland. "Why didn't you guys ever nail Huey Newton?" I asked him. "Oh," he said, "We never wanted to get a call from that side of town, because you guys and your lawyers would be all over us." The cops were just working stiffs with jobs to protect. There were no Kojaks, and there was no repressive state.

In creating a protective shield around the Panthers, we had repeated a figure of the progressive past. Trotsky had described the communist parties of the world as frontier guards for the Soviet Union. Their function was to explain away Stalin's crimes, put obstacles in the path of those who resisted his policies, and discredit witnesses who testified against him. The New Left had formed a similar frontier guard around the Panthers and their crimes.

An episode involving Bobby Seale now illustrated the wide latitude the Panthers enjoyed because of the protection their supporters provided. After being beaten by Newton and threatened by Elaine, the former chairman of the Black Panther Party had disappeared. In 1975, in democratic America, one of the most prominent figures in the political culture simply vanished. And no one publicly noticed or cared that he was gone: not the press, not his political supporters in the white left, not his former followers. It turned out that Seale was in hiding, in fear for his life. A year and a half after Seale's disappearance, Charles[7] told me that Seale had fled because of Elaine's threats, and no one knew where he was—not even his mother. Seale was easily the most public and popular of the Panther leaders, personally known to most of the prominent figures on the left, including his co-defendants in the Chicago conspiracy case—Dave Dellinger, Tom Hayden, Jerry Rubin, and Abbie Hoffman—and their lawyer, William Kunstler. In all the time he was missing, not one of these champions of the persecuted and oppressed raised his voice to ask where Bobby Seale was, and thus provide him with protection. None of them was willing to do so, because Seale's persecutors were the Panthers themselves.

The entire episode seemed such an unlikely occurrence that fifteen years later I began to wonder that it had happened at all. Then, in the course of doing research for a piece I was writing, I came across a 1976 article about Eldridge Cleaver in *Rolling Stone* called "Revolution On Ice." The article mentioned in passing that Bobby Seale had disappeared, and noted that his family had not heard from him and was "concerned." What the article did not say was that many people knew why he was missing, but their lips were sealed.

The silence that enveloped Seale's disappearance resurrected the feelings I had after Betty's death: the loneliness that closed around a person identified as an "enemy of the people"; the immoral core of the community of the left; its lack of conscience when the victims were among those it had politically damned. Lenin had called his opponents "insects" that the revolution must exterminate. If you were merely a peasant and got in the way of the revolution, your life was flattened into a single abstraction, as in "The achievement of socialism requires the liquidation of the *kulak*." The particular individual with distinctive features simply disappeared. Stalin's innovation was to make these condemned souls "unpersons" even before their deaths. Even heroes of the revolution were not immune. You could be as famous as Trotsky, and it would count for nothing when the revolution turned against you. Not only would Stalin kill you to the applause of the people, but it would be as if you had never existed. Your achievements would be removed from the historical record, and even your image would be erased from the photographic memory of the time. When socialist justice was complete, there would be nothing left of you at all.

For awhile, Bobby Seale became an unperson in America. Among all those who had once considered him a hero and friend, nobody cared. Or they were too terrified to care. This was how Itzhak Feffer had disappeared—forgotten and abandoned by his friends.[8] Of course, it was still America, the Panthers did not control the state, and (in the end) Bobby Seale survived. But what if the Panthers, or radicals like them, eventually did succeed?

Thinking about this caused me to reflect on the difference between our adversaries and us. There was plenty of injustice in the system we opposed. But it had created procedures and institutions designed to redress grievances, correct injustices, and put checks on the power of government. In rejecting our radical agendas, our opponents had always stressed the importance of "process" and following rules, even when the issues seemed obvious. As radicals, we were impatient with order and had contempt for process. We wanted "direct rule" and "people's justice," unconstrained by such legalisms and the hierarchies they required. We had no use for law that pretended to be neutral between persons and classes, that failed to recognize historical grievances or the way rules were shaped by social forces. We did not believe in bourgeois legality and objective standards. The revolutionary will embodied justice and truth. We were going to eliminate "checks and balances" and let the people decide.

As a result, we had no justice. There were no means to redress the crimes committed by the Panthers or other tribunes of the people—in America or anywhere else. There was no institutional recourse, and no moral standard, to which we were committed. And there was no rationale to create them. This contempt for order, for objective values, for moralities that transcended particular interests, separated us from our enemies, and made their justice superior to ours—even when they were wrong. The Smith Act decisions that had sent communist leaders to jail during the McCarthy era had been reversed by the courts a short time later. The Rosenbergs had received no such reprieve, but at least the system had allowed their cause to be heard. As a result of this respect for individuals and rights, the prosecutions of the McCarthy era had become the object of a national soul-searching and many judicial and political reversals. The truth—whatever it was—eventually had a chance to breathe.

Socialist justice provided no such opportunity and no such reprieve. It had been forty years since Stalin's purges. The victims were

dead, their memories erased. They were unpersons without public defenders, expunged even from the consciousness of the living. Those
who knew the truth had to keep their silence, even as I had to keep
mine. If we actually succeeded in making a revolution in America, and
if the Panthers or similar radical vanguards prevailed, how would our
fate be different from theirs? Our injustice, albeit mercifully smaller in
scale, was as brutal and final as Stalin's. As progressives, we had no law
to govern us, other than that of the gang.

—

After Betty's murder, I ceased to be politically active. I couldn't even
think about politics apart from these events. In my heart, I knew that
it would not be possible for me to work for a cause again until I had
resolved the issues of her death. As New Leftists, we felt ourselves
immunized from crimes that the left had committed in the past, both
by acknowledging that they had occurred and by resolving to change
the attitudes that had caused them. But we had changed the attitudes,
and now the crimes were being repeated. I began to ask myself whether
there was something in marxism, or in the socialist idea itself, that was
the root of the problem.

I was not alone in raising this question now. The Polish philosopher Leszek Kolakowski had been an intellectual leader of the New
Left until his defection to the West in 1968, after the Soviet invasion
of Czechoslovakia. Five years later, Kolakowski organized a conference
at Oxford, which asked: "Is There Anything Wrong with the Socialist
Idea?" In a paper delivered to the conference, he suggested that there
was: the goals which socialists had historically pursued contained the
seeds of the socialist nightmare.

The ideal of human unity was one. The end of "self-alienation"
was really the core of the socialist hope. Socialists believed that private
property divided human beings, making some rich and some poor, some
oppressors and others oppressed, and was the root cause of social conflict.
Socialists proposed to abolish property and unite people in the state.
But the abolition of property was really the abolition of private asso-

ciation and civil society, and of the bourgeois rights they underpinned. Socialist unity could only be achieved as a totalitarian solution.

Kolakowski then turned to the goal of equality and showed that it led to a similar impasse. Even if one assumed all human beings to be equal by nature (a dubious proposition), historical circumstance had made them unequal. After the revolution, these historical inequalities would have to be redressed. But the class of people that decided who would be made equal, and at what rate, would—by the very fact of that power—become a new ruling caste. The quest for equality would create a new inequality. There was no exit from the cycle of human fate.

Along with Kolakowski's questions came others. I had been reading *Political Messianism* by J. L. Talmon, which described nationalism and socialism as secular religions that lacked a doctrine of original sin. After reading Talmon's account, I began to wish that I had inherited such a concept. The idea of original sin—that we are born flawed, that the capacity for evil is lodged within us (no matter how our consciousness may be raised)—would have instilled in me a necessary caution about individuals like Huey Newton, and movements like ours. There were people who had a will to evil that no amount of political enlightenment could overcome. Nor could any movement (no less humanity) hope to purge itself of the potential for evil that lurked in us all.

Solzhenitsyn had formulated this insight in the following way: "The line separating good and evil passes not through states, nor between classes, nor between political parties, but right through every human heart—and through all human hearts." But if this was true, what could socialist liberation mean? If evil was a choice that any individual could make, then human beings would always pose a danger to each other, and there could be no "withering away of the state." There would always be a need for law above individuals, for police to enforce the law, and for prisons to contain those who broke it. We could never dispense with the apparatus of repression, even after socialist justice had been instituted. But if this was true, how could we dispense with "bourgeois" law, the best system of rules and institutions yet devised to protect individuals from the predations of their government and each other? If we really cared about liberty and justice, we would have to give up our superior status as revolutionary opponents of "bourgeois" order, and enter the universe of its morality and thought.

Bourgeois morality was not all that we would have to accept. If there was indeed an element in human nature that could not be re-shaped by socialist ideas, then not only was the rule of law necessary, but the rule of the market as well. As radicals, we had decried the absence of a social plan, and what Marx called the "fetishism of commodities"—the fact that in capitalist economies "things were in the saddle" and the market ruled, instead of man. But if human beings were corrupt in their nature, they would corrupt the plan as well. How could there be a social plan not driven by ego and self-serving desire? Better to be governed by markets that were impersonal, by neutral rules that were not subject to human will.

The unraveling continued. If it was necessary to "seize power" and "smash the state," the individuals who rose to the fore in revolutions were likely to be fanatics with an aptitude for violence. The readiness of Lenin and Stalin to be ruthless and brutal—to do what was "necessary"—had caused others to follow them, and the rest to get out of their way. My own political experience confirmed the rule. In volatile situations, the momentum was always seized by those most certain in their conviction, least impressed by ambiguity, and most ready to take risks or manipulate facts to achieve their objectives. When you went into combat, it was only natural to put your trust in warriors who were prepared to be ruthless and brutal. But these characteristics of the revolutionary vanguard were not the traits of good rulers, in whom judiciousness, moral scruple, and caution would be obvious virtues. Yet how could the conquerors be persuaded to step down?

I wrestled with these questions for a long time, unable to find satisfactory answers and equally unable to pursue them to their logical conclusion. To give up the socialist idea was still unthinkable. It had been the standard by which I judged right and wrong, the principle that had created my communities and friendships and shaped my actions. The pursuit of the ideal had made me what I was, until I had no conception of myself without it. When I thought of leaving the socialist movement, the feeling was the same as leaving my own life.

But I could not drop the issue, either. I began to discuss my questions with friends and in informal groups, and even arranged to conduct a class at a radical institute on the topic "Is Socialism a Viable Idea?" This formulation was the closest I was ready to come to the precipice in front of me. I hoped the announcement would attract peers who could persuade me that my intuitions were wrong. But the only participants who showed up were new to the left. When I confronted friends, they evaded the issue—responding instead to its dangerous subtext, which I was trying so hard to suppress: "If you are asking such questions, David, you must be planning to leave us." Michael Lerner, who came to recruit me into a vanguard he was calling the New American Movement, summed up their reactions with characteristic crudeness.[9] "Even to raise such questions," he said to me, "is counter-revolutionary." Like a person being pushed unwillingly out a door, I protested passionately against these charges. My intentions were constructive, I argued; there was no reason to conclude that the questions I was raising were unanswerable. But over time my reassurances to myself grew less and less convincing.

The attempts to involve others in my quest came to an end, finally, when I was invited by a sociologist friend, William Kornhauser, to attend a seminar on "Marxism and Post-marxism" at UC Berkeley. The seminar was held under the auspices of the Institute for Social Relations, which was headed by Troy Duster, the black sociologist whom I had taken to see Newton. I looked forward to the group because it was made up of veterans of the movement who would be knowledgeable about the issues I wanted to discuss. Among them were Robert Blauner (who had written books on alienation and race), former SNCC activist Hardy Frye, Todd Gitlin, Jeff Lustig, Victoria Bonnell, and David Wellman. Wellman's father had been one of the communist leaders prosecuted under the Smith Act in the 1950s. I was the only one attending the seminar who was not on a university faculty.

Once the sessions got under way, however, it became apparent that the others present had different agendas than mine. They divided themselves into marxists and "structuralists." The latter were marxists who thought that the practical failures of socialist revolutions had made

Marx's analysis untenable, and who sought to rescue the marxist agenda by sophisticating its radical theory. But I wanted to question radical theory itself, specifically its destructive attack on "bourgeois" culture and institutions in the absence of practical ideas of what to do when the destruction was accomplished. To "annihilate" bourgeois society in the name of an abstract ideal seemed to me intellectually empty and politically irresponsible. To carry on a radical critique of the existing order without any practical idea of what would replace it was nihilism.

When I attempted to raise these questions, I encountered a wall of resistance. Instead of a response, there was only an awkward shuffling into the next subject. I began to feel permanently "out of order," an intruder into someone else's conversation. My own thinking, at the time, had been shaped by a book I was reading, *The Ordeal of Civility* by John Murray Cuddihy, which had won a National Book Award. In Cuddihy's view, the theories of Marx and Freud were strategies for dealing with their predicament as members of a despised social group. European Jews had been given rights and were admitted to civil society only after the French Revolution. But they had been denied full acceptance through a kind of "institutional racism," a code of civility that continued to keep them in their place. It was Cuddihy's thesis that the revolutionary ideas of Marx and Freud were attempts to deconstruct these civil orders and replace them with a universal order in which they would finally be granted the acceptance they craved. Freud claimed to show that bourgeois civility was a mask for sexual repression, while Marx argued that it mystified economic exploitation. Each had a vision of liberation—science for Freud, socialism for Marx— that would provide a universal solvent in which the significance of ethnic identities disappeared.

Earlier in my life, I would have thought Cuddihy's idea merely peculiar. But the events of the past year had made me acutely conscious of my own ethnicity. In the aftermath of Betty's and Ellen's deaths,[10] I thought about how vulnerable we were because we were white; how this had made it difficult for me, for example, to plead Betty's cause. For the first time in my life, I had felt isolated and made helpless by my race.

I thought of how we had extended ourselves to bring justice to others because they were black. How for myself and Ellen this had begun when we were still adolescents, and yet how little this care seemed to be reciprocated. I thought of how Troy Duster had known the Panthers were dangerous, but had done nothing to warn me. Nor could I have reasonably expected him to do anything to help me after Betty was killed. In all my efforts on behalf of black people, I had never thought to ask: would my black comrades extend themselves to gain justice for *me*?

I began to review events of the past to which I had paid little attention before, like the expulsion of the Jews from the civil-rights movement in 1966. Jews had funded the movement, devised its legal strategies, and provided support for its efforts in the media and in the universities—and wherever else they had power. More than half the freedom riders who had gone to the southern states were Jews, although Jews constituted only 3 percent of the population. It was an unprecedented show of solidarity from one people to another. Jews had put their resources and lives on the line to support the black struggle for civil rights, and indeed two of their sons—Schwerner and Goodman— had been murdered for their efforts. But even while these tragic events were still fresh, the black leaders of the movement had unceremoniously expelled the Jews from their ranks. When Israel was attacked in 1967 by a coalition of Arab states calling for its annihilation, the same black leaders threw their support to the Arab aggressors, denouncing zionism (the Jewish liberation movement) as racism. Rarely had a betrayal of one people by another been as total or as swift. Yet radical Jews like myself had continued our dedication to the black movement for civil rights—to their struggle and their cause. What was it that made us so willing to support those who would treat us like this, who would not support us in return? Why did we think it was all right— even noble—to operate according to standards so different from those that governed others?

Just two months before Betty's disappearance, I had written a cover story for *Ramparts*, "The Passion of the Jews," in which I defended the denials of progressives like myself.[11] It opened with an encounter that posed the same question. A Jewish doctor had asked me: "Do you have any Christian friends whom you could trust with your life?" I was appalled by the question, by his implication that there could be none. It was such a "plummet into tribal depths," I wrote, that I did not want to confront it. Comfortable and safe as he was in America, this doctor could not forget the fate of Germany's Jews, who had also felt comfortable and safe before being turned in by their Christian friends. In my answer, I attempted to place his anxiety in the frame of the revolution I still believed in and which I still believed would provide a solution. By rejecting their own societies, radicals had entered a state-less diaspora, like the Jews before the creation of Israel. Having no state to defend them, they identified with those who were powerless and oppressed. Out of this identification, a new community was form-ing—a "community of faith" in the revolutionary future which would rescue us all from this dilemma:

> The revolutionary belongs to a community of faith that extends beyond the classes and the nations and reaches across the bound-aries that divide and oppress. Within every national group it forms the basis of a new human community and a new human identity. Today the revolutionary is isolated, obstructed by the divisions that form the cultural and political legacy of the past; the revolu-tionary is of the nations, but not in them. For the revolutionary's eye is on the future. Today there is Black and Jew, American and Russian, Israeli and Arab. But within each nation—Russia, America, Israel, Egypt—there are the aliens, the persecuted, the unassimilated, the "Jews" who know the heart of the stranger and who struggle for human freedom. Today they are separated; to-morrow they will be joined.

Betty's death killed this fantasy in me. There was no revolutionary community. There would be no redemptive future. There is no one to save us from who we are.

One day Troy Duster interrupted our seminar to talk about Harry Edwards, a black sociologist who had recently been denied his tenure at the university. Edwards was a former athlete and well-known activist who had led the protests at the 1968 Olympics, where black medalists raised clenched fists during the playing of the national anthem after their victories, instead of saluting the American flag. He was denied tenure when a slim departmental majority decided that his publications, which were about the sociology of sports, did not merit an appointment. Edwards had denounced the decision as "racist." Now he was considering a new twist in the strategy to save his job. "Harry has been approached by the Russians," Troy announced. "They want to bring his case to the UN, as a human-rights violation. What do you think?"

When it came to human rights, the UN was not a friend of the Jews. In the Middle East conflict, the General Assembly had censured Israel many times, but not the Arab states who had declared war on Israel. It had recently given a standing ovation to the African dictator and cannibal Idi Amin, who had massacred tens of thousands of his countrymen, but had voted to condemn zionism as "racism." It had turned a blind eye toward the Russian police state, where the Brezhnev regime was accelerating the persecution of Jewish dissidents like Andrei Sakharov and Natan Sharansky amidst growing fear about where the attacks would lead. Jews had only one powerful ally in the UN, the new administration of Jimmy Carter, which had proclaimed a policy of defending "human rights" and which had put pressure on the Kremlin to halt its repression of Soviet Jews. This was why the Russians had approached Harry Edwards: to neutralize Western protests over the persecution of Soviet Jews.

I was outraged that Edwards would even consider cooperating with the Russians in this situation. Vicki Bonnell, whose husband was a Soviet dissident (and Jewish), described the severity of the repression in Russia, and argued that making Edwards' case parallel would be inappropriate and would compromise their struggle. Others agreed that the move would be misinterpreted, and was therefore unwise. Later, I thought about how respectfully everybody had treated the proposal, and how the terms of the discussion had been confined to "dissidents," skirting the issue of the Jews. What if the roles were reversed? What if blacks in the Soviet Union were being denied basic civil rights and thrown into psychiatric institutions as a punishment for dissent? What if a Jew had proposed compromising their cause? The response would have been immediate and direct. The two blacks in the room—Troy Duster and Hardy Frye—would have said: "If you don't support us there, we're not going to support you here." And that would have been that. Black radicals had a clear sense of their ethnicity and the threat they faced, even if we did not.

The issue came to a head when Robert Blauner presented a paper to the seminar. Blauner argued that marxist theory had overlooked the most powerful forces in the modern world—nationalism and racism—because Marx had come from a relatively "homogeneous" society. Our task was to correct those deficiencies in his theory. When Blauner finished, I spoke. Far from being part of a homogeneous society, I said, Marx belonged to a despised minority that had only recently won its civil rights. He was descended from a long line of famous rabbis, but his own father had given up the family religion in order to retain his government post. Marx had written a notorious essay ("On the Jewish Question") identifying capitalist exploitation with Judaism. He had built his entire theoretical edifice on a concept—class—which was pointedly free of ethnic and national characteristics, in order to formulate the idea of socialism as a community liberated from these distinctions. Socialism would "solve" the Jewish question by eliminating Judaism, along with all other ethnic and national identities. What we had to ask ourselves—and here I paused for effect—was whether Marx wasn't a self-hating Jew, and whether socialism was anything more than a wish to be included.

"B-u-l-l-shit" boomed the voice next to me. It was Jeff Lustig: "We've heard this all before, and I find it boring," he said. When he finished, I spoke again: "I'm glad that Jeff has settled these questions," I said, "but just out of curiosity I'd like to hear how the other marxists in the room identify themselves ethnically." I knew, of course, that they were all Jews, and that not one would demean himself to acknowledge that fact. As the words left my mouth, and as if to prove my point, David Wellman began a tirade at the end of the table, his face turning apoplectic red: "I'm sick and tired of Horowitz's questions," he sputtered, "his interrogations, his attempts to obstruct this seminar with questions that don't interest anyone else."

When Wellman finished, I offered to leave. I didn't want to interfere with the seminar's work, I said, and if everyone felt as he did, I would go. Vicki Bonnell, Kornhauser, and one or two others spoke up for me. The rest, including Gitlin (whom I had known since my days at the Russell Foundation[12]), sat sullen and silent. When it was over, no one except Wellman had said that I should leave. But at the next session, only three others besides myself showed up. The seminar never met after that. When I discussed this strange conclusion to an intellectual enterprise with Kornhauser, he pointed out that Troy Duster's institute, which had sponsored the seminar, was financed by a foundation grant that had been given to Wellman. It was his "marxist" explanation as to why the others had joined the boycott. He also told me that Wellman was only half-Jewish and had become visibly upset at a gathering two weeks before, when someone had referred to him as a Jew and he had denied that he was.

Shortly afterward, Harry Edwards was given his tenure when the chancellor of the university overruled the sociology department. For a faculty body to be overruled by an administrator on a matter of tenure was an unprecedented infringement of a jealously guarded prerogative. It was said that the Soviets had directly intervened with the Carter administration on behalf of Edwards, and that President Carter himself had called the chancellor. There were no protests over this blatant political intrusion and violation of academic freedom. Professor Edwards subsequently became a national figure as an adviser to the major sports leagues and a spokesman on issues of racism. At Berkeley he caused a commotion in the Jewish community—but nowhere else—by assigning exams during Jewish high holy days and refusing to allow Jewish students, absent for religious reasons, to take makeup exams.

The seminar had provided an answer of sorts to my questions. If these issues could not be discussed in a left-wing institute in a university setting, where could they be discussed? How could the left be reformed if it didn't have the courage to confront itself? How could it propose to change the world if it was unwilling to ask whether its ideas were valid? How could it transform the world if it couldn't transform itself?

The seminar also provoked a new question: why was the socialist dream so hard to look at? Freud had suggested an answer. In *Civilization and Its Discontents* he had analyzed the expectations of socialists—that the world would be governed by justice and love—as an adult fairy tale. Socialism was a wish for the comforting fantasies of childhood to come true. I had an additional thought: the revolutionary was a creator, just like God. Socialism was not only a childish wish, but a wish for childhood itself: security, warmth, the feeling of being at the center of the world.

One evening shortly after the seminar collapsed, I went to Moe's Books on Telegraph Avenue, to browse. As a writer, I always had a difficult time in bookstores, and especially Moe's, which was an entire building, four stories high, and contained books in every conceivable category of knowledge. Like the revolutionary, every writer creates his own universe. Even if he is not the subject of the work, the writer's eye is still the center of its world. In every artistic creation there is the same impulse, as in childhood, to be the center of attention. Visiting Moe's, I would sometimes get a headache just trying to take in the multiplicity of works and put them into some order in my mind. There were so many titles competing for others' attention, so many competing with mine.

That evening, my difficulties were unusually intense. I envisioned not only the universe of authors, but the universe of audiences as well. Audiences that did not know or care the others existed. There were entire worlds of readers who devoured nothing but mysteries, or romances, or works on the occult, or science fiction—all of which were as foreign to me as the worlds of sociology and political economy were to them. Whole tiers of Moe's were occupied with these disparate universes, sufficient in themselves to exclude awareness of others. While I was thinking these thoughts, I had a sudden shock of recognition. Although my own books were confined to a tiny portion of a single shelf in this vast array of human learning, I had always found security in the belief that a hierarchy ordered it. I visualized a pyramid whose apex was marxism, which was my life's work, and which provided the key to all other knowledge. Marxism was the theory that would change everyone's world. And put mine at the center. But in that very moment a previously unthinkable possibility also entered my head: the marxist idea, to which I had devoted my entire intellectual life and work, was false.

All around me, the room went black. In the engulfing dark, the pyramid flattened and a desert appeared in its place, cold and infinite, and myself an invisible speck within it. *I am one of them,* I thought. *I am going to die and disappear like everyone else.* For the first time in my conscious life, I was looking at myself in my nakedness, without the support of revolutionary hopes, without the faith in a revolutionary future, without the sense of self-importance conferred by the role I would play in remaking the world. For the first time in my life, I confronted myself as I really was in the endless march of human coming and going. I was nothing.

Left Illusions

F OR MOST OF MY ADULT AND PROFESSIONAL LIFE, I regarded myself as a man of the left. The identification was stronger. Ever since marching in my first May Day parade down New York's Eighth Avenue thirty years ago, I had looked on myself as a soldier in an international class struggle that would one day liberate all humanity from poverty, oppression, racism, and war. It was a romantic conception, to be sure, but then revolution as conceived in the marxist and socialist canons *is* a romantic conception. It promises the fulfillment of hopes that are as old as mankind; it posits a break with the whole burdened progress of history, freedom from the chains that have bound master and slave, lord and peasant, capitalist and proletariat from time immemorial.

Not long after the end of the Vietnam War, I found myself unable to maintain any longer the necessary belief in the marxist promise. Along with many other veterans of the 1960s struggles, I ceased to be politically active. It was a characteristic and somewhat unique feature of our radical generation, as distinct from previous ones, that we did

---

This article was published in the December 8, 1979 issue of the *Nation* as "A Radical's Disenchantment"—a title provided by the editors. I wrote it at the instigation of E. L. Doctorow, who was on the *Nation*'s board, and whom I had recently met. It turned out to be my farewell to the left (see *Radical Son*, 305-7). This is the first time it has been reprinted, and it has been edited for this book.

not join the conservative forces of the *status quo*. Instead, politics itself became suspect. We turned inward—not, I would say, out of narcissism, but out of a recognition, unfamiliar and in some ways threatening to our radical ideas, that failure (like success) is never a matter merely of "the objective circumstances." It has a root in the acting self.

Few of us, I think, felt at ease with the political limbo in which we found ourselves. It was as though the radicalism we shared was in some deep, perhaps unanalyzable sense a matter of character rather than commitment. It was as though giving up the vision of fundamental change meant giving up the better part of oneself. So we continued to feel a connection to the left that was something more than sentimental, while our sense of loss led to conflicts whose appearance was sometimes less than fraternal. Such feelings, I believe, were an unspoken but significant element in the controversy over Joan Baez's open letter to the Vietnamese, and the Ronald Radosh-Sol Stern article on the Rosenbergs in the *New Republic*.[1]

Antonio Gramsci once described the revolutionary temperament as a pessimism of the intellect and an optimism of the will. For the veterans of my radical generation, the balance was tipped when we sustained what seemed like irreparable injury to our sense of historical possibility. It was not even so much the feeling that the left would not be able to change society; it was rather the sense that, in crucial ways, the left could not change itself.

Above all, the left seems trapped in its romantic vision. In spite of the defeats to its radical expectations, it is unable to summon the detachment to look at itself critically. Despite the disasters of twentieth-century revolutions, the viability of the revolutionary goals remains largely unexamined and unquestioned. Even worse, radical commitments to justice and other social values continue to be dominated by a moral and political double standard. The left's indignation seems exclusively reserved for outrages that confirm the marxist diagnosis of the sickness of capitalist society. There is protest against murder and repression in Nicaragua but not Cambodia, Chile but not Tibet, South Africa but not Uganda, Israel but not Libya or Iraq. Political support is mustered for oppressed minorities in western countries but not in

Russia or the People's Republic of China, while a Third World country that declares itself "marxist" puts itself—by the very act—beyond reproach. In the same vein, almost any "liberation movement" is embraced as just that, though it may be as unmistakably atavistic and clerically fascist on first sight as the Ayatollah Khomeini's in Iran.[2]

This moral and political myopia is compounded by the left's inability to accept responsibility for its own acts and commitments. Unpalatable results (for instance, the outcome of the revolution in Russia) are regarded as "irrelevant"—and dismissed—as though the left in America and elsewhere played no role in them, and as though they have had no impact on the world the left set out to change. Or they are analyzed as anomalies—and dismissed—as though there were in fact a standard of achieved revolution by which the left could have confidence in its program and in its understanding of the historical process.

Recently, the shock of events in Indochina—mass murder committed by Cambodia's communists, the invasion and unacknowledged occupation of Cambodia by Vietnam, and the invasion of Vietnam by China—has produced new and promising responses among radicals still committed to the socialist cause.[3] Paul Sweezy, dean of America's independent marxists, wrote in the *Monthly Review* this June of "a deep crisis in Marxian theory" because none of the existing "socialist" societies behave the way Marx and "most marxists . . . until quite recently—thought they would." Classes haven't been eliminated, nor, he observes, is there any visible intention to eliminate them; the state, far from disappearing, has grown more powerful, and "they go to war not only in self-defense but to impose their will on other countries—even ones that are also assumed to be socialist."

The current dimensions of the left's intellectual crisis are more readily grasped, however, in a writer like Noam Chomsky, who, as an anarchist, has never had illusions about existing "socialisms," and who has no attachment (intellectual or visceral) to pristine marxism.[4] Chomsky's intellectual integrity and moral courage, to my mind, set a standard for political intellectuals. Yet, in a manner that is not only characteristic of the non-trotskyist left but seems endemic to its political stance, Chomsky refuses to devote his tenacious intelligence to a systematic scrutiny of "socialist" regimes or even anti-western regimes of the Third World.

Thus, in a passage from his new book *Language and Responsibility*, Chomsky criticizes the absence of socialist journalists in the mass media and comments, "In a sense, we have over here the 'mirror image' of the Soviet Union, where all the people who write in *Pravda* represent the position they call 'socialism'—in fact, a certain variety of highly authoritarian state socialism." Chomsky attributes this conformity to "ideological homogeneity" among the U.S. intelligentsia and to the fact that the mass media are capitalist institutions. Chomsky then offers examples of press conformity regarding the Vietnam War and concludes: "It is notable that despite the extensive and well-known record of Government lies during the period of the Vietnam War, the press, with fair consistency, remained remarkably obedient, and quite willing to accept the Government's assumptions, framework of thinking, and interpretation of what was happening."

The question that I find myself asking, when I read these words just now, is by what standard does Chomsky judge the obedience of the American press remarkable? Is there a national press that is not obedient in the sense described? Does Chomsky mean that the American press was remarkably *more* obedient to its government during the Vietnam War than other national presses would have been in similar circumstances? Looking back at those events from the present historical juncture, one would be inclined to say exactly the reverse. Not only did the American press provide much of the documentation on which the antiwar movement's indictment of the American war effort was based—including the My Lai atrocities—but in *defiance* of its government and at the risk of prosecution for espionage and treason, it published classified documents known as the "Pentagon Papers," which provided a good deal of the record of official lies to which Chomsky refers.[5]

This is not to say that Chomsky's characterization of press subservience is wrong, but rather to put the criticism in perspective. Within the framework of ideological conformity and institutional obedience, which Chomsky rightly deplores, a body of dissent developed during the 1960s which has continued to influence the conduct of American foreign policy and the structure of international relations in the present decade. Who would have thought ten years ago that the anti-American revolution in Iran, the linchpin of America's imperial interests in the Middle East, would not trigger an immediate American military intervention? Who would have believed that the twenty-five thousand military "advisers" in Africa's conflicts in the 1970s would be Cubans rather than Americans?

Consider, too, for a moment, Chomsky's misleading comparison of the Soviet and American presses as "mirror images." In fact, the ignorance imposed on the Soviet public by government-controlled media and official censorship is mind-boggling by western standards. At a bare minimum, the information necessary to carry on a public debate over government policies in areas such as foreign policy and defense is not available to the Soviet citizen (who would be forbidden to use it if it were). Censorship is carried to such an extreme that the Soviet citizen may be uninformed about such non-controversial threats to his wellbeing as natural disasters, man-made catastrophes or even military provocations by the United States. When Washington mined Haiphong Harbor and dared Russian vessels to challenge the blockade, a crisis—compared at the time to the 1962 confrontation over Cuban missiles—ensued. For twenty days during this crisis, the Soviet people were not informed that the mining had taken place! (The purpose of the blackout was to allow the Soviet leadership to capitulate to the American threat without domestic consequences.)

Why bring this up? Why dwell on the negative features of the Soviet system (or of other communist states) which in any case are widely reported in the American media? What is the relevance?

These are questions the apologists of the left raise when they are confronted by the Soviet case. Unfortunately, the consequences of ignoring the flaws of practical communism are far ranging and real. To begin with, the credibility of the left's critique is gravely undermined. Chomsky's article is a good example. The American press does not look inordinately servile when compared with its real-world counterparts—and especially its socialist opposites. Only when measured against its own standards and the ideals of the democratic society of which it is part does it seem so. Yet it is Chomsky who raises the Soviet comparison (precisely because the United States and the Soviet Union *are* in an adversary relationship—a political fact of prime importance that the left often prefers to ignore), and he does so in a misleading way. The result is that his argument is vitiated or at least seriously weakened for anyone who has not internalized the special expectations of the left that a future socialist press would be independent, critical, and accurate.

Latent in Chomsky's critique is a comforting illusion—namely that the left's failure to sustain itself as a political force with a radical alternative social vision is due to the absence of socialist journalists in the capitalist media rather than to its own deficiencies; the failure of its ideals in practice; its moral inconsistency; its inability to formulate—and fight for—realistic programs. In short, the fact that it cannot command moral and political authority among its political constituencies.

The blind spot toward the Soviet Union provides a good instance of the left's lack of political realism. The Soviet Union is one of the two predominant military powers in the world. That alone makes it a crucial subject of any contemporary political analysis that claims to be comprehensive. Radicals often seem to think that western policy can be explained independently of Soviet behavior by reference to the imperatives of the system, the requirements of the "disaccumulation crisis," and the like. This was always a weakness in the radical perspective, but as a result of the continuing development of Soviet power in the last decade, it has passed a critical point and has become crippling.

During the 1950s, and even in the 1960s, the Soviet Union was significantly weaker militarily than the United States. The celebrated missile gap was all on the other side. Hence, whatever Soviet intentions, Washington's influence on the dynamics of the arms race and the Cold War was preponderant. This is no longer the case. The Soviet Union has now achieved nuclear parity with the United States for the first time since the onset of the atomic era. This profoundly affects, among other things, the Soviet ability to intervene in political and military conflicts outside its borders. The political pendulum has also swung in its favor. Compare the days when John Foster Dulles used to attack the non-aligned states for "immoral" neutrality, with the recent conference of non-aligned countries in Havana, where the policy of Washington's representatives was to *keep* the participants neutral (that is, not aligned with the Soviet bloc).

These changes and the trend they represent make a realistic analysis of Soviet policies crucial for any political movement. Yet, in a special issue of the *Nation* concerned with "Intervention" (June 9),[6] only one of ten articles was even partially devoted to the Soviet Union.[7] The article, by Michael Klare, employed a comparative analysis of U.S. and Soviet military forces to *discount* the impression that the Soviet Union is now or intends to become an interventionary power.

Klare achieved this feat by defining "interventionist forces" in such a restrictive manner as to exclude the Soviet invasion of Czechoslovakia and the occupation forces it maintains there, and by describing Soviet intervention in the Middle East, Africa, and Asia as "aid" to "beleaguered allies"—in short, by taking a page from the apologists for American intervention. When Klare was compelled under his own rules to admit that some Soviet missions had the look of interventionist forces, he quickly denied it, saying, "but it is important to remember that the units involved are seen by Moscow as being 'on loan' from their normal, defensive mission, and so would be recalled the moment they were needed at home." And so, presumably, would the U.S. "advisers" that began America's involvement in Vietnam, if they had been needed at home.

Failure to appreciate the world role of a major power—the depressing history of leftist apologias for that power aside—would be serious enough. But the Soviet Union, despite all the qualifying circumstances of its origins and development, is the country in which the revolutionary socialist solution—state ownership of the means of production—has been tested and found wanting. For this reason, far more than for the others, it requires radical attention. The point was forcefully made a few years ago by the Polish philosopher, Leszek Kolakowski:

Why the problems of the real and the only existing communism, which Leftist ideologies put aside so easily ("all right, this was done in exceptional circumstances, we won't imitate these patterns, we will do it better" etc.), are crucial for socialist thought is because the experiences of the "new alternative society" have shown very convincingly that the only universal medicine these people have for social evils—state ownership of the means of production—is not only perfectly compatible with all disasters of the capitalist world, with exploitation, imperialism, pollution, misery, economic waste, national hatred and national oppression, but that it adds to them a series of disasters of its own: inefficiency, lack of economic incentives, and, above all, the unrestricted role of the omnipotent bureaucracy, a concentration of power never known before in human history.

Can the left take a hard look at itself, at the consequences of its failures, at the credibility of its critiques, at the viability of its goals? Can it begin to shed the arrogant cloak of self-righteousness that elevates it above its own history and makes it impervious to the lessons of experience?

In a previous essay, Kolakowski wrote that the left was defined by its "negation" of existing social reality. But not only this: "It is also defined by the direction of this negation, in fact by the nature of its utopia." Today, the left's utopia itself is in question. That is the real meaning of the crisis of marxism. Yet, paradoxically, the way for the left to begin to regain its utopia, to fashion a new, more adequate vision of radical commitment and radical change, is to take a firmer grip on the ground under its feet.[8]

12

My Vietnam Lessons

WHEN I SEE PROTESTERS in the flush of youthful idealism holding signs that proclaim "No Vietnams in Central America," a feeling of ineffable sadness overtakes me. For twenty years ago I was one of them. In 1962, as a graduate student at Berkeley, I wrote the first book of New Left protest, *Student*,[1] and helped to organize the first "anti-war" demonstration opposing what we denounced as U.S. intervention in Vietnam.

In the mid-1960s, I went to England and helped to organize the Vietnam Solidarity Campaign, which supported what we called the Vietnamese struggle for independence from the United States, as well as the International War Crimes Tribunal, which brought American war atrocities under intense and damning scrutiny but ignored atrocities committed by the communist forces in Vietnam. While in England, I also wrote *The Free World Colossus*, a New Left history of the Cold War, which was used as a radical text in colleges and in the growing movement against the Vietnam War. At the end of the 1960s, I returned to America as an editor of *Ramparts*, the most widely read New Left magazine. Our most famous cover appeared during Richard

---

This is the text of a speech that I made to a congressional seminar on the tenth anniversary of the fall of Saigon, April 10, 1985. It was reprinted in *Deconstructing the Left* (1995).

Nixon's campaign in 1972 for a second term. It featured a photograph of the My Lai massacre with a sign superimposed and planted among the corpses saying, "Re-Elect the President."

Let me make this perfectly clear: those of us who inspired and then led the anti-war movement did not want merely to stop the killing, as so many veterans of those domestic battles now claim. We wanted the communists to win. It is true that some of us may have said we only wanted the United States to get out of Vietnam, but we understood that this meant the communists would win. "Bring the troops home" was our slogan; the fall of Saigon was the result.

There was a political force in American life that did want a peace that would not also mean a communist victory—a peace that would deny Hanoi its conquest and preserve the integrity of South Vietnam. That force was led by our archenemy President Richard Nixon, whose campaign slogans were "Peace with Honor" in Vietnam and "Law and Order" at home. Just as we did not want honor that meant preserving the government of South Vietnam, so we did not respect law and order, because respecting the democratic process would have meant that the majority in America, which supported President Nixon and South Vietnam, would have prevailed.

Like today's young radicals, we 1960s activists had a double standard when it came to making moral and political judgments. We judged other countries and political movements—specifically socialist countries and revolutionary movements—by the futures we imagined they could have if only the United States and its allies would get out of their way. We judged America, however, by its actual performance, which we held up to a standard of high and even impossible ideals. We were, in the fashionable term, "alienated" from what was near to us, unable to judge it with any objectivity.

Some of this alienation—a perennial and essential ingredient of all political leftism—could be attributed to youth itself, the feeling that we could understand the world better and accomplish more than our elders could. There was another dimension to our disaffection, however, an ideology that committed us to "truths" behind the common sense surface of things.

I myself was a marxist and a socialist. I believed in the "dialectic" of history, and therefore, even though I knew that the societies calling themselves marxist were ruled by ruthless dictatorships, I believed that they would soon evolve into socialist democracies. I attributed their negative features to underdevelopment and to the capitalist pasts from which they had emerged. I believed that marxist economic planning was the most rational solution to their underdevelopment and would soon bring them unparalleled prosperity—an idea refuted as dramatically by the experience of the last seventy years as the ancillary notion that private property is the source of all tyranny and that socialist states would soon become free.

On the other hand, the same marxist analysis told me that America, however amenable to reform in the past, was set on a course that would make it increasingly rigid, repressive, and ultimately fascist. The United States was the leviathan of a global imperialist system under attack at home and abroad. Its ruling class could not afford to retreat from this challenge; it could only grow more reactionary and repressive. This expectation, wrong in every respect, was not an idiosyncratic theory of mine but was the basis of the New Left's political view of the world generally and of its strategy of opposition to America's war in Vietnam in particular.

The New Left believed that, in Vietnam, America's corporate liberal empire had reached a point of no return. As a result, electoral politics and any effort to reform it were futile and counterproductive. The only way to alter America's imperial course was to take to the streets— first to organize resistance to the war and then to "liberate" ourselves from the corporate capitalist system. That was why we were in the streets. That was why we did not take a hard stand against the bomb throwers in our midst.

What happened to change my views and cause me to have second thoughts? As our opposition to the war grew more violent and our prophecies of impending fascism more intense, I had taken note of how we were actually being treated by the system we condemned. By the decade's end, we had (deliberately) crossed the line of legitimate dissent and abused every First Amendment privilege and right granted us as Americans. While American boys were dying overseas, we spat on the flag, broke the law, denigrated and disrupted the institutions of government and education, gave comfort and aid (even revealing classified secrets) to the enemy. Some of us provided a protective propaganda shield for Hanoi's communist regime while it tortured American fliers; others engaged in violent sabotage against the war effort. All the time I thought to myself: if we did this in any other country, the very least of our punishments would be long prison terms and the pariah status of traitors. In any of the socialist countries we supported—from Cuba to North Vietnam—we would spend most of our lives in jail and, more probably, be shot.

And what actually happened to us in repressive capitalist America? Here and there our wrists were slapped (some of us went to trial, some spent months in jail), but basically the country tolerated us. And listened to us. We began as a peripheral minority, but as the war dragged on without an end in sight, people joined us: first in thousands and then in tens of thousands, swelling our ranks until finally we reached what can only be called the conscience of the nation. America itself became troubled about its presence in Vietnam, about the justice and morality of the war it had gone there to fight. And because the nation became so troubled, it lost its will to continue the war and withdrew.

Thus was refuted all the preconceptions we had had about the rigidity of American politics, about the controlled capitalist media (which, in fact, provided the data that fueled our attacks on the war), and about the ruling-class lock on American foreign policy. That policy had shown itself in its most critical dimension responsive to the will of ordinary people and to their sense of justice and morality. As an historian, I believe I am correct in my judgment that America's withdrawal from the battlefront in Vietnam because of domestic opposition is unique in human history: there is no other case on record of a major power retreating from a war in response to the moral opposition of its own citizenry.

If America's response to this test of fire gave me an entirely new understanding of American institutions and of the culture of democracy that informs and supports them, the aftermath of the U.S. retreat gave me a new appreciation of the communist opponent. America not only withdrew its forces from Vietnam, as we on the left said it could never do, but from Laos and Cambodia and, ultimately, from its role as guardian of the international status quo.[2]

Far from increasing the freedom and wellbeing of Third World nations, as we in the left had predicted, however, America's withdrawal resulted in an international power vacuum that was quickly filled by the armies of Russia, Cuba, and the mass murderers of the Khmer Rouge. All this bloodshed and misery was the direct result of America's post-Vietnam withdrawal, of the end of *Pax Americana*, which we had ardently desired and helped to bring about.

In Vietnam itself, the war's aftermath showed beyond any doubt the struggle there was not ultimately to achieve or prevent self-determination but—as various presidents said and we denied—a communist conquest of the south. Today, the National Liberation Front of South Vietnam, whose cause we supported, no longer exists. Its leaders are dead, in detention camps, under house arrest, in exile, powerless. America left Vietnam ten years ago; but today Hanoi's army is the fourth largest in the world, and Vietnam has emerged as a Soviet satellite and imperialist aggressor in its own right, subverting the independence of Laos, invading and colonizing Cambodia.

These events confronted me with a supreme irony: the nation I had believed to be governed by corporate interests, a fountainhead of world reaction, was halted in mid-course by its conscience-stricken and morally aroused populace; the forces I had identified with progress, once freed from the grip of U.S. "imperialism," revealed themselves to be oppressive, predatory, and unspeakably ruthless. I was left with this question: what true friend of the South Vietnamese, or the Cambodians, or the Ethiopians, or the people of Afghanistan, would not wish that *Pax Americana* were still in force?

There was yet another Vietnam lesson for me when I pondered the question put by Jeanne Kirkpatrick to the still-active veterans of the New Left: "How can it be that persons so deeply committed to the liberation of South Vietnam and Cambodia from Generals Thieu and Lon Nol were so little affected by the enslavement that followed their liberation? Why was there so little anguish among the American accomplices who helped Pol Pot to power?" Indeed, why have such supposedly passionate advocates of Third World liberation not raised their voices in protest over the rape of Afghanistan or the Cuban-abetted catastrophe to Ethiopia?

Not only has the left failed to make a cause of these marxist atrocities, it has failed to consider the implications of what we now know about Hanoi's role in South Vietnam's "civil war." For North Vietnam's victors have boldly acknowledged that they had intruded even more regular troops into the South than was claimed by the Presidential White Paper used to justify America's original commitment of military forces—a White Paper that we leftists scorned at the time as a fiction based on anti-communist paranoia and deception. But today's left is too busy denigrating Ronald Reagan's White Papers on Soviet and Cuban intervention in Central America to consider the implications of this past history to the present.

My experience has convinced me that historical ignorance and moral blindness are endemic to the American left, necessary conditions of its existence. It does not value the bounty it actually has in this country. In the effort to achieve a historically bankrupt fantasy—call it socialism, call it "liberation"—it undermines the very privileges and rights it is the first to claim.

The lesson I learned from Vietnam was not a lesson in theory but a lesson in practice. Observing this nation go through its worst historical hour from a vantage on the other side of the barricade, I came to understand that democratic values are easily lost and, from the evidence of the past, only rarely achieved, that America is a precious gift, a unique presence in the world of nations. Because it is the strongest of the handful of democratic societies that mankind has managed to create, it is also a fortress that stands between the free nations of the world and the dark, totalitarian forces that threaten to engulf them.

My values have not changed, but my sense of what supports and makes them possible has. I no longer can join "anti-war" movements that seek to disarm Western democracies in the face of the danger that confronts them. I support the current efforts of America's leadership to rebuild our dangerously weakened military defenses, and I endorse the conservative argument that America needs to be vigilant, strong, and clear of purpose in its life-and-death struggle with its global totalitarian adversaries. As an ex-radical, I would only add that in this struggle Americans need to respect and encourage their own generosity—their tolerance for internal dissent and their willingness to come to the aid of people who are fighting for their freedom.

13

Semper Fidel:
The Battle over Nicaragua

TWENTY-FIVE YEARS AGO, as one of the founders of the New Left, I was an organizer of the first political demonstrations on this campus—and indeed on any campus—to protest our government's anti-communist policies in Cuba and Vietnam. Tonight, I come before you as a man I used to tell myself I would never be: a supporter of President Reagan, a committed opponent of communist rule in Nicaragua. I make no apologies for my present position. It was what I thought was the humanity of the marxist idea that made me what I was then; it is the inhumanity of what I have seen to be the marxist reality that has made me what I am now. If my former comrades who support the Sandinista cause were to pause for a moment and then plunge their busy political minds into the human legacies of their activist pasts, they would instantly drown in an ocean of blood.

The real issue before us is not whether it is morally right for the United States to arm the *contras*,[1] or whether there are unpleasant men

---

This is the text of a speech given in a debate over Nicaragua at a pro-Sandinista teach-in at the University of California, Berkeley, on April 4, 1986. It appeared in the June, 1986, issue of *Commentary* as "Nicaragua: A Speech to My Former Comrades in the Left" and was reprinted in *Deconstructing the Left* (1995).

among them. The issue before us and before all people who cherish freedom is how to oppose a Soviet imperialism so vicious and so vast as to dwarf any previously known. An "ocean of blood" is no metaphor. As we speak here tonight, this empire—whose axis runs through Havana and now Managua—is killing hundreds of thousands of Ethiopians to consolidate a dictatorship whose policies against its black citizens make the South African government look civilized and humane.

There is another issue, especially important to me: the credibility and commitment of the American left, whose attitudes towards American power have gained a far-reaching influence since the end of the Vietnam War.

In his speech on Nicaragua, President Reagan rightly invoked the precedent of the Truman Doctrine, the first attempt to oppose Soviet expansion through revolutionary surrogates in Greece. The first protest of my radical life was against the Truman Doctrine in a May Day march in 1948. I was with the left defending revolutions in Russia and China, in Eastern Europe and Cuba, in Cambodia and Vietnam, just as the left defends the Sandinistas now.

And I remember clearly the arguments and "facts" with which we made our case in forums like this, and what the other side said, too— the presidents who came and went and the anti-communists on the right, the William Buckleys and the Ronald Reagans. And, in every case, without exception, time has proven the left wrong—tragically and destructively wrong. Wrong in its views of the revolutionaries' intentions and wrong about the facts of their revolutionary rule. And just as consistently, the anti-communists were proven right.

Just as the left now dismisses the president's warnings about Soviet expansion—calling them anti-communist paranoia, a threat to the peace, and a mask for American imperialism—so we attacked President Truman as the aggressor. Russia's control of Eastern Europe, we said, was only a defensive buffer, a temporary response to American power—first because Russia had no nuclear weapons, and then because it lacked the missiles to deliver them.

Today, the Soviet Union is a nuclear superpower, missiles and all, but it has not given up an inch of the empire it gained during the

Second World War—not Eastern Europe, not the Baltic states that Hitler delivered to Stalin and whose nationhood Stalin erased and who are now all but forgotten, not even the Kurile islands that were once part of Japan.

Not only have the Soviets failed to relinquish their conquests in all these years—years of dramatic, total decolonization in the West—but their growing strength and the wounds of Vietnam (a scab liberals and leftists have continued to pick) have encouraged them to reach for more. South Vietnam, Cambodia, Laos, Ethiopia, Yemen, Mozambique, and Angola are among the nations that have recently fallen into the Soviet orbit. To expand their territorial core—which their apologists still refer to as a "defensive perimeter"—Moscow has already slaughtered a million peasants in Afghanistan, an atrocity warmly endorsed by the Sandinista government.

The Sandinista minister of defense, Humberto Ortega, describes the army of the conquerors—whose scorched-earth policy has driven half the population of Afghanistan from its homes—as the "pillar of peace" in the world today. To any self-respecting socialist, praise for such barbarism would be an inconceivable outrage—as it was to the former Sandinista, now *contra*, Eden Pastora. But praise for the barbarians is sincere tribute coming from the Sandinista rulers, since they see themselves as an integral part of the Soviet empire itself.

The struggle of man against power is the struggle of memory against forgetting. So wrote the Czech writer Milan Kundera, whose name and work no longer exist in his homeland. In all the Americas, Fidel Castro was the only head of state to cheer the Russian tanks as they rolled over the brave people of Prague. And cheering right along with Fidel were Carlos Fonseca, Tomas Borge, Humberto Ortega, and the other creators of the present Nicaraguan regime. One way to assess what has happened in Nicaragua is to realize that wherever Soviet tanks crush freedom in the future, there will now be two governments in the Americas supporting them all the way—Cuba, where Castro sells his young men as Soviet legionnaires for billions of dollars a year, and Nicaragua, whose time to provide Soviet conscripts for empire will come, if and when the American left manages to cut the *contras* adrift.

Memory against power: about its own crimes and for its own criminals, the left has no memory at all, which is the only reason it can wave its finger at President Reagan and the anti-communist right.

In the eyes of the left in which I grew up, as well as in those of the Sandinista founders, Stalin's Russia was a socialist paradise, the model of the liberated future of all mankind. Literacy to the uneducated, power to the weak, justice to the forgotten—we praised Russia then, just as the left praises the Sandinistas now. And just as they ignore warnings like Violetta Chamorro's—"With all my heart, I tell you it is worse here now than it was in the times of the Somoza dictatorship"— so we dismissed the anti-Soviet "lies" about Stalinist repression.

In the society we hailed as a new human dawn, tens of millions of people were put in slave labor camps, in conditions rivaling Auschwitz and Buchenwald. Between thirty and forty million people were killed— in peacetime, in the daily routine of socialist rule. While leftists applauded their progressive policies and guarded their frontiers, Soviet marxists killed more peasants, more workers, and even more communists than all the capitalist governments together since the beginning of time.

And for the entire duration of this nightmare, the William Buckleys and the Ronald Reagans and the other anti-communists went on telling the world exactly what was happening. And all that time, the pro-Soviet left and its fellow travelers went on denouncing them as reactionaries and liars, using the same contemptuous terms with which the left attacks the president today.

In fact, the left would still be denying the Soviet atrocities if the perpetrators themselves had not finally acknowledged their crimes. In 1956, in a secret speech to the party elite, the Soviet leader Nikita Khrushchev made the crimes a communist fact; but it was only the CIA that actually made the fact public, allowing radicals to come to terms with what they had done. Khrushchev and his cohorts could not have cared less about the misplaced faiths and misspent lives of their naive supporters in the left.

The Soviet rulers were concerned about themselves. Stalin's mania had spread the slaughter into their own ranks. His henchmen wanted to make totalitarianism safe for its rulers—Stalinism without Stalin. In place of a dictator whose paranoia could not be controlled, they instituted a dictatorship by directorate—which (not coincidentally) is the form of rule in Nicaragua today. In the future, Soviet repression would work one way only: from the privileged top of society to the powerless bottom.

The year 1956—which is also the year Soviet tanks flattened the freedom fighters of Budapest—is the year that tells us who the Sandinistas really are. In this year, because the truth had to be admitted at last, the left all over the world was forced to redefine itself in relation to the Soviet facts. China's communist leader, Mao, decided he liked Stalin's way better. For Mao's sinister folly, twenty-five million people died in the "great leaps" and "cultural revolutions" he then launched. But in Europe and America a new anti-Stalinist left was born. This New Left, of which I was one of the founders, was repelled by the evils it was now forced to see and embarrassed by the tarnish the totalitarians had brought to the socialist cause. It turned its back on the Soviet model of Stalin and his heirs.

In Nicaragua, the Sandinista vanguard was neither embarrassed nor repelled. The following year, 1957, Carlos Fonseca, the revered founding father of the Sandinista Front, visited Russia and its new and improved totalitarian state. To Fonseca, as to Borge and his other comrades, the Soviet monstrosity was their revolutionary dream come true. In his *A Nicaraguan in Moscow*, Fonseca proclaimed Soviet communism his model for Latin America's revolutionary future.

A second step in this vision of a communist America is now being realized in Nicaragua. The *comandante* directorate, the army, and the secret police (socialism's three most important institutions) are already mirrors of the Soviet state, not only structurally but in their personnel, trained and often manned by agents of the Soviet axis.

Yet the most important figure in this transformation is not a Nicaraguan at all, but Cuba's communist dictator, Fidel Castro. From 1959, when Carlos Fonseca and Tomas Borge first arrived in Havana, and for twenty years after, the Sandinista leaders became disciples of Castro in Havana and with his blessings travelled on to Moscow, where Stalin's henchman completed their revolutionary training. Humberto Ortega, Daniel's less visible but more important brother, is Fidel's personal protégé. Ortega is the author of the *tercerista* strategy, which allied their minuscule sect to a coalition of democrats contending for power.

Fidel is not only the image in which the Sandinista leadership has created itself and the author of its victorious strategy, but the architect of its politburo, the *comandante* directorate. The directorate was personally created by Fidel in Havana on the eve of the final struggle, sealed with a pledge of military aid against the Somoza regime. Without Castro's intervention, Arturo Cruz and the other anti-Somoza and pro-democratic *contras* would be the government of Nicaragua today. And it was Fidel who showed the Sandinistas how to steal the revolution after the victory and to secure their theft by manipulating their most important allies: the American left and its liberal sympathizers.

Twenty-five years ago, when the Sandinistas began their apprenticeship, Fidel was our revolutionary hero, too. Like today's campus radicals, we became "coffee-pickers" and passengers on the revolutionary tour, wrote glowingly about literacy campaigns, health clinics, and other wonders of the new world a-coming. When Fidel spoke, his words were revolutionary music to our ears: "Freedom with bread. Bread without terror." "A revolution neither red nor black, but Cuban olive-green." And so in Managua today, "Not (Soviet) communism but Nicaraguan *Sandinismo*" is the formula his imitators proclaim.

So persuasive were Fidel's political poems, that radicals all over the world fell under his spell. Jean-Paul Sartre wrote one of the first and most influential books admiring the new leader: "If this man asked me for the moon," the philosopher wrote, "I would give it to him. Because he would have a need for it."

When I listen to today's enthusiasts for the Sandinista redeemers with their scorn for the *contra* rebels, the fate of a Fidelista hero comes to my mind, one of the liberators of Cuba, whose role in the revolution was once the equal of Che. For in the year that Jean-Paul Sartre came to Havana and fell in love with the humanitarian Fidel, Huber Matos embarked on a long windowless night of the soul.

Huber Matos's fate was sealed in Fidel's second revolution. All the fine gestures and words with which Fidel seduced us and won our support—the open marxism, the socialist humanism, the independent path—were calculated lies. For even as he proclaimed his color to be olive green, he was planning to make his revolution Moscow red. So cynical was Fidel's strategy that at the time it was difficult for many to comprehend. One by one, Fidel removed his own comrades from the revolutionary regime and replaced them with Cuban communists. At the time, the communists were a party in disgrace. They had opposed the revolution; they had even served in the cabinet of the tyrant Batista while the revolution was taking place. But this was all incidental to Fidel. Fidel knew how to use people. And Fidel was planning a new revolution that he could trust the communists to support. He had decided to turn Cuba into a Soviet state. Moreover, Fidel also knew that he could no longer trust his Fidelista comrades, because they had made a revolution they thought was going to be Cuban olive green.

Although Fidel was a party of one and the Sandinistas were a party of nine, and though he removed socialists and they removed democrats, the pattern of betrayal has been the same in Nicaragua as it was in Cuba: to gain power, the Sandinistas concealed their true intention (a Soviet state) behind a revolutionary lie (a pluralist democracy). To consolidate power, they fashioned a second lie (democracy, but only within the revolution), and those who believed in the first lie were removed. At the end of the process, there will be no democracy in Nicaragua at all, which is exactly what Fonseca and the Sandinistas intended when they began. When the Sandinistas removed their anti-Somoza allies, of course, they did not need Nicaraguan communists to replace them, because they had Fidel behind them and thousands of agents and technicians from the communist bloc.

When Huber Matos saw Fidel's strategy unfolding in Cuba, he got on the telephone with other Fidelistas to discuss what they should do. This was a mistake. In the first year of Cuba's liberation, the phones of revolutionary legends like Huber Matos were already tapped by Fidel's secret police. Huber Matos was arrested.

In the bad old days of Batista oppression, Fidel had been arrested himself. His crime was not words on a telephone but leading an
attack on a military barracks to overthrow the Batista regime. Twelve
people were killed. For his offense, Fidel spent a total of eighteen months
in the tyrant's jail, writing a book about his deeds. Huber Matos was
not so lucky. Fidel was no Batista, and the revolution was no two-bit
dictatorship, like the one it replaced. For his phone call, Huber Matos
was tried in such secrecy that not even members of the government
were privy to the proceeding. Afterwards, he was consigned to solitary
confinement in a windowless cell for the next twenty-two years. And
even as Fidel buried his former friend and comrade alive, he went on
singing his songs of revolutionary humanism and social justice.

In another setting, Milan Kundera explains the meaning of this
revolutionary parable of Huber Matos and Fidel. Recalling the French
communist, Paul Eluard, who wrote poems praising brotherhood while
his friend was murdered by the communist regime in Prague, Kundera
remarked: "The hangman killed while the poet sang." He explained
these words thus: "People like to say: Revolution is beautiful, it is only
the terror arising from it which is evil. But this is not true. The evil is
already present in the beautiful; hell is already contained in the dream
of paradise. To condemn gulags is easy, but to reject the totalitarian
poetry which leads to the gulag by way of paradise is as difficult as
ever." Words to bear in mind today as we consider Nicaragua and its
revolution of poets.

To believe in the revolutionary dream is the tragedy of its supporters; to exploit the dream is the talent of its dictators. Revolutionary
cynicism, the source of this talent, is Fidel's most important teaching
imparted to his Sandinista disciples. This is the faculty that allows the
comandantes to emulate Fidel himself: to be poets and hangmen at the
same time, to promise democracy and organize repression, to attack
imperialism and join an empire, to talk peace and plan war, to champion justice and deliver Nicaragua to a fraternity of inhumane, repressive, militarized, and economically crippled states.

"We used to have one main prison, now we have many," laments a
former Fidelista surveying the socialist paradise to which Nicaragua

aspires. "We used to have a few barracks; now we have many. We used to have many plantations; now we have only one, and it belongs to Fidel. Who enjoys the fruits of the revolution? The houses of the rich, the luxuries of the rich? The *Comandante* and his court."[2]

Nicaragua is in the grip of utterly cynical and utterly ruthless men whose purpose is to crush its society from top to bottom, to institute totalitarian rule, and to use Nicaragua as a base to spread communist terror and regimes throughout the hemisphere. The Sandinista anthem that proclaims the Yankee to be the "enemy of mankind" expresses precisely the revolutionaries' sentiment and goal. That goal is hardly to create new societies—the sordid record of communist states would dissuade any reformer from choosing the communist path—but to destroy the societies that already exist.

For Nicaragua, a *contra* victory would mean the restoration of the democratic leadership from whom the Sandinistas stole the revolution, the government that Nicaragua would have had if Cuba had not intervened in the first place. For the Americas, it would mean a halt to the communist march that threatens its freedoms and its peace. Support for the *contras* is a first line of defense. If they fail, it will hasten the time when Americans will have to defend themselves.

A final word to my former comrades and successors in the left: It is no accident that the greatest atrocities of the twentieth century have been committed by marxist radicals; and it is no accident that they have been committed by radicals in power against their own peoples. Hatred of self, and by extension one's country, is the root of the radical cause. As American radicals, the most egregious sin you commit is to betray the privileges and freedoms ordinary people from all over the world have come to this country to create—privileges and freedoms that ordinary people all over the world would feel blessed to have themselves. But the worst of it is this: that you betray all of this tangible good that you can see around you for a socialist pie-in-the-sky that has meant horrible deaths and miserable lives for the hundreds of millions who have already fallen under its sway.

— 14 —

The Road to Nowhere

The self-deification of mankind, to which marxism gave philosophical expression, has ended in the same way as all such
attempts, whether individual or collective: it has revealed itself
as the farcical aspect of human bondage.

Leszek Kolakowski

October 1990
Dear Ralph,[1]

I T HAS BEEN OVER A DECADE since this silence, as durable as an
iron curtain, descended between us. In these circumstances, I have
had to depend on others to learn how you regard me these days:
how, at a recent social gathering, you referred to me as "one of the two
tragedies of the New Left" (the other being a former Brecht scholar
who now publishes guides to the nude beaches of America[2]); how my
apostasy has inflicted an emotional wound, as though in changing my
political views and leaving the left I had personally betrayed you.

I understand this. How could it be otherwise for people like us,
for whom politics (despite our claim to be social realists) was less a

---

From *The Politics of Bad Faith* (1998). An abridged version was first published in the
December 1990 issue of *Commentary* under the title "Socialism: Guilty As Charged."
This excerpt has been edited for this book.

matter of practical decisions than moral choices? We were partisans of a cause that confirmed our humanity, even as it denied humanity to those who opposed us. To leave such ranks was not a simple matter, like abandoning a misconception or admitting a mistake. It was more like accusing one's comrades, like condemning a life.

Our choice of politics was never a matter of partial commitments. To choose the left was to define a way of being in the world. (For us, the personal was always political.) It was choosing a future in which human beings would finally live as they were meant to live: no longer self-alienated and divided, but equal, harmonious, and whole.

What persuaded us to believe that socialism, having begun everywhere so badly, should possess the power to reform itself into something better? To be something other than it has been? To pass through the inferno of its Stalinist tragedies and to become the paradiso of our imaginations?

For we did believe in such a transformation. We were confident that the socialized foundations of Soviet society would eventually assert themselves, producing a self-reform of the Soviet tyranny. This was our New Left version of the faith we inherited. This refusal to accept history's verdict made socialism a reality still. In the 1960s, when the booming capitalist societies of the West made radical prospects seem impossibly remote, we had a saying among us that the first socialist revolution was going to take place in the Soviet Union.

In 1953, Stalin died and a New Left generation convinced itself that the long-awaited metamorphosis was at last taking place. With Stalin's death came the Khrushchev thaw, the famous speech lifting the veil on the bloody past, and a relaxation of the Stalinist terror. To those on the left who had refused to give up, these were signs that the totalitarian caterpillar, having lodged itself in the cocoon of backwardness, was about to become the socialist butterfly of which they had dreamed.

We had our own prophet to explain the transformation. Our mutual friend, Isaac Deutscher, had emerged from the prewar battles over Trotskyism to become the foremost interpreter of the Russian Revolution to our radical generation. Deutscher began with the reality that was given to us: the fact of Stalinism, as it had taken root in the empire of the czars. Deutscher began to explain why Stalinism, in spite of itself, was being transformed into socialism.

Stalinism, he wrote, was "an amalgamation of marxism with the semi-barbarous and quite barbarous traditions and the primitive magic of an essentially pre-industrial . . . society." In short, Stalinism was the fulfillment of Lenin's famous prescription that with barbarism the Bolsheviks would drive barbarism out of Russia. "Under Stalinism . . . Russia rose to the position of the world's second industrial power. By fostering Russia's industrialization and modernization Stalinism had with its own hands uprooted itself and prepared its 'withering away.'"[3]

We will leave aside, for a moment, the unfounded optimism of this description of Stalinist economic development, looking only at the theoretical perspective it made possible. In Deutscher's view, the backwardness of Russian society had provided the Bolsheviks not only with a revolutionary opportunity, but also a historical advantage. They could avail themselves of modern technologies and social theories. Instead of relying on the anarchic impulses of capitalist investment, they could employ the superior methods of socialist planning. The result of these inputs would be a modern economy more efficient and productive than those of their capitalist competitors.

According to Deutscher, in mid-century the socialist bloc, which had hitherto provided such grief for radicals like us, was poised for a great leap forward: "With public ownership of the means of production firmly established, with the consolidation and expansion of planned economy, and—last but not least—with the traditions of a socialist revolution alive in the minds of its people, the Soviet Union breaks with Stalinism in order to resume its advance towards equality and socialist democracy."

The ultimate basis of this transformation was the superior efficiency of socialist planning: "Superior efficiency necessarily translates itself, albeit with a delay, into higher standards of living. These should lead to the softening of social tensions, the weakening of antagonisms between bureaucracy and workers, and workers and peasants, to the further lessening of terror, and to the further growth of civil liberties."[4]

Deutscher wrote these words in 1957, a year in which the Soviets celebrated the fortieth anniversary of the revolution by launching the first space satellite ("Sputnik") into orbit. The feat dramatized the progress that had been achieved in a single generation and heralded the end of the Soviets' technological "apprenticeship" to the West. The message of Sputnik to the faithful all over the world, Deutscher predicted, was "that things may be very different for them in the second half of the century from what they were in the first." For forty years, their cause had been "discredited . . . by the poverty, backwardness, and oppressiveness of the first workers' state." But that epoch was now coming to an end. With the industrial leap heralded by Sputnik, they might look forward to a time when the appeal of Communism would be "as much enhanced by Soviet wealth and technological progress as the attraction of bourgeois democracy has in our days been enhanced by the fact that it has behind it the vast resources of the United States."[5]

This was the vision of the socialist future that the Soviet leadership itself promoted. In 1961, Khrushchev boasted that the socialist economy would "bury" its capitalist competitors, and that by 1980 the Soviet Union would overtake the United States in economic output and enter the stage of "full communism," a society of true abundance whose principle of distribution would be "from each according to his ability to each according to his needs."

As New Leftists, we took Khrushchev's boast with a grain of salt. The Soviet Union was still a long way from its marxist goals. Moreover, as Deutscher had warned, any future Soviet progress might be "complicated, blurred, or periodically halted by the inertia of Stalinism, by war panics, and, more basically, by the circumstance that the Soviet Union still remains in a position of overall economic inferiority vis-à-vis its American antipode."[6] Soviet socialism was still a myth that Stalinism had created. But it had a redeeming dimension: the myth had helped "to reconcile the Soviet masses to the miseries of the Stalin era," and Stalinist ideology had helped "to discipline morally both the masses and the ruling group for the almost inhuman efforts which assured the Soviet Union's spectacular rise from backwardness and poverty to industrial power and greatness."[7]

Because it seemed credible, Deutscher's sober assessment was for us intoxicating. Its mix of optimism and "realism" became the foundation of our political revival. The turn marxism had taken in 1917, creating a socialist economy within a totalitarian state, posed a seemingly insoluble riddle. How could socialist progress be reconciled with such a stark retreat into social darkness? What did this portend for Marx's insight that the modes of production determined the architecture of social relations? Building on Trotsky's prior analysis, Deutscher pointed to a way out of the dilemma that would preserve our radical faith.

And no doubt that is why, thirty years later, even as the tremors of *glasnost* and *perestroika* were unhinging the empire that communists had built, you returned to Deutscher's prophecy as a revolutionary premise. "Much that is happening in the Soviet Union [you wrote in the *Socialist Register*, 1988] constitutes a remarkable vindication of [Deutscher's] confidence that powerful forces for progressive change would eventually break through seemingly impenetrable barriers."[8]

Nothing could reveal more clearly how blind your faith has made you. To describe the collapse of the Soviet Empire as a vindication of Deutscher's prophecies (and thus the marxist tradition) is to turn history on its head. We are indeed witnessing a form of "revolution from above," but it is a revolution that refutes both Deutscher and Marx. The events of the past years are not a triumph for socialism, but its death knell. The rejection of a planned economy by the leaders of actually existing socialist society, the pathetic search for the elements of a rule of law (following the relentless crusades against "bourgeois rights"), the humiliating admission that the military superpower is in all other respects a Third World nation, the incapacity of the socialist mode of production to enter the technological future and the unseemly begging for the advanced technology that it has stolen for decades from the capitalist West—all this adds up to a declaration of socialism's utter bankruptcy and historic defeat. This bankruptcy is not only moral and political, as we all recognized before, but economic as well.

It is precisely the economic dimension of this bankruptcy that Deutscher did not foresee, and that forecloses any possibility of a socialist revival. For all of these post-Khrushchev decades, that revival has been premised on the belief in the superiority of socialist economics. This is the meaning of the claim, so often repeated in leftist quarters, that the "economic rights" and "substantive freedoms" of socialist states took precedence over the political rights and (merely) procedural freedoms guaranteed by the capitalist West. Faith in the socialist future had come to rest on the assumption that abundance would eventually flow from socialist planning, and that economic prosperity would then lead to political deliverance, the Deutscherian thesis.

In our New Left fantasies, the political nightmare of the socialist past was to be redeemed by the deus ex machina of socialist plenty. The economic bankruptcy of the Soviet bloc buries this faith and brings to an end the socialist era in human history.

This is the reality you have not begun to face.

It is important to understand this reality, which signals the close of an historical era. But this can be accomplished only if we do not deny the history we have lived. You can begin this retrieval of memory by recalling your critique of Leszek Kolakowski ten years ago, which set down the terms of your defense of the cause to which we were all so committed.

Your complaint against Kolakowski, you remember, was that in demolishing the edifice of marxist theory, he had slighted the motives of those who embraced it and thus failed to explain its ultimate appeal. Kolakowski had portrayed marxism as the secular version of a religious quest that went back to the beginning of human history: how to reconcile contingent human existence to an essence from which it was estranged, how to return humanity to its "true self."[9] As Kolakowski viewed it, marxism was the messianic faith of a post-religious world. Naturally, such an explanation would be insulting to you. You rejected it as "superficial," inadequate (you said) to explain marxism's attraction to "so many gifted people."

In your view, marxism's appeal was not to those hungry for religious answers, but to people who responded to the call "to oppose great evils and to create conditions for a different kind of world, from which such evils would be banished." The call to fight these evils was the crucial factor in enlisting people in the cause of the left, and you named them: "exploitation, poverty and crisis, war and the threat of war, imperialism and fascism, the crimes of the ruling classes."[10]

Let us pass for a moment over the most dramatic of these evils—exploitation, crisis, war, imperialism, fascism, and the crimes of "ruling classes," including the vast privileges of the nomenklatura—from which you will agree marxist societies themselves have not been free since their creation. Let us consider, rather, the simple poverty of ordinary people, whose redress was the most fundamental premise of the revolutionary plan. Let us look at what has been revealed by *glasnost* about the quality of the ordinary lives of ordinary people after seventy years of socialist effort—not forgetting that twenty million human beings (the figure is from current Soviet sources) were eliminated to make possible this revolutionary achievement.

Official Soviet statistics released during *glasnost* indicate that following seventy years of socialist development, 40 percent of the Soviet population and 79 percent of its older citizens live in poverty.[11] Of course, judged by the standards of "exploitative" capitalist systems, the entire Soviet people live in a state of poverty.

The Soviet Union's per capita income is estimated by Soviet economists as about one-seventh that of the United States, more or less on a par with Communist China.[12] In the Soviet Union in 1989, there was rationing of meat and sugar—in peacetime. The rations revealed that the average intake of red meat for a Soviet citizen was half of what it had been for a subject of the czar in 1913. At the same time, a vast supermarket of fruits, vegetables, and household goods, available to the most humble inhabitant of a capitalist economy, was permanently out of reach for the people of the socialist state. Indeed, one of the principal demands of a Siberian miners' strike in 1989 was for an item as mundane and basic to a sense of personal wellbeing as a bar of soap.

In a land of expansive virgin forests, there was a toilet paper shortage. In an industrial country with one of the harshest and coldest climates in the world, two-thirds of the households had no hot water, and a third had no running water at all. Not only was the construction of housing notoriously shabby, but space was so scarce, according to the government paper *Izvestia*, that a typical working-class family of four was forced to live for eight years in a single eight-by-eight-foot room, before marginally better accommodation was available. The housing shortage was so acute that at all times 17 percent of Soviet families had to be physically separated for want of adequate space.

After sixty years of socialist industrialization, the Soviet Union's per capita output of nonmilitary goods and services placed it somewhere between fiftieth and sixtieth among the nations of the world. More manufactured goods were exported annually by Taiwan, Hong Kong, South Korea or Switzerland, while blacks in apartheid South Africa owned more cars per capita than did citizens of the socialist state. The only area of consumption in which the Soviets excelled was the ingestion of hard liquor. In this, they led the world by a wide margin, consuming 17.4 liters of pure alcohol or 43.5 liters of vodka per person per year, which was five times what their forebears had consumed in the days of the czar. At the same time, the average welfare mother in the United States received more income in a month than the average Soviet worker could earn in a year.

Nor was the general deprivation confined to private households and individuals. The public sector was equally desolate. In the name of progress, the Soviets had devastated the environment to a degree unknown in other industrial states. More than 70 percent of the Soviet atmosphere was polluted with five times the permissible limit of toxic chemicals, and thousands of square miles of the Soviet land mass were poisoned by radiation. Thirty percent of all Soviet foods contained hazardous pesticides, and 6 million acres of productive farmland were lost to erosion. More than 130 nuclear explosions had been detonated in European Russia for geophysical investigations to create underground pressure in oil and gas fields, or just to move earth for building dams.

The Aral Sea, the world's largest inland body of water, was dried up as the result of a misguided plan to irrigate a desert. Soviet industry operated under no controls, and the accidental spillage of oil into the country's ecosystems took place at the rate of nearly a million barrels a day. In the words of a comprehensive study of this disaster, "No other great industrial civilization so systematically and so long poisoned its air, land, water, and people. None so loudly proclaiming its efforts to improve public health and protect nature so degraded both. And no advanced society faced such a bleak political and economic reckoning with so few resources to invest toward recovery." [13]

Even in traditional areas of socialist concern, the results were catastrophic. Soviet spending on health was the lowest of any developed nation, and basic health conditions were on a level with those in the poorest of Third World countries. Thirty percent of Soviet hospitals had no running water, the training of medical personnel was poor, equipment was primitive, and medical supplies scarce. (By way of comparison, U.S. expenditures on medical technology alone were twice as much as the entire Soviet health budget.) The bribery of doctors and nurses to get decent medical attention and even amenities like blankets in Soviet hospitals was not only common but routine.

So backward was Soviet medical care thirty years after the launching of Sputnik, that 40 percent of the Soviet Union's pharmacological drugs had to be imported, and much of these were lost to spoilage due to primitive and inadequate storage facilities. Bad as these conditions were generally, in the ethnic republics they were even worse. In Turkmenistan, fully two-thirds of the hospitals had no indoor plumbing. In Uzbekistan, 50 percent of the villages were reported to have no running water and 93 percent no sewers. In socialist Tajikistan, according to a report in *Izvestia*, only 25 to 30 percent of the schoolchildren were found to be healthy. As a result of bad living conditions and inadequate medical care, life expectancy for males throughout the Soviet Union was twelve years less than for males in Japan and nine years less than in the United States, and less for Soviet males themselves than it had been in 1939.

Educational conditions were no less extreme. "For the country as a whole," according to one Soviet report, "21 percent of pupils are trained at school buildings without central heating, 30 percent without water piping and 40 percent lacking sewerage." [14] In other words, despite sub-zero temperatures, the socialist state was able to provide schools with only outhouse facilities for nearly half its children. Even at this impoverished level, only nine years of secondary schooling were provided on average, compared to twelve years in the United States, while only 15 percent of Soviet youth were able to attend institutions of higher learning, compared to 34 percent in the U.S.

In Deutscher's scheme, Soviet schools ("the world's most extensive and modern education system," as he described it) were the keys to its progressive project. But, as *glasnost* revealed, Soviet spending on education had declined in the years since Sputnik (while U.S. spending tripled). By the 1980s, it was evident that education was no more exempt from the generalized poverty of socialist society than other non-military fields of enterprise. Seduced by Soviet advances in nuclear arms and military showpieces like Sputnik, Deutscher labored under the illusion of generations of the left. He too believed that the goal of revolutionary power was something other than power itself.

For years the left had decried the collusion between corporate and military interests in the capitalist West. But all that time the entire socialist economy was little more than one giant military-industrial complex. Military investment absorbed 25 percent of the Soviet gross product (compared to only 6 percent in the United States), and military technology provided the only product competitive for export. Outside the military sector, as *glasnost* revealed, the vaunted Soviet industrial achievement was little more than a socialist mirage, imitative, archaic, inefficient, and one-sided. It was presided over by a sclerotic nomenklatura of state planners, incapable of adjusting to dynamic technological change. In the 1930s, the architects of the Soviet economy had overbuilt a heavy industrial base, and then, as if programmed by some invisible bureaucratic hand, had rebuilt it again and again.

Straitjacketed by its central plan, the socialist world was unable to enter the "second industrial revolution" that began to unfold in countries outside the Soviet bloc after 1945. By the beginning of the 1980s, the Japanese already had thirteen times the number of large computers per capita as the Soviets and nearly sixty times the number of industrial robots (the U.S., on the other hand, had three times the computer power of the Japanese). "We were among the last to understand that in the age of information sciences the most valuable asset is knowledge, springing from human imagination and creativity," complained Soviet President Gorbachev in 1989. "We will be paying for our mistake for many years to come."[15]

While capitalist nations, including recent Third World economies like South Korea, were soaring into the technological future, Russia and its satellites were caught in the contradictions of an archaic mode of production and stagnating in a decade of zero growth, becoming what one analyst described as "a gigantic Soviet socialist rust belt."[16] In the 1980s, the Soviet Union had become a military superpower, but the achievement bankrupted its already impoverished society.

Nothing illustrated this bankruptcy more poignantly than the opening of a McDonald's fast-food outlet in Red Square about the time the East Germans were tearing down the Berlin Wall. In fact, the semiotics of the two were inseparable. During the last decades of the Cold War, the Wall had come to symbolize the borders of the socialist world, the Iron Curtain that held its populations captive against the irrepressible fact of the superiority of the capitalist societies in the West. When the Wall was breached, the terror was over, and with it the only authority ever really commanded by the socialist state.

The appearance of the Moscow McDonald's revealed the prosaic truth that lay behind the creation of the Wall and the bloody epoch that it had come to symbolize. Its Soviet customers gathered in lines exceeding in length those of the idolaters waiting outside Lenin's tomb, the altar of the revolution itself. Here was the capitalist genius for catering to the ordinary desires of ordinary people spectacularly displayed, along with socialism's systemic lack of concern for the needs of common humanity.

McDonald's executives even found it necessary to purchase and manage their own special farm in Russia, because Soviet potatoes, the very staple of the people's diet, were too poor in quality and unreliable in supply. On the other hand, the wages of the Soviet customers were so depressed that a hamburger and fries was equivalent in rubles to half a day's pay. And yet this most ordinary of pleasures—the bottom of the food chain in the capitalist West—was still such a luxury for

Soviet consumers that to them it was worth a four-hour wait and four hours' wages.

Of all the symbols of the epoch-making year, this McDonald's fest was perhaps the most resonant for leftists of our generation. Impervious to the way the unobstructed market democratizes wealth, the New Left had focused its social scorn precisely on those plebeian achievements of consumer capitalism that brought services and goods efficiently and cheaply to ordinary people.

Perhaps the main theoretical contribution of our generation of New Left marxists was an elaborate literature of cultural criticism made up of sneering commentaries on the "commodity fetishism" of bourgeois cultures and the "one-dimensional" humanity that commerce produced. The function of such critiques was to make its authors superior to the ordinary liberations of societies governed by the principles of consumer sovereignty and market economy. For New Leftists, the leviathans of postindustrial alienation and oppression were precisely these "consumption-oriented" corporations, like McDonald's,[17] that offered inexpensive services and goods to the working masses—some, like the Sizzler restaurants, in the form of "all you can eat" menus that embraced a variety of meats, vegetables, fruits, and pastries virtually unknown in the Soviet bloc.

These mundane symbols of consumer capitalism revealed the real secret of the era that was now ending, the reason why the Iron Curtain and its Berlin Walls were necessary, why the Cold War itself was an inevitable byproduct of socialist rule: in 1989, for two hours' labor at the minimum wage, an American worker could obtain, at a corner Sizzler, a feast more opulent, more nutritionally rich and gastronomically diverse than anything available to almost all the citizens of the socialist world (including the elite) at almost any price.

—

In the counterrevolutionary year 1989, on the anniversary of the Bolshevik Revolution, a group of protesters raised a banner in Red Square

that summed up an epoch: "Seventy Years on the Road to Nowhere."
They had lived the socialist future and it didn't work.

This epic of human futility reached a climax the same year, when
the socialist state formally decided to return the land it had taken from
its peasants half a century before. The collectivization of agriculture in
the 1930s had been the very first pillar of the socialist plan and one of
the bloodiest episodes of the revolutionary era. Armies were dispatched
to the countryside to confiscate the property of its recalcitrant owners,
conduct mass deportations to the Siberian gulag, liquidate the kulaks
and herd the survivors into the collective farms of the marxist future.

In this "final" class struggle, no method was considered too ruthless
to midwife the new world from the old. "We are opposed by everything that has outlived the time set for it by history," wrote Maxim
Gorky. "This gives us the right to consider ourselves again in a state of
civil war. The conclusion naturally follows that if the enemy does not
surrender, he must be destroyed." The destruction of the class enemy—
the most numerous and productive element of Soviet society at the
time—was accomplished by massacres, by slow deaths in concentration camps and deliberately induced genocidal famine. In the end,
over ten million people were killed, more than had died on all sides in
World War I.[18]

But the new serfdom the Soviet rulers imposed in the name of
liberation only destroyed the peasant's freedom and incentive, and thus
laid the foundations of the final impasse. Before collectivization, Russia had been the "breadbasket of Europe," supplying 40 percent of the
world's wheat exports in the bumper years 1909 and 1910.[19] But socialism ended Russia's agrarian plenty and created permanent deficits—
not merely the human deficit of those who perished because of Stalinist
brutalities during the collectivization, but a deficit in grain that would
never be brought to harvest because of the brutality inherent in the
socialist idea. Half a century after the socialist future had been brought
to the countryside, the Soviet Union had become a net importer of
grain, unable to produce enough food to feed its own population.

These deficits eventually forced the state to allow a portion of the
crop to be sold on the suppressed private market. Soon, 25 percent of

Soviet grain was being produced on the 3 percent of the arable land reserved for private production. Necessity had compelled Soviet rulers to create a dramatic advertisement for the system they despised. They had rejected the productive efficiencies of the capitalist system as exploitative and oppressive. Yet, the socialist redistribution of wealth had produced neither equity nor justice, but scarcity and waste instead.

At the end of the 1980s, amid growing general crisis, Soviet youth were using loaves of bread as makeshift footballs because its price had been made so artificially low that it was now less than the cost of the grain used to produce it. This was a microcosm of the socialist economy. Irrational prices, bureaucratic chaos, and generalized public cynicism (the actually existing socialist ethos in all marxist states) had created an environment in which 40 percent of the food crop was lost to spoilage before ever reaching the consumer. And so, half a century after ten million people had been sacrificed to "socialize the countryside," those who had expropriated the land were ready to give it back.

The road to nowhere had become a detour. (Soviet joke: "What is socialism? The longest road from capitalism to capitalism.") Now the Soviet rulers themselves had begun to say that it had all been a horrible "mistake." Socialism did not work. Not even for them.

Of all the scenarios of the communist *Gotterddmmerung*, this denouement had been predicted by no one. Ruling classes invariably held fast to the levers of their power. They did not confess their own bankruptcy and then proceed to dismantle the social systems that sustained their rule, as this one had. The reason for the anomaly was this: the creators and rulers of the Soviet Union had indeed made a mistake. The system did not work, not even in terms of sustaining the power of its ruling class.

The close of the Soviet drama was not predicted, because the very nature of the Soviet Union was without precedent. It was not an organic development, but an artificial creation, the first society in history to be dreamed up by intellectuals and constructed according to plan. The crisis of Soviet society was not so much a traditional crisis of legitimacy and rule as it was the crisis of an idea, a monstrously wrong idea that had been imposed on society by an intellectual elite, an idea so passionately believed and yet so profoundly mistaken that it had caused more misery and suffering than any single force in history.

This suffering could not be justified by the arguments of the left that the revolutionary changes were "at least an improvement on what existed before." Contrary to the progressive myth that radicals invented to justify their failures, czarist Russia was not a merely pitiful, semi-barbaric state when the socialists seized power. By 1917, Russia was already the fourth industrial power in the world. Its rail networks had tripled since 1890, and its industrial output had increased by three-quarters since the century began. Over half of all Russian children between eight and eleven years of age were enrolled in schools, while 68 percent of all military conscripts had been tested literate.

A cultural renaissance was underway in dance, painting, literature, and music, Blok, Kandinsky, Mayakovsky, Pasternak, Diaghelev, Stravinsky already figures of world renown. In 1905, a constitutional monarchy with an elected parliament had been created, in which freedom of the press, assembly, and association were guaranteed, if not always observed. By 1917, legislation to create a welfare state, including the right to strike and provisions for workers' insurance was already in force and, before it was dissolved by Lenin's Bolsheviks, Russia's first truly democratic parliament had been convened.[20]

The marxist revolution destroyed this achievement, tearing the Russian people out of history's womb and robbing whole generations of their minimal birthright, the opportunity for a decent life. Yet even as this political abortion was being completed and the nation was plunging into its deepest abyss, the very logic of revolution forced its leaders to expand their lie: to insist that the very nightmare they had created was indeed the kingdom of freedom and justice the revolution had promised.

It is in this bottomless chasm between reality and promise that our own argument is finally joined. You seek to separate the terror-filled actualities of the Soviet experience from the magnificent harmonies of the socialist dream. But it is the dream itself that begets the reality and requires the terror. This is the revolutionary paradox you want to ignore.

Isaac Deutscher had actually appreciated this revolutionary equation, but without ever comprehending its terrible finality. The second volume of his biography of Trotsky opens at the end of the civil war with a chapter called "The Power and the Dream," in which he describes how the Bolsheviks confronted the situation they had created: "When victory was theirs at last, they found that revolutionary Russia had overreached herself and was hurled down to the bottom of a horrible pit." Seeing that the revolution had only increased their misery, the Russian people began to ask: "Is this . . . the realm of freedom? Is this where the great leap has taken us?" The leaders of the revolution could not answer and retain their power. They began to equivocate and then to lie. "[While] they at first sought merely to conceal the chasm between dream and reality [they] soon insisted that the realm of freedom had already been reached—and that it lay there at the bottom of the pit. If people refused to believe, they had to be made to believe by force."[21]

So long as the revolutionaries continued to rule, they could not admit that they had made a mistake. Though they had cast an entire nation into a living hell, they had to maintain the liberating truth of the socialist idea. And because the idea was no longer believable, they had to make the people believe by force. It was the socialist idea that created the terror.

Because of the nature of its political mission, this terror was immeasurably greater than the repression it replaced. Whereas the czarist police had several hundred agents at its height, the Bolshevik Cheka began its career with several hundred thousand. Whereas the czarist secret police had operated within the framework of a rule of law, the Cheka (and its successors) did not. The czarist police repressed extralegal opponents of the political regime, that is, people who were breaking czarist law. To create the socialist future, however, the Cheka targeted whole social categories as enemies of the revolution—regardless of individual attitudes or acts—and targeted them for liquidation.

The results were predictable. "Up until 1905," wrote Aleksandr Solzhenitsyn in his searing record of the gulag, "the death penalty was an exceptional measure in Russia." From 1876 to 1904, 486 people were executed or seventeen people a year for the whole country (a figure which included the executions of non-political criminals). During the years of the 1905 revolution and its suppression, "the number of executions rocketed upward, astounding Russian imaginations, calling forth tears from Tolstoy and . . . many others; from 1905 through 1908 about 2,200 persons were executed—forty-five a month. This, as Tagantsev said, was an epidemic of executions. It came to an abrupt end."[22]

But then came the Bolshevik seizure of power: "In a period of sixteen months (from June 1918 to October 1919) more than sixteen thousand persons were shot, which is to say more than one thousand a month." These executions, carried out by the Cheka without trial and by revolutionary tribunals without due process, were executions of people exclusively accused of political crimes. And this was only a drop in the sea of executions to come. The true figures will never be known, but in the two years 1937 and 1938, according to the executioners themselves, half a million "political prisoners" were shot, twenty thousand a month.

To measure these deaths on a historical scale, Solzhenitsyn also compared them to the horrors of the Spanish Inquisition, which during the height of its existence condemned an average of 10 heretics a month.[23] The difference was this: the Inquisition only forced unbelievers to believe in a world unseen; socialism demanded that they believe in the very lie that the revolution had condemned them to live.

—

The author of our century's tragedy is not Stalin, nor even Lenin. Its author is the political left that we belonged to, that was launched at the time of Gracchus Babeuf and the Conspiracy of the Equals, and that has continued its assault on bourgeois order ever since. The reign of socialist terror is the responsibility of all those who have promoted the socialist Idea, which required so much blood to implement, and then did not work.

If socialism was a mistake, however, it was never merely innocent in the sense that its consequences could not have been foreseen. Before marxists had spilled their first blood, the critics of Marx had warned that his schemes would end in tyranny and would not work. In 1844, Marx's collaborator Arnold Ruge predicted that Marx's dream would result in "a police and slave state." And in 1872, the anarchist Mikhail Bakunin, Marx's arch-rival in the First International, described the political life of the future that Marx had in mind: "This government will not content itself with administering and governing the masses politically, as all governments do today. It will also administer the masses economically, concentrating in the hands of the State the production and division of wealth, the cultivation of land. . . . All that will demand . . . the reign of scientific intelligence, the most aristocratic, despotic, arrogant, and elitist of all regimes. There will be a new class, a new hierarchy . . . the world will be divided into a minority ruling in the name of knowledge, and an immense ignorant majority. And then, woe unto the mass of ignorant ones!"[24]

If a leading voice in Marx's own International could see with such clarity the oppressive implications of his revolutionary idea, there was no excuse for the generations of marxists who promoted the idea even after it had been put into practice and the blood had begun to flow. But the idea was so seductive that even marxists who opposed the Soviet state continued to support the socialist idea, saying this was not the socialism that Marx had in mind, even though Bakunin had seen that it was.

So powerful was the socialist fantasy that even those on the left whom Bakunin inspired and who opposed the communists, could not bring themselves to abandon the idea that had put the civilized West under siege. Like Bakunin, they were sworn enemies of capitalism, the only industrial system that was democratic and that worked. Their remedies for its deficiencies—abolishing private property and the economic market—would have led to generalized poverty and revolutionary terror as surely as those of Marx. By promoting the socialist idea of the future and by participating in the war against the capitalist present, these non-marxist soldiers of the political left became ideological partners in the very tragedies they deplored.

Of all Marx's critics, only the partisans of bourgeois order understood the mistake that socialists had made. They appreciated—as socialists did not—the only practical, and therefore real, social bases of human freedom: private property and economic markets. As the Bolsheviks completed the consolidation of their political power, the Austrian economist Ludwig von Mises, in 1922, published his classic indictment of the socialist idea and its destructive consequences.

Von Mises already knew that socialism could not work and that no amount of bloodshed and repression could prevent its eventual collapse. "The problem of economic calculation," he wrote, "is the fundamental problem of socialism" and cannot be solved by socialist means. "Everything brought forward in favor of Socialism during the last hundred years, . . . all the blood which has been spilt by the supporters of socialism, cannot make socialism workable." Advocates of socialism might continue "to paint the evils of Capitalism in lurid colors" and to contrast them with an enticing picture of socialist blessings, "but all this cannot alter the fate of the socialist idea."[25] Von Mises's thesis was elaborated and extended by Friedrich Hayek, who argued that the information conveyed through the pricing system was so complex and was changing so dynamically that no planning authority, even with the aid of the most powerful computers conceivable, could ever succeed in replacing the market.[26]

Across the vast empire of societies that have put the socialist idea to the test, its fate is now obvious to all. Von Mises and Hayek, and the other prophets of capitalist economy, are now revered throughout the Soviet bloc, even as the names of Marx, Lenin and Trotsky are despised. Their works, once circulated only in *samizdat*, were among the first of *glasnost* to be unbanned. Yet, in the progressive press in the West, in articles like yours and in the efforts of your comrades to analyze the "meaning" of the communist crisis, the arguments of the capitalist critics of socialism, who long ago demonstrated its impossibility and who have now been proven correct, are nowhere considered, as if they had never been made.

For socialists, like you, to confront these arguments would be to confront the lesson of the history that has passed: the socialist idea has been, in its consequences, one of the worst and most destructive fantasies to ever have taken hold of the minds of men.

And, despite your protestations, it is the very idea that Marx conceived. For two hundred years, the promethean project of the left has been just this: to abolish property and overthrow the market, and thereby to establish the reign of reason and justice embodied in a social plan. "In marxist utopianism, communism is the society in which things are thrown from the saddle and cease to ride mankind. Men struggle free from their own machinery and subdue it to human needs and definitions."[27] That is Edward Thompson's summary of Marx's famous text in the first volume of *Capital*: "The life-process of society, which is based on the process of material production, does not strip off its mystical veil until it is treated as production by freely associated men, and is consciously regulated by them in accordance with a settled plan."[28]

The "fetishism of commodities" embodied in the market is, in Marx's vision, the economic basis of the alienation at the heart of man's estate, "a definite social relation between men, that assumes, in their eyes, the fantastic form of a relation between things."[29] The aim of socialist liberation is mankind's reappropriation of its own activity and its own product—the reappropriation of man by man—that can only be achieved when private property and the market are replaced by a social plan.

The slogan Marx inscribed on the banners of the communist future, "From each according to his ability, to each according to his need," is really an expropriated version of Adam Smith's Invisible Hand, under which the pursuit of individual interest leads to the fulfillment of the interests of all. But, in the socialist future, there is no market to rule over individual human passions and channel self-interest into social satisfaction, just as there is no rule of law to protect individual rights from the human passions that rule the state. There is only the unmediated power of the socialist vanguard, which it now exercises from its bureaucratic throne.

All the theorizing about socialist liberation comes down to this: the inhabitants of the new society will be freed from the constraints of markets and the guidelines of tradition and bourgeois notions of a rule of law. They will be masters in their own house and makers of their own fate. But this liberation is, finally, a Faustian bargain. Because it will not work. Moreover, the effort to make it work will create a landscape of human suffering as great as any ever imagined.

Toward the end of his life, our friend Isaac Deutscher had a premonition of the disaster that has now overtaken the socialist left. In the conclusion to the final volume of his Trotsky trilogy, *The Prophet Outcast*, he speculated on the fate that would befall his revolutionary hero if the socialist project itself should fail: "If the view were to be taken that all that the Bolsheviks aimed at—socialism—was no more than a *Fata Morgana*, that the revolution merely substituted one kind of exploitation and oppression for another, and could not do otherwise, then Trotsky would appear as the high priest of a god that was bound to fail, as Utopia's servant mortally entangled in his dreams and illusions."

But Deutscher did not have the strength to see the true dimensions of the catastrophe that socialism had in store. Instead, his realism only served to reveal the depths of self-delusion and self-justifying romanticism that sustain the left. Even if such a failure were to take place, he argued, the revolutionary hero "would [still] attract the respect and sympathy due to the great Utopians and visionaries. . . . Even if it were true that it is man's fate to stagger in pain and blood from defeat to defeat and to throw off one yoke only to bend his neck beneath another—even then man's longings for a different destiny would still, like pillars of fire, relieve the darkness and gloom of the endless desert through which he has been wandering with no promised land beyond."[30]

This is the true self-vision of the left: an army of saints on the march against injustice, lacking itself the capacity for evil. The left sees its revolutions as pillars of fire that light up humanity's deserts, but burn no civilizations. It lacks the ability to make the most basic moral accounting, the awareness that the Marxes, Trotskys, and Lenins immeasurably increased the suffering of humanity and destroyed many of the blooms that existing civilizations had managed to put forth.

The quest for a new world consumed the lives of entire nations. The effort to produce a super race of socialist men and women created monstrosities instead. And these horrors were predictable, indeed were predicted by critics who saw that the radical ideals would create the very demons that ultimately consumed them.

For behind the revolutionary pursuit of the impossible ideal lies a deep hatred for the human norm, an unquenchable desire for its annihilation. It was the inhumanity of our radical ambition that made the evil of the communist epoch so total. Self-hatred is the dark side of the ambition to exceed all previous human possibility, and the ultimate root of the revolutionary ideal. Terror is the necessary means for an agenda whose aim is to erase the past and remake the human soul. The totalitarian state was not an aberration of the progressive spirit, but its consummation. The radical project is a war against nature.

This is the reason that the socialist effort to reconstruct humanity achieved Orwellian results, the promise of freedom a terrorist state, the promise of wealth a minimalist existence. In the end, the Adam and Eves of the liberated future proved to be only grotesque masks of their pre-revolutionary selves. It was their all-too-human desires that shaped the socialist terror, while the old humanity reasserted itself the instant the terror was removed.

Why should we have expected anything different? What else could have resulted from so calculated a rupture with the human past? What positive outcome could be achieved by so radical a rejection of tradition, and the wholesale destruction of existing institutions? What could an experiment like this produce other than the social equivalent of Frankenstein's monster?

Yet, without socialism, the peoples of the Russian Empire might have moved into the front ranks of the modern industrial world (like the Japanese) without the incalculable human cost. Instead, even the most productive of the Soviet satellites, East Germany, once the Prussian powerhouse of European industrialism, is now condemned to a blighted economic standard below that of Italy, South Korea, or Spain.

Consider now the history of our century. On whose heads does the responsibility lie for the blood that was shed to make the socialist experiment possible? If the socialist idea is a chimera and the revolutionary path a road to nowhere, can the revolutions themselves be noble, even in intention? Can they be justified by the lesser but known evils they sought to redress?

Consider: if no one had believed Marx's idea, there would have been no Bolshevik Revolution; Russia might have evolved into a modern, democratic, industrial state; Hitler would not have come to power; there would have been no Cold War. For seventy years, the revolutionary left put its weight on the totalitarian side in the international civil war that Lenin had launched, and against the side that promoted human freedom and industrial progress. And it did so in the name of an idea that could not work.

The communist idea is not the principle of the modern world, as Marx supposed, but its antiprinciple, the reactionary rejection of political individualism and the market economies of the liberal West. Wherever the revolutionary left has triumphed, its triumph has meant economic backwardness and social poverty, cultural deprivation and the loss of political freedom for all those unfortunate peoples under its yoke.

This is the real legacy of the left of which you and I were a part. We called ourselves progressives, but we were the true reactionaries of the modern world. The Iron Curtain that divided the prisoners of socialism from the free men and women of the West has now been torn down. The iron curtain that divides us remains. It is the utopian dream that is so destructive and that you refuse to give up.

Your ex-comrade,
David

IV

REFLECTIONS ON RACE

15

Memories in Memphis

ON A TRIP TO THE SOUTH I found myself in Memphis, the city where Martin Luther King Jr. was struck down by an assassin's bullet just over thirty years ago. Memphis, I discovered, is home to a "National Civil Rights Museum," created by a local trust of African Americans active in civil rights causes. Tucked out of the way on a city side street, the museum is housed in the building that was once the Lorraine Motel, the very site where Dr. King was murdered. I decided to go.

Except for two white 1960s Cadillac convertibles, the parking lot outside the motel was empty, part of the museum's plan to preserve the memories of that somber day in April three decades ago. The cars belonged to King and his entourage, and have been left as they were the morning he was killed. Above them, a wreath hung from a balcony railing to mark the spot where he fell. Beyond is the room where he had slept the night before. It, too, is preserved exactly as it was, the covers pulled back, the bed unmade, the breakfast tray laid out, as though someone would be coming to pick it up.

Inside the building, the first floor of the motel has vanished completely. It has been hollowed out for the exhibits, and the cavernous room has become a silent stage for the dramas of the movement King

From *Hating Whitey & Other Progressive Causes*, 1999.

once led. These narratives are recounted in documents and photographs, some the length of wall frescoes, bearing images as inspirational today as then. In the center of the hall, the burned shell of a school bus recalls the freedom rides and the perils their passengers once endured. Scattered about are small television screens whose tapes recapture the moments that once moved a nation. On one screen a crowd of well-dressed young men and women braves police dogs and water-hoses, vainly attempting to turn them back. It is a powerful tribute to a movement and leader who were able to win battles against overwhelming odds by exerting moral force over an entire nation.

As a visitor reaches the end of the hall, however, a corner turns to a jarring, discordant sight. Two familiar faces stare out from a wall-size monument that seems strangely out of place. The faces are those of Malcolm X and Elijah Muhammad, leaders of the Nation of Islam. Aside from one of King himself, there are no other portraits of similar size in the museum. It is clear that its creators intended to establish these men along with King as spiritual avatars of the civil rights cause.

For one old enough to have supported King, I found such a presentation incomprehensible, even bizarre. At the time of these struggles, Malcolm X was King's great antagonist in the black community, leading its resistance to the civil rights hope. The Black Muslim publicly scorned King's March on Washington as "ridiculous" and predicted the failure of the civil rights movement King led because the white man would never willingly give black Americans such rights. He rejected King's call to non-violence and his goal of an integrated society, and in so doing earned the disapproval of the American majority that King had wooed and was about to win. Malcolm even denied King's racial authenticity, redefining the term "Negro," which King and his movement used to describe themselves, to mean "Uncle Tom."

King was unyielding before these attacks. To clarify his opposition to Malcolm X's separatist vision, King refused to appear on any platform with him, effectively banning Malcolm from the community of respect. The other heads of the principal civil rights organizations, the NAACP's Roy Wilkins and the Urban League's Whitney Young joined King in enforcing this ban. It was only in the last year of Malcolm's life, when the civil rights cause was all but won and when Malcolm had left the Nation of Islam and rejected its racism, that King finally relented and agreed to appear in the now famous photograph of the two that became iconic after their deaths.

Yet this very reconciliation—more a concession on Malcolm's part than King's—could argue for the appropriateness of Malcolm's place in a "civil rights" museum. Malcolm certainly earned an important place in any historical tribute to the struggle of the descendants of Africans to secure dignity, equality, and respect in a society that had brought them to its shores as slaves. Malcolm's understanding of the psychology of oppression, his courage in asserting the self-confidence and pride of black Americans, might make him worthy of inclusion in the temple of a man who was never a racist and whose movement he scorned.

But what of Elijah Muhammad? What is a racist and religious cultist doing in a monument to Martin Luther King? It is a truly perverse intrusion. The teachings of Elijah Muhammad mirror the white supremacist doctrines of the southern racists whose rule King fought. According to his teachings, white people were invented six thousand years ago by a mad scientist named Yacub in a failed experiment to dilute the blood of the original human beings, who were black. The result was a morally tainted strain of humanity, "white devils" who went on to devastate the world and oppress all other human beings, and whom God would one day destroy in a liberating Armageddon. Why is the image of this bizarre fringe racist blown up several times life-size to form the iconography of a National Civil Rights Museum? It is as though someone had placed a portrait of the leader of the Hale-Bopp Comet cult in the Jefferson Memorial.

After I left the museum, it occurred to me that this image reflected a truth about the afterlife of the movement King created, and whose moral legacy was in large part squandered by those who inherited it after his death. The moral decline of the civil rights leadership is reflected in many episodes of the last quarter century: the embrace of racist demagogues like Louis Farrakhan and Al Sharpton, and indefensible causes like those of Tawana Brawley, O. J. Simpson, the Los

Angeles race rioters, and the Million Man March on Washington, organized by the Nation of Islam, cynically designed to appropriate the moral mantle of King's historic event.

The impact of such episodes was compounded by the silence of black civil rights leaders over racial outrages committed by African Americans—the anti-Korean incitements of black activists in New York, the mob attacks by black gangs on Asian and white storeowners during the Los Angeles race riot, the lynching of a Hasidic Jew by a black mob in Crown Heights, and a black jury's acquittal of his murderer. The failure of current civil rights leaders like Jesse Jackson, Kweisi Mfume, and Julian Bond to condemn black racists and black outrages committed against other ethnic communities has been striking in contrast to the demands such leaders make on the consciences of whites, and the moral example set by King when he dissociated his movement from the racist preachings of Malcolm X.

The moral abdication of black civil rights leaders is integrally related to (if not fully explained by) their close association with a radical left, whose anti-white hatreds are a by-product of its anti-Americanism. This left's own attitudes towards blacks are so patronizing that one disillusioned activist was inspired to write a book about them titled *Liberal Racism*.[1] As a result of this alliance, ideological hatred of whites is now an expanding industry not only in the African American community, but among white "liberals" in elite educational institutions as well. Harvard's prestigious W. E. B. DuBois African American Studies Institute, for example, provided an academic platform for lecturer Noel Ignatiev to launch "whiteness studies," an academic field promoting the idea that "whiteness" is a "social construct," that is oppressive and must be "abolished."

The magazine *Race Traitor* is the theoretical organ of this academic cult, emblazoned with the motto: "Treason to Whiteness is Loyalty to Humanity." This is hardly a new theme on the left, echoing as it does Susan Sontag's perverse claim that "the white race is the cancer of history." (Sontag eventually expressed regrets about her remark, not because it was a racial smear, but out of deference to cancer patients who might feel unjustly slurred.) According to the *Race Trai-*

tor intellectuals, "whiteness" is the principal scourge of mankind, an idea that Farrakhan promoted at the Million Man March when he declared that the world's "number one problem . . . is white supremacy."

"Whiteness," in this view, is a category imposed on American society by its ruling class to organize the social order into a system of marxist-type oppression.[2] Consequently, "the key to solving the social problems of our age is to abolish the white race." This new racism expresses itself in slogans lifted right out of the radical 1960s. According to the whiteness studies revolutionaries, "the abolition of whiteness" must be accomplished "by any means necessary." To underscore that this slogan means exactly what it says, the editors of *Race Traitor* have explicitly embraced the military strategy of American neo-Nazis and the militia movement, and call for a John Brown-style insurrection that would trigger a second American civil war and that would destroy the symbolic (and oppressive) order of whiteness.

Such language is incendiary and fuels a widespread denigration of Americans—including Jews, Arabs, Central Europeans, Mediterranean Europeans, East Indians, Armenians—who are multiethnic and often dark-skinned, but who for official purposes (and under pressure from left-wing groups like the NAACP) are designated "white." Unlike anti-black attitudes, which are universally decried—and which would trigger the expulsion of their purveyors from any liberal institution in America—this racism is not only permitted, but encouraged, especially in the academic culture responsible for the moral and intellectual education of tomorrow's elites.

An anthology of the first five years of *Race Traitor*, for example, has been published by a prestigious, academic-oriented publishing house (Routledge) and was the winner of the 1997 American Book Award. Its jacket features praise by a prestigious Harvard professor, Cornel West, who writes: "*Race Traitor* is the most visionary, courageous journal in America." West's coziness with the racist Louis Farrakhan (he was a speaker at the Million Man March) has done nothing to tarnish his own academic reputation, his popularity with students, or his standing in the civil rights community. Afrocentrist racists like Leonard Jeffries, the late John Henrik Clarke, Derrick Bell, and Tony Martin—

to name just a few—have also been integral parts of the academic culture for decades, often running entire academic departments. By contrast, a distinguished Harvard scholar, Stephan Thernstrom, who is white, was driven out of his classroom by black student leftists who decided that his lectures on slavery were politically incorrect because they didn't reflect prevailing leftist views.

In recent decades, anti-white racism has, in fact, become a common currency of the "progressive" intelligentsia. Examples range from communist Professor Angela Davis, whose ideological rants are routinely laced with racial animosity, and who recently told an audience of undergraduates at Michigan State (following Farrakhan) that the number one problem in the world was white people, to Nobel laureate Toni Morrison, whose boundless suspicions of white America amount to a demonization almost as intense as Elijah Muhammad's. In her introduction to an anthology about the O.J. Simpson case, *Birth of a Nation 'Hood*, for example, Morrison compared the symbolic meanings of the O.J. Simpson case to D.W. Griffith's Ku Klux Klan epic in order to imply that white America acted as the KKK in pursuing Simpson for the murder of Ron Goldman and Simpson's ex-wife.

With full support from America's most prestigious universities, *Race Traitor* intellectuals in the field of "whiteness studies" have produced an entire library of "scholarship" whose purpose is to incite hatred against white America, against "Euro-American" culture, and against America's institutions in general. Thus, according to the editors of *Race Traitor*, "Just as the capitalist system is not a capitalist plot, race is not the work of racists. On the contrary, it is reproduced by the principal institutions of society, among which are the schools (which define 'excellence'), the labor market (which defines 'employment'), the law (which defines 'crime'), the welfare system (which defines 'poverty'), and the family (which defines 'kinship')."[3] Left-wing racists like the editors of *Race Traitor* characterize the presence of whites on this continent as an unmitigated catastrophe for "peoples of color" and an offense to everything that is decent and humane. In the perspective of these race radicals, white America is the "Great Satan." In academic cant, they replicate the poisonous message of the black racists of the Nation of Islam.

I once occupied the other side of the political divide. My views on race, however, have remained entirely consistent with my previous commitments and beliefs. I opposed racial preferences in the 1960s, and I oppose them now. Then I believed that only government neutrality towards racial groups was compatible with the survival of a multi-ethnic society that is also democratic. I still believe that today.

Where my views have changed is in the appreciation I now have for America's constitutional framework and the commitment of the American people to those ideals. America's unique political culture was indeed created by white European males, primarily English and Christian. It should be obvious to anyone with even a modest historical understanding, that these antecedents are not incidental to the fact that America and England are the nations that led the world in abolishing slavery and in establishing the principles of ethnic and racial inclusion. Moreover, we are a nation besieged by peoples "of color" trying to immigrate to our shores to take advantage of the unparalleled opportunities and rights our society offers them.

The creation of America by Protestant Christians within the framework of the British Empire was historically essential to the development of institutions that today afford greater privileges and protections to all minorities than any society extant. White European-American culture is a culture that the citizens of this nation can take enormous pride in, precisely because its principles—revolutionary in their conception and unique in their provenance—provide for the inclusion of cultures that are non-white and non-Christian (and which are not so tolerant in their lands of origin). That is why America's democratic and pluralistic framework remains an inspiring beacon to people of all colors all over the world, from Tiananmen Square to Haiti and Havana, who have not yet won their freedom, but who aspire to do so. This was once the common self-understanding of all Americans and is still the understanding of those who have resisted the discredited and oppressive worldview of the "progressive" left.

The left's war against "whiteness," and against America's demo-cratic culture in the 1990s is integrally connected to the Cold War that America fought against the marxist empire after World War II. It is in many respects the Cold War come home. The agendas of contempo-rary leftists are merely updated versions of the ideas and agendas of the marxist left that once supported the communist empire. The same radicals who launched the social and political eruptions of the 1960s have now become the politically correct faculties of American univer-sities. With suitable cosmetic adjustments, the theories, texts (and even leaders) of this left display a striking continuity with the radicalism of thirty and sixty years ago. Their goal remains the destruction of America's national identity and, in particular, of the moral, political, and economic institutions that form its social foundation.

The left's responses to my observations is not difficult to predict. Impugning the motives of opponents remains the left's most durable weapon, and there is no reason to suppose that it will be mothballed soon. In the heyday of Stalinism, the accusation of "class bias" was used by communists to undermine and attack individuals and institutions with whom they were at war. This accusation magically turned well-meaning citizens into "enemies of the people," a phrase handed down through radical generations from the Jacobin Terror through the Stalinist purges and the blood-soaked cultural revolutions of Chair-man Mao. The identical strategy is alive and well today in the left's self-righteous imputation of sexism, racism, and homophobia to any-one who dissents from its party line. Always weak in intellectual argu-ment, the left habitually relies on intimidation and slander to impose its increasingly incoherent point of view.

It is not that no one else in politics uses such tactics; it is just that the left uses them so reflexively, so recklessly, and so well. In the battle over California's Civil Rights Initiative to outlaw racial preferences, for example, the left's opposition took the form of a scorched earth strat-egy whose purpose was to strip its proponents of any shred of respect-ability. The chief spokesman for the anti-discrimination initiative, Ward Connerly, was accused of anti-black racism and of being a bedfellow of the Ku Klux Klan, despite himself being black. (The left even invited former Klan member David Duke to California, paying his expenses for the trip, to forge the non-existent connection.)

During the campaign, NAACP and ACLU lawyers who debated the initiative with its proponents relied almost exclusively on charges of racism and alarmist visions of a future in which African-Americans and women would be deprived of their rights should the initiative pass. In television spots, the anti-Initiative groups actually featured hooded Klan figures burning crosses to make their case. A fearful voice-over by actress Candace Bergen explicitly linked Ward Connerly, California Governor Pete Wilson, and Speaker Newt Gingrich with the KKK, claiming that women would lose all the rights they had won, and blacks would be thrown back to a time before the Civil Rights Acts, if its proponents succeeded. They even suggested that maternity leave for pregnant women would become illegal if the law was passed.

In the years since the passage of the California Civil Rights Initiative, not a single one of the left's dire predictions has been realized. Women have not lost their rights and blacks have not been thrown back to the segregationist era. Even the enrollment of blacks in California's system of higher education has not significantly dropped,[4] although demagogues of the left—including the president of the United States at the time, Bill Clinton—have used a short-fall in admissions *at the very highest levels* of the system (Berkeley and UCLA) to mislead the public by suggesting that an *overall* decline has taken place. One year after the initiative passed, enrolment had significantly fallen at only six out of seventy-four elite graduate, law, and medical school programs. Yet there has been no apology (or acknowledgment of these facts) from Candace Bergen, the NAACP, the ACLU, People for the American Way, or the other leftist groups responsible for the anti-Civil Rights Initiative campaign and the inflammatory rhetoric and fear mongering that accompanied it.

For maintaining my commitment to the ideals of the civil rights movement that King led, I have been attacked many times by the very people who betrayed those ideals. Among these attacks was a letter from the award-winning Berkeley novelist Ishmael Reed, who suggested that I was obsessed with blacks but did not really care what happened to them.[5] There is no real answer to such inversions of the truth. Nonetheless, I wrote him back: "I have three black granddaughters for whom I want the absolute best that this life and this society have to offer. My extended black family, which is large and from humble origins in the deep South, contains members who agree and who disagree with my views on these matters. But all of them understand that whatever I write on the subject of race derives from a profound desire for justice and opportunity for everyone in this country, including my extended black family. It springs from the hope that we can move towards a society where individuals are what matters and race is not a factor at all."

16

Liberals and Race

SOMETIMES THE EASIEST TRUTHS TO UNDERSTAND are actually the hardest to learn. "Thinking doesn't make it so" is one. "Just because it feels good, doesn't mean it's good" is another. The failure to learn these distinctions is actually the cause of liberalism, and lies at the heart of the liberal confusion about race.[1] Liberals begin by taking a stand that feels morally right; but the true appeal of liberalism lies in its making believers feel good about *themselves*.

Because liberalism begins and ends in a moral posture, it doesn't require the difficult assessment of facts on the ground to validate its conclusions. In recent years, these facts have not been hospitable to liberal views of a pervasive racism in American life. Some years ago, a distinguished black sociologist—himself a liberal—wrote a book about "the declining significance of race" in America.[2] The book was received with great consternation and the author soon stopped talking about the subject.

In the 1960s, the Civil Rights Acts put the power of the federal government on the side of the victims of racial prejudice and effected a sea change in American attitudes and institutions. But instead of declaring victory, the civil rights movement discovered "racism" in new

---

This article first appeared on FrontPageMagazine.com July 29, 2001, and has been edited for this book.

"subtle" and even "invisible" forms. Liberal historian Diane McWhorter, who wrote a book about the murder of four black children in Birmingham in 1963—an act of real, visible bigotry—summarized this phenomenon: "In the late 1960s, the civil rights movement was flummoxed by the insidious, clandestine racism of the North."[3]

But the North was the region whose political power had vanquished racial segregation in the South. How could it be anti-racist and insidiously racist at the same time? What is "clandestine racism" then, except an excuse to see something that is not there? Of course racial attitudes persist (and they come in all colors). But attitudes can remain just that, and have no real world consequences. Mere attitudes are not what civil rights leaders mean when they speak of racism that is "institutional." They mean racism that has a real world effect. But if attitudes express themselves in actions, they are no longer "clandestine" or "subtle" and in contemporary America they are punishable by law.

It is an interesting and important feature of modern liberalism that not only is its moral posture almost irrelevant to the facts, but it is also a pressure on the facts. The more racism you think there is and the bigger the obstacle you think it presents, the more liberal you are—the more "politically correct." One could plot the entire political spectrum using political correctness as a measure. A centrist liberal will think there is more racism and it is a bigger problem than a conservative will. A leftist will be convinced that there is more racism and it is an even bigger problem than a liberal. In short, the more racists you can find under any given bed, the more progressive you will be judged, and the more guilt free you will feel.

Thus, there is a psychological pay off. The more racism you are able to see, the better you can feel about yourself. In discovering racism, even where it may not exist, you are able to realize your own virtue and its self-reward.

But just because it feels good doesn't make it good. Feeding the appetite for self-love can hurt the very people one sets out to serve.

Suppose an athletic team with a roster of black stars is having a poor season. Suppose the coach explains his players' poor performances by blaming the racism of the referees. For all the internal satisfaction he might get from having a social conscience, his message will be crippling. By advising them to blame others, he is denying his players the only chance they have to improve their game, which is to hold themselves accountable for what they do. That, in a nutshell, is the conservative critique of liberalism on race: it is a crippling message for black Americans.

Every survey of public attitudes on race shows that over the last sixty years there has been a dramatic decline of racist attitudes among white Americans. For example, overwhelming majorities embrace or accept school, work, and housing integration and even intermarriage. Paralleling these changes in attitude, there has been an equally dramatic advance in the status of black citizens over the same interval. To take one telling index, in 1940 only 1 percent of blacks were middle class (defined as having twice the income of the poor). The figure is now 49 percent.[4] If that isn't an indication of revolutionary progress, what is?

But liberal denial and liberal confusion over race persist. A recent article written by commentator Chris Matthews offers an illustrative case. Matthews' column is called "White Blindness," by which he means blindness to the impact of contemporary racism on blacks. His observations were inspired by a recent poll that showed a majority of white Americans believe that blacks have "about the same opportunities in life [as] whites have," and that there is not a lot of discrimination against blacks remaining. Quipped Matthews, "I accept the accuracy of the survey . . . It's the white people I don't believe."[5]

According to Matthews, white people lie to themselves (or to pollsters) about race, because "many whites do not want to admit racial discrimination for fear it will be used to justify affirmative action." Liberals, being more moral than other whites, support affirmative action with the following line of reasoning: By holding blacks back, racism gives unfair privileges to whites. Justice requires that privilege be redistributed to blacks to "level the playing field." Since whites are adversely affected by affirmative action (they lose a race privilege) the unenlightened will oppose it. But they don't want to appear racist, so they will deny that racism exists (or that it is a significant obstacle to black aspirations). Hence "white blindness."

The problem with this argument is that the principal opposition to affirmative action derives from two perspectives that are not grounded in racism or self-interest. The first is the belief that any kind of racial preference is an offense to the American idea. Individuals should be judged on their merits, and incorporating racial policies into the law violates the American principle of equality before the law. The second is the pragmatic judgment that affirmative action policies work badly in the real world not only for whites but for minorities themselves.[6]

The fiftieth question on the same poll that Matthews cites (but doesn't quote) is this: "In order to give minorities more opportunity, do you believe race or ethnicity should be a factor when deciding who is hired, promoted, or admitted to college, or that hiring, promotions, and college admissions should be based strictly on merit and qualifications other than race or ethnicity?"

Ninety-four percent of the whites interviewed answered this question negatively, which would seem to confirm Matthews' point. But 86 percent of blacks also answered the question negatively and 88 percent of Hispanics.

Matthews thinks it's obvious that opportunities for blacks are dramatically less available than opportunities for whites: "Can a white American, with Harlem, Watts or any of this country's huge racial ghettos in mind, defend his or her claim that blacks have the same 'opportunities'?" he writes.

It's an odd, but typically liberal idea that all blacks live in Harlem or Watts, or some "huge racial ghetto." It certainly makes putting scare quotes around the word "opportunities" an easier task. But the reality is that 74 percent of blacks have incomes above the poverty line,[7] and don't live in inner cities or "ghettos." This wasn't always the case. In 1940, 87 percent of blacks were poor and lived in places like Harlem and Watts. Job and housing discrimination had a big effect in limiting black choices then.[8] But things are obviously different now. How is it that the remaining 26 percent of blacks are still living in poverty? Can their failure really be blamed on white racism? Are whites forcing some blacks to live in inner cities, while allowing the vast majority to escape?

Part of the problem is the now habitual use of the word "ghetto" itself. Blacks in America don't live in "ghettos." When Jews lived in ghettos in Europe—which is the origin of the word—they were actually forced to live there. They couldn't leave. By law. The word "ghetto" like many other emotionally charged terms—"Holocaust" and "Diaspora" are two—has been appropriated from the annals of Jewish suffering by black activists for obvious reasons. But for the same obvious reasons, these words carry with them many false implications in their new context.

The Middle Passage, for example, which brought black slaves to America and which Toni Morrison and others refer to as a "Black Holocaust," was actually not a calculated genocide, like Hitler's extermination of the Jews. The slave traders were businessmen who had money invested in their grim cargos, and did not buy slaves in Africa to kill them on the way to plantations across the sea.

The term "Diaspora," on the other hand, refers to the forced dispersal of the Jews from Israel and their existence for two millennia as a pariah group, without a homeland or citizen rights of their own. The population of black Africa was not dispersed by an external power. Black Africans sold their brothers and sisters into slavery, while retaining continuous sovereignty in their own lands. The slaves who were sent into exile lost their connection so thoroughly in the process that there is no significant movement among American blacks to return to a "homeland." American blacks are not living in a diaspora where they are permanent aliens. They are home.

The disconnection of these terms from reality notwithstanding, the use of them heightens the perception of victimization beyond the circumstances. That is their purpose. But thinking doesn't make it so.

Matthews and other liberals refuse to accept this analysis. Matthews writes that blacks are "consigned" to live in certain neighborhoods as though they cannot leave. To be fair, he is too smart to state this claim baldly. Instead he asks it as a rhetorical question: "What does consign blacks to…." as though the question of whether they were "consigned" in the first place has already been settled. He answers his falsely posed question with more insinuating questions: "Because they are not wanted in nicer neighborhoods, and would rather not have their families put up with the hassle? Because real estate agents steer black buyers away from the better openings? Or because the black homebuyer simply doesn't have the money to buy better homes? Whatever answer you choose involves a denial of equal opportunity."

But the notion that blacks can't buy nice middle class homes is false to begin with. The existence of a large black middle class answers the question about money. Exclusion by race is illegal. Suppose some real estate agents do it anyway. Are there no black real estate agents? The civil rights complaint industry is a large one these days, with powerful support agencies in the federal government. Is it likely that widespread illegal housing discrimination exists and yet there are no widespread protests and lawsuits? Recently, black organizations raised a national hue and cry about the Confederate flag. It raised a lot of hackles. Does Chris Matthews seriously believe that the reason black "civil rights" activists are not protesting rampant racial exclusion in real estate is to avoid a hassle? If this kind of exclusion were systematically keeping middle class blacks from living where they wanted to, doesn't it seem more likely that this powerful constituency, which controls large cities like Atlanta, Detroit, Washington, DC, and Baltimore, would have long ago thrown its weight into this battle?

A more interesting question Matthews might want to ask is whether there are in fact large numbers of middle class blacks who want to live in predominantly white neighborhoods in the first place. Does he think that the persistence of "historically black" colleges is the result of white colleges keeping blacks out? Perhaps Matthews missed the article by a black reporter in the *Washington Post* who announced she was proudly relocating in "Chocolate City" and didn't want any "Vanilla" there. Recent studies show, in fact, that black segregation in housing is largely a product of self-selection.[9]

A while back, I was thinking about liberals' perception problems in a different context. It was July 4, and I was looking out over miles of ocean beaches stretching from the Pacific Palisades to Malibu crowded with holiday bathers. What drew my attention was the fact that there was not a black person in sight. It occurred to me that a liberal would immediately conclude that this was "segregation," and explain it as a product of "institutional racism."

South Central, where blacks are "consigned" to live in Los Angeles, is quite far away from the ocean coast. Black people can't afford to live in Malibu or the Pacific Palisades, or even in the white suburbs near them. Even if black people were inclined to make the trip, they probably wouldn't want the "hassle" of spending time on the beach with whites "who don't want them." Such would be a liberal's musings. The absence of blacks taking in the holiday sun and surf could only be the result of white racism—clandestine maybe, institutional of course—but effective all the same.

The problem with this analysis is that about three-quarters of the people who were in fact enjoying the surf that day were Mexican-Americans from East Los Angeles. East Los Angeles is even farther from the coast than Compton or Watts, and just as impoverished. Moreover, there are a lot more black actors and music moguls living in Malibu and the Palisades than there are Mexicans. The problem with the liberal viewpoint is that it fails to take into account people's cultural choices—their free will to decide for themselves what they want to do and where they want to go or live.

"Ever watch an NBA game [asks Matthews] and notice that the players are black but that nearly 100 percent of the seats within a hundred feet of the court are filled with whites? Ever go anywhere and not see the whites in the better seats, the better houses, the better jobs?" For Matthews, these questions answer themselves and add up to a case that discrimination is responsible for denying blacks the opportunities that would get them those better seats and houses. It all reminds Matthews of a Groucho Marx line: "Are you going to believe me or your lying eyes?"

Well, it all depends on whose eyes are doing the lying. The fanciest house in my neighborhood is owned by Laurence Fishburne, the black star of *In Search of Bobby Fisher, Othello, The Matrix,* and other Hollywood features. Somewhere out there, the growing black middle class is living well, even if Chris Matthews is a stranger to their neighborhoods. The black middle class has some pretty respectable jobs, too, like running Atlanta, Washington, DC, Detroit, Baltimore, and other major American cities, just to pick a non-entertainment, non-sports field of endeavor, with six-figure salaries, that will be familiar enough to make the case.

As for the NBA, if Matthews had looked at the other seats in the house, he wouldn't have found many blacks there either. But if he had looked at the far more expensive front row seats for a Mike Tyson fight in a Las Vegas resort, he would have seen Jesse Jackson, Don King, the late Tupac Shakur, the record mogul Suge Knight, and other Armani-suited fans of a darker hue. What accounts for the difference at NBA games? I don't pretend to have an answer, but then I couldn't tell you why there are almost no black hockey players or black hockey fans. Nor could I tell you why if you were hiking in the Sierras, or any national park—where the fees are nominal—a black person would be harder to find than a Hobbit. Disneyland, which is quite expensive, is crowded with working-class Mexicans, but there are almost no blacks. Cultural choices are inscrutable. But they are choices. And one thing is certain: it's not money or opportunity that's keeping blacks from occupying the high dollar seats at NBA games.

Unfortunately, the feel-good racial fantasies of liberals cause a real world blindness whose consequences are destructive. Some years ago, the liberals in the state education establishment in Michigan set up aggressive affirmative action programs to overcome the "institutional racism" they imagined was keeping blacks out of Michigan universities. Of course, Michigan schools already couldn't discriminate against blacks even if they wanted to, since it was against the law. The purpose of the new programs was to rig the entrance requirements at these institutions so that black students who were not adequately prepared could get in anyway, thus achieving "diversity." Liberals could feel good. So even though the students were not prepared, liberals recruited them aggressively anyway to give them those front row seats that were just out of reach. When black enrollment swelled, liberals looked at these plums and said, "My, what good boys (and, of course, girls) we are."

But the *Detroit News* recently spoiled the fun by showing what was wrong with the picture. The *News* conducted an investigation of the program results at seven Michigan universities, which revealed that among black students who were freshman in 1994, only 40 percent got their diplomas after six years. Sixty percent had failed or dropped out. "We're throwing them out after taking their money and they're getting nothing out of it," summed up a history professor at Ferris State University who helped to start one of the programs designed to keep minority students in college. "We're mugging [the majority] of them, taking their money, taking their dignity. I feel like I am participating in a vast criminal conspiracy."[10]

The road to hell (the poet William Blake once observed) is paved with good intentions.

17

*Ten Reasons Why Reparations
Are a Bad Idea—and Racist, Too*

I N THE SPRING OF 2000, the idea that taxpayers should pay reparations to black Americans for the damages of slavery and segregation ceased to be a fixation of the political margin and began to
emerge as the next big "civil rights" thing. Congressman John Conyers
had already introduced legislation to set up a commission that would
examine the impact of slavery, as a foreordained prelude to legislated
compensation. A coalition of African-Americans has claimed a debt of
$4.1 trillion. A coalition of African nations has claimed a debt of $777
trillion against a collection of governments including the United States.
Distinguished black intellectuals like Henry Louis Gates have given it
their imprimatur, while Randall Robinson, who led the successful South
African boycott movement a decade ago, has written a strident manifesto called *The Debt: What America Owes to Blacks*, which has become
a bible of the reparations cause.

<hr/>

This article first appeared on *Salon.com* on May 30, 2000. In the spring of 2001, based
on the article, I mounted an ad campaign against reparations for slavery. The ads were
rejected by forty college papers and were greeted by demonstrations and outcries on
the campuses where they did appear. The campaign garnered national attention and
generated more than four hundred news stories about the controversy. I recount the
history of the campaign in *Uncivil Wars: The Controversy over Reparations for Slavery*
(2001).

Moreover, it is not just in the realm of ideas that the payback demand has gained ground. The Chicago City Council has voted 46-1 in favor of a reparations resolution. The lopsided nature of the vote persuaded Mayor Richard Daley to apologize for slavery (in *Chicago*?). The primary sponsor of the resolution, Alderman Dorothy Tillman, has announced she intends to organize a "national convention" to push the issue of reparations.

So what is wrong with the idea? In what follows, I have listed ten reasons why all Americans—African-Americans in particular—should reject it. The bottom line is that it will alienate African-Americans from their American roots and further isolate them from all of America's other communities who are themselves blameless in the grievance of slavery, cannot be held culpable even for racial segregation, and who, in the last generation, have made significant contributions to ending discrimination and redressing lingering injustices suffered by Americans of African descent.

ONE

Who Owes the Debt?

Assuming there actually is a debt, it is not at all clear who owes it. Chicago Alderman Dorothy Tillman articulated the claimants' argument for the debt this way: "America owes blacks a debt because when we built this country on free labor, . . . wealth was handed down to the white community." Randall Robinson reaches back in time even further: "Well before the birth of our country, Europe and the eventual United States perpetrated a heinous wrong against the peoples of Africa, and benefited from the wrong through the continuing exploitation of Africa's human and material resources."

To sustain this claim, Robinson's book devotes entire sections to the alleged depredations of whites against blacks hundreds and even thousands of years before the "eventual United States"—that is, the government that is expected to pay the reparations—was created. It is necessary to insert the qualifier "alleged," because like so many who wave the bloody racial shirt these days, Robinson makes little effort to establish causal responsibilities, but invokes any suffering of blacks where whites were proximate as evidence that whites were to blame.

Slavery itself is the most obvious example. As even Henry Louis Gates will admit, it was not whites but black Africans who enslaved their brothers and sisters. They were abetted by dark-skinned Arabs—since Robinson and his allies force us into this unpleasant mode of racial discourse—who organized the slave trade. This raises a question: Are reparations going to be assessed against the descendants of Africans and Arabs for their role in slavery? There were also three thousand black slave owners in the antebellum United States. Are reparations to be paid by their descendants too?

TWO

African-Americans Have Also Benefited from Slavery

The idea that only whites benefited from slavery is factually wrong and is also attitudinally racist. By accusing the U.S. government of crimes against black people in advance of its existence, Robinson reveals the ugly anti-white attitudes that lie beneath the surface of many arguments for reparations, especially his.

Assuming America was built on the labor of slaves, as Robinson and other reparations proponents claim, then obviously the wealth in which black Americans share today is the fruit of slave labor as well. It is often claimed by black leaders that black America is the tenth richest "nation" in the world. Where did this wealth come from if not the same source as American wealth generally? If slavery created any part of this wealth, then obviously it created wealth for black Americans. Slave-owning blacks in the antebellum United States clearly benefited from the free labor of slaves, along with whites. Are their descendants to be exempted from payment of the debt, just because they are black?

How much have the descendants of slaves benefited from the system they now claim has stolen their labor? American blacks on average enjoy per capita incomes in the range of twenty to fifty times that of blacks living in any of the African nations from which they were kidnapped. What about *this* benefit of slavery? Are the reparations proponents going to make black descendants of slaves pay themselves for benefiting from the fruits of their ancestors' servitude?

THREE
What About the Descendants of Union Soldiers Who Gave Their Lives to Free the Slaves?

In terms of lineal responsibility for slavery, only a tiny minority of Americans ever owned slaves during the slavery era. This is true not only of those who lived in the north, but even those who lived in the antebellum South where only one white in five was a slaveholder. Why should their descendants owe a debt? What about the descendants of the 350,000 Union soldiers who died in the war that freed the slaves? They gave their lives. What possible morality would ask them to pay (through their descendants) again?

FOUR
Most American Whites Have No Connection to Slavery

Most Americans living today (white and otherwise) do not have even an indirect, lineal connection to slavery. In fact, they have no connection to slavery at all. The two great waves of American immigration occurred after 1880 and after 1960. Is there an argument worth considering that would, for example, make Jews (who were cowering in the ghettos of Europe at the time), or Mexicans and Cubans (who were suffering under the heel of Spain), responsible for this crime? What reason could there be that Vietnamese boat people, Russian refuseniks, Iranian refugees, and Armenian victims of the Turks, or Greek, Polish, Hungarian, and Korean victims of communism, should pay reparations to American blacks? There is no reason, and no advocate of reparations has so much as bothered to come up with one.

FIVE

The Cases of Jewish and Japanese Reparations
Are Not Comparable and Therefore Do Not Provide Precedents

The historical precedents generally invoked to justify the reparations claim—that Jewish and Japanese-Americans received reparations from Germany and the United States—do not hold up under scrutiny. The circumstances involved bear no resemblance to the situation of American blacks, and are not really precedents at all. The Jews and Japanese who received reparations were individuals who actually suffered the hurt. Jews do not receive reparations from Germany simply because they are Jews. Those who do were corralled into concentration camps and lost immediate family members or personal property. Other Jews have not received compensation. Nor have all Japanese-Americans received payments, but only those whom the government interned in relocation camps and who had their property confiscated. This is also true of the black inhabitants of Rosewood and Oklahoma City and the victims of the Tuskegee experiment who have received reparations. The reparations claims now being advanced by black leaders seem to imply that the only qualification required for reparations is the color of one's skin. Robinson's book is pointedly subtitled "What America Owes To Blacks." If this is not racism, what is?

SIX

What about Successful Blacks?
What Is Their Economic Grievance?

Behind the reparations argument lies the unfounded claim that every black in America suffers economically from the consequences of slavery and discrimination. Of course this presumes that any blacks do. (See argument two, above.) It would seem a hard case to prove individual damages over a hundred-and-fifty year (or even fifty-year) gap in the first place. But no real effort has been made by any researcher to do this. The only evidence really offered by the reparations party is the existence of contemporary "income disparities" and "inequalities" between the races. What about the income disparities between West Indian-born and descended blacks in America and American-born and descended blacks? This gap is as large as the black-white income gap, and yet West Indians are also the descendants of slaves. But the reality is that, as far as the reparations claimants are concerned, no actual connection need be proved. The rhetorical connection is enough.

On the other hand, African-American success stories that contradict the claims are abruptly dismissed. To take the most obvious case, Oprah Winfrey may have been a slave's great-granddaughter and a sharecropper's granddaughter in the most segregated of all southern states, Mississippi. But—victim of slavery and segregation or no—she had the opportunity (and was able) to become the richest woman in America by her own efforts. On the strength of her appeal to (non-racist) white consumers, she earned over $700 million. Would she have had this opportunity if her ancestors had never been brought as slaves to America?

To be sure, Oprah Winfrey's achievement is extraordinary. But it is reprised in millions of other, more modest, success stories of America's prosperous black middle class—including those of every prominent promoter of the reparations claim, Randall Robinson and Henry Louis Gates included. No wonder the only argument that is offered against these obvious counter-facts is that every black success story must be an exception to the rule.

But the reality is that this black middle class—composed exclusively of descendants of slaves—is not only a prosperous middle class, but also one that is now larger in absolute terms than the black underclass, which is really the only segment of the black population that can be invoked in behalf of the case. Is this black middle class majority—numbering millions of individuals—really just a collective exception of unusual people? Or does its existence suggest that the failures of the black underclass may be failures of individual character, and hardly, if at all, a result of lingering aftereffects of racial discrimination, let alone a slave system that ceased to exist over a century ago.

West Indian blacks in America may be descended from slaves, but their average incomes are equivalent to the average incomes of whites, and nearly 25 percent higher than the average incomes of American born blacks of all classes. How is it that slavery adversely affected one large group of descendants but not the other? And how can government be expected to decide an issue—did slavery impact an individual's failure to make the most of his or her opportunity—that is so subjective? Why can a penniless Mexican, who is in America illegally and unable even to speak English, find work in America's inner cities, while blacks cannot? Can nineteenth-century slavery or even the segregation of fifty years ago really explain this? The fact is that nobody has demonstrated any clearly defined causal connection between slavery and the economic disparities that are alleged to require restitution.

These questions don't even broach the problem of those who will be expected to pay the "debt," however. How are blue-collar whites and ethnics expected to understand their reparations payments to African-American doctors, lawyers, executives, and military officers, let alone multimillionaire entertainers and athletes who are descendants of slaves?

SEVEN

Reparations Will Increase Victim Mentalities, Negative Attitudes, and Alienation within the African-American Community

The campaign for reparations will inevitably fuel a renewed sense of grievance among African-Americans, since even if reparations are paid, they will never amount to sufficient compensation for the injustices of the past. The reparations claim is not a constructive or helpful message for black leaders to be sending their community at this moment in history. As America enters the twenty-first century, it is more than ever a nation of immigrants, and increasingly a nation of immigrants "of color." Virtually every group that has come to seek refuge and opportunity in America has its own grievances to remember. For millions of immigrants, the suffering is recent, and can be as serious as ethnic cleansing or genocide.

What attitude are these people going to have to the payment claims from African-Americans, whose slavery experience lies in the distant past and was not the actual experience of any blacks alive today? Won't the demand for reparations be seen as just another claim for special treatment, for an extravagant new handout? Even if the experience of segregation (now nearly fifty years old) is added to slavery, won't these immigrant communities—Hispanic, Indian, Asian—regard this as a crutch made necessary only because some blacks can't seem to locate the ladder of opportunity within reach of others (many of whom are even less privileged than themselves)?

To focus the social passions of African-Americans on what some Americans may have done to their ancestors fifty or a hundred and fifty years ago is to burden this community with a crippling sense of victimhood. It is also to create a new source of conflict between African-Americans and other American communities.

A young black intellectual sent me the following comments about reparations: "I think the reparations issue will be healthy. It will show all Americans (white, Hispanic, Asian) how much blacks contributed to helping build this country." Actually, as *The Debt* makes clear, what it will accomplish is just the opposite. It will provide black leaders with a platform from which to complain about all the negative aspects of black life—to emphasize inner city pathologies and failures, and to blame whites, Hispanics, and Asians for causing them. How is this going to impress other communities? How is it going to build bridges to them? It is really just a prescription for sowing more racial resentment, creating greater racial antagonism, and throwing more obstacles in the path of African-American progress.

EIGHT
What about the Reparations that Have Already Been Paid?

Since the passage of the Civil Rights Acts and the advent of the Great Society in 1965, trillions of dollars in *net* transfer payments have been made to African-Americans[1] in the form of welfare benefits and racial preferences (in contracts, job placements, and educational admissions)—all under the rationale of redressing historic racial grievances.[2] These funds have been paid by taxpayers who are mainly white. And while it is true that most welfare recipients are also white, the proportion of the African-American community which is on welfare is far greater, and since welfare reform, has become absolutely greater. Moreover, these African-American welfare recipients are the only blacks in America who can plausibly be said to be disadvantaged as a result of the fact that their ancestors were brought here as slaves.

Reparations advocates have an answer to this argument—and it is a revealing one. Here is how Randall Robinson refers to this massive gesture of generosity and contrition on the part of the white political majority in America during the last thirty-five years: "It was only in 1965 [that America] began to walk away from the social wreckage that centuries of white hegemony had wrought." *Take that* white, Hispanic, and Asian America! If a trillion dollars in restitution and a wholesale rewriting of American law is nothing, then what will fill the bill?

NINE
What about the Debt Blacks Owe to America?

This raises another question that black leaders might do well to reflect on: what about the debt blacks owe to America—to white Americans—for liberating them from slavery?

Slavery existed in all societies, and for thousands of years before a white person set foot in Africa or the Atlantic slave trade began. But in thousands of years of its existence, there never was an anti-slavery movement until white Christian Englishmen and Americans created one. If not for the anti-slavery attitudes and military power of these white Christians, the slave trade would not have been ended. If not for the sacrifices of white soldiers and a white American president who gave his life to sign the Emancipation Proclamation, blacks in America would still be slaves. If not for the dedication of Americans of all ethnicities and colors to a society based on the principle that all men are created equal, blacks in America would not enjoy the highest standard of living of blacks anywhere in the world, and indeed one of the highest standards of living of any people in the world. They would not enjoy the greatest freedoms and the most thoroughly protected individual rights. Where is the gratitude of black America and its leaders for those gifts?

TEN

Blacks Are Virtually the Oldest Americans.
Why Not Embrace Their American Destiny?

The final reason for African-Americans themselves to reject the reparations claim is a recognition of the enormous privileges African-Americans enjoy as Americans, and therefore of their own stake in America's history, slavery and all.

For the African-American community to isolate itself even further from America by asserting claims for reparations would be to embark on a course whose consequences are troubling to contemplate. Blacks were here before the Mayflower. Who is more American than the descendants of African slaves? Yet the black community has had a long flirtation with separatists and nationalists in its ranks who are thinly veiled racists and want African-Americans to have no part of America's multiethnic social contract. This separatist strain in black America's consciousness has now been joined with the anti-Americanism of the political left to form the animating force of reparations movement.

In this regard, Randall Robinson—himself a political leftist—is a movement archetype. Anti-white sentiments and anti-American feelings leap out from every page of *The Debt*, including a chapter devoted to praising Fidel Castro, one of the world's longest surviving and most sadistic dictators. A rhapsody for Fidel Castro's marxist police state would seem a bizarre irrelevance to a book on reparations for American blacks, except for Robinson's belief that Castro is a quintessential victim of American "oppression" and therefore a hero regardless of his crimes. Randall Robinson despises America that much. "Many blacks— most perhaps," he claims in his discussion of Castro, "don't like America." But apparently they should like Cuba's gulag.

This unthinking anti-Americanism is the crux of the problem the reparations movement poses for African-Americans, and for all Americans. Behind the reparations idea is an irrational fear and hatred of

America. It is about holding America responsible for every negative facet of black existence, as though America were God, and God had failed. Above all, it is about denying the gift America has given to all of its citizens, including its black citizens, through the inspired genius of its founding.

In the eyes of Randall Robinson, an American founder like Thomas Jefferson was merely "a slave owner, a racist and—if one accepts that consent cannot be given if it cannot be denied—a rapist." (Robinson is referring to Jefferson's affair with his slave Sally Hemings, despite the fact that there is no evidence establishing Jefferson as the father of Hemings' children.[3]) The fact that Americans still honor the author of the Declaration of Independence makes his personal sins into archetypes that define America itself: "Does not the continued un-remarked American deification of Jefferson tell us all how profoundly contemptuous of black sensibilities, American society persists in being? How deeply, stubbornly, poisonously racist our society to this day remains?"

This hatred for America, and specifically, for white America, blinds Robinson—and those who think like him—to a truth far more important than Jefferson's dalliance with Sally Hemings, which may or may not have been unwilling (consent obviously can be given, even if it cannot be denied). For it is the proclamation Jefferson wrote—"all men are created equal"—which white Americans died for, that accomplished what no black African did: they set Randall Robinson's ancestors free.

For all America's faults, African-Americans have an enormous stake in America and in the heritage individuals like Thomas Jefferson helped to shape. To denigrate Jefferson is to denigrate themselves. The heritage enshrined in the American founding, and the institutions and ideas to which it gave rise, is what is really under attack in the reparations movement. This assault on America, conducted by racial separatists and the political left, is not only an attack on white Americans, but on all Americans—and on African-Americans especially.

America's black citizens are the richest and most privileged black people alive—a bounty that is a direct result of the heritage that is under assault. The American idea needs the support of its African-

American citizens. But African-Americans also need the support of the American idea.

Dredging up a new reason to attack this idea is not in the interest of the African-American community. What would serve this community better would be the rejection of the ideas of the political left articulated by leaders like Randall Robinson who endorse this claim. African-Americans would be better served by embracing America as their home, and defending its good: the principles and institutions that have set them—and all of us—free.

18

Racism and Free Speech

I am not tragically colored. There is no great sorrow dammed up in my soul, nor lurking behind my eyes. . . . I do not belong to the sobbing school of Negro-hood who hold that nature somehow has given them a low-down dirty deal and whose feelings are all hurt about. Even in the helter-skelter skirmish that is my life, I have seen that the world is to the strong regardless of a little pigmentation more or less. No, I do not weep at the world—I am too busy sharpening my oyster knife.

Zora Neale Hurston

THE ATTACKS ON THE REPARATIONS AD I attempted to place in college papers in the spring of 2001 were more extensive and attracted more attention than any previous campus incident involving freedom of the press or freedom of speech. Forty papers rejected the ad outright, and on the thirty-odd campuses where it was published, there were demonstrations, protests and attacks on the papers that printed it. At Brown University, student leftists stole the entire edition of the *Brown Daily Herald* and destroyed it. Yet despite

From *Uncivil Wars: The Controversy over Reparations for Slavery* (2001).

their unprecedented scope, these incidents were niether a new nor an isolated phenomenon.

According to the Student Press Law Center, an organization that provides free legal help to student papers under attack, there have been 205 incidents of "offensive" student papers being stolen and burned since 1993.[1] In one celebrated case, black students destroyed fourteen thousand copies of the *Daily Pennsylvanian* because they were upset over the appearance of two op-ed columns by the same author. One had criticized Martin Luther King's personal ethics; the other had challenged the racial double standards displayed by the Penn authorities when they failed to discipline a black honor society called Onyx, whose members had hazed blindfolded initiates and shouted anti-white slogans in the middle of the night, waking up students in the dorms. No actions were taken against the members of Onyx, but the author of the columns was investigated for thirty-four student-initiated charges of "racial harassment" for what he had written. The charges were eventually dismissed.[2]

While racial issues were obviously a factor prompting the efforts to suppress my ad, these efforts would have been made even if race had been no part of the issue at all. That someone should challenge the hegemony of the left on campus was enough to invite retribution. This was made clear by a new ad campaign conducted by members of the Independent Women's Forum (iwf) during the last weeks of the spring semester. The iwf attempted to place an ad titled "Take Back the Campus! Combat the Radical Feminist Assault on the Truth" in five college papers. The ad was written by Christina Hoff Sommers, author of two well-known books, *Who Stole Feminism?* and *The War Against Boys*, that had angered radical feminists. Taking a cue from my efforts, the iwf ad listed the "Ten Most Common Feminist Myths," among them the claim that one in four women was a rape victim and that women earned only 75 percent of what men were paid. (In fact, if work experience, skill level, and educational background were taken into account, women earned about 98 percent what men did, according to government figures.[3]) The *Columbia Spectator* rejected the iwf ad; the Harvard *Crimson* wanted changes made that were not approved by the time the school year ended; the *Dartmouth Review*, the Yale *Daily News*, and the UCLA *Daily Bruin* all published it.[4]

The response at UCLA was particularly revealing. A demonstration was held to protest what the organizers described as "hateful misinformation," "violent" and "hostile."[5] They demanded a free page to respond and an apology from the paper's editors as well. One of the student leaders, Christie Scott, told a reporter the IWF statement was "just as detrimental as the Horowitz ad" and reiterated: "We want an apology, but most of all we want this not to happen again."[6] The most ominous statement came from LeAnn Quinn, a psychology senior and member of the Coalition for the Fair Representation of Women, who said: "They're trying to infiltrate campuses with their lies and myths."[7] Defense of the university as a fortress of left-wing purity indicated how far doctrines of political correctness had themselves "infiltrated" the education of undergraduates at UCLA.

It also showed that the underlying issue in the controversies over the ad was ultimately not racial, but political. Civil libertarian Nat Hentoff drew attention to this fact in noting the ironic parallel between the attacks on the campus papers that printed the reparations ad and the destruction of abolitionist newspapers by pro-slavery mobs in the era before the Civil War.[8] Writing in the New York *Village Voice*, Hentoff described a meeting he had attended at Columbia University,[9] hosted by the International Socialist Organization, a campus player in the events at Brown and the attacks on student papers at other colleges. The ISO flier advertising the event proclaimed: "Right-Wingers Try To Buy Free Speech! Anti-Racist Protester From Brown Speaks Out!"

Buying space for a political ad was actually not that different from submitting an article, except that it allowed the purchaser to publish his opinions more swiftly and efficiently, and it allowed editors to establish some distance from the contents. This relieved the editors of some of their oversight responsibilities while allowing the writer more freedom in expressing his views. On the other hand, both the op-ed column and the ad purchase were privileges, not rights. Every paper has the right to reject any ad it chooses and any article as well. The First Amendment enjoins government from interfering with free speech. It does not compel editors to publish everything submitted to them. There is one caveat, however, because the courts have held that if a paper is funded and overseen by a state institution and prints an ad on one side of a political debate, it cannot deny ad space to the other side. I was able to use this ruling in the case of the *Minnesota Daily* at the University of Minnesota. The *Daily* originally rejected the ad, but after being apprised of the law, agreed to print it. [10]

The issue of free speech arose in the case of my ad, not because I had a right to have it printed, but because there was a concerted political effort to prevent me from doing so. At the Columbia protest event, the Brown activist said: "The *Village Voice* printed the ad, and we need to organize against it and shut the paper down!"[11] Commented Hentoff: "This is hardly the first time that there have been threats to shut us down, but the totalitarian mind-set of these traducers of the civil rights movement on campuses around the country is worth more attention than has been paid by the mainstream press."

The failure to confront the "totalitarian" dimension of the controversy made the press treatment somewhat less reassuring than would otherwise have been the case. It was one thing to provide a vigorous defense of anyone's right to say anything (he may be a "racist" but let him speak). It was quite another to defend the integrity of views that were under attack. Suppose radicals hadn't stolen the paper at Brown, suppose they hadn't demonstrated at the editorial offices of the *Duke Chronicle*, and suppose the editor of the *Daily Californian* had not apologized under pressure. Few people would have heard about the ad. But more importantly, fewer still would be aware that forty campus papers had refused to print a perfectly reasonable statement, for fear of being labeled "racist" by unscrupulous censors.

None of the editorial defenses of the ad in *USA Today*, the *Boston Globe*, the *Philadelphia Inquirer* and other papers found anything racist in the ad itself. Yet none defended the ad (or its author) against racial smears either. In other words, no one defended my right to make a reasonable argument on an issue like reparations without being subject to racial attacks. In my view, this was almost as important as the right to publish the ad itself.

The problem was underscored by a backhanded defense of my speech rights in a *Newsweek* column by Jonathan Alter.[12] In the center of the page on which the column appeared, there was a photograph of one of the Spartacist protesters at Berkeley. She was carrying a sign that said in big letters: "David Horowitz, Racist Ideologue." There was no caption to the photograph, and there was no reference to the photo in Alter's piece. In other words, none of the four million readers of *Newsweek* was informed that this woman belonged to a totalitarian sect, was a self-described "communist" who wanted a Bolshevik America, and was prepared to denounce anyone whose views opposed her own as a "tool of the bosses" and a "racist" as well.

On the other hand, the same media that subliminally spread these slanders would not have dared to characterize the minority students and faculty who smeared me as hate-mongers.[13] That would fall under the category of "insensitive." Yet I was the one in danger of being marginalized as a bigot.

This was not a concern easily dismissed. My career as a writer and commentator is dependent in part on the attitudes of thousands of people in media and political circles who know me only by reputation. In innumerable incidents like the *Newsweek* photo, the reputation I depended on was being injured in ways I had no means to redress. How many editors, after seeing Alter's article, would think a second time before asking me to write? What institutions would decide not to invite me to speak because of my "controversial" image? Which politicians would avoid me in order to forestall the possibility of guilt by association? I would never know.

The column Alter had written was itself an exercise in McCarthyism, racial and otherwise. He began by misrepresenting me as an "agitator" of the "extreme right." In fact, I have a middle-of-the-road position on abortion, am a libertarian on issues of media censorship, and have a long record of defending gays against right-wing attacks.

I am also an outspoken critic of Republicans for not being concerned enough about the plight of minorities in America's inner cities.[14] This last fact is material because of the concluding paragraph in Alter's column, which attributed to me a view that was the opposite of everything I had ever said or believed: "The not-so-subtle subtext [of the ad] was that we've given 'them' enough, and so should give up on addressing the continuing problems of race and poverty in America." To drive home this idea, without any supporting evidence, Alter wrote: "The ad reminds me of one of those tiresome rants supporting a NAAWP (National Association for the Advancement of White People)."

Alter could easily have consulted the hundreds of thousands of words I had written on the Internet which refuted his claim. But even this "research" was unnecessary since the ad provided its own rebuttal. Its text was difficult, in fact, to misread. Its final point had emphasized that there was no group with a longer standing claim to be American than African-Americans. I had said that America needed African-Americans as much as African-Americans needed America. The ad was a plea to African-Americans not to listen to their own racists and separatists, but to embrace America's heritage with its creed that all men are created equal. What could be less racist than that? Yet, without a second thought as to the damage it might inflict, Alter casually applied the stigma to me.

Alter's thoughtless attack reflected the double standards of the political culture that had shaped the debate, and that habitually tarred other conservative writers like Dinesh D'Souza and Ward Connerly without any regard for what they actually thought or wrote. *Washington Post* columnist Richard Cohen inadvertently illuminated the problem in an article devoted to the controversy, which he called "Specious Speech." Unlike Alter, Cohen not only defended the publication of the ad but also the argument itself: "Word for word, the ad makes sense." But then he took away a lot of what he had just given when he also said the ad was guilty of being "offensive" as my critics had claimed: "But word for word is not, I learned a long time ago, how people read. They take in a message, a tone. The interior message of Horowitz's ad is smug, cold—dismissive. It's not racist, as some have charged. It just feels that way." [15]

The question that Cohen's article begged was this: offensive to *whom*? My arguments were not directed at African Americans, nor intended to dismiss their interests or feelings. My arguments were directed at partisans of a political idea that claimed that all America was guilty for the sins of slavery and that its poisons had continued into the present. Like others involved in the controversy over the ad, Cohen was finally unable to make the distinction between the political advocates of reparations, and the African American community itself.

Long before I wrote the ad, black conservatives like Thomas Sowell and Walter Williams had made many of the arguments that appeared in it, including the most controversial one—that African Americans owed a debt to their country.[16] The blunt tone I adopted was a response to the abrasive one my political opponents had used in making their case. It was also an *homage* to Sowell and Williams and other black conservatives for the vicious way in which their views were regularly stigmatized and dismissed by the same people. This was something that Cohen and the rest of my critics never considered. The double standard in the culture prevented them.

Reparations advocates accuse America of being uniquely responsible for slavery; they ascribe malicious intent to every compromise with political reality; they deny America's achievement in ending slavery; they accuse every living citizen who is not black of benefiting from slavery and of being responsible for all economic disparities that black Americans suffer; they dismiss Americans' efforts in the realm of human rights and describe America as being "built on genocide, and theft, and slavery."[17] They accuse contemporary Americans of being "deeply, stubbornly, poisonously racist,"[18] and threaten that unless their demands are met "America can have no future as one people."[19]

Are these statements *not* offensive? Yet who would publicly dare to say so? Who would take reparations advocates like Randall Robinson and Charles Ogletree to task for their hostility to America generally and to white Americans in particular? Of course, this is precisely what my ad did, and that is the reason for the reaction it provoked.

Randall Robinson, who is the leading spokesman for reparations, is certainly never criticized for *his* tone, which is often inflammatory. His book, *The Debt: What America Owes Blacks*, has become the manifesto of the cause, and he speaks frequently to college audiences, who always treat him with deference, an attitude shared by the nation's media.

In 1998, Robinson published an autobiography called *Defending the Spirit*, which chronicled a public career that had made him a national figure as a leader of the successful movement to impose economic sanctions on South Africa, a standing he has tried to transfer to the reparations issue. On the first page of his autobiography, Robinson informs the reader of his racial perspective: "I am obsessively black," he writes, and "race is an overarching aspect of my identity." So, he admits, is victimhood. "White Americans," Robinson claims, "have made me this way."[20] Two pages later he amplifies the confession: "White-hot hatred [of whites] would seem the proper reflex" for the "pain" that he feels. But prudence prevents him from expressing himself directly. As he puts it, "There is no survival there." Instead, he is forced into a muted self-reflection: "In the autumn of my life, I am left regarding white people, before knowing them individually, with irreducible mistrust and dull dislike."[21]

Robinson's attitude would inevitably be described as racist if confessed by a white writer. But in a black writer it is regarded as "gasp-out-loud frank,"[22] "provocative . . . honest, bluntly told,"[23] "brutally frank"[24] and all-in-all, "an unfiltered, uncensored, smart black voice in your ear." This last is the verdict pronounced on Robinson's book by Richard Cohen's paper, the *Washington Post*.

A page after confessing his obsession with race, Robinson offers the following reminiscence: "My father died in 1974 at the age of sixty-eight, of what the family now believes to have been Alzheimer's disease. Toward the end, and not lucid, he slapped a nurse, telling her not to 'put her white hands on him.' His illness had afforded him a final brief honesty. I was perversely pleased when told the story."[25] The honesty, along with the pleasure, evidently lies in the fact that his father's well-meaning helper was white, and any gesture other than hostility towards a white person would be a lie.

The facts of Randall Robinson's life, as he relates them, make this bigotry difficult to comprehend, despite the fact that he was born in Richmond, Virginia, in the segregated South. Robinson's family was poor because of discrimination, although Robinson's father, Max, was a college graduate. When Randall was fourteen, the Supreme Court made its landmark decision to end segregation in the public schools. As a result of the changes that followed, the children of Max Robinson did better than he had. Much better. Randall's older brother, Max Jr., for example, became a famous newsman who eventually joined Peter Jennings as a co-anchor on ABC's *World News Tonight*.

The younger Randall was a poor student and went to Virginia Union University, a small college attended only by blacks. He dropped out of school before graduating to join the military, where, in 1963, he was stationed at Fort Benning, Georgia. Just before his battalion was shipped overseas, a white Army major with a "bluff manner" and a "voice [that] held a detectable trace of Old South money," encouraged Robinson to go back to school. The officer told Robinson that if he applied to school, he would be eligible for an early discharge, and he offered to expedite the application. That August, the major and his unit were shipped to Vietnam to fight one of the bloodiest engagements of the war. In September, Robinson returned to college. A month later, he recalls, "more than half of my former army battalion died in the battle of the Ia Drang Valley."[26]

Robinson graduated from his small black college and was recruited to Harvard Law School. Upon graduating Harvard, he decided not to become a lawyer, but to dedicate himself, as an activist, to the "empowerment and liberation of the African world." Over the years, his crusades brought him great material success, so that he was able to send his own teenage daughter to an exclusive $15,000 a year private school, while he pursued a public career, traveling to exotic locales around the world. In his own words, he "conferred with presidents, and more than once altered the course of American foreign policy."[27]

In his own lifetime, Randall Robinson witnessed the greatest revolution in race relations of any society in human history. He was born in 1940, in poverty, which was normal then for blacks, in the capital of the old slave South. Segregation was the law. This was before more than half of black America rose up from poverty and into the American middle class. It was before the nation's military and schools and professional athletic leagues were integrated, before discrimination in government and business was outlawed, before a black could marry a white in many parts of the country, before a black American had served as the nation's military chief or as a cabinet member in the White House or as a justice of the Supreme Court; it was before mayors and governors and more than six thousand elected officials from states all across America were black, many of them representing districts that are white. Yet for Robinson, the American glass is not even half empty. "I am convinced that I will die in a society as racially divided as the one into which I was born more than a half century ago."[28]

Bob Herbert, a black columnist for the *New York Times*, wrote that "*Defending the Spirit* [is] Mr. Robinson's account of his inability, despite a world-class education and tremendous professional success, to escape the humiliating trap of racism."[29] An anecdote at the beginning of the book captures what Herbert has in mind. It is told as a preface to the story of his father's final aggression.

In the spring of 1995, Robinson found himself "in back of a small country hardware store somewhere off Route 13 near Nassawadox on the Eastern Shore of Virginia." He had climbed onto a loading platform and was looking for the proprietor. As he did so, there were voices behind him. In front of the store, a young man in bib overalls was talking to another man who turned out to be the proprietor Robinson was seeking. "A boy jus went in theah looking fuh ya," the young man was saying in a thick southern drawl. The word "boy" stung Robinson, and the hurt grew worse when he realized he could not shake the rage he felt, even after the incident was past. Aware of his own elevated position in life, and the fact that the social disparities in the situation work entirely in his favor, Robinson experiences a retrospective cognitive dissonance as he analyzes the event: "My rage is complicated by the balm of comparative material success. I tell myself that I cannot be wounded by a red-faced hayseed. But I am. The child lives on in the man until death."

Well, it does if you let it. The "insult," as Robinson describes it, seems motiveless and impersonal. Why react at all? It is a vestige of the past. But it is a past that Robinson keeps on exhuming until it assumes an aura so bright it manages to eclipse everything else: "The 'boy' to whom the semiliterate corn farmer is referring is I. And I have traveled a long way to nowhere."[30]

Nowhere? Can Randall Robinson—and Bob Herbert who validates these sentiments—be serious? Robinson has traveled to places beyond anything his white irritant could imagine, and equally beyond the segregated poverty from which Robinson himself had emerged. If there is a wound here, it is self-inflicted. Robinson's view that his rage reflects the persistence of an inner child is certainly correct. But the remedy is to give up on the intellectual thumb-sucking and grow up.

Robinson and other upper middle-class black intellectuals who hold on so obsessively to fantasies of racism would do well to recall the life of the African-American novelist, Zora Neale Hurston, born fifty years before Robinson, who died in poverty after having to forge a career in the teeth of Jim Crow segregation. Hurston took an entirely different attitude to her racial harassers. In Hurston's lifetime, racial prejudices were not vestigial traces of a receding past, but the harsh mores and entrenched passions of the time. This, however, did not deter her. "Sometimes I feel discriminated against," Hurston wrote in 1927, "but it does not make me angry. It merely astonishes me. How can any deny themselves the pleasure of my company?"[31] Hurston even recognized advantages in her position as a racial underdog: "No one on earth ever had a greater chance for glory. The world to be won and nothing to be lost. It is thrilling to think—to know that for any act of mine, I shall get twice as much praise or twice as much blame. It is quite exciting to hold the center of the national stage with the spectators not knowing whether to laugh or to weep. The position of my white neighbor is much more difficult. No brown specter pulls up a chair beside me when I sit down to eat. No dark ghost thrusts its leg against mine in bed. The game of keeping what one has is never so exciting as the game of getting."[32]

As a result of the changes that have taken place in America, the issue is less one of race than of perspective on race. The moral trumps, the laws, the institutions of power in American society are today all arrayed on the side of the "victims" in these dramas. Racism exists and racists persist, but they are irretrievably on the defensive. If DuBois was right in saying that the problem of the twentieth century was the color line, it would also be correct to say that one of the problems of the twenty-first century will be the persistence of memories about that experience. In America, racism of the kind that provides Robinson a frisson of authenticity is an heirloom of the past. There is no war in the open that racists have the slightest hope of winning. There is racial injustice, but it is injustice in the shadows. In America today, no racial prejudice, whether in institutions or individuals, can withstand exposure to the public light. That is the revolutionary transformation between the life spans of Randall Robinson and Zora Neale Hurston. In this millennium, there is no reason to be a victim. But in order not to be one, you have to stop thinking like one first.

19

Conservatives and Race

O N JULY 16, 2002, MY WEBSITE[1] RAN A STORY about the "Wichita Massacre," the brutal execution of four white youths by two criminal brothers who happened to be black. It was our second look at this tragic incident. We ran it as a special feature—this time on the occasion of the trial of the perpetrators—because it crystallized for us a national hypocrisy on race. It is an attitude that regards the murder of blacks by whites as indicating the existence of a characteristically *American* racism and therefore is banner news, while the far more prevalent murder of whites by blacks is routinely regarded as without racial overtones and—as in this Wichita case—not newsworthy at all.

The more recent article had originally appeared on the website of American Renaissance, a white racialist group founded by Jared Taylor. Reposting it from this site seemed to require some explanation. In the commentary I wrote to accompany our feature, I described Taylor as "a man who has surrendered to the multicultural miasma that has overtaken this nation and is busily building a movement devoted to white identity and community," agendas we "did not share":

This essay originally appeared on FrontPageMagazine.com on August 27, 2002, under the title "American Conservatism: An Argument with the Racial Right." It has been edited for this book.

What I mean by "surrendering" is that Taylor has accepted the idea that the multiculturalists have won. We are all prisoners of identity politics now. If there is going to be Black History Month and Chicano Studies, then there should be White History Month and White Studies.[2] If blacks and Mexicans are going to regard each other as brothers and the rest of us as "Anglos," then whites should regard each other as brothers as well. . . . Within the multicultural framework set by the dominant liberalism in our civic culture, Taylor's claim to a white place at the diversity table certainly makes sense. But there is another option and that is getting rid of the table altogether and going back to the good old American ideal of *E Pluribus Unum*—"out of many one." Not just blacks and whites and Chicanos, but Americans.

Jared Taylor replied to these comments in the *American Renaissance* and raised the fundamental question of whether America is or should be a multiethnic, multiracial society, or whether it was conceived and should be preserved "as a self-consciously European, majority-white Nation." Among literate conservatives, Jared Taylor is the most blunt in expressing such a vision, but it is a theme of others who might be called "Euro-racialists." (This is a bastardized and somewhat incoherent coinage, but one that adequately describes a bastardized and somewhat incoherent perspective).

Prominent among the articulators of Euro-racialism are the writers for the website www.Vdare.com and Pat Buchanan, whose best-selling book *The Death of the West* articulates its most familiar version. If Buchanan's last electoral run is any indication, Euro-racialism is a still a fringe prejudice among conservatives. But if it were to emerge as the view of conservatives themselves, it would in my view mean the death of the American conservative movement. Since I consider the American conservative movement the last bulwark in the defense of America and the West, it would ironically also fulfill the prophecy in the title of Buchanan's book.

Taylor describes me as a "neoconservative," but I have no idea what this has to do with my opinions or my work. The two most prominent theoreticians of neoconservatism announced its death some time ago, because it had always defined the defection of a group of New York liberals from liberalism over liberalism's failure to stay the course in fighting the anti-communist battle during the Cold War. Since the end of the Cold War, neoconservatism—at least in the view of its founders—has become indistinguishable from conservatism itself.

I have never identified myself as a "neo-conservative" because, belonging to a younger political generation, I did not share some of the social attitudes of the neoconservative founders. Since attitude is fundamental to some conservative perspectives, I have preferred to define my own. To be a conservative in America from my perspective is to defend where possible and restore where necessary the framework of values and philosophical understandings codified in the American Founding.[3] This should not be taken to mean a strict constructionist attitude toward every clause of the documents that constitute the Founding. If the framers of the Constitution had presumed to see the future, or had wanted to rigidly preserve the past, they would not have included an amendment clause in their contract.

My brand of conservatism is based on a belief in the fundamental truths of these ideas: individualism; the idea of rights that are derived from "Nature's God" and therefore inalienable; the conservative view of human nature and the philosophy of limited government that flows therefrom; and the recognition that property rights are the foundation of all human liberties.

For me, Taylor's challenge goes to the heart of what it means not only to be an American, but also to be an American conservative. Because America is a nation "conceived"—and not just a nation evolved (although it is that too)—the meaning of the American Founding is and will always be a contested issue for Americans. The answer to these questions about the meaning of the American idea and therefore of the American nation, will always affect its direction and its future.

It is not coincidental, therefore, that the issue of the Founding is the very first to which Taylor turns. Taylor contends that the national motto "*E Pluribus Unum*"—out of many, one—refers not to many races or ethnicities when it comes to forming an American people but simply to the thirteen colonies. But this is a rhetorical argument rather than a comment on reality, since it ignores the actual populations of the thirteen colonies, which even at that time were multi-ethnic and multi-racial. In 1776, American citizens included, among others, not only ethnic Englishmen, but Dutchmen, Germans, French, Scotch-Irish, Jews and free blacks.

In an attempt to anchor his rhetorical case in the attitudes of the Founders themselves, Taylor quotes John Jay to the effect that Americans were a united and connected people because they had common ancestors. But Jay is obviously mistaken because this was certainly not true in any ethnic or racial sense. Even insofar as Americans were European in origin, "European" is not an ethnicity, and the history of Europe is the history of wars *between* its ethnicities and its racial groups.

An acquaintance of mine, of Scotch-Irish descent, maintains that his forebears came to the New World expressly for the opportunity to fight the English. Whether the memory is accurate or not, it illuminates the error made by both John Jay and Jared Taylor. America was created out of a British Empire that was virtually global, and its various peoples, European and otherwise, far from being a cohesive group with a common ancestry, had heritages of mutual hostility and war.

The fundamental mistake of the Euro-racialists is to confuse ethnicity and culture. How is race or ethnicity integral to the American idea or the American culture? Are not Francis Fukuyama, Dinesh D'Souza, and Thomas Sowell quintessential Americans despite their Japanese, Indian, and African lineage? The Jews have remained a people united by culture and—until recently—a language for two thousand years; but as a people with a common heritage, they still embrace a world of ethnicities and races.

It is a culture that is the crucial factor in shaping the American identity, not an ethnicity or race. John Jay's observation that speaking a common English language is an indispensable element in transmitting this culture and creating an American people is probably correct. Here, there is ground for agreement. An American identity cannot exist outside an American culture. Even though that American culture can and must evolve and incorporate new elements, it cannot leave behind its European roots without losing, in some fundamental sense, itself. It is this American culture, not a racial or ethnic heritage, that we need to preserve.

Ironically, Taylor and the Euro-racialists have fallen into a trap set by the "multicultural" left. The left's multicultural offensive is an attack on America's national culture, not on its racial or ethnic composition. "Inclusion" and "diversity" are not the real agendas of the left—America has always honored both principles, however imperfectly. The idea of the melting pot *is* an American idea. The left, however, has never been interested in a "melting pot" that would assimilate diverse ethnicities into an American culture.

The left is hostile to the very idea of assimilation. Its agenda is the deconstruction of America's national identity and culture, and particularly the American narrative of inclusion and freedom. The multiculturalist narrative is not about the assimilation of minorities into the crucible of American freedom, but their liberation from American "oppression." The Euro-racialists become allies of the left by accepting the left's view of itself as a movement for diversity and inclusion and responding with a call for Euro-centricity and exclusion.

Under the smokescreen of ethnic inclusion, the left has injected an anti-American curriculum into the American educational system which it hopes will alienate America's youth from their heritage. How can Americans be proud of their history if is a relentless tale of theft of the land, enslavement of a race, oppression of minorities, exploitation of classes, and ambition for an empire abroad? Under the smokescreen of "diversity," the left has rewritten America's laws and subverted its Constitution. In an effort to undermine the American foundation, it has worked to institutionalize group rights and racial privileges in place of individual rights and a legal framework that is race neutral. If successful, it will have abrogated the American social contract without having had to fire a shot.

It is perfectly diabolical: in the name of diversity and inclusion, the left has set out to destroy the framework of individualism and the rule of law that make diversity and inclusion possible. But instead of fighting this sinister attack on American pluralism, Jared Taylor and the Euro-racialists are eager to validate it. They have even embraced the destructive narrative devised by the left, whose purpose is to kill the American dream. Taylor's construction of American history directly parallels the maliciously distorted version of the nation's history in the works of such anti-American fanatics as Noam Chomsky and Howard Zinn.

In Taylor's telling of the American story, America is in fact the racist nightmare of leftist fantasy. Taylor begins his historical reconstruction with Thomas Jefferson who "thought it had been a terrible mistake to bring blacks to America, and wrote that they should be freed from slavery and then 'removed from beyond the reach of mixture.'" Taylor then describes a pantheon of notable Americans who were officers of the American Colonization Society designed to promote the same "solution," including Andrew Jackson, Francis Scott Key, and Supreme Court Chief Justice John Marshall. He observes that Monrovia, the capital of Liberia, is named after the chief architect of the Constitution, James Monroe, "in gratitude for his help in sending blacks to Africa." Naturally Taylor includes the chief icon of the left's deconstruction project, Abraham Lincoln, who "also favored colonization" and invited the first delegation of blacks to visit the White House in order to "ask them to persuade their people to leave."

Taylor's purpose in assembling this perverse pantheon of American leaders is transparent. Since politicians "are cautious people who re-circulate the bromides of their times," the racist reality of America must be much worse even than this list would suggest. In sum, racism is the American creed.

But this selective portrait is no less a caricature coming from Jared Taylor than when it comes from Louis Farrakhan or Howard Zinn. Many motives could have prompted nineteenth-century American statesmen to consider "colonization" a reasonable alternative to the problem of assimilating people who had been brought to America in chains and who had suffered grievous injustice at the hands of those who brought them. But even granting, for example, the racial prejudice of a figure like Jefferson, the presumption that this exhausts the complexity of his attitude, let alone of his historic role in shaping the racial question in America, is both vulgar and absurd. This is the same man who proclaimed that God had created men *equal* and endowed them with the inalienable rights to liberty, who sowed the ideological seed not only of the Thirteenth Amendment that emancipated the slaves but also the Fourteenth Amendment that guaranteed all Americans, black as well as white, equal citizenship rights under the law.

If Jefferson planted the seeds of black liberation, it is the American people who made the flowering possible, through the sacrifice of hundreds of thousands of lives in a civil war. The denigrators of Lincoln hate that he resolved the schism in the American mind in favor of Jefferson's idea that America was a nation conceived in liberty and dedicated to equality. Reactionaries like Taylor may want to take the country back to the pre-American social order that existed before 1776, but there are few Americans alive today who will follow them. Moreover, it is a gross historical misrepresentation to call this project "American," as Taylor and his followers do.

Taylor's recounting of the legislative past is equally selective and ahistorical. The fact that the first American naturalization bill made citizenship available only to "free white persons" or that it took more than a hundred years to expand citizenship rights to all races and ethnicities, as he writes, would bear the significance he wants to assign it *only* if the weight of American history were not on the side of the expansion of these rights, and *only* if the premise of that expansion were not—as they are—the very principles embedded in the Founding itself. The text of the Constitution does not contain the terms "black" and "white" *because* it does not recognize racial distinctions among its citizens or their rights. The delay in granting the rights of citizenship to blacks is regrettable, but the granting of these rights is nonetheless the fulfillment of the American promise.

This development of rights established in the Founding is not to be confused with the seemingly limitless expansion of rights promoted by the left under the doctrine of a "living Constitution." The "rights" the left seeks to create are not rights recognized in the classical liberal doctrines the Founders embraced, but antithetical to them. They are the redistributionist rights of the radical tradition the Framers despised and that Madison described as "wicked" in the *Federalist*, Number 10.[4] Racial preferences, which have become the "civil rights" cause of the left and which have been made constitutional by so-called liberal courts, are in fact an offense to the Constitution and the values it enshrines. Equality of citizenship for all races, on the other hand, is clearly an expression of the principles inscribed in the constitutional documents, which are the foundations of the republic.

To conclude his argument Taylor turns personal, which may be appropriate for a discussion that attempts to address both the universal and the particular:

> Mr. Horowitz deplores the idea that "we are all prisoners of identity politics," implying that race and ethnicity are trivial matters we must work to overcome. But if that is so, why does the home page of Frontpagemag.com carry a perpetual appeal for contributions to "David's Defense of Israel Campaign"? Why Israel rather than, say, Kurdistan or Tibet or Euskadi or Chechnya? Because Mr. Horowitz is Jewish. His commitment to Israel is an expression of precisely the kind of particularist identity he would deny to me and to other racially-conscious whites. He passionately supports a self-consciously Jewish state but calls it "surrendering to the multicultural miasma" when I work to return to a self-consciously white America. He supports an explicitly ethnic identity for Israel but says America must not be allowed to have one. . . . If he supports a Jewish Israel, he should support a white America.

There is a lot that is wrong with this picture. Not to be a "prisoner" of identity politics is not the same as regarding race and ethnicity as "trivial matters," and I don't. To portray me as a political Jew, who identifies primarily with Jewish causes, or who would not rally to the defense of Israel if he were of some other ethnicity is very wide of the mark. My political causes are public record and go back more than fifty years, and in my autobiography, *Radical Son*, I have even recorded my interior thoughts about why I took on these causes. None of them

were ethnically motivated, which I believe is true for most people involved in similar ones. If there has been an ethnic group to which I
have devoted the major portion of my political energies over the course
of a lifetime, it has been black Americans, not Jews.

As a marxist, of course, I was a deracinated Jew—never *bar
mitzvahed* and a stranger to synagogues. As an editor of the leftwing
magazine *Ramparts*, I did write a cover story called "The Passion of
the Jews,"[5] and did defend the existence of Israel as a "raft state" for
survivors of the Holocaust, rejected everywhere else. But the article
itself was a case against Jewish particularism, while recognizing its va-
lidity in a world in which Jews had become the objects of a program
for their extermination. At the time, however, I still believed in a socialist revolution that would dissolve these prejudices and forge an
international community free from such atavisms.

This utopian delusion was killed in me shortly after I wrote the
piece in circumstances I have described elsewhere. But to recognize
the fact of ethnic particularity is not equivalent to becoming a racialist
or a nationalist in the narrow, tribal sense to which Jared Taylor aspires. Of course, Israel is important to me in a way that other countries
are not. Yes, this is part of my heritage with which I identify. But even
after I rejected the progressive illusion, I did not become the prisoner
of an ethnic calculus in selecting my (now conservative) causes. I am
an American. This is the nation I identify with first. The American
creed is universal, and as an American who believes in preserving and
defending these principles, I will defend them wherever they inspire
others. Call this American ethnocentrism if you will. It is a lot more
inclusive than the white European nation for which Jared Taylor longs.

I do not fool myself for a moment into thinking that it would not
matter to me as a Jew if the Arabs succeeded in their determination to
destroy the state of Israel. But I also do not expect any American of
any national origin to be unaffected by the infliction of great harm to
his or her ancestral community. Despite this concession, I do not think
ethnicity defines the way I, or most Americans, measure right and
wrong or decide to commit our political passions.

Israel is under attack by the same enemy that has attacked the United States. Israel is a point of origin for the culture of the West and it is under attack for the same reasons that America is under attack by radical Islam as the "Great Satan." Palestinian terrorists were involved in the first World Trade Center bombing. In defending Israel, as I have defended other countries—Afghanistan for example, when it was attacked by the Soviets—I have no ambivalence about my national identity, which is American, not Israeli, and most certainly not "white."

If I support an ethnic Jewish state in principle, it is because if Arabs were to become a majority in Israel, they would persecute, kill, and expel the Jews—as they have for a thousand years. No sober person could believe otherwise. But I also support an ethnic Jewish state because this is merely the granting of equality to Jews by the family of nations. Would a Frenchman feel sanguine about a German majority in France?

America is different from most other nations. It is a nation that from the beginning has encompassed many ethnicities and more than one race. It was created as a "new nation" and its creators defined its identity not by blood or soil, but in a document articulating principles that are universal.

One could argue, of course, that this very fact of America's uniqueness proves the reactionaries' case—that human beings are incapable of transcending their ethnic and racial particularities to form a common national bond. But that would require arguing that the two and a quarter centuries of the American experiment have failed. I am not ready to believe this, even if Jared Taylor and the Euro-racialists are. I could very well be mistaken. But I would rather be wrong as an American, than the president of Jared Taylor's Euro-white alternative. Moreover, I remain certain of at least one thing. America *is* such a multi-ethnic and multi-racial experiment, and Jared Taylor and the Euro-racialists are wrong in contending that it is not.

V

THE GRAMSCIAN MOMENT

20

The Intellectual Class War

A FEW YEARS AFTER THE FALL of the marxist utopias, I found myself sitting on a sofa in Beverly Hills next to a man who was worth half a billion dollars. His name was Stanley Gold and he was chairman of a holding company that was the largest shareholder in Disney, the largest media corporation in the world. Since I was currently engaged in a conservative project in the entertainment community and the occasion was a cocktail reception for a Republican senator, I turned the conversation to a pitch for support. But I had only run through a few bars of my routine before Gold put a fatherly hand on my arm and said, "Save your breath, David. I'm a socialist."

I am reminded of this story every time a critic pulls out the marxist canard that I have "sold out" my ideals, or suggests that an opinion I've expressed can be explained by the "fact" that somewhere a wealthy puppetmaster is pulling my strings. I am not alone, of course, in being the target of such attacks, which are familiar to every conservative who has ever engaged in political debate.

Of course, those who traffic in socially conscious abuse have a ready answer for anecdotes like this one, namely, that it is an isolated and aberrant case. In other words, even if it is true, it is false. There is a larger marxist "truth" that trumps little facts like this, which is that

---

From *Hating Whitey & Other Progressive Causes* (1999). It has been edited for this book.

conservative views express the views of corporate America, serve the status quo, defend the rich and powerful, and legitimize the oppression of the poor. The same trump presumes that leftist views, however well paid for by the wealthy, are inherently noble because they oppose those injustices.

In the fantasy world of the left, Stanley Gold can only be understood as a human oxymoron: a uniquely good-hearted capitalist who is a friend to humanity and a traitor to his class. But, then, so are such famous left-wing billionaire (and centimillionaire) moguls as Ted Turner, David Geffen, Oprah Winfrey, Steven Spielberg, Michael Eisner, Bill Gates, Warren Buffett, Ron Burkle, and a hundred others less famous (but equally wealthy).

In fact, Stanley Gold is only exceptional in being a witty and candid fellow, and in being ideological at all. For, unlike the publicly self-identified progressives named above, the CEOs of most major corporations studiously avoid ideological politics, whether left or right, because such politics are not in the corporate interest at all. To become identified with a hard political position is perhaps to alienate customers, but more importantly to become a sitting target for one's ideological political opponents who may control the machinery of regulation and taxation, or exert other life-and-death powers over their enterprises. For a corporate leader, ideological politics is obviously not a prudent path and consequently is not generally pursued. Besides, from a business point of view most politicians are fungible. This politician's favor can be had as easily as the next. It is safer to stay above the fray and purchase influence as necessary. Money, rather than ideological passion, is the currency of corporate interest, power rather than ideas its political agenda. Therefore, politicians rather than intellectuals are the normal objects of its attention.

There can be exceptions to the corporate rule of political neutrality. If an administration chooses to declare war on a wealthy individual or a corporate entity, or a particular industry, that can result in a political alignment. Big Tobacco, Microsoft, and Michael Milken all became the targets of government assaults and adopted a defensive strategy of embracing the political opposition (Tobacco and Microsoft went strongly Republican, Milken became a Democrat). Another exception is the political shakedowns of large corporations by community activists, which is almost exclusively a province of the left. Under attack from radical Greens, for example, major companies like ARCO have become generous subsidizers of the environmental movement. Through similar extortionist efforts, Jesse Jackson's Rainbow/Push coalition has received more corporate underwriting than any dozen conservative groups combined.

But the norm for corporate interests is holding themselves aloof from any ideological politics, which in the long run can only damage their business interests. The same applies to freewheeling individuals who are serious financial players. I have had very conservative billionaires tell me that whatever their personal views, they cannot afford to support conservative efforts like mine and risk the ire of my political antagonists.

A consequence of this standoff is that most of the contributions available to ideological activists of the left or right are either small individual donations solicited through direct mail campaigns or large institutional donations from tax-exempt foundations. In this area, too, the active imaginations of the left have created a wildly distorted picture in which well-funded goliaths of the right, Olin, Scaife and Bradley, overwhelm the penurious Davids of the left. Edward Said, for example, used the platform of the once distinguished Reith lectures to attack Peter Collier and me over the "second thoughts" movement we had launched as a critique of the left: "In a matter of months during the late 1980s, Second Thoughts aspired to become a movement, alarmingly well funded by right-wing Maecenases like the Bradley and Olin Foundations."

Some years later, a report appeared on "The Strategic Philanthropy of Conservative Foundations," documenting the annual disbursements of what were deemed the key conservative grant-giving institutions. The annual sum of the subsidies from twelve foundations was calculated at $70 million. This may seem a large sum until one looks at the Ford Foundation, which dispenses more than $900 million per year—or more than ten times as much—to mainly liberal and left-wing causes.

Ford is the principal funder of academic multiculturalism and ideological black studies and women's studies programs. For nearly twenty years it was virtually the sole funder of the leftist Mexican-American Legal Defense Fund (MALDEF), which lacks any visible root in the Mexican-American community, but has been the spearhead of "open borders" policies and the driving force behind the multibillion dollar failure of bilingual education programs in public schools. The Ford Foundation invested $25 million in MALDEF during these years.

In these agendas, Ford is typical rather than exceptional. In fact, the biggest and most prestigious foundations, bearing the most venerable names of the captains of American capitalism—Ford, Rockefeller, Mellon, Carnegie, and Pew—are all supporters of the left, as are many newer but also well-endowed institutions like the MacArthur, Markle, and Schumann foundations. MacArthur alone is three times the combined size of the "big three" conservative foundations, Olin, Bradley, and Scaife.

Moreover, these foundations do not even represent the most important support the corporate "ruling class" and its social elites provide to the left. That laurel goes to the private and public universities that have traditionally been the preserve of the American aristocracy and now—as Richard Rorty has approvingly observed—are the "political base of the left." With its multi-billion dollar endowment and unmatched intellectual prestige, Harvard provides the exemplary case, its relevant faculties and curricula reflecting the absolute unchallenged hegemony of leftwing ideas in the academic culture. The Kennedy School of Government at Harvard—to take an emblematic case—is arguably the most prestigious and important reservoir of intellectual talent and policy advice available to the political establishment. Cabinet officials are regularly drawn from its ranks. Yet of its 150-plus faculty members, only five are identifiable Republicans, a ratio that is as extraordinary, given the spectrum of political opinion in the nation at large, as it is common in the university system.

The institutional and financial support for the left—through its dominance in the universities, the book publishing industry, the press, television news, and the arts—is so overwhelming it is hardly contested. There are no prestigious universities where the faculty ratio in the liberal arts and social sciences is 150 Republicans to five Democrats or even fifty Republicans to one hundred Democrats. There is not a single major newspaper in America whose features and news sections are written by conservatives rather than liberals—and this includes such conservative-owned institutions as the *Wall Street Journal, the Los Angeles Times, the Orange County Register* and the *San Diego Union.* (The *Times* has a left-wing editorial page as well.)

The left, it can hardly be disputed, is funded and supported by the very "ruling class" it whines is the Sugar Daddy of the right, and the oppressor of minorities, the working class, and the poor. Moreover, institutional support and funds provided to the intellectual left by the greedy and powerful far exceed any sums it provides to the intellectual right, as any one with a pocket calculator can compute. How is this possible? Could it be that the marxist model itself is wrong? Oh, perish that thought. We're all post-marxist marxists anyway now.

According to the leftist model, the interest of the corporate rich lies in preserving the status quo. But if the Clinton years did nothing else, they should certainly have put this canard to rest. The Clinton administration's most important left-wing projects were the comprehensive government-controlled healthcare plan and the effort to preserve racial preferences. Both received the enthusiastic support of corporate America: the healthcare plan by the nation's largest health insurance companies, and racial preferences by Fortune 500 corporations across the board.

In the 1999 presidential primary campaign, Bill Bradley was the Democratic candidate running from the left. The chief points of Bradley's platform were a plan to revive the comprehensive Clinton healthcare scheme that had been rejected, and to press left-wing racial grievances. Bradley's most recently acquired African-American friend was the anti-Semitic racist Al Sharpton who had become, for Democratic Party candidates, the black leader to appease. But despite his radical agendas, as everyone knows, "Dollar Bill's" $30-plus million campaign war chest was largely filled by Wall Street, where he himself had made millions as a stockbroker over the years.

Unless one is blinded by the discredited marxisms of the political left, there is no reason that the rich should be adversaries of the poor or oppose their interests. Not in a dynamic market society. Only if the economic market were a zero sum game, as leftists believe—"exploited labor" on the one side and capitalist profit on the other—would leftist ideas make any sense. But they don't. The real world relation between labor and capital is quite the opposite of what the left proposes. Entrepreneurs generally want a better-educated, better-paid, more diverse working force, because that means better employees, better marketers, and better consumers of the company product. That is why, historically, everywhere capitalism has been embraced, labor conditions have improved and inequalities have diminished over time whether there has been a strong trade union presence or not.[1] That is why the capitalist helmsmen of the World Trade Organization are better friends of the world's poor than any of the luddite demonstrators in Seattle who protested in their behalf.

The twenty-first century political argument is not about whether to help the poor or whether to include all Americans in the social contract. Republicans embrace these objectives as firmly as Democrats, conservatives as well as liberals. The issue is how best to help the poor and how best to integrate the many cultures of the American mosaic into a common culture that works. Twenty years after the welfare system was already a proven disaster for America's inner city poor, Democrats and leftists were still demanding more welfare and opposing significant reforms. Clinton himself vetoed the Republicans reform bill twice and only signed it when he was told he could not be re-elected if he didn't. Welfare reform has liberated millions of poor people from dead end dependency and given them a dose of the self-esteem that comes from earning one's keep.

If the left were serious about its interest in the poor, it would pay homage to the Republicans who made welfare reform possible, and in particular the despised former House speaker Newt Gingrich. If hypocrisy weren't their stock-in-trade, self-styled champions of the downtrodden like Cornel West and Marian Wright Edelman would be writing testimonials to Gingrich as a hero of America's downtrodden.

But that won't happen. Instead, the left will go on tarring Gingrich and his political allies as "enemies of the poor" and lackeys of the rich.

The conservative party in America is not the Republicans who are responsible for the major reforms of the Clinton years. The mantle of reaction is better worn by the left, given its resistance to change and its rearguard battles against the market and free trade. But the left controls the culture, and with it the political language. Therefore, in America, reactionaries will continue to be called "progressives," and reformers, conservative.

21

Missing Diversity

I N THE FALL OF 2001, I spoke at a large public university in the
eastern United States, which will remain nameless to protect the
innocent. It was one of more than thirty colleges I had visited
during the school year and, as usual, my invitation had come from a
small group of campus conservatives who also put together a small
dinner for me at a local restaurant. Our conclave reflected the current
state of conservatism in the American university. Not only were our
numbers small, there were no deans or university administrators present,
and only one professor. Open conservatives are an isolated and harassed minority on today's college campuses, where they enjoy little
respect and almost no support from institutional authorities.

Although I am a nationally known public intellectual, the author
of many books, and a *Fox News* contributor, the absence of administration representatives at these dinners that normally precede my campus
speeches is entirely predictable. (In nearly two hundred campus appearances in the last ten years, I can think of only two exceptions.)
When I spoke to one thousand students at the University of Michigan
in the spring of 2002, there were three university vice presidents seated
in the balcony, but not one thought to introduce himself to me before

This article appeared on Salon.com, June 20, 2002, under the title "Closed Doors,
Closed Minds." For other thoughts on this subject, see the section "Progressive
Education" in *Hating Whitey and Other Progressive Causes.*

or after my remarks. My experience as a conservative in this regard is not unique. By contrast, if I were an anti-American radical like Angela Davis, deans of the college would wait on me and professors would give academic credit to students for attending my lectures. On many occasions, my speech would be an official campus event.

Angela Davis—a lifelong communist zealot with no identifiable scholarly achievement—is a celebrated campus figure (there is even an "Angela Davis Lounge" at the University of Michigan to honor her). Consequently, her attraction for like-minded peers now entrenched in university administrations is understandable, however regrettable. But the same disparity would be discernible between a less well-known leftist and almost any comparable conservative. It reflects a reality of campus life. While conservatives often make up a large proportion of the student body—and in some cases even a plurality—conservative professors and administrators are notably hard to find. Not only are the overwhelming majority of college professors fashionably "liberal" and Democratic Party partisans, most faculties also feature a strong contingent of hard leftists whose views can only be regarded as extreme and whose concentrated numbers allow them to dominate (and even define) entire academic fields. These faculty radicals are also available to sponsor an impressive array of campus political groups. If the university is large enough, these left-wing activists may well receive hundreds of thousands of dollars from general student funds.

Among those invited to my dinner was a silver-haired history professor at the university, who served as the faculty sponsor of the Young America's club that invited me. This man represented a dying breed of faculty conservative who had been tenured in an era when hiring committees were not yet excluding those whose political views were not suitably left. The transformation in higher education that followed the emergence of the politicized academy was succinctly described by the distinguished intellectual historian John P. Diggins at an annual meeting of the American Studies Association in Costa Mesa a decade ago. Diggins told the assembled academics: "When my generation of liberals was in control of university faculties in the 1960s, we opened the doors to the hiring of radicals in the name of diversity. We thought you would do the same. But you didn't. You closed the doors behind you."[1]

Diggins' observation provides the template for what has happened to American universities in the last thirty years. The liberal academy of the 1950s and 1960s, whose ideals were shaped by Charles Eliot and Matthew Arnold and whose mission was "the disinterested pursuit of knowledge," is no more. Leftists tenured after the 1960s first transformed these institutions into political battlegrounds and then redefined them as "agencies of social change." In the process, they defeated and then excluded peers whom they perceived as obstacles to their politicized academic agendas.

Some years ago a distinguished member of this radical generation, Richard Rorty, summarized its achievement in the following words: "The power base of the left in America is now in the universities, since the trade unions have largely been killed off. The universities have done a lot of good work by setting up, for example, African-American studies programs, Women's Studies programs, Gay and Lesbian Studies programs. They have created power bases for these movements."[2] Rorty is a professor of comparative literature and philosophy at Stanford University and one of the nation's most honored intellectuals. Rorty is also a leading light of the democratic socialist magazine *Dissent* and a "moderate" in the ranks of the left. That such a figure should celebrate the conversion of academic institutions into political "power bases" speaks volumes about the tragedy that has befallen the university.

On the occasions of my campus visits, I am always curious to discover the local circumstances that conspire to create a situation so otherwise inexplicable in an open society. How, in particular, does an institution that publicly promotes itself as "liberal" and "inclusive," as dedicated to "diversity" and the "free exchange of ideas," devolve into such a political monolith? The conservative history professor who had come to my dinner was obviously a senior member of his academic department, which was really the only status a conservative faculty member could have, since the hiring doors had been closed nearly a quarter of a century earlier. So I asked how his faculty colleagues treated conservatives like him.

Catching my drift, he replied, "Well, they haven't allowed me to sit on a search committee since 1985." He was referring to the committees that interview prospective candidates to fill faculty openings. "In 1985, he continued, "I was the chair of the search committee and of course we hired a marxist." "Of course," I said, knowing that for conservatives who believed in the traditional mission of academic inquiry, diversity of viewpoints would make perfect sense. Others might be guided by different imperatives. Their very dedication to "social change" would commit them to an agenda that is about power and that would inspire them to clear rivals from their path.

The professor went on: "This year we had an opening for a scholar of Asian history. We had several candidates but obviously the most qualified one was from Stanford. Yet he didn't get the job. So I went to the chair of the search committee and asked him what had happened. 'Oh,' he said, 'you're absolutely right. He was far and away the most qualified candidate and we had a terrific interview. But then we went to lunch and he let out that he was for school vouchers.'"

In other words, if one has a politically incorrect view on K-12 school vouchers, one must be politically incorrect on the Ming Dynasty, too. This is almost a dictionary description of the totalitarian mentality. But there is more than dogmatism at work in this calculation. This attitude also reflects the priorities of an entrenched oligarchy, which fears to include those it cannot count on to maintain its control.

A certain focus on control is normal for bureaucrats in any institution. But in an institution like the university, whose very structures are elitist, there are few natural limits to such political agendas. Outside the hard sciences and the practical professions, what is the penalty for bad ideas? None. Once a discredited dogma like marxism is legitimated through the hiring process, there is no institutional obstacle to its expansion and entrenchment as a scholarly philosophy.

The normal structural support for ideological conformity in the academy is intensified by the introduction of overt political agendas. These agendas were originally imported into the university by radicals acting as self-conscious disciples of an Italian marxist named Antonio Gramsci. As an innovative Stalinist in the 1930s, Gramsci pondered the historic inability of communist parties to mobilize workers to seize the means of production and overthrow the capitalist ruling class. Gramsci's new idea was to focus radicals' attention on the means of intellectual production. He urged radicals to acquire "cultural hegemony," by which he meant to capture the institutions that produced society's governing ideas. This would be the key to controlling and transforming society itself.

To illustrate how ingrained this attitude has now become and how casually it is deployed to justify the suppression of conservative ideas, let me cite an e-mail I received from a professor at Emory University in Atlanta. The professor was responding to an article I had written about the abuse of conservative students by administrators at Vanderbilt and the exclusion of conservatives from the Vanderbilt faculty.[3]

The author of the e-mail was not especially radical, yet he did not have so much as a twinge of conscience over the picture I drew of a faculty cleansed of conservative opinions. "Why do I and other academics have little shame here?" he asked rhetorically. Then he answered his own question: "We are not the only game in the marketplace of ideas. We are competing with journalism, entertainment, churches, political lobbyists, and well-funded conservative think tanks."

In other words, contemporary academics see themselves not primarily as educators, but as agents of an "adversary culture" at war with the world outside the university. They are contemptuous of the fact that the university was not created, and is not funded, to compete with other institutions. It is designed to train a productive citizenry and leadership class, endowing them with appropriate knowledge and skills. Because of its strategic function as an educator of elites, however, the university can also be effectively used, in the way Gramsci proposed, to subvert those other institutions.

There is thus an organic connection between the political bias of the university and the political bias of the press. It was not until journalists became routinely trained in university schools of journalism in the post-1960s era that mainstream media began to mirror the perspectives of the adversary culture. As Professor Rorty observed, universities have now become a power base of the political left. The Emory professor's argument only makes sense from the vantage of someone who is part of this left and who is so alienated from his own society as to want to subvert it. His suggestion that universities somehow are there to "balance" conservative think tanks, on the other hand, is preposterous. "Well-funded" conservative think tanks may stand in intellectual opposition to subversive agendas, but what wealthy think tank can compete with Harvard, its centuries of tradition, its hundreds of faculty members, its government subsides, and its $18 billion, tax-free endowment? The really well-funded think tanks are the universities the left controls.

The power of the academic left does not derive merely from the numbers in its own ranks. Academics who are not particularly radical may also harbor resentments against the larger culture and be inspired to seek like-minded colleagues. When these viewpoints are imbued with a sense of social mission that requires ideological cohesion for success, the result is the growth of an intellectual monolith. How monolithic? In the spring of 2001, I organized college students to investigate the voting registrations of university professors at more than a dozen institutions of higher learning. The students used primary registrations to determine party affiliation. Here is a representative sample:

- At the University of Colorado—a public university in a Republican state—94 percent of the liberal arts faculty whose party registrations could be established were Democrats, and only 4 percent were Republicans. Out of eighty-five professors of English who registered to vote, none were Republicans. Out of thirty-nine professors of history, one. Out of twenty-eight political scientists, two.[4]

  How Republican is Colorado? Its governor, two Senators and four out of six congressmen are Republican. There are two hundred thousand more registered Republicans in Colorado than there are Democrats. But at the state-funded University of Colorado, Republicans are a fringe group.

- At Brown University, 94.7 percent of the professors whose political affiliations showed up in primary registrations last year were Democrats, only 5.3 percent were Republicans. Only three Republicans could be found on the Brown liberal arts faculty, but none in the English, history, political science, sociology, or African studies departments.

- At the University of New Mexico, 89 percent of the professors were Democrats, 7 percent were Republicans, and 4 percent were Greens. Of two hundred professors, ten were Republicans, but none in the political science, history, and journalism departments, and only one each in the sociology, English, women's studies, and African-American studies departments.

- At the University of California, Santa Barbara, 97 percent of the professors were Democrats, 1.5 percent were Greens, and an equal 1.5 percent were Republicans. Only one Republican professor could be found.

- At the University of California, Berkeley, of the 195 professors whose affiliations showed up, 85 percent were Democrats, 8 percent were Republicans, 4 percent were Greens, and 3 percent were American Independent Party, Peace and Freedom Party, and Reform Party voters. Out of fifty-four professors in the history department, only one Republican could be found, out of twenty-eight sociology professors, none, out of fifty-seven English professors, none, out of sixteen women's studies professors, none, out of nine African American Studies professors, none, out of six journalism professors, none.

- At the University of California, Los Angeles, of the 157 professors whose political affiliations showed up, 93 percent were Democrats, only 6.5 percent were Republicans.

- At the University of North Carolina, the *Daily Tar Heel* conducted its own survey of eight departments and found that, of the professors registered with a major political party, 91 percent were Democrats, while only 9 percent were Republicans.

In an ideological universe in which university administrators claim that "diversity" is their priority, these are striking facts. How can students get a good education if they're only being told half the story? The answer is, they can't.

The present academic monolith is an offense to the spirit of free inquiry. The hiring practices that have led to this situation are discriminatory and illegal. They violate the Constitution, which prevents hiring and firing on the basis of political ideas and also patronage laws that bar state institutions from servicing a particular political party. Yet university administrators have not shown any inclination to address this problem or to reform the practices that perpetuate it. Nor have self-identified "liberal" professors who are themselves the source of the problem. If there is to be reform, it will have to come from other quarters.

22

Wake Up America:
My Visit to Vanderbilt

V ANDERBILT UNIVERSITY is a venerable academic institution in Nashville, and the premier seat of higher learning in the state of Tennessee. Like every one of the nearly two hundred colleges I have visited in the last ten years, it has long ceased to be a liberal institution in the meaningful sense of that term. In the hiring of its faculty and in the design of its curriculum, in the conduct of its community dialogue and in the shape of its public square, Vanderbilt—like most American universities—is for all intents and purposes an intellectual monolith, an ideological subsidiary of the Democratic Party and a base for the far side of the political left.

No aspect of the university system exposes this bias so readily as the process by which tribunes of the nation's culture wars are invited to speak at college forums. Only authorized student groups with faculty sponsors can extend such invitations. Moreover, they must come up with funds to underwrite travel and lodging arrangements, along with an honorarium that can range from $1,000 to $20,000, depending on the speaker's celebrity. If the speaker is a political activist, these ap-

This article appeared on *Salon.com* on September 4, 2002, under the title, "On Campus, Nobody's Right." It has been edited for this book.

pearances can provide a substantial supplement to personal income and a significant subsidy to the speaker's political cause.

I spoke at twenty-three universities in the spring of 2002, appearing at Vanderbilt on April 8. The invitation came from a conservative student group called Wake Up America, which was formed three years earlier for the purpose of bringing speakers to campus. Despite its dedicated agenda, however, Wake Up America had only managed to put on four events in the three years of its existence. This was not because of a scarcity of conservative speakers ready to speak on college campuses. It is because Vanderbilt refuses to provide funds to Wake Up America to underwrite its aspirations. Vanderbilt's attitude towards Wake Up America is in fact anything but supportive. Vanderbilt officials have treated the group like an alien presence from the moment of its conception.

Thus, when Wake Up America's founder, Dan Eberhart, approached Assistant Vice Chancellor Michelle Rosen to gain approval for his group, she told him, "there is no need for your organization because a student group already exists, namely the Speakers Committee." This was an Orwellian subterfuge. The Assistant Vice Chancellor knew that the Speakers Committee was a partisan student group dedicated to bringing left-wing speakers to the Vanderbilt campus. James Carville, Ralph Nader, Kweisi Mfume, and Gloria Steinem, for example, have been recent visitors, courtesy of the Committee. These are pricey celebrities, and the Vanderbilt student activities fund had granted the Speakers Committee $50,000 a year to make their wish list real. This year, the Student Finance Committee, which administers the fund, increased the Speakers Committee grant to $63,000. By contrast, in its entire three-year existence, Wake Up America has never been granted a single cent to bring conservatives to the Vanderbilt campus.

The Speakers Committee is actually only one of an array of left-wing groups that are the beneficiaries of Vanderbilt funds. In a recent press release announcing the disbursement of $1,143,963 to student groups, the Student Finance Committee defined its purpose in these noble words: "to fund activities that will have broad campus appeal and that will guarantee a diversity of activities within our community."

A glance at the roster of funded groups reveals that the diversity does not extend to the realm of ideas.

While Wake Up America receives no funds at all, the Vanderbilt Feminists receive $10,620; the Vanderbilt Lambda Association (a group of gay leftists) receives $12,000; the (left-wing) Middle Eastern Student Association receives $4,700; the (left-wing) Black Students Alliance receives $12,400; the (left-wing) Organization of Black Graduate & Professional Students receives $13,120; the (left-wing) Vanderbilt African Student Association receives $1,500; the (left-wing) Vanderbilt Association of Hispanic Students receives $14,200; and the (left-wing) Vanderbilt Asian American Student Association gets $15,000.

How do I know that these ostensibly ethnic associations are "left-wing"? I know it as a result of my inquiries at Vanderbilt and by my own broad range of experience with similar groups on campuses across the country. They are not only political and to the left, but they are more often than not at the extreme end of that spectrum as well. For example, when I spoke at Denison College in Ohio a few weeks before my Vanderbilt appearance, I had been preceded the month before by Angela Davis, Denison's official Martin Luther King Day speaker. Davis is a lifelong communist apparatchik who received a "Lenin Prize" from the East German police state during the Cold War, and remained a party member after the fall of the Berlin Wall. The official Denison website, on the other hand, describes her as "known internationally for her ongoing work to combat all forms of oppression in the United States and abroad."[1] The university closed its offices during her speech so that the entire campus could hear her unreconstructed, anti-American, marxist views.

When I spoke at Michigan State, I had been preceded by columnist Julianne Malveaux, who was also the official Martin Luther King Day speaker, and who had received $15,000 from student funds, some of which were supplied by the Black Student Association. As in the case of Davis, Malveaux's views are antithetic to King's. She is a crudely racial marxist who once asserted that there were "two hundred million white racists in America" and on another occasion expressed her wish that Clarence Thomas would have a heart attack. Her speech was called "Economic Justice: The Struggle Continues," and included attacks on Ward Connerly, Laura Bush, the idea of a colorblind society and of King as its visionary.

I had been preceded at Duke by Aaron Magruder, a black cartoonist who had gained fame through his comic strip "Boondocks" and notoriety for attacking America after the World Trade Center was bombed. Magruder was also the university's official Martin Luther King Day speaker. In his speech, Magruder noted that 90 percent of the American people supported the war and said, "I would like to believe the 10 percent leftover is black." He then told the students, "your vote means nothing; you can protest if you want, they'll throw you in jail." Davis, Malveaux, and Magruder all reflected the extremist sentiments of the black student groups on campus without whose imprimatur no Martin Luther King Day speaker could be selected in the first place.

At Vanderbilt, the university annually provides roughly $130,000 for left-wing agitations, including the visits of left-wing speakers. This is balanced by none for conservative groups and speakers. Ironically, the faculties of these schools are strong proponents of campaign finance reform in the political world they don't control.

In the academic world, the situation at Vanderbilt is completely normal, with the exception of a handful of small conservative and religious schools like Hillsdale College and Liberty University. At the University of Wisconsin, the Multicultural Students Association responded to the reparations ad I placed in the *Badger-Herald* in the spring of 2001 by attacking the paper as "a racist propaganda machine"— a ludicrous but damaging smear—and attempting to shut it down. The MSA was rewarded for its bad behavior the following fall with a student government grant of $1 million to fund its extremist agendas. On the same campus, the same student government gave the Students for Objectivism—a conservative group—$500 in program funds. In the wake of my reparations ad and the demonstrations that attended it at Duke University, President Nan Keohane announced a grant of $100,000 in additional funds for student groups. By the time I arrived at Duke, a day after my visit to Vanderbilt, $50,000 of Keohane's grant had already been disbursed—$500 to the Duke Conservative Union and $49,500 to left-wing organizations.

Because university funds were unavailable, my Wake Up America hosts had to raise the money from outside contributions, not an easy task for students. They managed to secure funding from three individuals and from two conservative organizations—Young America's Foundation, which underwrites the lion's share of my campus tours, and the Leadership Institute. The money they raised allowed them to bring me to campus, house me, and provide about one-fifth the honorarium I would have received if I were a left-wing ideologue like Julianne Malveaux or Angela Davis. If I were Malveaux, or Cornel West, or Gloria Steinem, in other words, I could have collected more than $200,000 in three months for attacking America and spouting marxist and racist clichés to college students. There is probably not a single prominent left-wing activist working the campus circuit who is not making a six-figure income for spreading such toxins.

A frustrating but typical trait of college conservatives is that they don't complain about the inequities that are routinely inflicted on them. Because they do not make trouble for abusive and illiberal campus administrators, nothing is done to correct these problems.

Discriminatory funding policies are actually only a small part of the injustices that conservative students suffer and that seem like normalcy to them. They also adjust to the rampant political bias in their expensive curricula, which is the result of a faculty hiring process that bars conservatives and limits the education of all students to a relentlessly one-sided view of the world they live in. Obtaining a faculty sponsor for Wake Up America was thus even more difficult than getting the assistant vice chancellor to approve its formation.

Dan Eberhart scoured the campus for a professor that would sponsor his club. He put letters of request in professors' mailboxes. He approached them directly. In the end, out of a thousand faculty members at Vanderbilt, he was able to come up with only one who would sponsor a group whose intention was to bring conservative speakers to a college campus. Vanderbilt is not only an old and traditional institution, but it is hosted by a state with a Republican governor and two Republican senators, and a citizenry whose majority voted Republican in the last presidential election. The successful purge of conservatives from the faculty of Vanderbilt is thus a sobering commentary on the politically debased condition of the American university, which has fallen victim to an academic McCarthyism more insidious and effective than the academic witch-hunts of the past.

The lone professor willing to sponsor a non-left student group at Vanderbilt turned out to be a business school professor from outside the Vanderbilt community. Because his primary occupation is actually business rather than teaching, this professor flies from his home in San Francisco to Nashville twice a week to teach his course. In other words, there are really no conservative professors in residence at Vanderbilt University who are willing to publicly sponsor a group whose purpose is to bring an under-represented viewpoint to the Vanderbilt community—even though it is a viewpoint shared by a majority of Tennessee voters and half the American public.

My Vanderbilt talk was scheduled for Monday, April 8, and Wake Up America had long before reserved a room for it (January 12). But on Thursday, April 4, the Vanderbilt administration informed Dan Eberhart that a professor now needed the room for a review class, and that my speech would have to be cancelled. Vanderbilt is a very large university, and even the building I gave my speech in seemed virtually deserted that night. I didn't think it was coincidental that this happened to me on at least three other occasions during this spring tour. The University of Oregon cancelled my appearance the day I arrived in state on the grounds that a request for security for the event made two weeks earlier was one day too late and the room had been given to another event. My sponsors were informed of this the day before my announced appearance. NYU cancelled the room for my talk the day I arrived in New York, also because of an alleged room-scheduling problem, and James Madison University cancelled, as I was about to depart for Florida, for the same reason.

In other circumstances, a young, well-mannered conservative like Eberhart might have capitulated to this petty harassment and cancelled the event. Fortunately, he held his ground, strengthened in his resolve perhaps by the fact that my office had been able to arrange a c-SPAN taping of the event.[2] His resistance bore fruit, and permission was given to proceed, but not until Eberhart agreed to pay "for the wear and tear to the foyer" of the hall where the speech took place. A $100 clean-up fee was also tacked on, even though no food and beverages were served and there was no refuse to clean up.

Despite a downpour, about 250 people showed up for the speech in Wilson Hall and listened civilly while I described "How the left Undermined America's Security."[3] The attendance was even more gratifying than usual because the *Vanderbilt Hustler*, which was the student paper, did not—as it usually does—publish an advance article about the speech or inform the campus community of what I said when it was over.

Afterwards I signed books and answered questions of those who stayed to ask them. One of my interlocutors was a professor of philosophy who handed me a yellowing copy of my very first book, *Student*, published exactly forty years earlier. In that book, I described the first student demonstrations of the 1960s at Berkeley, where I was pursuing a graduate degree. I didn't realize at the time that we were going to transform American universities into politicized institutions where only approved ideas would be welcome. I hope I would have had second thoughts then about my actitvies if I had realized this would be the outcome.

When I asked the professor what kind of philosophy he taught at Vanderbilt, he said with a smirk, "marxist philosophy," then asked me to write the following in his book: "To my political enemy from a foaming-at-the-mouth, rightwing ideologue." I signed the book, but with a different inscription ("Second thoughts are best"[4]), and he left. I was then approached by a group of undergraduates who showed by their appearance and questions that they were not politically conservative. A young woman with a diffident demeanor asked in earnest tones what I thought of racial profiling.

Her question was inspired by a portion of my talk that addressed the problem of airport security. I had pointed out that nine of the World Trade Center terrorists were actually stopped by airport security on 9/11 because they had faulty identification. But they had been allowed to board the planes anyway. I said that the Clinton administration's failure to institute adequate security measures prior to the attack was due in part to an ideological aversion to profiling Muslim terrorists.

I tried to explain to the student the difference between factoring race into a profile and using race as the profile itself. I referred her to Heather MacDonald's article in the conservative magazine *City Journal*, "The Myth of Racial Profiling," fully realizing as I did so that this undergraduate would never have heard of Heather MacDonald or *City Journal*. Nor would she be familiar with the writings of virtually any living conservative writer including myself. I gave her the name of the website where MacDonald's article was posted and could be located. But I did so with a heavy heart, because I knew that she would probably forget the website address, that she had many questions, not one, and that her parents were paying $30,000 a year to give her a good education, but that at Vanderbilt she would only be getting one side of the story and only one perspective on the ideological conflicts that would affect her life.

I have met students like this throughout my campus sojourns. The encounters are the saddest memories I take away with me. Millions of students like this young woman pass through universities like Vanderbilt, which routinely betray their trust. In their quest for knowledge, they are given decks that are stacked, instruction that is partisan and partial. And there is nothing I or a small contingent of conservatives can do in one hour or during one event to alter these facts.

The Era of Progressive Witch-Hunts

I N THE EARLY 1990s, some years before Bill Clinton accosted a twenty-two-year-old intern named Monica Lewinsky and before his spouse claimed that a "right-wing conspiracy" invented the affair, I was invited by conservative students at Portland State University to enter a fire zone of the culture war. The topic I was to speak on was of my choosing: "Political Correctness and the Epidemic of AIDS." It was a subject calculated to join the war at one of its flash points.

At the time of my trip in the spring of 1992, Oregon was in the throes of a battle over how public authorities should deal with homosexuality. There was controversy over whether a curriculum on homosexuality should be introduced into the elementary schools and whether government should take a position on the morality of homosexuality itself. Anti-homosexual conservatives had put a constitutional initiative on the Oregon ballot, known as Proposition 9, which would prohibit educational programs that promoted acceptance of homosexuality. More aggressively, Proposition 9 would require the state of Oregon to declare homosexuality a condition that was "abnormal, wrong, unnatural and perverse."[1]

Unknown to me when I accepted the invitation was that my student hosts had been recipients of financial support from backers of the

---

This article is previously unpublished.

anti-homosexual proposition. When the leader of the group called to invite me to the campus, and I told him the subject I wanted to speak about was AIDS, he became uneasy and wanted to know what I was going to say. "Hold on," I said, "You've already invited me. You don't want to put yourself in the same position as the left by telling me I'm only welcome if what I have to say is politically correct, do you?" This put him off, as he had no ready answer, and my trip went ahead.

My host's anxiety was justified. While I strongly opposed the agendas of the gay left, unlike many conservatives I have no particular problem with homosexuality itself, which I regarded as most probably a fact of nature, not a product of moral choices. Some conservatives support their anti-homosexual strictures by comparing homosexuality to alcoholism. But alcoholism is a destructive behavior in itself, which homosexuality is not. Whatever moral or theological views others might take, my view is that homosexuals deserve the same respect and legal protections as other citizens. Consequently, I was opposed to the anti-gay initiative that conservatives had placed on the ballot, with its blanket condemnation of homosexual behavior. It was especially important, I thought, for conservatives to oppose all attempts by government to make pronouncements on moral choices where harm to others was not an issue.

I expressed these opinions in an interview prior to my speech for the student paper, the *Vanguard*. I said that conservatives who supported Proposition 9 were abandoning their own core principles, including the commitment to individual liberty and limited government. If the initiative passed, what principle, I asked, would prevent a future government from declaring conservatives themselves "abnormal, wrong, unnatural and perverse"?

Such views should have pleased the leftists who came to hear me speak at Portland State. But I was also identified as a defector from their cause and someone who had warned about the perils of a public health policy on AIDS shaped by ideology rather than science. In an article written with Peter Collier in 1983, I had warned that sex clubs where promiscuous activity took place were not being closed and that traditional public health methods for combating epidemics were not

being employed because the left had mounted a ferocious and successful campaign to taint them as "homophobic" or "politically incorrect."[2]

In this charged atmosphere, my views were considered treason to
the leftist cause and were crime enough to condemn me in the eyes of
the faithful. As far as these "progressives" were concerned, no deviation
from the party line was tolerable, not even one that would save gay
lives. As a result, the welcome waiting for me in Portland was not
going to be friendly.

Prepared though I may have been for resistance to what I had to
say, the rancid hatred that greeted my arrival came as something of a
surprise. A *Vanguard* editorial published on the day of my arrival contained the following morbid throat clearing: "We all know that some
of us would like to snuff David Horowitz." The editorial went on to
say that despite this death wish, I should be allowed my First Amendment right to be heard. For its part, the university administration made
no effort to contact me before the event, nor at any time during my
appearance on its campus or thereafter (which has been my typical
experience in these matters). But university officials did think enough
of my visit to arrange for six armed guards in the auditorium where my
speech was to be delivered.

The lecture had been scheduled for the noon hour. When I entered the auditorium, there were about 150 students—some seated, some
milling around—along with the security guards, who were eyeing them
intently. A professor was scurrying about the aisles with a somewhat
frantic air. My student hosts identified him as "the other David
Horowitz." I realized that I had actually met this Professor Horowitz
twenty years earlier when I had visited the same campus to speak as a
radical. Then he was honored to meet me. Now he was distributing a
handout to inform anyone who would listen that the two of us were
not the same person. His own views, as the flier attempted to make
clear, were politically correct. *I am not now and have never been* this
David Horowitz.

The students who had invited me constituted a small group among
those attending. In fact, most of those settling into their seats proved
to be curious but neutral—the kind of attitude one would hope to
expect from college students. The conservatives had been able to find

only a single member of the faculty who was bold enough to sponsor their organization, but he had chosen not to attend the event and expose himself unnecessarily to the wrath to come. Instead, the conservative student leader introduced me. Before the proceedings began, a worried administrator urged the audience to accord me the privilege of a hearing, no matter what they thought of my ideas. I was appreciative of this, but noticed that he had also avoided contact with me as one might the carrier of a plague, a fact more eloquent than his words.

As soon as I began to speak, the anti-Horowitz demonstrations started. The second row of seats had been entirely occupied by members of ACT-UP the militant AIDS organization that had made headlines by bursting into a Mass at New York's St. Patrick's Cathedral and throwing condoms on the altar. To my event they brought giant white signs with black lettering, which they now thrust into the air in response to each statement I made. This sea of signs served to block the podium I was speaking from, screaming in giant capital letters: "LIES!" "PIG!" "BIGOT!" As if this were not enough of a statement, when especially provoked, individual activists would leap from their chairs to rant at the podium.

The first blast of the heckling threw me off balance: "What's the matter with you?" I said to them. "I'm a conservative and I've come all the way to Portland to defend your rights to be who you are. Why are you trying to prevent me from speaking? Are you *nuts?*" This was oil on the fire, so I tried a different tack: "This is a university. If we can't have reasoned and civil discourse *here*, where could such a dialogue take place? You'll have plenty of time in the question period to make your statements. Why don't you just let me say my piece and perhaps learn something?" The signs went into the air: LIES! PIG! BIGOT!

Throughout my talk, which lasted almost an hour, the interruptions and the sign-waving continued. The harassers had no interest in what I was saying. Their agenda was to obstruct my message and—more important—to stigmatize me as a moral outcast, as someone who should not be heard at all.

Eventually I was able to get through my remarks, enduring several declamations during the question period. I had survived, but to what end? Departing Oregon, I thought about the students I was leaving behind. The university would not be changed by my brief visit, and in my absence the only views heard from anyone on campus except my marginalized hosts would be those that were politically acceptable. In this case that meant there would be no challenging of a status quo that was killing tens of thousands of young people every year.

What I had left behind me was a college administration that looked on anti-intellectual behavior from the left as a normal feature of the campus environment. The guardians of the intellectual community at Portland State apparently agreed that conservative views, like mine, were an ideological contagion that should be stamped out. The students I had left behind were being educated in an atmosphere of intellectual intimidation. Their silences signaled either that they agreed with the prevailing orthodoxy or that they had made decisions to keep their own counsel until graduation afforded an escape.

—

Rather than being a unique episode, the intolerance I experienced at Portland State University is a pervasive reality on the nearly two hundred American campuses I have personally visited—not only in elite centers like Columbia and Yale, but in rural settings as far-flung as Ferrum College in the Blue Ridge Mountains of Virginia and the University of Idaho in Pocatello. Book-length studies have already been written about the repression of speech and thought through means both formal and informal on American college campuses in the post-1960s era.[3] In my own travels, although the degree of intimidation varied, there was not a single campus I visited where I did not encounter conservative students who confessed an unwillingness to speak their minds in the classroom for fear of being harassed by radical students or punished by grades given by leftist professors. On no campus were there more than a handful of openly conservative professors willing to sponsor the small student groups who invited me.[4]

So intense and pervasive is the atmosphere of fear created by the progressive witch-hunt and its political orthodoxy that progressives themselves cannot be assured of immunity from attack. In 1993, I had the opportunity to interview Harvard law professor Alan Dershowitz on a show I hosted for public radio station KCRW in Los Angeles.[5] In the course of the interview, Dershowitz observed that the atmosphere at Harvard was so hostile to the free expression of ideas in politically charged areas that he would no longer deliver his regular lecture on rape law without preparing a legal defense for the expected feminist assault. "A lot of classes at law school are video-taped for archival purposes. When I teach rape, though, these days I will not teach the subject without having a recording."[6] The precaution was necessary because of the existence of radical sexual harassment laws concerning "hostile environments," which could be invoked by radical feminists to criminalize ordinary speech. In the course of the interview, Dershowitz also volunteered that one of his law faculty colleagues, who was a leading expert in the field, had stopped giving lectures on the subject of rape altogether.

If one of the most prominent legal defense attorneys in the nation was afraid to give a public lecture at the Harvard Law School because the subject is a flashpoint for the political left, what did that say about the freedom of others, particularly students, to speak or think freely in the university culture?

Six years after my interview with Dershowitz, some law students at the University of California, Berkeley, published a book called *The Diversity Hoax* —a reference to the intellectual monolith the university had become.[7] It was a collection of testimonies about political intimidation at Boalt Hall, the prestigious law school of the University. The testimonies included the views of liberal as well as conservative students, relating episodes of classroom harassment whose purpose was to bring everyone into line on affirmative action and other issues considered litmus tests of human decency by the political left.

The Berkeley campus had been recently affected by the passage of Proposition 209, known as the California Civil Rights Initiative, which enjoined the state government from discriminating against citizens on the basis of gender or race.[8] The political left fervently supported the racial preferences outlawed by the initiative. Inflamed by agitators like Jesse Jackson, political activists at Boalt attacked as "racists" students who either supported the initiative or expressed uncertainty about it. No dissension from the extreme viewpoint was tolerated.

To advance their agenda, radicals staged a demonstration at Boalt in which they brought blacks and Hispanics into the classrooms who were not students. Law students were challenged to give up their seats to the newcomers or be labeled racists. The implication was that students who had passed the rigorous admissions requirements to attend Boalt were really admitted because of a racist bias in society. "When I expressed my outrage at being asked to give up my seat to a minority at a recent classroom protest staged in support of affirmative action," observed law student Isabelle Quinn, "[it] caused a classmate to call me a 'racist white conservative idiot.'" A second law student wrote "I felt I could not tell anyone [at law school] my personal philosophies—that I wanted to increase opportunities for students of diverse backgrounds but did not support affirmative action."

Even those who supported affirmative action were not immunized from attack. In a discussion of the tort of intentional infliction of emotional distress, a Boalt student named Jim Culp offered the following reasonable observation: "Unlike physical abuse, inflicting emotional distress is not an issue specific to women, as men and women are equally perpetrators and victims of it." His comment was met with a negative reaction as swift as it was intense: "There was a roar of scorn from many women in the class. Many stood up screaming unintelligible insults. Some even threw objects at me." But this classroom outburst—intimidating in itself—was not the extent of his ordeal. He had been flushed out as an enemy and "oppressor." "In one swoop I had successfully defined myself as a misogynist and chauvinist. For months groups of women would snicker as I walked by. . . . I had unknowingly become the male-pig poster child for the militant feminists at Boalt Hall."[9]

In another class attended by Culp, a professor attempted to discuss facets of "racial profiling." The professor chose a case that concerned a particular racial group responsible for a disproportionate number of crimes. In discussing the example, the professor related a personal experience in which he had modified his behavior in the presence of the unnamed group out of fear that he might become another victim. Although the experience was well in the past, he still felt uncomfortable with his reaction, in which he stereotyped particular individuals based on their group profile. But the professor's obvious sympathy for the racial group did nothing to appease the radicals in his class. "The professor asked for opinions concerning his experience and . . . was verbally attacked by several minority students. In ugly tones they called him, amongst other things, a 'racist,' and characterized his behavior as evil. I believe tears welled up in his eyes, and then he simply replied that he didn't think he would share such experiences with students in the future."[10]

Political correctness achieved a kind of apotheosis in an incident that occurred at Bowling Green State University, one of Ohio's premier liberal arts colleges. A tenured sociologist named Richard Zeller decided to propose a new course on the very subject of political correctness—what it is and its impact on the university. In particular, was the idea of political correctness itself at odds with academic freedom? The idea for the course was prompted by testimonies Zeller had received from students about professors who had used grade pressures to force them to agree to progressive shibboleths, for example, that all whites were racist or to reverse positions on emotionally and ideologically charged issues like abortion.

Zeller submitted the course for approval to his peers in the sociology department, but they voted to reject it. Zeller then sought an administrative home for the course in other departments, but was similarly rebuffed. Dr. Kathleen Dixon, director of women's studies, a field generally known for its ideological rectitude and exclusion of dissent, told the Bowling Green student newspaper: "We forbid any course that says we restrict free speech." What could be more Orwellian?

Far from being alone, Dixon was merely giving voice to the prevailing attitude among her progressive colleagues. Concurring with Dixon, an ethnic studies professor explained that Zeller's course would lead students to "feel good about the ruling paradigm, which since the inception of the United States has said that genocide is good, racism is better, and exploitation of women and the poor is the best way to go." In typical totalitarian fashion, the faculty leftists maintained that any attempt to question a prevailing orthodoxy was to align oneself with exploitation, racism, and genocide.[11] Zeller's department chairman, sociology professor Gary Lee, then pronounced an official anathema on his colleague, who had committed no offense prior to proposing the course in question: "Unfortunately, tenure protects the incompetent and malicious; [Zeller] has tenure, so he cannot be fired without cause."

The transformation of Zeller into an academic pariah was now complete. Beleaguered, isolated, and weary of the struggle, he decided to retire, rather than continue his career as a despised heretic. In his letter of resignation, he wrote:

> Don't cry for me. I'm doing just fine, thank you. Cry out, instead, for the students who regularly get intellectually mugged on the Bowling Green State University Campus . . . the traditionalist who believes that marriage is between a man and a woman, but can't say so for fear of failing; the conservative who believes in minimizing government interference in our lives and says so in a sociology class, the woman who believes that abortion is murder, but must write a pro-choice essay to pass English, and all of those who have "adjusted" and "self-censored" their ideas so that they can pass their classes. . . . BGSU has sold its soul to the thought police of political correctness. There was a time that honorable people could disagree honorably; now, any challenge to the campus sacred cows—feminism, affirmative action, and multiculturalism—is denounced as evil.[12]

Multiculturalism, which is not so much about the appreciation of diverse human cultures as it is about the theology of gender, race, and class oppression, is the academic religion that sanctions these campus witch-hunts. Its imperatives are established in the "student orientation" sessions required of every entering freshman. "A central goal of these [orientation] programs," as an authoritative study of these repressive practices sums them up, "is to uproot 'internalized oppression,' a crucial concept in the diversity education planning documents of most universities."[13]

At orientation, students are divided according to their membership by ethnicity and race into oppressed and oppressor groups. They are indoctrinated through training films with titles like "Blue Eyes" and "Skin Deep," in which blue and white are symbols of the oppressor group and brown eyes and skin that of the victims. "Programmatic differentiation by race is now typical in higher education. Half a century after the defeat of Nazism, our universities distinguish by blood and equate blood with culture. Sixty years after the Nuremberg Race Laws, we ask our students to check off their bloodlines and to act accordingly. The justification for this submergence of the individual into the tribe is the same as it was under fascism: The individual is a function—politically, morally, and historically of genetic and cultural collectivities. Campus life begins with the sorting out of students into oppressors and victims."[14] Once this orthodoxy is established, the mechanism of the witch-hunt follows directly. Every dissenter from the orthodoxy—every one who refuses to validate the theology of oppression—is doing the work of the devil, the oppressor.

These episodes are just the tip of an iceberg. Why then are the last thirty years not known as the era of progressive witch-hunts, especially since there have been many more victims of political correctness than there were of the McCarthy investigations? The obvious reason is that in this case the repressive orthodoxy is rooted in the academic culture. In contrast, McCarthy was hated, feared, and demonized by the intellectual left because of its sympathies with McCarthy's victims. These victims were indeed part of a conspiracy as McCarthy charged, though he certainly overstepped the bounds of veracity and decency in pursuing his targets. The opening of the Soviet archives has shown that while McCarthy was an unscrupulous demagogue, the internal communist threat in the 1950s was real, and there was—as McCarthy claimed—an organized "fifth column" of progressives ready to collaborate with the Soviet enemy. [15] The left he opposed, on the other hand, survived to get its revenge by writing the history of the era.[16]

Nor is the McCarthy period the only example of inverted priorities in historical characterization. Consider the Palmer raids of the

1920s, when the government rounded up anarchists from immigrant communities in the Northeast for interrogation about terrorist plots. This period is known in academic histories as the "Red Scare." In point of historical fact, however, the roundups were a response to a failed anarchist attempt to blow up the Attorney General of the United States, Mitchell Palmer, along with J. P. Morgan and nearly 100 other prominent individuals targeted by bombs sent through the U.S. mails. Palmer was wounded and his chauffeur killed by the bomb earmarked for him.

On the basis of the historical record, a more appropriate designation for this entire episode would more likely be the "Red Threat." Calling it the "Red Scare" is tantamount to calling the mob roundups after the St. Valentine's Day Massacre, the "Mob Scare." Of course mobsters usually don't acquire PHDS or occupy academic chairs from which to rewrite their own history, while anarchists and their intellectual sympathizers do.

The era of the progressive witch-hunt has been far worse in its consequences to individuals and freedom of expression than was the McCarthy era. The McCarthy era could not come close to producing the environment that has become commonplace in today's university for the simple reason that in the McCarthy era, the witch-hunters were outside the university community, while the agents of the progressive witch-hunts are inside and in control.[17] A second reason for the greater impact of progressive political repression in the academic world today lies in the changed self-conception of the university itself. In the 1950s, the academic ethos was one in which "the disinterested pursuit of knowledge" was an ideal to be honored, not deconstructed. The tradition of academic freedom that had developed in the first Progressive Era supported intellectual independence and dissent and could be invoked to support the targets of an intellectual inquisition.

In the post-1960s university, by contrast, the enforcers of political orthodoxy are tenured leftists backed by university administrators, a situation that contrasts strikingly with the liberal academy of the 1950s, which was under assault from Washington politicians. On today's campus the promotion of progressive politics is considered integral to the academic mission, a natural consequence of the university's new self-conception as an "agency of social change." This is a self-conception more appropriate to a political party than an institution devoted to intellectual inquiry. The university administration has, in consequence, become an enforcer of attitudes that are politically correct, and has created a bureaucratic apparatus to punish students who are not, who cross the ideological line.[18] Worse, unlike the McCarthy era witch-hunt, which lasted only a few years, the one enforced by left-wing "progressives" is now entering its third decade and shows no signs of abating.

VI

PROGRESSIVE WITCH-HUNTS

— 24 —

Carl Bernstein's
Communist Problem and Mine

SOMETIME IN THE LATE 1960S OR EARLY 1970S, an elderly woman named Ann Colloms,[1] who was the mother of my best childhood friend, came to see me. Like my own parents and, indeed all the adults I knew in the years when I was growing up, Ann had been a member of the Communist Party. She had come to me because she wanted to discuss an incident that occurred long in the past, when she was a member of the Party and which still troubled her nearly twenty years later. Although I considered myself part of the left, I had already developed some publicly expressed doubts about the radical heritage we all shared, and it was for this reason that Ann now sought me out to confess her complicity in a crime committed when she was a communist long ago.

Ann and my parents belonged to a colony of Jewish Communists who, in the early 1940s, had settled in a ten-block neighborhood of working-class Catholics in Sunnyside, Queens. The members of this colony lived two lives. Outwardly they were middle class, scrupulous

This essay was originally published as "Still Taking the Fifth" in *Commentary*, July 1989. It was reprinted in *Deconstructing the Left: From Vietnam to the Clinton Era*, 1995. It has been edited for this book.

in their respect for the mores of the community, and unfailing in their obedience to its civil laws. They always identified themselves publicly as political "progressives," espousing views that were superficially liberal and democratic. They thought of themselves (and were perceived by others) as "socially conscious" and "idealistic" and were active in trade unions and civil rights groups and in the "progressive" wing of the Democratic Party.

The picture is consistent with a myth now struggling to be born in our literary culture that these people were small "c" communists, whose belief in democratic values far outweighed their commitment to big "C" Communism, with its pro-Soviet, anti-American agendas.[2] In fact, nothing could be further from the truth. The members of this colony, including Ann and my parents, also inhabited another, secret world as soldiers in the Third International founded by Lenin. In their eyes, a sixth of humanity had entered a new stage of history in Soviet Russia in 1917. This path to the future would be made accessible to people all over the world by the actions of the loyal Communist vanguard they had joined. Outsiders may have perceived them as "liberals" and "progressives," but their secret membership in this revolutionary army was the political commitment that really mattered to *them*. It was the commitment that gave significance and meaning to what otherwise were modest and rather ordinary lives.[3]

In their own minds, Ann and my parents were secret agents. When they joined the Communist Party, they had even been given secret names for the time when their true objective would require them to abandon the facade of their liberal politics and go "underground" to take the lead in the revolutionary struggle. All their legitimate political activities were merely preparations or fronts for their real agendas, which they could discuss only with other secret agents like themselves. Their activities in the democratic organizations they entered and controlled and in the liberal campaigns they promoted were all part of their secret service. Their real purpose in pursuing them was not to advance liberal or democratic values but to serve the interests of the Soviet state—because in their minds the Soviet Union was where the future had already begun.

For those in the Party, the revolutionary role was not the fantasy it seems in retrospect, and its consequences were real, as the story that Ann told me reveals. No more than five-feet tall in her stocking feet, Ann had been a high school teacher of foreign languages. Her only flirtation with a reality beyond the prudent bounds of her middle-class existence was in fact her membership in the Communist Party But even her party life—despite its little Bolshevik rituals and con-spiratorial secrets—was organized around activities that were quite or-dinary: raising funds for the Spanish volunteers, marching for civil rights, and playing the part of a loyal cadre in the New York City Teacher's Union, Local 555, which the party controlled. But on one occasion Ann was chosen for a task that was not like the others and that would burden her with guilt for the rest of her life.

In 1940, when Ann had just become a mother for the first time, the party singled her out for a special mission. The nature of the mission required that its purpose not be revealed, even to her, and that its details be concealed even from her Party comrades. In any other area of Ann's life, the intimations of illegality and danger inherent in such a proposal would have provoked intolerable anxieties and suspicions for a person of her sheltered experience and temperament. But it was the Party that had made the request. And because it was the Party, the same elements had an opposite effect. The fear that was present only emphasized the honor that the Party was intending to bestow on her. The prospect of danger only heightened the importance of the call to serve the noble cause. She understood instinctively that it was the very insignificance and unobtrusiveness of her life that made her suitable for the task. It was the Party that spoke, but it was History that called.

Ann agreed to undertake the mission. Leaving her infant son with her husband in New York, she took a plane to Mexico. There she deliv-ered a sealed envelope to a contact the Party had designated. After making the delivery, she flew back to New York and resumed the life she had lived before. It was as simple as that. Yet it was not so simple at all. As Ann soon discovered, she was a small but decisive link in a chain by which the Soviet dictator Joseph Stalin intended to rescue the as-sassin he had sent to put an ice pick in Leon Trotsky's head.[4]

In retrospect, one of the most disturbing elements in Ann's story lay in the fact that she had waited so long to tell it, and then only to me and privately. She did so nearly twenty years after she and my parents had left the Communist Party, following Khrushchev's report on the crimes of Stalin. She told her story to me now to relieve her guilt. Neither she nor my parents had ever thought to tell me stories like this when I was young and starting out on my own career in the left, which might have warned me about the minefields I was entering. They never told their stories publicly nor would they approve of my doing so now. The attitude of progressives like Ann and my parents towards historical truth was ruthless. Nothing should be told that might hurt the cause. Like thousands of others, they had left the Party, but they could never leave the faith.

We learn in a new book by Watergate journalist Carl Bernstein that that his father Al was a secret agent in the same army as Ann and my parents.[5] Like them, he is one of those progressives who left the party but could never leave its political faith. When Carl approached his father about the book he intended to write on "the witch-hunts leading up to the McCarthy era," Al Bernstein stonewalled him, refusing to be interviewed. He did not approve his son's quest for the truth about his communist past. He did not want his son to discover the truth about his experience in the Communist Party or about the Party's role in American life. He did not want him to write about it. To even ask the questions his son was asking indicated that his political attitude was incorrect: "I think your focus on the Party is cockeyed. You're up the wrong tree. The right tree is what people did.... I worry about your premise. The *right* premise, the premise of a lot of recent books about the period, is that people were persecuted because of what they did, not because of their affiliation. Because once you admit affiliation you get into all that Stalinist crap."[6]

In the eyes of progressives like Al Bernstein, not to accept the "right" premise was more than politically incorrect—it was dangerous: "The premise people eventually accepted after the McCarthy period was that the victims weren't Communists. If you're going to write a book that says McCarthy was right, that a lot of us were Communists, you're going to write a dangerous book. . . . You're going to prove McCarthy right, because all he was saying was that the system was loaded with Communists. And he was right."

In Al Bernstein's view, even though McCarthy was right about the presence of Communists posing as liberals, and even though virtually all of McCarthy's victims were Communists, the fact that they were Communists (and lied about being Communists) had nothing to do with their being singled out: "Was I 'oppressed' because I was a Communist? . . . No. It was incidental. I was 'oppressed' because of what I did, because I was affiliated with a left-wing union."

No one should be misled by the disingenuousness of this paternal catechism. The sacrament the father rams down the throat of the son is brutal as well as tasteless. In point of fact, Al Bernstein was a communist; he was not merely "affiliated with" the United Public Workers of America, he was a leader of the union. The UPWA was not merely a "left-wing union," but a union under Communist Party control. And the fact that it was a union under Communist control—despite Al Bernstein's protestations—made it a different order of union entirely than other unions that were not Communist-controlled.

The difference was manifested most dramatically in the Cold War year 1948, which began with the communist coup in Czechoslovakia. Coming twenty years after Munich, this event sent shock waves through the capitals of the West. In an effort to halt the march of Soviet power, the Truman administration announced it was launching the Marshall Plan, an economic-aid program to revive the war-shattered economies of western Europe and to shore up its democracies against their own communist threats. While most American unions supported the Marshall Plan as an economic boon for their members and a necessary defense measure for the West, Al Bernstein's union did not. Along with the other Communist-controlled unions in America, Al Bernstein's United Public Workers attacked the Marshall Plan as a Cold War plot and launched an all-out campaign against it. On the political front, Al Bernstein and his comrades bolted the Democratic Party and organized the Progressive Party candidacy of Henry Wallace in the hope of unseating Truman and ending his anti-Communist program.

It was because of the Communist campaign to support the Soviet offensive in eastern Europe that Communist-controlled unions like Al Bernstein's were purged from the cio—and not by Senator McCarthy or Harry Truman and his Loyalty Board but by union leaders like Philip Murray and Walter Reuther. They were liberal socialists who opposed and condemned Stalinists like Al Bernstein for betraying their union members in the interests of the Soviet Union. Phillip Murray, who is cited in passing in Carl Bernstein's memoir for his principled opposition to the Loyalty Boards, also told the cio convention in 1948 that he opposed the Communists "because they have subverted every decent movement into which they have infiltrated themselves in the course of their unholy career."

More than three decades after Senator McCarthy's death, Al Bernstein at seventy-plus years of age is still actively practicing his old Stalinist deceits, still taking the Fifth Amendment in any inquiry, however innocent, into his commitments and beliefs, and still hiding his communist agendas behind a liberal facade. He pursues his deception not only towards the world at large but also towards his own pathetically inquisitive son. To be called a witch-hunter by your father, while only trying, however ineffectually, to sort out the Oedipal tangle must be a daunting experience.

Bernstein, whose memoir is utterly innocent of the vast literature on American Communism that refutes virtually every page of this book he took eleven years to write, measures the dimensions of his filial love in a passage that occurs less than halfway through the text: "Many years later . . . [I] realized that it is my father for whom I write, whose judgment I most respect, whose approval I still seek." *Loyalties* is a unilateral withdrawal from the Oedipal struggle.

In the end, it is the sheer desperation of this filial hunger that explains the deficiencies of the preposterous book he has had the bad judgment to publish as *Loyalties* (even the original title—*Disloyal*—has been changed to fit the fashions of the paternal party line). He resists his father's "correct premise" manfully at the outset, but by the final chapters of *Loyalties* he has capitulated and even joined up. Al

Bernstein's Communist Party loyalties didn't matter (either to him or to those who pursued him), Carl avows. He and all the other agents of the communist cause were targeted solely for their activities on behalf of trade unionism and civil rights. The internal security program of the Truman administration "really was a war against liberals."

This is not a book about the Communist Party and its discontents but a lecture on the need to keep the tattered faith at whatever cost to one's integrity. Rapidly expiring all over the world, this faith, strange to say, is alive and well in literary America. As Al Bernstein, the possessor of a shrewder, stronger intellect than his wayward son impatiently observes, "the right premise"—the Communist Party's premise—is "the premise of a lot of recent books about the period." Thus, the standard academic work on the subject of American universities in the loyalty-oath era—*No Ivory Tower* by Princeton professor Eleanor Schrecker—is written from this apologist perspective, as are most other recent studies by academic leftists about the early Cold War security conflicts.

Even more striking support for Al Bernstein's observation is offered by the notices of *Loyalties* in the most prestigious book reviews—the *Sunday New York Times*, the *Los Angeles Times,* and the *Washington Post*. In each, Carl had his literary knuckles rapped by leftist reviewers who chided him for not justifying his parents' communist politics *enough*. Thus, Paul Robeson's neo-Stalinist biographer Professor Martin Duberman complained in the *Washington Post*'s *Book World*: "In his dedication, Carl Bernstein asserts that he is proud of the choices his parents made. But he never provides enough argued detail about what went into those choices to allow most Americans to join him—as surely they should—in his approbation." In other words, Communism was the correct choice for right-thinking Americans to make.

What are the tenets of the neo-Stalinist faith that has so unexpectedly resurfaced in American letters in the 1980s? Basically there are two. The first is that Communists were peace-loving, do-gooding, civil-rights activists and American patriots; the second is that they were innocent victims of a fascist America. Carl has it down pat. Citing his father's judgment that, "[McCarthyism] was a reign of terror," Carl writes: "I have never heard my father talk like that, have never known him to reach for a cliché. But this was no cliché."[7]

No, it was not a cliché; it was a lie. No, Carl, there was no reign of terror—at least not in the way that phrase applies to the Stalinist world out of which our families both came and where it means blood in the gutters. My mother, for example, elected to take an early "disability" retirement from the New York school system, rather than answer questions about her membership in the Party. But with the help of Party friends and liberal sympathizers, she immediately went on to other more lucrative careers. Your father became a small-time entrepreneur and you got a job (through his personal connections) as a reporter at the *Washington Star*. When later you were at the *Washington Post* and about to help topple a sitting president and went to managing editor Ben Bradlee to reveal the terrible secret about your parents' communist past, what did he do? Remove you? No, in anti-communist, paranoid America, home of the reign of terror, the editor of the most politically powerful media organ in the nation told you to get on with the job of removing a president in the middle of an anti-communist war. And what did you learn from that experience? Exactly nothing.

And that is my bottom-line complaint about *Loyalties* and its pseudo-account of the anti-communist era. As in other recent memoirs of this time, whose real premise is to keep the progressive faith, the story of the post-war domestic conflict between communists and anti-communists is told from the Communists' point of view—or at least that of their fellow-traveling sympathizers. In a fleeting episode of *Loyalties*, for example, Carl's friend and former boss Ben Bradlee recalls over dinner that he had always thought of progressives like Carl's parents (whom personally he did not know) as "awful people." Even in the jagged structure of this book, the observation is jarring, but far more disconcerting is the fact that the famous investigative reporter of Watergate does not pursue the remark to inquire what memories might lie behind it. The same lack of inquisitiveness is seen in his feeble efforts to understand the nature of his parents' true commitments. He describes his mother, then in her seventies, as a woman who is "very forgiving." But when she refers to a political adversary of thirty years ago as a "vicious bastard," her son simply ignores the emotional signal, thus missing anything that it might tell us about the polarized psyches of political progressives like her.

Elsewhere, he describes how his grandfather would take him to a Jewish bookstore to buy the Yiddish-language Communist newspaper *Freiheit*. "Until the day he died in 1967 he had no use for the [non-communist] *Forward*—or the [non-Communist] *Socialist*. 'Fareters,' traitors of the cause, he called them, and he didn't much like having any of them into his house." The same mentality reacts with the anathema *reign of terror*, when the suggestion is made that Communists like Bernstein's family might have betrayed their own country in the Cold War with the Soviet Union.

This life-long hatred towards non-Communist leftists, coupled with casual vitriolic abuse, was a staple of the progressive personalities of Carl Bernstein's childhood *milieu* and the "victims" of the postwar "purge." At one point in the text, family friend (and fellow Communist Party member) Bob Treuhaft explains to Carl why Al Bernstein joined the Party: "There was a feeling that unless you joined and were with us you were the enemy." Carl lets this one slip by, too.

There were many enemies. John L. Lewis, head of the CIO's United Mine Workers, was once a Party ally, but when he refused to go along with the Communist-supported no-strike pledge after the German invasion of Russia, the party attacked him as a "pro-Nazi" who was committing "treason." The Communists also routinely denounced civil rights leader A. Philip Randolph, the organizer of the war-time March on Washington, as "a fascist helping defeatism," because Randolph refused to shelve the struggle for civil rights—as the party dictated—in favor of joining the effort to help save the USSR from defeat.[8] So much for the fantasy that Communist Party members were at bottom only unionists and civil-rights idealists.

Not only were the Party progressives, not libertarians, they were also—despite their pious wails later on—notorious masters of the political blacklist in all the organizations they managed to control. It was partly for these reasons that when the loyalty boards and the congres-

sional committees finally did come to town, there were a lot of people—
a lot of liberal people—waiting to settle scores with the communists.
To these liberals, the Communists were not the compassionate pilgrims of Carl Bernstein's book, but political conspirators who had
infiltrated and manipulated and taken over their own organizations to
subvert them for hidden agendas. They were left-wing zealots who
had slandered, libeled, and blacklisted *them* when they had opposed
the Party line. They were self-conscious subversives who lied to the
public, pretending that they were not marxists or loyal to Soviet Russia when in fact they were.

The Communists lied to everyone then, and the new keepers of
their faith are still lying today. "If you're going to write a book that
says McCarthy was right, that a lot of us were Communists, you're
going to write a dangerous book," Al Bernstein warned. Consider the
logic: to admit the truth is to lend credence to the claims of the enemy.
Why is this dangerous nearly *forty years* later? Is not McCarthy himself the most irretrievable political corpse of the McCarthy era? It is
dangerous not because it will bring persecution on progressive heads,
but because it will puncture the final illusion that allows a progressive
life of that era to appear to be something more than service to the
totalitarian cause.

It is not fear of libeling an "innocent" association that haunts the
political left; it is something more like the fear that haunted the conscience of deconstructionist scholar Paul De Man (whose Nazi sympathies were recently revealed): embarrassment over a guilt that was
real. "'Look,' [Al Bernstein] snapped, 'you've read Lillian Hellman's
book.[9] She skirts these questions [about Communist Party member-
ship] very neatly. She's too sharp to leave her self open to that kind of
embarrassment.'"

As always, Al Bernstein's old Stalinist politics reveal a sharper judgment than that of his born-again son. For the guilty, lying is good
politics. Embarrassment is the problem, not a sham "reign of terror"; it
is the shame of possible exposure as a loyal supporter for all those years
of a mass murderer like Stalin.

The struggle over the past is not over the fact of communism, but over what it meant to be a communist. Here Bernstein *pere* and *fils* are in agreement. Civil rights, trade unionism, human brotherhood, and peace: *that's* what we really were they stubbornly claim as their final defense (all others having been refuted); that was our cause. Communism? Marxism? Socialism? Those were incidental features of our profile, irrelevant to who we were and what we did.

Loyalties reveals the secret of how the left aims to be born again— by erasing the embarrassment of its disreputable past; by hiding the shame of having supported Stalin and Mao and Fidel and Ho and all the purges, mass murders, and other "necessary" means that finally served no beneficial ends. But the real embarrassment for the left is to have been so stubbornly and perversely on the wrong side of history; to have embraced "solutions" that were morally, politically and economically bankrupt in the important struggles of our time. As Joseph Stalin was the first socialist to truly understand, the airbrushing of history is the only sure means to preserve the honor of the left. In this, as no doubt in other things in his undiscovered life, Al Bernstein follows right along the Stalinist path. And his son walks in lockstep behind him, picking up his mess.

25

Et Tu, John?

ABOUT THE TIME THAT A WHITE HOUSE INTERN named Monica Lewinsky became a household name in January 1998, I received a call from Ronald Radosh an old political friend who had recently written an article for *Heterodoxy*, a magazine I edited with my writing partner Peter Collier. The gravamen of Radosh's message was that he had just been warned by an editor at the *New Republic* not to have anything to do with Collier or me. The reason? We were "Nazis."

To be identified as a Nazi, would be disturbing under any circumstances—and not just for a Jew like myself. The fact that John Judis, the author of this slander, was a thoughtful leftist—someone who knew me and whom I considered a friend—and was an editor at a well-thought-of institution of the liberal-left culture (albeit it one that had placed a silent ban on Collier and myself), made the surface implications much worse.

The pretext for Judis's attack seemed innocent enough. He was outraged at the fact that I had come to the defense of Matt Drudge, the Internet reporter who had broken the story that Lewinsky was having an affair with the president in the Oval Office. About a month

This article first appeared on FrontPageMagazine.com on January 1, 1998, and was reprinted in *Sex, Lies & Vast Conspiracies* (1998). It has been edited for this book.

before Judis's call, Drudge had become the target of a libel suit filed against him by White House aide Sidney Blumenthal, a former writer for the *New Republic* who played a prominent role as Clinton's hatchet man and who was particularly ruthless when it came to discrediting the reputations of the women who came forward to complain about their mistreatment by the nation's commander in chief.

Drudge had made himself anathema to the White House (and thus to Blumenthal) when, in August 1997, he broke a previous story concerning a female supporter of President Clinton's named Kathleen Willey. Willey claimed to have visited the Oval Office to ask the president's help, shortly after her husband's bankruptcy and suicide had left her insolvent, and had been sexually groped instead.

At the time of the Blumenthal suit, Drudge was already famous because of this story, but he was also a journalistic loner, operating out of a one-bedroom apartment in Hollywood, on a $30,000-a-year income, with no means of mounting a legal defense in the absence of outside help. It was my offer to organize a defense fund that inspired John Judis's attack

The suit that Blumenthal had filed against Matt Drudge was itself tangentially connected to the scandal that had emerged out of the Lewinsky affair. The left eventually came up with a telling phrase—"sexual McCarthyism"—to describe the attack from the right that the Lewinsky affair inspired. For the left, which still clung to the belief McCarthy's victims were innocents, it was an odd construction. It suggested that the president's critics were attempting to taint him for something he did not do. Or, if he did do it, one for which he was not morally culpable. But the very people leveling the charge had previously made political fodder out of the sexual lives of their own opponents, which had included figures like Senator Robert Packwood and Justice Clarence Thomas. Nor did considerations of hypocrisy prevent them from dredging up dirt on the sexual lives of Republicans involved in the subsequent impeachment battle.

In the days following the discovery of Monica Lewinsky, a reporter for the left-wing magazine *Mother Jones* managed to locate some old court records from a bitter divorce and custody battle involving a prominent Republican political consultant named Don Sipple, whose estranged wife had accused him of spousal abuse. Democrats seized on the story as a kind of retributive justice for the Republicans' sins in persecuting Clinton, although the only connection seemed to be that an intimate relationship was involved and the target was a Republican. (Talk about guilt by association.) The *Mother Jones* attack caused Sipple to lose his job, and some irate Republicans retaliated by spreading an old Washington rumor that Blumenthal had been arrested once for beating his wife. It was this story that Drudge published, prompting Blumenthal's suit.

The "politics of personal destruction" was another phrase Democrats had coined while defending their president. Since it was an indispensable weapon in Blumenthal's own professional arsenal, there was an element of poetic justice in his having become the target of such an attack. It was Blumenthal who invented the phrase "vast right-wing conspiracy," which Hillary Clinton used to mark her enemies while denying that her husband had been having an affair. This vague and comprehensive accusation that a conspiracy lay at the root of her husband's troubles was easily the most inflammatory invitation to a witch-hunt since McCarthy's famous speech in West Virginia about Communists at the State Department working for the Kremlin.

Unlike the First Lady's accusation, Drudge's assertion about Blumenthal was not submitted as a fact. Nor had he put his own authority behind the claim. Instead, he had described it as a "rumor," and explained its background as an act of political revenge. Despite these qualifications, Blumenthal's attorneys responded to the posted story with a threatening letter. On receipt of the letter, Drudge instantly removed the piece and posted a retraction which he kept on his site for thirty days. More people probably saw the disclaimer than read the original story. But this attempt at rectification did not satisfy Blumenthal, who proceeded with a $30 million lawsuit against Drudge (which he eventually lost). Simultaneously, he mobilized his numerous and powerful friends in the media to scorch the earth around the meddlesome newshound. These developments in the days that followed Drudge's post appeared to me a thinly veiled White House attempt to crush the Internet upstart and drive him out of business.

It was at this juncture that I entered the story by calling Drudge and offering to set up a fund for his defense. I had been involved in efforts to defend First Amendment rights since 1992, when I had created the Individual Rights Foundation, a public interest group of lawyers who fought campus speech codes designed to produce politically correct thinking among college students. We defended the speech rights of all who were in jeopardy, feminists and Afro-centrists, as well as conservatives. We even attained some notoriety when we forced a vice-chancellor at the University of California, Riverside, to undergo "sensitivity training" in the First Amendment after he had banned a fraternity for producing a T-shirt the left didn't like.

In other words, we were in the field defending free speech well before Blumenthal's vindictive suit against Matt Drudge. The fact was that I had never met Drudge before calling him up and arranging a meeting to discuss his defense. At first he didn't seem to think that he particularly needed one. But I introduced him to Manny Klausner, a libertarian and one of the nation's leading intellectual property lawyers, who convinced him that he should have representation and agreed to take up the case. The Individual Rights Foundation paid the bill.

In the months that followed the First Lady's attack on the alleged "right-wing conspiracy," I was one of many who received calls from the press about my connections to two points on the chart that Blumenthal was said to have constructed to map the sinister web of the right-wing cabal. (The *Nation* magazine actually published a version of this chart for the edificaton of its readers.) The points in the web that intersected with my activities were Matt Drudge (through the defense fund) and the philanthropist Richard Mellon Scaife, who had underwritten some journalistic investigations of the Clinton administration and whose philanthropic foundation also sponsored some of the activities of the Individual Rights Foundation, just as it had the Johns Hopkins Medical Institute and other non-profit enterprises.

I have only met or exchanged words with Richard Mellon Scaife twice in my life. He appears from the public record (and my brief encounters) to be a decent and honorable man whose only offense in this case was to believe that Bill Clinton was a scoundrel and should be investigated by an independent press. What is the difference between this activity and, say, Ben Bradlee's assignment of Woodward and Bernstein to pursue the Watergate affairs of Richard Nixon? Nonetheless, in the months following the "vast right-wing conspiracy" charge, Scaife was so demonized by the nation's left-wing media as the dark figure behind Clinton's troubles that mere association with him became a taint. I cannot count the number of times I have been attacked for my own slight connection by individuals ranging from well-known Clinton spear-carriers James Carville, David Brock, and Joe Conason, to obscure letter-writers to the journals my articles appear in.

The atmosphere eventually became so thick with vague suspicion and groundless paranoia that in 1999 Scaife became the target of an actual assassination attempt. A deranged Las Vegas loner who managed porn sites and a leftist information center on the Internet became so alarmed at Scaife's alleged influence that he traveled across country to Scaife's headquarters in Pittsburgh intending to kill him. When the would-be assassin arrived at his destination, however, he apparently lost his nerve. Instead of completing his plan, he went into a men's room across from Scaife's office and turned his gun on himself.

How does it feel to be the focus of such volatile suspicions? To someone like myself, who was raised by Communists in the McCarthy era, it feels quite familiar. As a youngster in the 1940s, I could observe the FBI agents who regularly staked out the streets of our neighborhood, a center of communist activity, to chart people's comings and goings. Unfair as the treatment of my family and our communist friends may have seemed to us at the time, there was a reasonable explanation for it, and a large element of truth to the conspiracy charges themselves. As the recently opened Soviet archives attest, American Communists were willing enlistees in a secretive movement that did take its orders (and money) from Moscow. This movement was self-consciously dedicated not only to the overthrow of American democracy, but to the undermining of America's security. My own parents hid an East German communist in their house who later became the Mayor of the Soviet-controlled sector of Berlin. They and their friends and most of those who fell into McCarthy's net were indeed loyal to a foreign dictatorship and actively supported its anti-American agendas.[1]

Yet most people agree, and I am one of them, that McCarthy's investigations were conducted in an irresponsible manner that caused injury to some people who were innocent of any connection to the actual communist conspiracy and others who, while involved in the conspiracy, were guiltless of any actual criminal deeds. (The number of these innocents, on the other hand, has been greatly exaggerated in accounts of this era written by academics sympathetic to the Communist cause.[2]) More than Communists whom the FBI was already pursuing, McCarthy's primary target seemed to be his political opponents in the Democratic Party, who he (sometimes correctly) believed were protecting them.[3]

Since institutions like the *New Republic*, abhorred "McCarthyism" even when it was directed at people with treasonous intentions, it seems reasonable to ask why they are now so eager to support a White House witch-hunt whose purpose is to smear and destroy Clinton critics who are not abetting an enemy power. In any case, what right wing conspiracy could the first lady have had in mind? The story that he was having an affair with Lewinsky was true.

Lewinsky was in the White House not as the result of any Republican plot, but because her parents were Democratic Party contributors. It was *Newsweek*—hardly a conservative institution—that had originally developed the story which Matt Drudge made public. Clinton had the affair and lied about it. It was his lying that forced others to undertake the arduous and sometimes risky task of holding him to account. Lewinsky was identified because of Clinton's perjury in the Paula Jones case, not as the result of a right-wing witch-hunt. Finally, the "right" isn't organized as the Communist left was through a conspiratorial organization with secret codes and top-down discipline. Nor is it united around a party line the way the Communists and their fellow travelers were in the early years of the Cold War. Richard Scaife, for example, may have funded investigations suggesting that the suicide of Vince Foster was a more sinister event than many suspected. But a conservative special prosecutor, Kenneth Starr, wrote the official report clearing Clinton of any malfeasance and supporting the original suicide report. What kind of conspiracy is that?

What triggered John Judis's attack on Peter Collier and me was a suggestion by Radosh that Judis read the article he had written for our magazine *Heterodoxy*. Judis replied that he wouldn't read anything printed in *Heterodoxy* because Peter and I were, well, "Nazis." When Peter heard the story, he fired off an e-mail to Judis whose message was: *Heterodoxy*, Nazis, Yikes! Judis replied:

> I assume your letter was prompted by a conversation I had with Ron Radosh this afternoon, since I haven't talked to you in ages. You need to know a little background. Ron brought up *Heterodoxy*. I said, as I have said before to him, that I was pissed off about Horowitz's defense of that scumbag Drudge. Radosh attributed my position to my being friends with Sid Blumenthal, and instead of blowing up at him as I should have, I started railing about Nazis. I don't think Horowitz is a Nazi, but I do think that his position is detestable. I wrote him a letter at the time but it was returned because he no longer lives at the address to which I sent it. Assuming you are in cahoots on this stuff, I'll send it to you and you can forward it to him if you desire.

Judis then sent the letter he had written to me (that never arrived) to Peter.[4]

> Dear David: This morning, a mutual friend of ours urged me to read your articles on Sid Blumenthal and the *Drudge Report*. Rather than responding simply to him (I think I said something to the effect that I'd rather eat dog shit), I thought I would tell you what I thought of your leading the defense of Mr. Drudge.
>
> Let me make the point indirectly through two anecdotes:
>
> 1) When the *Drudge Report* first came out, one of my friends called me that afternoon to ask whether I'd seen it and what I knew of Sid's private life. This person, who didn't know Sid, assumed the report was true. I read it myself, and reading about court records, wondered, too, whether Sid hadn't concealed a part of himself from me all these years. Afterwards, I talked to several people who knew Sid and Jackie socially better than I did who

thought the report was preposterous, but until the hoax was fully revealed, I still had lingering doubts. The point is this: there is no slander so insidious or so subversive to a person's reputation and character as a charge of wife-beating, especially when backed up with claims about court records. It can lead a friend of twenty years to harbor doubts about them. That's why law schools use this kind of charge as a model for slander and defamation.

2) After the hoax was revealed, I suggested to one of the editors at the *New Republic* that they run a short about it, noting, among other things, the connection to AOL,[5] but this editor, knowing Mike Kelly's[6] animosity toward Sid (at least the equal in ferocity of your own) hesitated to suggest it. To my surprise, Kelly brought it up himself and insisted on running a short. His one concern was that even mentioning such a charge in the course of explaining it was a hoax could lend credence to it. In this case, Kelly was willing to put aside his feelings toward Sid because it was a question of principle—of someone attacking someone's reputation in the most scurrilous manner and using the new power of the internet to do so. Kelly also believed, as I do, that it was important to sue in this instance, because it is important to establish a precedent so that other would-be journalists are deterred from following the example of Mr. Drudge and so that publishers, such as America Online, are deterred from promoting these kinds of scumbags.

I'd draw a very sharp contrast between your conduct and Kelly's. The mark of a moral person is the ability, upon occasion, to transcend one's own resentments and hatreds, as well as one's loves and enthusiasms. Kelly was able to do it. You are not. The main difference between your defense of Drudge in the 1990s and your defense of Huey Newton or Los Siete[7] during the 1960s is that in the latter cases, you still had a smidgen of principle. I detest what you are doing. Yours, John.

Peter replied to Judis's letter himself,[8] saying that he had put it in the trash receptacle of his e-mail, but that Judis could send it on to me if he wanted:

If I know David [he wrote], he will take you to task particularly for the last paragraph of this still-unsent letter of yours, which won't be difficult, since you've given him a target as big as a barn with what could easily be interpreted as a morally imbecilic proposition about supporting criminal gangs in the 1960s being some sort of misguided principle that can still be said to travel well, in extreme rhetorical instances such as the case at hand, in the 1990s. Innocently supporting murderers in the 1960s: morally OK. Less innocently supporting an Internet gossipmonger in the 1990s: morally criminal. This is a weird moral calculus, my friend.

Peter did forward Judis's letter to me, and I replied to it:

Dear John:[9] I have Peter's copy of your e-mail of November in which you explain why you have washed your hands of me, and "detest" what I do, apparently because I have come to the defense of Matt Drudge. This evidently makes me a conspirator in the plot to wound Sidney Blumenthal through unkind and inaccurate words that misrepresent the person you presume him to be. Peter has also sent me the reply he wrote in my behalf, and while I concur in his observations, they seem incomplete. For me the attack in your letter also broaches basic issues about the nature of our political discourse. I am, therefore, answering you in my own voice.

Over the last ten years I have kept in touch with you, partly for old times' sake, and partly because I thought you were a man of integrity and would keep faith with the past we shared. Though we no longer share agendas, I thought there might even come a time when you would provide testimony against the powerful attacks and distortions of my life and Peter's by the left that have resulted from our political defection.

As you can see this touches directly on the issues you raise about the misrepresentation of your friend at the hands of Matt Drudge. For Peter and I have been the target of far more more calculated slander than your friend Sid. In terms of actual wounds inflicted by mean-spirited and vicious misrepresentations,

Blumenthal does not begin to know what pain is. Or, evidently, how to deal with it.

In view of your attack on me now, it is something of an irony that I thought you might be up to the task of one day defending us against political slanders. I was perhaps misled by the fact that you were willing to entertain any overtures at all from me, when almost everyone Peter and I had known and befriended in the community of the left had turned on us with an irrational hatred when our politics changed. The passion of these newly minted enemies was so intense that we could no longer count on those who had witnessed what we had done to remember or respect the integrity of a single fact about our lives, once that fact was put into question. Were Peter and David holy rollers of the ideological sects, partisans of mindless extremes? Were they the real authors of the crimes they accused others of committing?[10] Because of the silence of people like you on these matters, it was left to us—and to others who had second thoughts—to remember that we were not.

Consider how total this attack on our reality has been. While an almost universal hatred has been directed at Peter and me by our former comrades, we are the ones accused by them of malice; of having acted out extremist fantasies in the past and of being driven only by our hatred of old friends in the present.

Your personal warmth towards me was not the only factor that encouraged my misplaced trust. I was also impressed that in your own writing you made a significant effort to be fair to intellectual opponents on the right, like Bill Buckley, whose biographer you became. You developed a modest specialty as a portraitist of conservative intellectuals and of "renegades" from the left like James Burnham and Whittaker Chambers. I respected this, and it encouraged me to hope that this spirit of fairness (rare enough among left-wing intellectuals) might one day prompt you to examine our careers and counteract the politically motivated efforts to defame us and deny us a hearing. Only this month, for example, your friend Paul Berman referred to me as a 'demented lunatic' in the pages of *Dissent*—probably the leading intellectual journal of the left, portraying me as someone who was a Leninist fanatic before his second thoughts and after—defamatory lies on both counts.

From the time Peter and I announced our political change of heart in a piece in the *Washington Post* some thirteen years ago, and organized a conference of other 'second thoughters,' we were greeted by a wall of hate erected by our former comrades. Your friend Sidney played a significant part in creating that wall. In a signature piece on our "Second Thoughts" conference that appeared in the *Washington Post*, he caricatured us as political buffoons and right-wing extremists. It was the beginning of a campaign to degrade our humanity and marginalize us in the political culture. In the same article, Sidney portrayed me as a callow narcissist who had abandoned his principles and his children to flee to the flesh-pots of Beverly Hills. Every word he wrote was false, but there was no way for me to respond or to clear my name.[11]

And that was just the beginning. Over the last ten years, the attacks on Peter and myself have continued unabated. We have been portrayed as murderers (by your friends Hertzberg and Berman[12]), as political criminals, as racists and homophobes, and always as shrill and monomaniacal ideologues to whom no self-respecting intellectual should pay the slightest serious attention. This is the culture war, John, and it has been successfully waged against us in the very precincts that you roam.

Peter and I have written the only books by veterans of the 1960s left that challenge its myths. They are primary sources for the period as well as analytical texts about its meanings. But in the two hundred courses devoted to the 1960s in college curricula across the country, you will rarely find references to *Destructive Generation* or *Second Thoughts about the Sixties*, or *Deconstructing the Left* or *Radical Son*. The tenured left has seen to that. Instead you will find texts by 1960s loyalists Angela Davis, Todd Gitlin, and even Huey Newton. The campaign of political libel conducted by Sidney and your friends, though it has not silenced us as they intended, has not been lacking in successes either.

Now I will tell you something that you may not believe, but that is true nonetheless. I don't harbor any personal malice towards Blumenthal, nor is any such animus the reason I came to the defense of Matt Drudge. Any discomfort that Sidney inflicted through his caricature of me in the *Post* was washed away when I was able to write my own story in *Radical Son* and thus correct his misrepresentations about my family and my motives (although I was not able to undo the damage he had done me in the political culture during the preceding ten years). Moreover, the malice towards Peter and me and the general misrepresentation of our politics is so generic to the left that it would be foolish to load responsibility on one unscrupulous man. Moreover, if Matt Drudge had deliberately libeled Sidney for political ends and revealed a malicious intent to destroy him in the process, I assure you I would not have come to Drudge's aid.

Nor would I hesitate to have done what Michael Kelly did in printing a correction of the Drudge error. The fact is, as Peter has pointed out, Drudge did this himself and did so immediately on being informed of his mistake. And his retraction was reported throughout the press and to a far greater audience than the original error.

What then is the purpose of Sidney's thirty-million-dollar lawsuit? Surely not to send a warning to other writers as you suggest. The suit and the retraction already perform that function. My own piece in *Salon* about the affair was censored in several of its parts simply because the editors were afraid of a similar suit. I reported, for example, that Sidney had been shifted to the Style section of the *Post* when his editors became unhappy about his less than scrupulous journalistic methods. This was factually true, but still too risky for *Salon*'s editors in the litigious climate Sidney and his lawyers have created. Is this an atmosphere that you, as a writer, want to encourage?

You make the claim that Drudge's offense is especially heinous because there is no slander so insidious or subversive of character as the charge of wife-beating. Really? More insidious than

Berman's baseless and outrageous charge that Peter and I were complicit in the murder of our friend and then sought to shift the blame to others?

But let's take your claim about wife-beating charges at face value. Have you considered the case of Don Sipple, the Republican pollster accused of wife-beating by your political friends at *Mother Jones*? Do you have any idea what the basis for the charge against Sipple was? The impression given in the media was that he had actually been convicted of beating his wife. When I looked at the original article in *Mother Jones*, it was somewhat of a shock to discover that the charge was actually an unproven claim made by a scorned ex-wife in the course of a bitter custody battle. I have no idea as to the truth of the accusation, but neither do the editors of *Mother Jones* or you. Yet a man has been seriously damaged as a result.[13] Where is your outrage over the insidious subversion of *this* life?

Here is what is so perverse in your anguish over Sid. Unlike Sipple (or Peter and myself), Blumenthal commands enormous resources and influence as a presidential aide with a large network of friends in the press. He was quickly able to reach millions with his side of the story. In context, such pain as he incurred, though it may have been intense, was fairly limited. By contrast, ten years ago, when I went to Richard Harwood, the ombudsman of the *Washington Post*, to point out the lies that Blumenthal had written about me and my family, Harwood merely shrugged his shoulders sympathetically, suggesting that I write a letter to the editor, a response that few would notice. He did remove the offending column from the *Post*'s weekly national edition, but that was all he was able to offer. On the other hand, your Sid, cognizant of the facts and wholly unrepentant, made sure that the slander would reach a wider audience by reprinting the lies he had written, uncorrected, in a book of his collected articles.

Certainly no one in politics is immune from name-calling, misrepresentation, or unfounded accusation. That is a deplorable state of affairs, but it is also the territory, and everyone knows it. In such an environment, all anyone can ask is to be able to respond to the slanders that are made and attempt to correct them. Occupy-ing a high political ground, Blumenthal had powers of redress that most of us lack. He should be the last to whine, let alone sue. That you and Blumenthal seem so refreshingly thin-skinned only reveals how protected you are, as members of the left, by a sympa-thetic media and by the relative civility of the conservative press.

In the end, Blumenthal's suit has only one set of agendas: to destroy Drudge, to discredit him, to run him out of the busi-ness—to shut him up along with all the other Clinton adversaries from Gennifer Flowers to Paula Jones. In these battles the White House is a Goliath from which, as a leftist, you would normally keep your distance. So why your hostility to the Internet David?

The error Drudge made in passing on the rumor about your friend hardly reflects a pattern in his journalism. His celebrity is fresh. He is still so innocent of such smears and of the suits that can attend them that he didn't even have an attorney until I put him in touch with one.

The same cannot be said for your friend Blumenthal, who no doubt has the best legal advice money and his proximity to the Clintons can secure. His lawyers showed no qualms about circu-lating his one-hundred-and-thirty-seven-page suit, filled with unsubstantiated charges against Drudge to the entire media (a practice that is normally frowned on by the legal community be-cause it invites a libel claim in return). Moreover, Blumenthal is supported by an armada of prominent left-wing journalists like Joe Conason, Frank Rich, Eric Alterman, Alex Cockburn, and Robert Scheer, for whom casual distortion and personal abuse are a kind of lingua franca of their craft.

It is Sid, isn't it, whose new career is that of the Clintons' shadow McCarthy, the architect of Hillary's "vast right-wing con-spiracy" charge that has reporters calling me daily? In the smog of paranoia that Sidney's efforts have generated, I have become a dot on his infamous conspiracy chart for setting up a fund to pay Drudge's legal bills. This ugly claim is what Maureen Dowd identifies as the Clinton "doomsday strategy" and which Stephano-poulos recently described as the president's determination "to take everybody down with him"—interns, witnesses, journalists—by exposing their dirty secrets to the public. I'm sure the 941 FBI files the Clintons illegally appropriated come in handy in these efforts.

It was only a year ago that Peter and I hosted an event in Los Angeles you attended as our guest. The meeting was warm with nostalgia, and for our part we made every effort to put you at ease in the unfamiliar environment you were entering. Yet, cordial as our relations seemed to be, you didn't call me when the Blumenthal matter came up or even bother to make sure that your letter was put in my hands. You chose instead to attack me behind my back and to warn our mutual friend Radosh of the contagion involved in any contact with us.

And so, you have developed your own way of dehumanizing Peter and me and of becoming part of the *Kulturkampf* against us. This must be why you have abandoned your usual judgment to embrace a scoundrel like Blumenthal (or at least his scoundrel acts). And this is why, while championing Sid, you have never thought to correct the insidious slanders directed at us in the magazines you write for and among the audiences you reach. An assessment of our work that recognized its seriousness and that corrected the caricatures of our character and allegiances would have been a natural sequel to your pieces on previously despised defectors like Burnham and Chambers. The difference is that they are safely dead and we are not. For the people you call your friends and whose praise and plaudits you seek, Peter and I are radioactive, political untouchables—as we have been for the nearly fifteen years since those first lies from Blumenthal's pen. What lawsuit is going to give us redress for that?

26

Michael Lind and the
Right-Wing Cabal

URING THE TIME I was at work on my autobiography, *Radical Son*, I was informed by Ron Radosh that an article had appeared in the socialist magazine *Dissent*, written by an author named Michael Lind and titled "The Death of Intellectual Conservatism." It was Lind's attempt to explain the political transformation that had led him to abandon his career as a writer on the right and join the anti-conservative forces on the left. Within a few months of Radosh's call, Lind had become a kind of celebrity as result of his political "conversion," which was celebrated with great fanfare by the prestige organs of the intellectual culture. It was a "God That Failed" in reverse.

Prior to these events, despite the fact that Lind and I were both members of a relatively small community of conservative intellectuals, I was only vaguely aware of his existence. Although I was an inveterate reader of the conservative press and was familiar with most if not all the intellectual lights of the movement, Lind was little more than a name on the masthead of Irving Kristol's foreign policy magazine, the *National Interest*, the author of a couple of articles I had glanced over, but whose subjects and arguments I did not remember.

From *Sex, Lies and Vast Conspiracies* (1998). Edited for this book.

Despite Lind's obscurity, there were reasons for the interest that the news of his apostasy had already inspired in me. He appeared to be someone stepping onto a path parallel to the one that both Radosh and I had previously trod, albeit in an opposite direction. Radosh and I had begun our journey in 1952, when we first encountered each other as thirteen-year olds at a chapter meeting of the Labor Youth League, an organizational successor to the Young Communist League that was run by the Party as a political front. The new name was to hide the relationship with the parent organization, which was then a target of investigation because of its ties to the Soviet state.

Although I lived in Queens, I was visiting the Manhattan group on a mission to recruit writers for the "youth page" of the *Daily Worker*, the Communist Party's official organ. The page lasted for only one issue, but Radosh and I became lifelong friends. In 1987, he was one of the ex-radicals Peter Collier and I invited to the "Second Thoughts" conference in Washington, D.C., to which we had invited a group of former 1960s radicals fed up with the anti-American passions and totalitarian romances of the political left. Among those who attacked the conference, none was more vocal than the group of *Dissent* intellectuals whom Michael Lind now counted as his comrades. In their eyes we were "renegades," "Reaganites," and generally "overwrought."

The second reason for my interest in Lind's political conversion was a long-running dialogue between Radosh and me about whether he and I should have ended up as conservatives at all. At the time, Radosh was still nominally on the editorial board of *Dissent*, though his relationship had become increasingly tenuous. Despite *Dissent*'s often reiterated commitment to the democratic idea, its editor and guiding spirit, Irving Howe, had banned Radosh from writing articles about Nicaragua in its pages, where the Sandinista marxists were still clinging to power. The transparent reason for the ban was Radosh's vocal opposition to the marxist dictatorship at a time when Howe and his magazine had formed a popular front with that part of the American left that was still enthralled with the Sandinistas.

As time passed, however, and Radosh continued to make his views available in the pages of the *New Republic* and other journals, Howe found even this situation intolerable and, using intermediaries, pressured Radosh to resign from the *Dissent* board. The rationale provided was that Radosh, who still described himself, even to me, as a "social democrat," no longer shared *Dissent*'s agendas. Howe was prevented from removing Radosh, because of his unwillingness to antagonize another board member—and funder—Martin Peretz, who edited the *New Republic* and found Radosh's views on Nicaragua salutary.

Radosh was fiercely hated by the left because of a book he had co-authored demonstrating that one of the most famous of its martyrs, Julius Rosenberg, was indeed a spy. It appeared to me that the intensity of the hostility directed towards Radosh (which inevitably became a pressure on Howe) developed because he still identified himself as a member of the left, albeit dissenting. Radosh even voted for Bill Clinton in the 1992 presidential election and often expressed to me (as I have already mentioned) his discomfort at being identified with the "right-wing" where the constant, calculated, and unprincipled vilification by his persecutors on the left had effectively placed him.

I myself had no such qualms. The image of the right that the left has concocted—authoritarian, reactionary, bigoted, mean-spirited—is an absurd caricature that has no relation to modern conservatism or to the reality of the people I have come to know in my decade-long movement along the political spectrum—or to the way I see myself. Except for a lunatic fringe, American conservatism is not about "blood and soil" nostalgia or conspiracy paranoia, which figure so largely in imaginations that call themselves "liberal," but are anything but. Modern American conservatism is a reform movement that seeks to reinvent free markets and limited government and to restore somewhat traditional values. Philosophically, conservatism is more accurately seen as a species of liberalism itself—and would be more often described in this way were it not for the hegemony the left exerts in the political culture and its appropriation of the term "liberal" to obscure its radical agendas.

In the course of my own political journey, I had rejected the ethnic aggressions, leveling illusions, and totalitarian longings embodied in the "progressive" vision and had no apologies to make for my new beliefs. My only political regret was that the leftist delusions Radosh and I had abandoned were proving more tenacious than I had expected. When Radosh phoned about Lind's article, the subtext of his call was really a question: "Well, is Lind right about intellectual conservatism? Should you be having third thoughts?"

Inevitably, I was compelled to regard Lind as a sort of *doppelganger,* whose political odyssey might reflect facets of mine and provide useful insights. I was also curious about the way his apostasy would be received by the intellectual world. It would provide a foil for what had happened to me. When Peter and I publicly rejected half a lifetime of leftism, the response was not one I had prepared for. I had expected the attacks from the left. But only Peter foresaw the real punishments that were in store for us from the broader establishment culture and, in particular, the penalties they would exact on our intellectual and literary careers. When Peter and I wrote our declaration of independence in 1985 in an article in the *Washington Post* called "Lefties for Reagan," we had not actually been active in the left for nearly a decade. After our disillusionment, we had allowed a "decent interval" to elapse before re-entering the political arena and had not betrayed or exploited the confidences of recent friends. We thought the long gestation of our move to what we called our "second thoughts" might help to preempt attacks on us as "renegades" and "traitors." We were naive to think so.

During the ten years we were not politically active, we had written a series of bestselling biographies and several celebrated magazine articles and had carved out new careers as literary figures. But when our apostasy became public, the retribution was swift and seemingly without limit. Before our declaration, the biographies we had written were regularly given front page treatment in the *New York Times Book Review,* which called them "hypnotically fascinating . . . irresistible" epics and put them on its list of the top ten books of the year. But once we announced our defection, all that changed. If before we had promising careers as literary figures, virtually overnight we had none.

Our most important literary booster, Christopher Lehmann-Haupt, described our first conservative book, *Destructive Generation,* as "extremist" while expressing his own contempt for the Republican president we had supported, George Bush. Despite our efforts not to be typed as political conservatives (the adoption of the term "second thoughts" was one) we found ourselves unwelcome in the pages that mattered in the high culture—the *New York Times*, the *Atlantic*, *Harper's*, the *New York Review of Books*, and even the *New Republic*.

Our first biography, *The Rockefellers*, had been nominated for a National Book Award. We now realized that as a consequence of our political apostasy, we would never be in line for literary prizes again. Nor were the issues we raised in our "second thoughts" the source of much attention or interest in these intellectual journals, even as political scandal. We had been among the founders of the New Left, had written some of its basic political texts, and had edited its flagship publication, *Ramparts*. Yet our defection was treated as trivial and our motives venal. Even our political careers were casually dismissed by writers like Gary Wills (in *Time*) as "marginal" to the 1960s movement that, in fact, we had helped to lead. None of the magazines that shaped the high culture (and that, as we now recognized, were themselves shaped by the left) made any effort to address the arguments that we and the other members of our group had raised at the "Second Thoughts" conference and in our subsequent writings. It was as though we no longer existed.

There was another unforeseen irony in our apostasy, which added to my curiosity about the fate of Michael Lind. The radical commitment is less a political than a moral choice. Leaving the faith is a traumatic experience because it involves an involuntary severing of communal ties. That is why "political correctness" is a habit of the progressive mind—it is the line of fear that holds the flock in check. No greater caution exists for those tempted to leave the faith than the charge of "selling out." Prior to the temptation, leaving the faith is inconceivable, a sign that one is no longer a good person. Only pathological behavior—a lust for money or some other benefit—could explain to a leftist the decision to join the opposition. To the progressive mind, no decent person could ever freely make such a choice. Even in the post-communist world, the most untheoretical progressive remains in this way a vulgar marxist despite all that has historically transpired.

The fact that Peter and I had actually lost opportunities for personal gain as a result of our change of heart made no impression on our former comrades, who labeled us "renegades" and accused us of selling out just the same.

The penalties we paid were a lesson for me in the pervasive control the political left exercised over the commanding heights of American culture. Lind's success in the aftermath of his *Dissent* piece now completed the instruction. Prior to his apostasy, Lind was an intellectual nonentity in the conservative movement, with no claim to importance other than having been sponsored and befriended by conservative intellectuals like William F. Buckley and Irving Kristol, hands that had fed him and that he now proceeded to bite.

But having done his about face, this obscure junior editor of an obscure magazine became an intellectual hot property. Whereas Peter and I had found ourselves unwelcome in the literary culture after our *Washington Post* valediction, Lind found himself flush with invitations to write lead articles and cover stories for the most prominent journals of the culture—the *New York Review of Books*, the *Atlantic, Harper's*, the *New York Times*, and the *Washington Post*—all of which proceeded to feature him as a new political *wunderkind*. Where Lind had been a third tier staffer at a small intellectual journal, he was now made a senior editor successively of *Harper's*, the *New Republic*, and the *New Yorker*, and was signed for three lucrative book deals, including an account of his apostasy, based on the *Dissent* article, called *Up from Conservatism: Why the Right Is Wrong for America*.

Up from Conservatism soon appeared, complete with deceptive flap copy describing Lind as "a former rising star of the right" and a blurb from Gore Vidal comparing him to Tocqueville and promoting the book as "a fascinating look—from the inside—at that web of foundations and other interested people, corporate and simply dotty, that now shape most of what passes for political commentary." Vidal, as usual, had it exactly backwards.

My first interest, both in reading Lind's *Dissent* article and now his book, was to examine the reasons for his break with the movement I had joined. I wanted to check for new illusions that might have insinuated themselves into my political commitments. In writing our own *explications de vie*, Peter and I had been careful to point out that for us there were no sudden revelations on the road to Damascus, no single moment or event that unraveled the skein of our former political selves. It was our perspective that had changed and the change had been worked over many events in the course of many years before we arrived at the conclusions that were summarized in our book *Destructive Generation*.

In *Up from Conservatism*, Michael Lind claims, in contrast, that he actually did experience a Damascus-style revelation on the way to his new career. His epiphany came with the publication, in 1991, of a book called *The New World Order* by Pat Robertson, which retailed "a conspiracy theory blaming wars and revolutions on a secret cabal of Jewish bankers, Freemasons, Illuminati, atheists, and internationalists." According to Lind, when confronted with this "threat" from Robertson, who had founded a new and powerful organization called the Christian Coalition, "the leaders of intellectual conservatism—William F. Buckley, Jr., Irving Kristol, and Norman Podhoretz—instead of protesting, chose unilateral surrender." Intrepid souls who criticized Roberston, like Lind himself, were "denounced as 'liberals' and even 'marxists.'" The result, according to Lind, was "an exodus of the major young intellectuals formerly associated with the right," himself among them. The overall consequence of these events, in Lind's view, is that "American conservatism is dead . . . . Today the right is defined by Roberston, Buchanan, and the militia movement."

Unfortunately, this account of the death of the intellectual right is pure fantasy. It is so—well—dotty, that it is hard to believe it is Lind's thesis (and the argument of his book), but it is. The claim about an "exodus" of major young conservative intellectuals caused me to do a "double take," since I am well acquainted with the intellectual right and was previously unaware of any such defection. Later in his text, Lind identifies "the major young intellectuals" who have defected. There are actually only three: Jeffrey Herf, Bruce Bawer, and Jacob Heilbrunn. Herf was, in fact, one of the featured speakers at our "Second Thoughts" conference in 1987 and is still a friend. It is news to me that Jeffrey

Herf ever thought of himself as a conservative. At our conference, he made it very clear that he still considered himself a member of the left, and described himself as a "feminist," to the consternation of some of the conservative elders present.

Bruce Bawer is a book and film critic, who may or may not still be a conservative. Jacob Heilbrunn is a Harvard graduate student who was briefly at the *National Interest* and is known only for the article he wrote about Pat Robertson in the *New Republic*, which he co-authored with Michael Lind. Some exodus. If Lind made such preposterous assertions about liberals, he would be hooted off the stage.

Restating his tendentious thesis, Lind claims "the 'right' now means the overlapping movements of the 'far right' . . . . The only movement on the right in the United States today that has any significant political influence is the far right." Lind summarizes the philosophy of this right in the following words: "The fact remains that a common worldview animates both the followers of Pat Robertson and Pat Buchanan and the far-right extremists who bomb abortion clinics, murder federal marshals and country sheriffs, and blow up buildings and trains. That worldview is summed up by three letters: ZOG. ZOG stands for 'Zionist-Occupied Government,' the phrase used by far-right white supremacists, anti-Semites, and militia members for the federal government."[1]

According to Lind it is not just a hateful philosophy these alleged leaders of conservatism share. "In the manner of the southern right from the Civil War until the civil rights revolution, which operated both through the Democratic Party and the Ku Klux Klan, or the modern Irish Republican movement, with its party (Sinn Fein) and its terrorist branch (the IRA), the contemporary American far right has both public, political wings (the Christian Coalition and Project Rescue) and its covert, paramilitary, terrorist factions." Naturally, Lind doesn't name any of these "factions" or attempt to link terrorist and paramilitary groups with their alleged "fronts," like the Christian Coalition, which has denounced such violence (unlike the IRA's front, Sinn Fein). For Lind, whose book is an exercise in slander, the accusation is all that matters.

How is it that William F. Buckley, who thirty years ago drummed anti-Semites and John Birchers out of the mainstream right, and one of whose books is an attack on anti-Semitism, or Norman Podhoretz, a vigorous defender of Israel and the Jews, would surrender unilaterally to anti-Semites and Ku Kluxers? Lind's answer is that Pat Robertson's Christian Coalition is electorally so powerful that conservatives like Buckley and neoconservatives like Podhoretz are afraid to challenge him and thereby jeopardize the Republican agenda. Or, as an unnamed *National Review* editor allegedly put it to Lind: "They're mad, but we need their votes."

The illogic of Lind's argument is breathtaking. If Robertson and Buchanan have identical worldviews (and such worldviews!) why would Robertson and the Christian Coalition support a non-ideological Republican like Robert Dole in the presidential *primaries*, as they did in 1996, rather than Buchanan? Lind elsewhere in the book identifies Robertson as "the kingmaker" of the Republican Party. What does that mean if it doesn't mean the ability to determine the party's candidate? And if so, why not himself? If the far right is the only "significant political influence on the right" why didn't Robertson engineer his own nomination, or at least secure it for a hard-core conservative (in addition to Buchanan, Phil Gramm and Bob Dornan were also running)? If fear of losing Robertson's votes was enough to intimidate Buckley, Podhoretz, and the neoconservatives, why were they so ready to condemn Pat Buchanan as an anti-Semite and even "fascist" (as the *American Spectator* and Bill Bennett called him), when he was winning 30 percent of the vote in two presidential primaries, about five times Robertson's own best effort?

Even if Robertston were half as important as Lind says he is, it needs to be pointed out, since Lind does not, that when Lind's original attacks on Roberston were taken up by the general media, Robertson responded to them publicly. In interviews and in paid advertisements in the *New York Times*, Robertson expressed his personal anguish and dismay at the implications that others had found in his works. He denied any intention to identify Jews as social conspirators, apologized to the Jewish community for any offense his book may have given, pointed out that nowhere in his book were the Jews explicitly singled out for blame, and recalled his longstanding efforts in behalf of Israel, which included marshalling crucial votes in Congress during the 1973 and 1990 Middle East wars, where Israel's survival may be said to have hung in the balance. He concluded his *mea culpa* by declaring that he was proud to be a strong supporter and dependable friend of both Israel and the Jews. Robertson's public disavowal of anti-Semitism—not fear—explain why Buckley and Podhoretz left Robertson relatively (but only relatively) unscathed while they were quick to descend on Buchanan, who refused to consider that his celebrated comments about Israel might be any cause for offense.

Robertson's behavior, it should be said, contrasts dramatically with that of other Israel-haters and anti-Semites, notably figures like Edward Said, Louis Farrakhan, and Gore Vidal, one of Lind's new friends, who once described Podhoretz and Midge Decter as "fifth columnists" for Israel. Farrakhan, unlike Robertson, actually preaches a virulent anti-Semitism to his flock and, moreover, through an infamous "covenant" with the Congressional Black Caucus, has been embraced by forty representatives of the party Lind has chosen for his new ideological home.

In composing *The New World Order*, Robertson did draw on tired conspiracy theories from anti-Semitic texts. But what is interesting about his use of those texts is his decision to remove most of their references to Jews, and specifically to the Jewish identity of the leaders of the alleged conspiracies. This is a peculiar quirk, to say the least, for an anti-Semite, let alone the neo-Nazi menace of Lind's imaginings.

Lind actually draws the reader's attention to this editorial process, but implies that Robertson's omission of the ethnic particulars of his conspirators is *additional* proof of Robertson's anti-Semitism: "Throughout *The New World Order*, as I shall show in further detail below, Robertson uses 'German' or 'European' where his anti-Semitic sources have 'Jewish.'" Lind quotes a passage from Robertson's text and inserts in brackets the offending connections Roberston has removed (the editorial ellipses are Lind's): "Later the European powers [i.e., bankers like the Rothschilds—Lind] began to see the wealth of North

America as a great treasure, and some of them still wanted to get their tentacles into America's economy [note the octopus metaphor, a staple of anti-Semitic and anti-capitalist rhetoric—Lind]. They eventually did so not by force, but by investing their money here, by sending people [i.e., Jewish bankers like Paul Warburg and Jacob Schiff—Lind], and by buying land." It is perfectly bizarre to suggest that the author took pains to hide his own anti-Semitic points, requiring an interlocutor like Lind to re-insert them, but that is exactly what Lind does.

Lind calls this "The Pat Roberston Scandal." The questions to ask, which he doesn't, are these: (1) Are Robertson's politics actually governed by these conspiratorial views (and if so how did he come to be an early supporter of Bob Dole)? (2) Are they shared by Ralph Reed, the director of the Christian Coalition, whom everybody, including his liberal opponents, agrees is a sophisticated political strategist and not a religious fanatic? (3) Are they shared by the 1.8 million members of the Christian Coalition, which as even Lind is forced to admit is a group connected only by direct mail solicitations and not a party or cult in the manner of the John Birch Society or the Nation of Islam? Lind makes no effort to assemble evidence that would illuminate or answer these crucial questions or ascertain whether Pat Robertson's conspiracy views are anything more than one man's hot air. In other words, Lind's "analysis" is completely devoid of any real world reference.

Lind goes on to lump Robertson with David Duke, who (unlike Robertson) is a card-carrying member of racist hate groups, and to assert, without argument or evidence, that a direct-mail group like the Christian Coalition is identical to a real membership organization like the John Birch Society. Lind takes Buckley's unwillingness to attack Robertson as an indication of the historic capitulation of mainstream conservatism to the anti-Semitic right. But he never allows for the possibility that Buckley might regard Robertson's views as eccentric and not reflecting widespread beliefs among his followers. The kooky doctrines of John Birch Society leader Robert Welch, which Buckley denounced, demonstrably infected Welch's politics and that of his followers. Welch publicly attacked Dwight Eisenhower, a moderate Re-

publican, as a communist, and his acolytes followed suit. Lind does
not mention a single occasion during the six years of the Christian
Coalition's existence that its policies have reflected a conspiratorial
mentality or an "anti-ZOG" agenda. Buckley's failure to attack Robertson
is the result of his (correct) judgment that Robertson is not a Robert
Welch.

One section of this malicious book held a perverse fascination for
me. It was Lind's effort to explain the world of intellectual conservatism, an environment with which I have become quite familiar. Lind's
analysis is contained in a chapter called the "The Triangular Trade:
How the Conservative Movement Works," and is as dishonestly constructed and argued as the title itself: "One might speak of the interac-
tion of money, ideas, and activists on the right as a 'triangular trade,'
like the Eighteenth Century cycle of rum-slaves-molasses." (In short
all the canards the left likes to peddle about conservatives are in place
in this mean-spirited little tract.)

According to Lind, the first leg of this "trade" is the "grass-roots"
right, which he identifies as the Goldwater-YAF-right, linked via Lind's
McCarthy-like leaps to the John Birch society, *National Review*, and
all the dread demons—the anti-Semites, the bigots, the militia storm
troopers, and killers of federal agents—that seem to crop up on every
other page of his book. The second leg in the trade is the "corporate
right," which turns out to be the hoary specter of Wall Street and Big
Business. The business elite, according to Lind, has "acquired its own
intelligentsia in the form of libertarians," specifically the Cato Institute, which in Lind's fantasies draft all the tax-cuts-for-the-wealthy-
legislation that incite Democratic fits of egalitarian bile. According to
Lind, "the strategy of the modern Republican party is based on a division of labor, with the grass-roots right serving as an electoral coalition,
and the libertarian right as a governing elite."

According to Lind, this arrangement presents a problem for Republicans, because the libertarians regard the grass-roots Goldwaterites
as "fascists," while the Goldwater fascists regard the libertarians as be-
trayers of their authoritarian dreams. Making this alliance work requires an "umbrella ideology," which is provided by the third part of

Lind's "triangular trade," the neoconservative "brain trust," a network of intellectual think tanks like the Heritage Foundation and the American Enterprise Institute. The purpose of the think tanks is to compel conservative intellectuals, through monetary bribes, to shill for the Republican agenda.

The picture that Lind paints is as remote from the realities of contemporary conservatism as Pluto from the sun. To take one example, Marshall Wittman, a former New Leftist and onetime head of the Waco, Texas, Free Angela Davis Committee, was until recently the legislative director of the Christian Coalition in Washington and thus in Lind's typology a crypto-fascist anti-Semite. Wittman, however, is a Jew. He is now the congressional liason for the Heritage Foundation, the biggest policy think tank on the right and actually the most influential in helping to formulate the Republican agenda. But the Heritage Foundation is not addressed at all in Lind's text (even though he worked there) because it is not libertarian and, therefore, completely refutes his thesis about how Republican policy may be shaped.

My friend Shawn Steel is a veteran of the Goldwater campaign, a former YAF-er, and a grassroots activist. He is also treasurer of the California Republican Party[2] and finance chair for Republican congressman Dana Rohrabacher's campaign organization. He is also on the board of the Center for the Study of Popular Culture (which I head), part of what Lind would call the neoconservative "brain trust." Both Steel and Rohrabacher are devout libertarians, farther from being "fascists" than any of my former comrades on the left including all of Lind's new friends. Both have been particularly active in recruiting Asian Americans to the Republican cause.

Neither, however, is unique. A reunion of Goldwater activists was held in Orange County during the presidential primaries four years ago, which I attended. Every significant right-wing Republican from the California congressional delegation and legislature was present to honor Howard Ahmanson, whom the *Los Angeles Times* described as the "king of the religious right" in the state. Ahmanson, however, opposed Proposition 187, California's anti-illegal immigration initiative. Nearly every speaker (there were twenty-seven), led by Representative

"B-1 Bob" Dornan, supported the moderate George Bush for president over Pat Buchanan. So much for Lind's guide to how the conservative movement works.

Lind's analysis amounts to little more than the kind of crackpot conspiracy theory he ostentatiously derides when Pat Robertson is the author. According to Lind, "the modern conservative brain trust originated in a scheme hatched in the 1970s by William E. Simon, Irving Kristol, and others." The plan was to make conservative intellectuals, hitherto an independent-minded, quirky, and diverse community, a controlled monolith that would function as the reliable tool of the Republican Party. "By the early 1990s, thanks to the success of the Simon-Kristol initiative, almost all major conservative magazines, think tanks, and even individual scholars had become dependent on money from a small number of conservative foundations." Lind has in mind the Olin, Bradley, and Scaife foundations.

At this point in Lind's text, the puppetmasters Simon and Kristol are being routinely referred to as the "Wall Street corporate raider" and "the ex-communist-apparatchik." For the record, it is worth noting that Irving Kristol's connection to "Communism" is this: he spent a year in 1938 in a Trotskyist splinter group arguing with the apparatchiks and showing what a poor Leninist he was.

Smears like this are not incidental to Lind's argument; they *are* his argument. Lind writes, "the conservative movement these ex-radicals [like Kristol] crafted was therefore one that adopted the characteristic institutions and strategies of communism while purveying an anti-communist (not merely a non-communist) message." Of course, the real Communist Party imposed conformity on its intellectuals through ideology and terror, something unavailable to conservatives in America. Kristol's "party," according to Lind, imposes identical uniformity through the dispensation of monies under the control of a few right-wing foundations. "What passes for intellectual conservatism is little more than the subsidized propaganda wing of the Republican Party. Public dissent on matters of concern to the U.S. business elite is not tolerated."

This is a pathetic rant. Joshua Muravchik and Ben Wattenberg, to name just two prominent fellows at the American Enterprise Institute (AEI), signed a public ad supporting Bill Clinton in 1992, without any consequences. Currently, there are at least three conflicting and hotly debated conservative positions on immigration reform, an issue of obvious concern to the business elite. In fact, the head of one conservative think tank has been hired by Silicon Valley computer firms to promote open immigration, while others call for greater restrictions. Jack Kemp and Bill Bennett, whose Empower America qualifies as a unit of the "brain trust," flew to California to oppose Proposition 187 in the midst of the election campaign, although the Initiative was supported by the heads of all of California's conservative think tanks, including Claremont and the Pacific Research Institute. Almost every conservative journal has published internal debates on this issue.

Irving Kristol, the grand puppetmaster himself, is (correctly) described by Lind as censorious on cultural issues. But then Lind doesn't explain how it is that congressional Republicans have led the fight against the V-Chip and censorship on the Internet. The range of issues on which conservatives disagree is almost endless. *National Review* recently published a cover feature by Bill Buckley calling for the legalization of drugs, to the dismay of Bill Bennett and most of the conservative intellectual community, including its own editorial board.

An even more instructive incident occurred on the publication of Dinesh D'Souza's *The End of Racism*. While the D'Souza book was funded in part by one of Lind's demonic right-wing foundations, it was publicly attacked by two foundation-funded conservative intellectuals and charter members of the "brain trust," Glenn Loury and Bob Woodson. So much for the party line.

High profile conservative intellectuals like Dinesh D'Souza and Charles Murray merit extra punishment at Lind's unscrupulous hands. Murray is indisputably one of the leading social scientists in America, but he and D'Souza are portrayed by Lind as intellectual whores—"subsidized conservative publicists"—hired to promote the political agendas of the Republican Party. "If this seems too harsh a judgment," writes Lind, "suppose that Murray's research had convinced him that in fact Head Start programs did work, and needed to be substantially expanded—and that to do so he recommended higher income taxes on the rich. One need not be a complete cynic to think that he might have trouble getting grants in the future from conservative foundations, or renewing his stay at the American Enterprise Institute."

If complete cynicism is not required to follow Lind's argument, a dose of ideological blindness might help. First, there has been little or no opposition to Head Start programs from conservative intellectuals. Second, how could anyone overlook the fact that Murray and D'Souza are best-selling authors and national celebrities who can command six-figure book contracts and lucrative speaking fees and thus are quite able to support themselves in the unlikely event that the American Enterprise Institute should decide to terminate them for such deviant views. But the American Enterprise Institute is hardly the only conservative institution available, while contrary to Lind's slander, the conservative universe is the opposite of monolithic. In fact, Charles Murray left another conservative think tank to come to the American Enterprise Institute precisely because the first did not want to support his work on *The Bell Curve*. Dinesh D'Souza eventually went to the Hoover Institution, a conservative brain trust where almost half the fellows are Democrats. So much for Lind's caricature.

Lind cannot even be trusted to tell the truth about himself. A brief autobiographical digression in Lind's book lets out that he is little more than a political poseur. The man who has exploited his minor league political metamorphosis for major personal gain reveals here that he was never actually a conservative at all: "My political journey has been far less dramatic than a switch from left to right," he confesses midway through *Up from Conservatism*. "My political views have scarcely changed since college."

Astoundingly, given the fanfare surrounding his "conversion," Lind's views are those of a centrist Democrat whose political hero is Lyndon Baines Johnson. Notwithstanding this fact, Lind was able to insinuate himself into the monolithic, ZOG-hating conservative movement while still at Yale, accepting a job at *National Review*, and proceeding mole-like for ten years to burrow through conservative institutions—the Heritage Foundation, the Bush administration, and ultimately the *National Interest*—taking advantage of the goodwill of conservative patrons along the way, only to turn them into the unlikely villains of his intellectually vapid, self-promoting tract.

Shortly after Peter Collier and I first entered the conservative world, I had a lunch with Norman Podhoretz, who warned me, "When you were on the left, you got away with everything. Now that you're on the right, you'd better be careful, because they won't let you get away with anything." Michael Lind has made the reverse crossing. "Getting Away with Everything" would have been a good title for this reprehensible, gutter-sniping book.

27

Defending Christopher Hitchens

L ET ME BEGIN BY ACKNOWLEDGING THE OBVIOUS: I may be the last person an ideological leftist like Christopher Hitchens would have wanted to see defending him in his imbroglio with White House henchman and ex-friend Sidney Blumenthal. This affair was triggered when Hitchens signed an affidavit to House investigators testifying that Blumenthal had lied to the federal grand jury in the Lewinsky scandal. Christopher and I were also once political comrades, though we were never quite close enough to become friends. But for nearly two decades we have been squaring off on opposite sides of the political barricades, and I knew that Christopher's detractors would inevitably use my support of him to confirm that he had lost his political bearings and betrayed them to the other side. Christopher has not had second thoughts about the left, nor is he ever likely to join Peter Collier and me as critics of the movement to which he has dedicated his life.[1] On the contrary. As everything Christopher has put on the public record attests, his contempt for Clinton and his decision to expose Clinton's servant as a liar spring from his deep passion for the left and for the values it claims to hold dear.

In two mordant and incisive articles in *Vanity Fair* before this epi-

This article first appeared on *Salon.com* on March 1, 1999. It was reprinted in *Hating Whitey & Other Progressive Causes* (1999).

sode, Hitchens demonstrated that the nation's commander in chief cynically and mendaciously deployed the armed forces of the greatest superpower on earth to strike at three impoverished countries, with no clear military objective in mind. Using the most advanced weaponry the world has ever seen, Clinton launched missiles into the Sudan, Afghanistan, and Iraq for only one tangible political purpose (as Hitchens put it): to "distract attention from his filthy lunge at a beret-wearing cupcake."

Hitchens' claim that Clinton's military actions were criminal and impeachable is surely correct. Republicans, it seems, were right about the character issue and failed only to show how this mattered to policy issues the public cared deeply about. Instead they got themselves entangled in legalistic disputes about perjury and constitutional impeachment bars and lost the electorate along the way. In making his own strong case against Clinton, Hitchens has underscored how Republicans botched the process by focusing on criminality that flowed from minor abuses of power—the sexual harassment of Paula Jones and its Lewinsky subtext—while ignoring a major abuse that involved corrupting the office of commander in chief, damaging the nation's security, and killing innocents abroad.

Reading Hitchens's riveting indictment stirred unexpected feelings of nostalgia in me for the left I had once been part of. Not the actual left that I came to know and reject, but the left of my youthful idealism, when I thought our mission was to be the nation's "conscience," to speak truth to power in the name of what is just. This, as is perfectly evident from what he has written, was Hitchens's own mission in exposing Blumenthal as the willing agent of a corrupt regime and its reckless commander in chief. In carrying out this mission, Hitchens stumbled on the Lewinsky matter, specifically Blumenthal's effort to smear the key witness to the president's bad faith. But that is because it was through Lewinsky that the Starr investigators had set up the character issue in the first place.

It is difficult to believe that a sociopathic personality like Clinton's could be compartmentalized to stop at the water's edge of sex, or that he is innocent of other serious accusations against him that Starr and the Republicans have been unable to prove. In fact, the same signature behavior is apparent throughout his administration (an idea aptly captured in the title of Hitchens's book about the president, *No One Left to Lie To*). The presidential pathology is evident not only in his reckless private dalliances (the betrayal of family and office), but also in his strategy of political "triangulation" (the betrayal of allies and friends), and in his fire sale of the Lincoln bedroom and advanced military technology to adversarial powers (the betrayal of country). Hitchens is quite right (if imprudent) to strike at the agent of the King, when the King is ultimately to blame.

Given the transparent morality of Hitchens's anti-Clinton crusade, it is all the more remarkable, and interesting, that so many of his comrades on the left, who ought to share these concerns, chose instead to turn on him so viciously. In a brutal display of comradely betrayal, they publicly shunned him in an attempt to cut him off socially from his own community. One after another, they rushed into print to tell the world at large how repulsed they were by a man whom only yesterday they still called "friend" and whom they no longer wish to know.

Leading this pack was Hitchens' longtime *Nation* colleague Alexander Cockburn, who denounced him as a "Judas" and "snitch." Cockburn was followed by a second *Nation* colleague, Katha Pollitt, who smeared Hitchens as a throwback to McCarthy era informers ("Let's say the Communist Party was bad and wrong. . . . Why help the repressive powers of the state? Let the government do its own dirty work.") She was joined by a thirty-year political comrade, Todd Gitlin, who warned anyone who cared to listen that Hitchens was a social "poison" in the same toxic league as Ken Starr and Linda Tripp.

Consider the remarkable nature of this spectacle. Could one imagine a similar ritual performed by journalists of the right? Robert Novak, say, flanked by Patrick Buchanan and William. F. Buckley, proclaiming an anathema on Bill Safire, because the columnist had called for the jailing of Ollie North during the Iran-Contra hearings? Not even North felt the need to announce such a public divorce. When was the last time any conservative figure (let alone a gathering of conservative figures) stepped forward to declare they were ending a private friend-ship over a political disagreement?

The curses rained on Hitchens' head were part of a ritual that has become familiar over generations of the left, in which dissidents are excommunicated (and consigned to various Siberias) for their political deviance. It is a phenomenon typical of religious cults, where purity of heart is maintained through avoiding contact with the unclean. To have caused the left to invoke so drastic a measure, Hitchens had evi-dently violated a fundamental principle of its faith. But what was it?

In fact, there seem to be at least two charges attached to Hitchens's transgression. On the one hand he was accused of "snitching" on a political ally; on the other he was said to have betrayed a friend. These are not obviously identical. Nor is it obvious that the left as a matter of principle is generally outraged about either. Daniel Ellsberg, to cite one example, is a radical snitch who betrayed not only his political allies but his own government. Yet Ellsberg is a hero to the left. David Brock, who also kissed and told, is not exactly persona non grata among leftists either. The left's standards for snitching on itself are entirely different from its standards for those who snitch on its enemies.

Hitchens's *Nation* editor, Victor Navasky, has written a whole vol-ume about the McCarthy era called *Naming Names* on the premise that the act of snitching is worse than the crimes it reveals *because* it involves personal betrayal. On the other hand, the bond of comrade-ship, of loyalty, of belonging, is exactly the bond that every organized crime syndicate exploits to establish and maintain its rule.

There was an immediate reminder of these connections in the Paul Robeson centennial that progressives were observing at the time Hitchens and Blumenthal ceased to be friends. In a variety of cultural and political events held across the nation, the left was celebrating the life and achievement of one of its great heroes on the hundredth anni-versary of his birth. Robeson, however, is a man who also betrayed his friend, in his case the Yiddish poet Itzhak Pfeffer, not to mention thousands of other Soviet Jews, who were under a death sentence im-posed by Robeson's own hero, Stalin. In refusing to help them, despite

Pfeffer's personal plea to him to do so, Robeson was acting under a code of silence that prevented communists like him from "snitching" on the crimes their comrades committed. They justified their silence in the name of the progressive cause, allowing the murderers among them to destroy not only millions of innocent lives, but their socialist dream as well.

That same spring, the Motion Picture Academy honored Elia Kazan, a theater legend who had been blacklisted for nearly half a century by the Hollywood left. He, too, was called a "Judas" by leftist members of the Academy protesting his award. Kazan's sin was to testify before a congressional committee about his fellow Communists who were also loyal supporters of Stalin's monstrous regime and who conducted their own blacklist of anti-Stalinists in the entertainment community. Kazan's most celebrated film, *On the Waterfront*, scripted by another disillusioned Communist, Budd Schulberg, depicts a longshoreman who "snitches" to a congressional committee that is investigating organized crime, specifically a mob that controls his own union and exploits its membership. It is a thinly veiled commentary on Kazan's and Schulberg's experiences in the left.

"Snitching" is how the progressive mob regards the act of speaking truth to power, when the power is its own. The mafia calls its code of silence omerta, because the penalty for speaking against the mob is death. The left's penalty for defection (in those countries where it does not exercise state power) is excommunication from its community of saints. This is a kind of death, too.

Cognizant of these realities, I avoided informing on friends or even "outing" them, during my own journey out of the left many years ago. In fact, my first political statements opposing the left were made a decade after I had ceased to be an active participant in its cause, and when the battles I had participated in were over. This did not make an iota of difference, however, when it came to my former comrades denouncing me as a "renegade," as though I in fact had become an informer. I was subjected to the same kind of personal betrayal Hitchens is experiencing now. With only a handful of exceptions, all the friends

I had made in the first forty years of my life turned their backs on me, refusing to know me, when my politics changed.

This tainting and ostracism of sinners is, in fact, the secret power of the leftist faith. It is what keeps the faithful, faithful. The spectacle of what happens to a heretic like Hitchens when he challenges the party line is a warning to others not to try it. This is why Alger Hiss kept his silence to the end, and why, even thirty and fifty years after the fact, the memoirs of leftists are so elusive and disingenuous when it comes to telling the hard political and personal truths about who they were and what they did. To tell a threatening truth is to risk vanishing in the progressive communities where you have staked your life ground. And to risk vanishing in memory too. Hitchens's crime is not the betrayal of friendship. It is the betrayal of progressive politics, the only bond the left takes seriously.

This is far from obvious to those who have never been insiders. Writing in the *Wall Street Journal*, the otherwise perceptive Roger Kimball described what has happened to Hitchens under the following title: "Leftists Sacrifice Truth on the Altar of Friendship." But this presumes either that they were closer friends of Blumenthal than of Hitchens or that friendship means more to them than politics. None of the denouncers of Hitchens claimed a closer friendship with Blumenthal as a reason for their choice. Moreover, there is not the slightest reason to suppose that these leftists would remain friends of Blumenthal should he, in turn, reveal what he really knows about Clinton's obstructions of justice and the machinations of the White House crew.

To examine an actual betrayal of friendship one need go no further than Cockburn's *New York Press* column outing Hitchens as a compulsive snitch. Friends can take different political paths and still honor the life that was once between them, the qualities and virtues that made them friends. Alex was once closer to Hitchens than Blumenthal ever was. They knew each other longer and their friendship was deeper. Hitchens even named his own son "Alex" out of admiration for his friend. But in his column, Alex gratuitously smeared

Hitchens (who is married) as an aggressive closet homosexual, an odorous, ill-mannered and obnoxious drunk, and a pervert who gets a sexual *frisson* out of ratting on his intimates. Not a single member of Hitchens' former community, which includes people who have known Hitchens as a comrade for thirty years, has stepped forward to defend him from the ugly slander.

What then inspires these auto da fes? It is the fact that the community of the left is a community of meaning, and is bound by ties that are fundamentally religious. For the non-religious, politics is the art of managing the possible. For the left, it is the path to a social redemption. This messianism is its political essence. For the left, the agenda of politics is ultimately not about practical options concerning which reasonable people may reasonably differ. It is about moral choices that define one as human. It is about taking sides in a war that will decide the future and whether the principle of justice will prevail. It is about *us* being on the side of the angels, and *them* as the party of the damned. In the act of giving up Blumenthal to the congressional majority and the special prosecutor, Hitchens put power in the hands of the enemies of the people. He acted as one of *them*.

Katha Pollitt puts it to Hitchens this way: "Why should you, who call yourself a socialist, a man of the left, help Henry Hyde and Bob Barr and Trent Lott? If Clinton is evil, are the forces arrayed against him better, with their 100 percent ratings from the Christian coalition, and their after-dinner speaking engagements at white supremacist clubs?" Of course, Katha Pollitt doesn't for a moment think that Clinton is evil. But Hitchens's new friends obviously are. Observe how easily she invokes the McCarthy stratagems to create the taint—the demonization of Hitchens's new "friends," the guilt by association that links him to them and them to the devil, the absurd reduction of the entire Clinton opposition to these links.

The casting out of Hitchens, then, was a necessary ritual to protect the left's myth of itself as a redemptive force. How could Blumenthal, who is one of them, who is loyal to their cause, be connected to something evil, as Hitchens suggests? How could *they*? All of Hitchens's attackers and all fifty-eight members of the congressional Progressive Caucus—yesterday's vanguard opponents of American military power—supported the wanton strikes against the Sudan, Afghanistan, and Iraq, without batting a proverbial lash. Every one of them found a way to excuse Clinton's abuse of disposable women like Paula Jones, Kathleen Willey, and Monica Lewinsky. The last thing they would want to do is confront Blumenthal's collusion in a campaign to destroy one of Clinton's female nuisances because she became a political threat. After all, it's they who want the reprobate in power. In blurting out the truth, Hitchens slammed the left up against its hypocrisies and threatened to unmask their sanctimonious pretensions. This is the threat the anathema on Hitchens was designed to suppress.

Here is my own message for the condemned man: You and I, Christopher, will continue our disagreements on many important things, and perhaps most things. But I take my hat off to you for what you have done. For your dedicated pursuit of the truth in these matters, and for your courage in standing up under fire. The comrades who have left you are incapable of such acts.

VII

THE POST-COMMUNIST LEFT

28

Marx's Manifesto: 150 Years of Evil

I

T HAS BEEN HARDLY A DECADE since the statues of Lenin were toppled throughout the Soviet empire. Yet in the West, leading intellectuals, including many who would not allow themselves to be called marxists, still profess to hear in Marx's words a message they insist is relevant to our times. On this 150th anniversary of the publication of the Communist *Manifesto*, they have rushed to celebrate the only text that most of the millions who served in marxist vanguards ever bothered to read.

The *Manifesto* is, as the historical record attests, an incitement to totalitarian ambitions whose results were even bloodier than those inspired by *Mein Kampf*. In it Marx announced the doom of free market societies, declared the liberal bourgeoisie to be a "ruling class" and the democratic state its puppet, summoned proletarians and their intellectual vanguard to begin civil wars in their own countries, and thereby launched the most destructive movement in human history.

Yet the celebration of this anniversary in the intellectual heights of our political culture is marked by fulsome praise for its "brilliant" analyses and, even more preposterously, for its prescience. Both the *New York Times* and the *Los Angeles Times* have embarrassed themselves,

This article first appeared on FrontPageMagazine.com on May 27, 1998. It has been edited for this book.

in fact, by proclaiming the indispensability of Marx's malevolent tract for understanding the failings of American capitalism, the very system that brought the marxist empire to its knees. The *Times*'s review is titled, "Marx's Masterpiece at 150."

We might expect such nonsense from a communist historian like Eric Hobsbawm, who contributed the gushing introduction to an anniversary edition of the *Manifesto* published by the *New Left Review*'s Verso Press. But it is unnerving to be presented with so historically unconscious a verdict from the *New York Times*. (Imagine: "Hitler's Masterpiece at 70.") Given the current state of the intellectual culture, it is no doubt appropriate that the *Times* would pick a professor of English literature for the task (university English departments being the last redoubts of the marxist faith this side of Pyongyang). But it is ironic that the author of this birthday ode to the demonic genius should be Columbia professor Steven Marcus, a protégé of Lionel Trilling, one of the most perceptive liberal thinkers.

According to Marcus and the *Times*: "The *Manifesto* was and is a work of immense autonomous historical importance. It marks the accession of social and intellectual consciousness to a new stage of inclusiveness. It has become part of an integral modern sensibility . . . and it remains so, after the demise of Soviet Communism and its satellite regimes, the descent into moribundity of marxist movements in the world, and the end of the Cold War."

To be sure, on America's benighted college campuses this description of marxism's currency is distressingly accurate. At Harvard and Yale, marxism, or some *kitsch* version of it, has indeed become "part of an integral modern sensibility." But elsewhere, outside the ivory tower, it has not. What should concern us is the *Times*'s endorsement of the intellectual degeneration reflected in this reverence for a text that inspired human catastrophe on an unprecedented scale. The *Times* does not digest the lessons of the Communist holocaust, chuck the *Manifesto* in the intellectual dustbin where it belongs, and turn to the volumes of those who actually understood how modern societies work and therefore predicted the Communist fall (von Mises and Hayek, for example). Instead, the *Times* apparently would like its progressive readers to believe that the horrifying facts of revolutionary history should not deflect the important task of continuing the civil war against capitalist democracies that the *Manifesto* incited: "A decade after those world-historical occurrences [i.e., the fall of Communism], the *Manifesto* continues to yield itself to our reading in the new light that its enduring insights into social existence generate. It emerges ever more distinctly as an unsurpassed dramatic representation, diagnosis and prophetic array of visionary judgments on the modern world . . . . A century and a half afterward, it remains a classic expression of the society it anatomized and whose doom it prematurely announced."

Prematurely! Are we to understand by this that the *Times* thinks the bloody apocalypse Marx gleefully hoped for is still to come? Apparently yes—if, as the *Times* suggests, the *Manifesto* has "enduring insights" into capitalist economies and the societies they sustain.

Is the *Manifesto* actually correct in what it says about "social existence?" In fact, the *Manifesto* is so self-evidently wrong in these matters that its author could not even begin to explain how the article praising his bankrupt and discredited war cry could appear in the *New York Times* at all. Marx famously proclaimed that "the ruling ideas are the ideas of the ruling class" and the *New York Times* is certainly a ruling class institution by marxist standards. How is it possible that the leading publication of the "ruling class," in the principal bourgeois nation, could serve up such marxist tripe to commemorate such an epochal event?

This question is hardly incidental to a text whose principal claim is that complex societies can be explained on the basis of a single social structure—economic class—an idea announced in its very first line: "The history of all hitherto existing society is the history of class struggle." This sentence is the essence and sum of the *Manifesto*, which is not an academic study but a call to arms. The reprehensible thesis argued by the *Manifesto* is that democratic societies are not different in kind from the aristocratic and slave societies that required violent revolutions to change. Despite surface appearances, despite that, in contrast to all previous political arrangements, democracy makes the people itself "sovereign"—Marx proposes to unmask democratic capitalism as an "oppressive" and tyrannical society like all the rest. It therefore requires (and this idea justifies) extra-legal, violent means to liberate the victims from its yoke. That is why those who have been inspired by the *Manifesto* have declared war on liberal society and have spilled so much blood and spread so much misery to achieve Marx's goals.

The argument of the first section of the *Manifesto* could not be clearer: All (non-socialist) societies are divided into classes that are "oppressed" and those who oppress them. Capitalism is no different, even though its revolutions may have established democratic political structures designed to enfranchise the "oppressed." The very idea of democracy in a society where private property exists is an illusion: "The executive of the modern state is but a committee for managing the common affairs of the whole bourgeoisie." In other words, democratic elections are a sham. Capitalists rule by force masked as electoral choice. In short, the only way to achieve authentic democracy and social well being is to answer force with force. Civil war is the political answer to humanity's problems. "Workers of the world unite, you have nothing to lose but your chains." In the vision of Marx and his radical disciples, the solution to all fundamental social problems—to war, to poverty, to economic inequality—lies in promoting a conflict that will rip society apart and create a new revolutionary world from its ruins. This is the enduring—and utterly poisonous—message of the *Manifesto*, the reason why its believers have left such a trail of human slaughter behind them on their way to the progressive future.

Almost every important analytic thesis of the *Manifesto*—including its opening statement—is demonstrably false. History is not the history of class struggle, a series of conflicts between economic oppressor and oppressed. Not even the French Revolution, the historical event, which provided the basis for Marx's theoretical model, is explicable in these terms. Historians like Simon Schama and Francois Furet have established, beyond reasonable doubt, that capitalism was already thriving under the monarchy, and that it was the French nobility, not the bourgeoisie, that upended the *ancien* régime. When we look at the twentieth century, whose course has largely been determined by the forces of nationalism and racism, which Marx utterly discounted, the inadequacy of his theories becomes impossible for those not blinded by faith to dispute.

According to Marx, the bourgeois epoch possesses a distinctive feature: "It has simplified the class antagonisms: Society as a whole is more and more splitting up into two great hostile camps, into two great classes, directly facing each other: Bourgeoisie and Proletariat." But, of course, it has done no such thing. It has introduced complexity into social structure, not simplified it. It has created a great middle class and a social mobility that refutes the idea of hierarchy so central to the marxist idea. But marxists love hierarchy and can't let go of it. In fact, much of the marxist critique of capitalism reflects nothing more than a romantic longing for a feudal past in which social status is pre-ordained and irrevocable and stamps every individual with a destiny and grace: "The bourgeoisie has stripped of its halo every occupation hitherto honored and looked up to with reverent awe [complains Marx]. It has converted the physician, the lawyer, the priest, the poet, the man of science, into its paid wage laborers."

Of course, it has not exactly done this either. Instead, it has turned physician, lawyer, scientist, and poet into entrepreneurs themselves. In the open societies created by capitalist revolutionaries, social identity is not fixed. Professionals can set up as independent contractors, incorporate themselves, and move up the social and economic ladder to heights undreamed of when their status, though it may have left others in "reverent awe," was also frozen by the immutable relations of an authentic class system, which bourgeois society is not. The complexity and fluidity of class structure in developed capitalist societies has made a mockery of the core principles of marxist belief.

However misguided as a social critic, Marx was a first-rate writer and therein lies much of his appeal. His memorable descriptions of the progressive expansion of market societies under the leadership of the "bourgeoisie" provide most of the basis for claims that the *Manifesto* is a "prescient" work. Marx famously extolled the capitalist class for constantly "revolutionizing the forces of production," concluding that "the bourgeoisie, during its rule of scarcely one hundred years, has created more massive and more colossal productive forces than have all preceding generations together."

But while praising its achievements, Marx casts the bourgeoisie as an illegitimate ruler whose productive forces have "outgrown" it, so that both progress and human freedom demand its extinction. In Marx's colorful prose: "Modern bourgeois society . . . is like the sorcerer, who is no longer able to control the powers of the nether world whom he has called up by his spells," and thus is doomed to a cycle of worsening economic crises: "In these crises there breaks out an epidemic that, in all earlier epochs, would have seemed an absurdity—the epidemic of over-production. Society suddenly finds itself put back into a state of momentary barbarism; it appears as if a famine, a universal war of devastation had cut off the supply of every means of subsistence."

Thus, according to Marx, the bourgeoisie is at war with the very forces of wealth it has called into being ("The weapons with which the bourgeoisie felled feudalism to the ground are now turned against the bourgeoisie itself"). In Marx's schema, the forces of production created by the bourgeoisie create a proletarian class, which is its victim and antagonist. Because the proletariat has no property, it is in a position to abolish private property, the very condition of bourgeois production and bourgeois oppression, and thus to remove the rulers from their corporate thrones and create a society in which the economy can be organized according to a social plan. According to Marx, this development has the inevitability of a natural force: "The advance of industry, whose involuntary promoter is the bourgeoisie, replaces the isolation of the laborers, due to competition, by their revolutionary combination, due to association. The development of modern industry, therefore, cuts from under its feet the very foundation on which the bourgeoisie produces and appropriates products. What the bourgeoisie, therefore, produces, above all, is its own gravediggers. Its fall and the victory of the proletariat are equally inevitable." Well, not really. History has destroyed the credibility of this vision (unless you are an English professor writing for the *New York Times*).

Under the spell of such prose, generations of "progressives" have been drawn into the socialist fantasy and encouraged to make war on the bounties and freedoms of capitalist societies in the name of "social justice" with catastrophic consequences. Socialism has failed, bringing hundreds of millions to their knees, while capitalism has created wealth and freedom for more human beings than any society in history. Despite these irrefutable facts, in the wake of the communist catastrophe, all that "progressives" are willing to concede is that Marx's economic categories are too narrow in scope (it is necessary to confront race and gender oppression as well), while claiming that "real socialism" has not been tried. So the names are changed, and the categories are expanded, while the model and the argument remain depressingly the same.

The core marxist model is as potent a force in western societies as ever before. The model proposes that democratic societies are systems of domination and oppression that must be destroyed; that democratic processes and institutions are shams, and that a just solution to social problems lies in confrontation and political war. This model is alive and well among radical feminists, racial separatists, queer nationalists, and the rag-tag intellectual army of post-modernists, critical theorists, and *kitsch* marxists who dominate our universities and, evidently, the editorial board rooms of our major press.

Contrary to the *Times* and the academic culture it reflects, what is important to remember on this 150th anniversary of the communist *Manifesto* is that Marx was wrong. He was wrong about the oppressive nature of the bourgeoisie and the outmoded nature of capitalist production, wrong about the increasing misery of the working class, and wrong about its liberating power, wrong about the increasing concentration of wealth and the increasing polarization of class, wrong about the labor theory of value and the falling rate of profit, and wrong about the possibility of creating an advanced, democratic, industrial society by abolishing private property and the free market and adopting a social plan.

Marx's economics was already outdated and unworkable when he wrote the *Manifesto*, but even worse was his political ignorance. He

was disastrously deaf to all the resonances of the Anglo-American political tradition and the accumulated democratic wisdom ascending
from the Magna Carta to the American Constitution. Here in all his
implacable arrogance is how the "visionary" who wrote the *Manifesto*
actually saw the political future:

> When, in the course of development, class distinctions have dis-
> appeared, and all production has been concentrated in the hands
> of a vast association of the whole nation, the public power will
> lose its political character. Political power, properly so called, is
> merely the organized power of one class for oppressing another. If
> the proletariat during its contest with the bourgeoisie is com-
> pelled, by the force of circumstances, to organize itself as a class,
> if, by means of a revolution, it makes itself the ruling class, and, as
> such, sweeps away by force the old conditions of production, then
> it will, along with these conditions, have swept away the condi-
> tions for the existence of class antagonisms and of classes gener-
> ally, and will thereby have abolished its own supremacy as a class.

One billion people have been impounded in totalitarian prison-
states, and one hundred million people have been murdered in our
lifetime by marxists acting on these false premises and illusions. The
root cause of social problems is the problematic individual. Political
power is not class power; it is the power of individuals and institutions. When the power of the state is unchecked by private property
and the power of private associations—as in socialism it inevitably is—
then, far from losing its political character, public power becomes absolute, totalitarian. This is what we should remember on the 150th
anniversary of Marx's destructive work. Political power is not "merely
the organized power of one class for oppressing another." In democratic market societies, where social mobility is fluid, the people are
sovereign and the rule of law prevails, social classes (and races and genders) do not "oppress" one another. Those who inflame the passions of
revolution, in such circumstances, are inciting their followers to criminal acts and inviting destructive social consequences.

Private property, which marxists want to abolish, has been proven by history to be the indispensable bulwark of human liberty, and the only basis for producing general economic prosperity and social wealth. There are no democratic societies or industrial societies or post-industrial societies that are not based on private property and economic markets. Those who make war on private property and the "profit motive" make war on human liberty and wellbeing.

In his *Times* review, Professor Marcus writes: "Whether it is regarded as capitalist democracy as civil society, as the welfare state in transition or as the modern social contract, bourgeois society remains alive and well which means of course, as it always has, that it is in a hell of a state."

The subtext of this deplorable but revealing remark is that American society is a hell, to be rejected and despised, that it is legitimate to subvert its institutions and destroy them. This is, indeed, the curriculum in all too many college classrooms today. These are the real meanings of the *Communist Manifesto* on its 150th anniversary, and of the celebrations of the *Manifesto* by an intellectual class whose own record in this bloodiest of centuries, is a sorry and sordid one of apology and support for the totalitarian enemies of America both abroad and within.

29

From Red to Green

I
N THE TWO HUNDRED YEARS since the French Revolution, conservatives have been waging a rearguard struggle in defense of freedom against the forces of the radical left. For the last hundred tears, this political combat has taken the form of an international civil war instigated by the marxist heirs of Robespierre and Saint-Just against the democratic market societies of the West. We are now witnessing the triumphant end of the marxist epoch that began with the Bolshevik coup in 1917 and that is being drowned by cries of freedom across the whole expanse of the Soviet empire seventy-two years later.

The events in France introduced the word "revolution" into our political vocabulary, meaning the absolute break with an existing order and the establishment of a radically new one, a government of Virtue to replace the despotism of Tradition, a cult of Reason to replace the religions of Faith, the true order of Nature to replace the artificial system of Society. It was no coincidence, therefore, that the French Revolution also introduced the concept and practice of political terror. For behind the radical impulse is a consciousness alien to all that is human, rejecting the historically given needs and desires of ordinary people as "backward" and artificial, which is why the radical effort to

---

This article first appeared in *National Review*, March 19, 1990, under the title "Making the Green One Red" and has been edited for this book.

maintain its order always requires radical force and, in the end, always fails.

The political radical differs from the reformer who seeks only to right particular wrongs; the radical seeks to annihilate the social order itself. His rebellion, in the words of Marx, is "not against any wrong in particular but against wrong as such." It is this idea that produces the radical's alienation from humanity, "an idea [in the words of Gerhart Niemeyer] that implies a declaration of war by some men on the historical existence of all men." The total critique of society entails its total deconstruction and leads inexorably to the revolutionary praxis— "total hostility, total suspicion, total terror: totalitarian power."[1]

What can justify the nihilism of the revolutionary agenda? Only a vision of the coming apocalypse. Only a vision of the existing order as totally unjustified, unnatural, destructive. "Better Red than Dead." To those of us who were radicals in the 1960s, this famous slogan had a different meaning than it had for liberals to whom it signified choosing the lesser of two evils. For radicals, it meant that if we did not achieve world socialism, we would all soon be dead. Our radical idea was that capitalism engendered conflict and war; unless capitalism were destroyed, the end of civilization was inevitable. On the eve of Lenin's conquest of power, the German revolutionary Rosa Luxemburg summarized this vision of a radical apocalypse in the slogan "Socialism or barbarism!"

The apocalyptic claim is the cornerstone of radical politics. For if the cause is absolute, everything is permitted, and the real work of revolution—radical nihilism, the destruction of what is—can be carried out with no looking back. Thus, in the name of everlasting peace, radicals wage permanent revolutionary war; in the name of a final human liberation, they enslave nations; in the name of ultimate justice, they commit unparalleled crimes.

For more than seventy years, the prospect of "socialism or barbarism" served to justify the destruction of the existing societies and to legitimize the Soviet future. But those seventy years of the socialist future have made Rosa Luxemburg's claim grotesque. Today—from Estonia to Armenia, from Alexanderplatz to Tiananmen Square—the sea of humanity liberated by marxists itself proclaims: Socialism *is* barbarism.

Even as its own inhumanity and inefficiency consume revolutionary socialism in the East, however, a specter can be seen rising from its ashes in the West. The colors are no longer red but green, the accents are those of Malthus rather than Marx, but the missionary project is remarkably intact. The planet is still threatened, the present still condemned, redemption through radical politics still presses: *Better Green than Dead.* In environmentalism, radicals have found a new paradigm for the paradigm lost.

Thus, the official program of France's new Green Party echoes Rosa Luxemburg's apocalyptic cry: "The future will be green or will not be at all." And the program of Germany's Greens exhibits the distinctive accents of the totalitarian voice: "The politics of radical ecology embraces every dimension of human experience—the old age is giving way to the new." Or, in the blunter expression of the founder of American "social ecology," Murray Bookchin: "We can't heal the environment without remaking society."

The old radical Adam is back: the apocalyptic ambition, the destructive resentment, the totalitarian project. "From all the knowledge we now have about environmental issues," writes Jonathon Porritt, a spokesman for Britain's Ecology Party and the director of Friends of the Earth, "the inevitable conclusion is that our way of life cannot be sustained; we cannot go on living as we do now." The revolutionary agenda requires a revolutionary strategy. When Porritt hears politicians saying that they care for the environment and therefore want to achieve "sustainable growth," it leaves him "spitting with rage." We cannot continue, he says, "with [our] same material living standard and at the same time be warriors on behalf of the planet."

Thus radical ecology leads to the familiar threat. The virtuous state must control and restrict social wealth and redistribute it according to the radical creed. In the radical view, property—the foundation of free societies—is mere theft whose spoils are to be divided up. As Porritt argues: "We in the West have the standard of living we do only because we are so good at stripping the Earth of its resources and oppressing the rest of the world's people in order to maintain that wealth." To achieve ecological balance means "progressively narrowing the gap to reduce the differences between the Earth's wealthiest and poorest inhabitants until there are 'more or less equal shares for all people.'"

Karl Marx described this prescription 150 years ago when he wrote, "Primitive communism is only the culmination of envy and leveling down on the basis of a preconceived minimum. How little this abolition of private property represents a genuine appropriation is shown by [its] abstract negation of the whole world of culture and civilization, and [its] regression to the unnatural simplicity of the poor, rough man without wants, who has not only not surpassed private property but has not yet even attained to it." Eco-socialism *is* barbarism.

Jonathon Porritt is a leader of the "moderate" wing of the radical environmental movement. David Brower, the founder of Porritt's organization, departed some years ago to create the more radical Earth Island Institute in Berkeley. Last June, Brower took his place alongside Nicaraguan dictator Daniel Ortega as co-sponsor of the fourth biennial meeting of the International Congress on the Hope and Fate of the Earth in Managua. One thousand delegates from more than seventy nations met at the Olaf Palme Center to denounce the United States and the other "imperialist" predators of the free world and to launch a new movement of "solidarity environmentalism," by establishing alliances with radicals in Third World countries. According to Brower's magazine, "the consensus at the Congress was that 'solidarity environmentalism' is the only kind that makes sense. . . . Would George Bush and Margaret Thatcher be able to call themselves environmentalists if the effort to protect the ozone layer and stop global warming was linked to the Third World movement's demands for a new, more equitable international economic system, an end to the Third World debt, and curbs on the free action of multinational corporations?"

In Managua, the political symbolism of the Green united front was all in place: Swedish social democracy, British eco-socialism. Third World marxism-Leninism, and American auto-nihilism. This development reflects the fact that the Green movement has grown to its present dimensions out of the crisis of the left—the necessity of establishing a face-saving distance from the catastrophe of marxist liberation in the socialist bloc. To avoid the taint of the socialist past, the Green parties of Europe and even primitive communists like Porritt constantly emphasize that their movement is "neither left nor right" and distinguish the "politics of ecology" from the "politics of industrialism" (i.e., of economic growth), which characterize both capitalist and socialist societies. But from a historical perspective, it would be more accurate to say that the Green movement is a phenomenon of both the political left and the political far right, uniting in itself the two traditions of radical totalitarian revolt against liberal order in the twentieth century—communism and fascism—and aspiring to be the third wave of the gnostic assault against freedom in our lifetime.

The fascist roots of the Green movement are well known. National Socialists were naturists long before the post-Khrushchev left discovered ecology, and the Nazis have been justly described as "the first radical environmentalists in charge of a state." Indeed, the enthronement of biological imperatives, of the virtues of blood and soil and the primitive communities of the Volk, the pagan rejection of the Judeo-Christian God, and the radical anti-humanism of the Greens are even more obviously derivative of fascist than strictly marxist political traditions. But despite tensions that exist between the deep ecologists of the environmental right wing and the eco-socialists of its left wing, they are indissolubly joined in the common embrace of a single illusion: the gnostic idea that humanity has been alienated from its natural self and that its redemption can be achieved by political means, implying a declaration of war by a chosen few against the historical existence of all.

Thomas Lovejoy has even expressed the radical anti-humanism of the Greens in a statement reminiscent of Susan Sontag's infamous indictment of the white race, during the 1960s, as the "cancer of history": "The planet is about to break out into a fever and we are the disease." Appearing to be a new ideological wrinkle at first, this in fact is the same old anti-humanism of the radical tradition, the very malevolence that has brought it to its present grief. For there is no "true self" of mankind to be liberated, as Marx maintained, other than the historical self that we see manifest in its historical acts. The liberation of humanity in the sense of a restoration of its natural self is a radical myth. The radical reality is its assault on humanity. What motivates radicals is not compassion for the lost soul of mankind, but hatred of human beings as they are. To the radical, whatever is, is wrong.

Ironically, however, it is this very antagonism to common humanity that, through the cunning of history, has proved to be the radicals' current undoing. In the name of injustice done to the proletariat, marxists were able to carry out their work of destruction against bourgeois society. But once in power, marxism—like fascism—exploited, oppressed, and ruined the very masses it claimed to liberate. Having soared to power on dreams of transcendence, the radical enterprise succumbed to the gravitational pull of human nature, which even massive doses of terror and repression could not undo.

The inability to remake humanity has now caused marxism to founder; the very victims in whose name its assault was carried out have now rejected it, so that marxism can no longer speak in their name or invoke their suffering to justify its destructive agendas. This is the real crisis of the radical left—and environmentalism is its solution.

In the environment, the left has found a victim to champion that cannot reject it, a victim that will provide endless justification for its destructive agendas. This is the truly new element in the Green revolution: a constituency—nature—that cannot speak for itself. The conflict between vanguard and victim that has plagued generations of the left has been thus eliminated. What remains is the hubris of the radical remnant, the self-chosen saviors for whom the human condition is not a reality we must come to terms with, but material that we must approach as gods and redeemers to subdue and transform.

What then is the conservative response to the environmental crisis and the radical threat? Conservatism is an anti-gnostic, anti-revolutionary attitude that accepts the fallen, unequal, alienated state of mankind and seeks to preserve the conditions of culture and freedom that human enterprise and moral imagination have created. That conservatives recognize and accept the problematic nature of human existence does not mean that they embrace a passive attitude towards the problems of human societies. On the contrary, their authentic concern about the fate and welfare of real human beings is attested to by their two-hundred-year struggle in defense of freedom. But now that the moment has come in which they are victors in this struggle and the left lies defeated on the plain of battle, they must reemphasize the active, progressive side of the conservative project, accepting their responsibility as captains of the democratic ship of state. For, as Burke admonished, "a state without the means of some change is without the means of its conservation."

Conservatives should not surrender the defense of the environment to the left, any more than we should surrender the defense of the Republic or of human rights to their historic enemies. Conservatives must not be blindly reactive, conceiving their role merely as a negative force, a check on radical hubris. Despite our commitment to liberty, indeed because of it, conservatives have maintained the peace and preserved the Republic as the foundation of our freedom by arming the state. Conservatives should not be afraid of the costs necessary to defend the environment as a foundation of our communal health and human heritage. Not all growth is good. (Metastasis is growth, too.) Nor is every event that calls itself a revolution bad. Two hundred years ago, conservatives took the lead in an American revolution to preserve their rights as Englishmen; today, they must take the lead in the reforms necessary to preserve the environment—both human and natural—as well.

30

V-Day, 2001

WHEN JANE FONDA WAS THIRTEEN YEARS OLD, her mother went into the family bathroom, closed the door, and slit her throat from ear to ear. Just beyond the threshold, she left a note for the maid saying that there was a mess inside, and to please clean it up. That evening Jane's father, Henry Fonda, went on stage, as usual, to perform the role of Mr. Roberts in the Broadway play in which he was starring. He never told his daughter her mother had committed suicide. She learned about it three years later in the pages of a movie fan magazine, which she read while at summer camp. Jane Fonda has spent the rest of her life trying to cope with a hurt that no human being can heal.

These biographical details are brought to mind by Jane Fonda's latest cause—the "Violence Against Women Day" or "V-Day" demonstrations that were held in 2001 in fifty cities, on two hundred college campuses and in Madison Square Garden. Fonda bankrolled the events to the tune of $1 million. The demonstrations were part of an effort by feminists across the country to transform Valentine's Day, a millennia-old celebration of romance and friendship, into a "Violence Against Women Day," a mass indictment of men. A novelist could not have

This article first appeared on *Salon.com* on February 13, 2001. It has been edited for this book.

formed the metaphor of Jane's childhood trauma and adult therapy more acutely: Valentine into violence.

While Jane Fonda has provided the organizing funds, the event is obviously not just an expression of personal distress; it is a social movement of the political left. In a manifesto prepared for the occasion, the organizers defined the purpose of the renaming as an effort to proclaim "Valentine's Day as V-Day until the violence stops. When all women live in safety, then it will be known as Victory Over Violence Day."

Of course, the idea that someday all women will "live in safety" is a utopian fantasy—the impossible dream of a heaven on earth, where the sick will be healed and the wounded made whole. How is this world—the real world of flesh and blood human beings, a world where people fail and abuse each other—ever going to be made safe for youngsters like Jane? There will always be troubled parents who will damage their own children. And those who are damaged will pass the damage on.

It was a messianic illusion that energized the thousands of women who flocked to Jane's cause, not so much a political movement as a false religious faith. It is a quest for salvation through political action, a yearning for redemption without God. It is, in fact, the yearning for a God who—for whatever reason—is absent from their hearts. The actress Glenn Close, who was one of the many celebrity adornments for the event, put the illusion into words when she described Eve Ensler—the woman who came up with the idea for V-Day—as a divine incarnation: "She is giving us our souls back."

Like all faiths that look to politics for redemption, the V-Day religion is also a creed of hate. Those who are saved, are saved only because others are damned. In authentic religions, the sacred is separated from the profane, the earthly from the divine. Final judgments are left to God. It is God who damns, God who forgives, and God who redeems. In authentic religions, each person understands himself as a sinner, and none mistakes himself for a savior.

But in political religions, human beings propose to act as saviors, judging and condemning, using their wisdom and power to redeem us all. But in politics, there is no redemption. There is only the bloody history of the left, its drama of guillotine and gulag, marching endlessly through time.

To celebrate and sanctify its false religious faith, the feminist left proposes to take the one holiday a year dedicated to the fallible love that men and women manage to show for each other, and turn it into a day of rage against men, as though men had the answers. As though vanquishing men, like defeating the devil himself, could redeem the world.

According to the organizers of V-Day, "22 to 35 percent of women who visit emergency rooms are there for injuries related to ongoing abuse." This makes the United States, in their eyes, one of the most repressive and barbarous places on earth. But, as Christina Hoff Sommers has noted, the actual figure of abuse according to Bureau of Justice statistics is one-half of one percent. Why the wild exaggeration? To establish the religion. To give the devil his due. As Sommers wrote: "The true numbers are apparently not high enough for V-Day proponents. They are determined to implicate the average American man in an ongoing social atrocity and to place the United States on a moral par with countries that practice genital mutilation and bride burnings."[1]

Jane Fonda's life has been consumed by hatreds in the name of love, like V-Day. During the Vietnam conflict, she traveled half-way around the world to commit treason, indicting American soldiers over Radio Hanoi as "war criminals," and abetting their torturers on a visit to the infamous "Hanoi Hilton." In her eyes, redemption would come in the victory of Communism. At a college rally in Michigan, she told her audience of students, "I would think that if you understood what Communism was, you would hope, you would pray on your knees that we would someday become Communist."

Jane's hatred for America and her love for communism have been central tenets of the leftist religion for nearly a century. Of course the left is not politically stupid or merely suicidal. It knows to veil its truest faith. Outwardly, leftists are all post-modernists now, and would not directly defend the gulag as they once did. Marxism itself has undergone revision. In the old days, marxists demonized "the ruling class." Now, there is a trinity of hate as whites, males, and heterosexuals are added to the old formulas of belief. In 2001, this new trinity was prominent in the chants of the left at the inauguration of a new Republican president: "Racist, sexist, anti-gay—George Bush go away." The same demonization of others, as in the communist generations before them; the same idolatrous belief in themselves as social redeemers.

The founder of V-Day is the author of "The Vagina Monologues," a compendium of feminist animus towards men. V-Day leaders Fonda and Close refer to themselves as soldiers in "Eve's Army." How fitting. Eve, the mother of us all, who was tempted by the serpent to "become as God," but who instead led our fall from grace into a vale of suffering and tears. It is this vale from which the left now proposes to save us.

31

AIDS: *Political Origins of an Epidemic*

WITH PETER COLLIER

L IBERTY BATHS MAY HAVE THE LOOK OF A SEXUAL YMCA—showers and a sauna, hair dryers, Coke machines, and gay men cruising the halls with towels wrapped around their waists—but it is actually part of a medical and political controversy over a sexually transmitted disease that is tearing San Francisco apart. In the basement are scores of private rooms with muffled sounds of ecstasy coming from behind closed doors. One door is open, and a man lies face down on a cot presenting himself seductively to anyone who might happen by. On the top floor is a carpeted viewing room where naked men watch gay porn on a movie screen while idly fondling each other. Down the hall a middle-aged man stands at one of the stalls that have "glory holes" cut in at waist level while a faceless stranger on the other side of the partition performs fellatio on him.

This article, written by Peter Collier and David Horowitz, first appeared in *California Magazine*, July 1983, under the title "Whitewash," and was reprinted in *Deconstructing the Left* (1995). It appeared just as the general public was becoming aware of AIDS and as the epidemic was about to break out of the three gay communities (San Francisco, Los Angeles, and New York) in which it had taken root. HIV had not yet been isolated and identified as a cause, and there were only fifteen hundred confirmed cases nationwide, compared to over 1 million today. What are now obvious truths regarding the spread of AIDS were condemned by gay activists as homophobic prejudice at the time. *California Magazine* was picketed after the article appeared.

The only place where there seems to be conversation is at the lunch counter, where two naked men are munching on hamburgers and talking about the AIDS epidemic that has begun to terrify the city. "I could get back into the closet right now," says one of the men, "and still get it in a year or two. So what would I have achieved? Celibacy?" The other nods enthusiastically. "I know," he says. "We're just little time bombs, aren't we?" Then he stands, stretches, and wipes his mouth with a napkin. "Well, I don't know about you, but I'm going to have some fun while I *tick*." After they have gone, the short-order cook shakes his head. "Did you hear that? It's like some straight joke about queers."

The humor *has* gotten grimmer in San Francisco. ("How does Anita Bryant spell relief?" goes one of the sicker jokes. "A-I-D-S.") And beneath this brittle bravado, the city exhibits the signs of profound anxiety and turmoil. Police requisition latex masks and surgical gloves when they have to deal with gays; gay landlords evict tenants showing the telltale purple lesions of Kaposi's sarcoma, a rare skin cancer associated with AIDS; patrons worry about frequenting the city's restaurants, where many of the service workers are gay; health workers who do not hesitate to deal with most grotesque street maladies treat hospitalized AIDS patients like lepers, shunting them off in remote rooms and sometimes allowing buttons to go unanswered.

It might be expected that the very organized and most powerful gay political machine in the country would have been able to deal with this situation. And in a limited way it has. Led by San Francisco's only gay supervisor, Harry Britt, and supported by mayor Dianne Feinstein, the San Francisco Board of Supervisors appropriated $4 million for the present fiscal year to combat AIDS, and the congressional offices of the late Phillip Burton (Democrat, San Francisco) and Barbara Boxer (Democrat, Marin Country) have vigorously lobbied Washington for more money. But for the most part, gay leaders have resolutely, and astonishingly, refused to speak out on the basic issue of AIDS—the medical consensus that it is contracted and spread through sexual contact—and they have failed to demand the prophylactic measures that could help contain the disease.

Recognizing this as an issue that threatens the political momentum that could lead to gay control of the board of supervisors within the next decade, gay leaders have made the matter of AIDS transmission into a "dirty little secret." As a result of their influence, until May of this year there was not a single piece of health department literature in the city's health clinics to inform their high-risk clientele of the fact that AIDS is transmitted through blood and semen. Public health officials have suppressed information about the extent of the epidemic. Attempts to close places such as the gay baths, where the anonymous public sex implicated in the spread of the disease takes place, have been preemptively crushed. And those gay public figures who have tried to provoke a discussion of the issues have often felt intimidation.

Catherine Cusic is a lesbian who heads the Gay/Lesbian Health Services Committee of the Harvey Milk Gay Democratic Club's AIDS Task Force. She is outraged by the dereliction of the gay leadership. "It is a pattern that goes back to the first appearance of AIDS," she says. "There are leaders in this community who don't want people to know the truth. Their attitude is that it is bad for business, bad for the gay image. Hundreds, perhaps thousands, are going to die because of this attitude. The whole thing borders on the homicidal."

As the medical community has worked to isolate and identify the virus it now feels certain causes AIDS, there has been a parallel struggle to define the disease socially. Some of the most violent talk has come from Christian fundamentalists, who compare AIDS to a biblical plague, and from secular moralists, who use the ready-made metaphor of Mother Nature finally striking back at transgressors against her laws. Gays, too, have been guilty of rhetorical excess. This may be understandable, given the history of discrimination and oppression from which they have so recently emerged. Carelessly using terms such as "genocide" and "holocaust," they view the slow progress of medical research as evidence of homophobia and compare it with the quick response to Legionnaire's Disease and Toxic Shock Syndrome. The AIDS virus just happens to have struck the gay community first, they say, but could as easily have had its malignant genesis in the heterosexual world.

In fact, the federal health bureaucracy has reacted forthrightly, if not especially swiftly, as AIDS has attained the critical mass necessary to make it a significant national health issue. Dr. Edward Brandt, assistant secretary of the U.S. Health and Human Services Department, has identified the disease as the "number-one priority" for the U.S. Public Health Service. In May, Congress moved to appropriate $12 million to fight the epidemic, which would bring the total federal expenditures to $26 million—considerably more than was spent battling either Legionnaire's Disease or Toxic Shock Syndrome over a longer period of time.

Gay leaders have reacted by charging that this money represents the tardy cynicism of a society worried that AIDS will jump the boundaries of the gay world and become a general menace. In fact, the disease has affected three narrowly defined high-risk groups in addition to bisexuals and gays with multiple partners: drug addicts, hemophiliacs, and Haitians. Moreover, while heterosexuals have been affected, there has often been a link to homosexuality: drug users sometimes share needles with gays; hemophiliacs receive blood from gay donors; and, according to Haitian officials, more than 30 percent of the victims in that country are homosexuals. In California, particularly, the epidemic has fallen heavily on gays, who constitute at least 90 percent of AIDS victims. Because the disease is communicable, spreading as a result of sexual contact, the only way in which the analogy with Legionnaire's Disease or Toxic Shock Syndrome would hold is if the Legionnaire's had insisted on returning to the hotel where they contracted their malady or if women had continued to use the dangerous tampons.

Columnist Herb Caen was one of the first to alert San Francisco to the confusion and schisms within the gay community. In late May he reported in the *San Francisco Chronicle* that a gay doctor had run into three of his AIDS patients in one of the baths and ordered them out, only to have them refuse to leave and threaten to sue him for breach of confidentiality. But the gay community's ambivalence in facing up to the disease is nothing new.

Several months ago, Catherine Cusic asked the city's public health department to put up posters about AIDS on buses and in other public places. The suggestion was presented to Pat Norman, a lesbian who coordinates the city's lesbian-gay health services, but no action was taken. Since then, while more and more gays have contracted AIDS, the department has been curiously uninvolved. Most public health experts, including gays, have come to the conclusion that the disease is sexually transmitted and that unprotected anal intercourse significantly increases the risk. "The agent is probably a blood-borne virus in many ways similar to Hepatitis B, which could be transmitted by direct inoculation of blood and through intimate sexual contact . . . where bleeding takes place," said Dr. Marcus Conant, who works with the gay-run Kaposi's Sarcoma/AIDS Foundation, at a recent city-sponsored AIDS symposium. However, in a pamphlet prepared by the foundation and distributed by the city, references to anal sex or any sex connected with trauma were omitted.

Cusic and other members of her committee have come to regard all this as a "conspiracy of silence," although at times it seems more to resemble a campaign of disinformation with clear political overtones. They point out that Pat Norman and the gay health activists who support her in the moderate Alice B. Toklas Memorial Democratic Club, a gay organization, have ties to the mayor's office and to political patronage. And the Toklas club apparently fears that taking a stand on the issue of the transmission of AIDS will cause a backlash against the city's institutionalized gay lifestyle and against gay businesses, which have become an important aspect of San Francisco's economy. When the Harvey Milk club recently joined a recall campaign against Mayor Feinstein, the Toklas club backed the mayor (who herself worried that the AIDS scare might keep the city from becoming a site for the 1984 Democratic Convention).

The politics involved in AIDS are not only intramural and civic but sexual as well. The philosophy of the Stonewall Gay Democratic Club is "Sex doesn't cause AIDS—a virus does." This has become the rallying cry of gays who fear the hidden message inherent in acknowledging that the disease is sexually transmitted: physician, heal thyself. In the words of one gay leader, "[People] worried that if they admitted the disease was spread sexually, everything that had been said about their lifestyle would seem true. They just wouldn't admit it, whatever the evidence."

The extent of this willingness to suppress information became clear earlier this year. Andrew Moss and Michael Gorman, two researchers at UC San Francisco Medical Center, completed a study showing that one of every 333 single men in the Castro area (including Noe Valley and the Haight) had already been diagnosed with AIDS. On January 16 and on several occasions over the following weeks, Moss and Gorman met with gay health activists from the Kaposi Sarcoma/AIDS Foundation, the Bay Area Physicians for Human Rights, three gay Democratic clubs, and public health officials to discuss their findings. Despite some dissent, however, the consensus at these meetings was against making the Moss-Gorman figures public, lest they be "misinterpreted."

At a meeting in early March to draft a statement on AIDS for the Lesbian/Gay Freedom Day Parade, Bill Kraus, an aide to the late Congressman Phil Burton, and Dana Van Gorder, of Supervisor Britt's office, strongly urged inclusion of the Moss-Gorman findings. Their proposal was defeated by Pat Norman and the other committee members, and the report languished until late that month, when it was leaked to Randy Shilts, a reporter on the *Chronicle*'s gay beat. Public health director Mervyn Silverman now says, "It didn't tell us anything we didn't already know." But he admits that he never saw the study, which was held back by health department officials. "There was never a decision that it should not be put out," Norman says, echoing Moss and Gorman's point of view, "but a question as to what context it should be put out in." Dr. Selma Dritz, assistant director of the health department's communicable disease division and a collaborator on the report, did not push the study, either. She says that the decision of whether or not to publish was up to Moss and Gorman.

Explaining his decision to publish the report, Shilts—who is gay—says, "The people in the Castro had a right to know this. If they're tricking in the bars, they've got a real good chance of tricking with someone who has the disease. I got a call from Gorman, telling me not to print the information. Gay political leaders called, including Randy Stallings [president of the Toklas club and co-chair with Norman of the Coalition for Human Rights, the umbrella organization for all the gay groups in San Francisco]. In eight years as a journalist, I've never been under such pressure to suppress a story. People keep telling me it would hurt business in the Castro, hurt the Gay Rights Bill in Sacramento. My feeling is, what the hell; if you're dead, what does the rest of it matter?"

Other gay leaders who had been pushing to get the conclusions of the Moss-Gorman study publicized and acted upon also found themselves under pressure. One of them was Kraus. "I kept saying that people have a right to know this," he says. "Those who wanted to keep the report under wraps said that if it got out, people would be afraid to come to the Castro, that AIDS patients would be thrown out of restaurants and all that. I went through an agonizing period saying to myself, 'What the hell is going on here? How can these people do this? How can they try to suppress this data?' It's still not entirely clear to me why they did it, but I do know how. They intimidate people into silence by saying that they're homophobic, anti-sex, and all kinds of other things people don't want to be called."

Ironically, during the time that this debate was going on, sixty-eight new cases of AIDS were reported. The connections between promiscuous sex and AIDS was by now so obvious to some gays that they had started masturbation clubs, were seeking more stable relationships, and had begun to criticize those who were spreading the disease. "We Know Who We Are," an article by Michael Callen and Richard Berkowitz, two gays who have AIDS, was circulating in something like *samizdat* form before finally being printed by the Sacramento gay newspaper *Mom . . . Guess What!* They cited medical evidence that gays are particularly susceptible to the disease because of repeated shocks to their immune systems from treatment for other sexually transmitted diseases, and concluded that gays must take personal responsibility for their condition. "The present epidemic of AIDS among promiscuous urban gay males is occurring because of the unprecedented promiscuity of the last ten to fifteen years," they wrote. "The commercialization of promiscuity and the explosion of establishments such as bathhouses, bookstores, and backrooms is unique in Western history. It has been mass participation in this lifestyle that has led to the creation of an increasingly disease-polluted pool of sexual partners."

Yet, while there were individual efforts to try to control the disease, there was not enough support to make it a majority movement. In a study conducted early this year, three gay psychotherapists—Leon McKusick, William Horstman, and Arthur Carfagni—compiled questionnaire responses from six hundred gay men and concluded that, while fears about AIDS were increasing and some modification of sexual activity had occurred, an alarming number of men were still engaging in high-risk behavior. An article about this study in the *Bay Area Reporter*, a leading gay paper, said that a large proportion of those interviewed were "continuing to engage in behavior that could transmit an AIDS infective agent—and at the same frequency as before they found out about AIDS." Perhaps most devastating was the finding that "gay men surveyed are still poorly informed about the disease transmission or are unwilling or unable to change sexual patterns."

The Lesbian/Gay Freedom Day Parade march, scheduled for June 26, presented an opportunity for some remedial education, but also for disaster. An estimated three hundred thousand gays from all over the United States would be coming to San Francisco and could spread the disease to uninfected communities through the country, especially if they patronized the city's bathhouses, which feature precisely the kind of sex most likely to spread AIDS. On May 24 the Harvey Milk club met and finally voted eighty to one to put out a pamphlet warning of the sexual transmission of the disease. Members of the club, among them congressional aide Bill Kraus, also joined with other concerned gay leaders to try to persuade bathhouse owners to dispense condoms and post warnings that oral and anal sex greatly increases the chances of contracting the disease. Kraus recalls that "not only were the bathhouse owners totally incensed that we'd suggest that they do something, but the Toklas club made a statement saying that what we were proposing did not represent their policy. We wound up on the defensive, spending our time explaining how we weren't really breaking ranks, et cetera, et cetera."

In desperation, Kraus joined with Cleve Jones, a gay aide to San Francisco assemblyman Art Agnos, and Ron Huberman of the Harvey Milk club and wrote a manifesto that was printed—after editor Paul Lorch sat on it for six weeks—in the *Bay Area Reporter*. "What a peculiar perversion it is of gay liberation to ignore the overwhelming scientific evidence, to keep quiet, to deny the obvious—when the lives of gay men are at stake," they wrote. "What a strange concept of our gay movement it is to care more about what they may do to us than about the need to spread the news about this disease to our people so that we can protect each other." The letter convinced Supervisor Harry Britt to take a stand on the bathhouse issue. "I didn't think he'd have the guts to do it," says Randy Shilts. "But after Kraus, Jones and Huberman published their letter, he finally saw that this was the side to be on and said in effect that we can't keep on humping like bunnies."

Others, however, saw the letter as treason to the gay cause. With the sophistry that was coming to dominate the debate, Toklas club president Randy Stallings wrote to the *Bay Area Reporter*: "No one knows what causes AIDS or how it is transmitted, but one thing is certain. If this illness is sexually transmitted, it can be transmitted from someone met in church as easily as someone met at a bathhouse. To single out one type of gay business as somehow 'responsible' for the epidemic is to begin the process of destroying our community. . . . Labeling San Francisco as unsafe for our people is inaccurate and a direct attack on the social and economic viability of our community."

But others tried to get Health Director Mervyn Silverman to close the bathhouses for the parade weekend. The public health director's response was, "It is not the bathhouses that are the problem—it's sex. People who want to have sex will find a way to have it." Shilts points out the consequences of such logic: "If one guy has sex with ten guys in a night—and some do—the risk becomes one in thirty-three for this guy. And he can take his dormant case of AIDS back to Iowa or wherever and start it going there." And Shilts sees an ultimate irony in all this: "People organizing the march want large numbers so they can have a show of force to press the federal government on AIDS research."

Shilts got so upset by the posturing and procrastination that he spent a day lobbying the board of supervisors and the mayor, eventually securing a commitment that literature specifying the risks of bathhouse sex would be distributed to patrons. At first, Silverman denied that he had the authority to enforce such a request. However, Mayor Feinstein (who was on the verge of signing sweeping legislation regulating smoking in the workplace) quoted to him the article of the city code giving him the power to act. Finally Silverman met with bathhouse owners in a new mood of realism. "Their businesses are likely to be affected if people keep dying from this damned thing," he said. "It is in everybody's interest—through altruism and humanitarianism, but also capitalism—to get this thing taken care of."

Privately, many gay spokesmen claim that they would like to see the bathhouses closed altogether. They worry about the conclusion that can be drawn from the spread of AIDS—that homosexuality can be hazardous to one's health. But some activists insist that the bathhouses must be defended precisely because they are the center of the most extreme form of public gay sexual behavior. And so the bathhouses have become a perverse and inchoate symbol of gay liberation itself.

Gay freedom parade co-chairman Konstantin Berlandt is a former editor of UC Berkeley's *Daily Californian* and antiwar activist. He sees the proposals to close the bathhouses as "genocidal" and compares them to the order requiring homosexuals to wear triangular pink shirt patches in Nazi Germany. Berlandt wrote a *Bay Area Reporter* account of the first closed meeting concerning gays and bathhouse owners, which was widely credited with torpedoing the effort to get them to inform patrons that they were at risk. "We fought Anita Bryant and John Briggs [anti-homosexual crusaders], and we'll fight against AIDS. Every time the community has been attacked the parades have been larger," he says, defending his opposition to the warning. "You have a situation where institutions that have fought against sexual repression for years are being attacked under the guise of medical strategy." Despite mounting medical evidence, Berlandt believes that transmission of the disease via bodily fluids is nothing more than a "theory" being used to attack the gay lifestyle. "I haven't stopped having sex," he says. "I feel that what we're being advised to do involves all the things I became gay to get away from—wear a condom, that sort of thing. So we have a disease for which supposedly the cure is to go back to all the styles that were preached at us in the first place. It will take a lot more evidence before I'm about to do that."

For gays who have worked hard and, so far, unsuccessfully to get the community to face up to the consequences of AIDS—to its symbolism and reality—such a statement represents denial at an elemental level. It is an inability to admit the magnitude of what is unfolding and an inability to accept responsibility for the role that personal excess has played in this health crisis. It also represents a mentality that insists on making a political and ideological argument out of what remains, above all, a personal tragedy.

Catherine Cusic, in addition to working with the Harvey Milk club's health service committee, is a respiratory therapist at San Francisco General Hospital. What she sees in the intensive care unit gives her a perspective that gay politicians and ideologues lack. "It's my job," she says, "to take care of patients unable to breathe on their own, without the help of the machine—in other words, the dying AIDS patients."

> You see these young people come in and die so quickly and in such agony. Their family comes in and watches. It's terrible when parents outlive their children. In some sense what I witness is political for me. I say to myself, "We're queers. They don't care about us. They're glad we're dying." But it's also personal. I watch these young men die. Their mothers start to cry. Their lovers have been sitting in the room, smiling and smiling, and then I see them at the elevator just standing and sobbing. It's horrible. And it's a horrible death. The patients waste away until they look like *Dachau* victims in the end. I see all this happen, and I have to admit that some of those responsible are gay leaders. In my mind they're criminally negligent. They've betrayed their own community.

32

An American Killing Field

A S COUNTLESS NEWS STORIES, articles, and editorials have reminded us, this is the twentieth anniversary of the onset of the AIDS epidemic in America. It is a grim anniversary. More than 450,000 Americans, mostly young, are dead.

The news story is this: after years of education efforts and billions of dollars in AIDS-related government programs, the infection rates for new AIDS cases are rising back to their peak levels. In related news, the new infection rates are highest among blacks and Hispanics, who now make up more than half the dead but who were hardly affected in the first years of the epidemic. In those years, when the numbers of those infected were small and effective public health methods might have contained its spread to new communities, more than 90 percent of those affected were white homosexuals living in New York, Los Angeles and San Francisco, IV drug-users in the same locations, and a tiny cohort of hemophiliacs and immigrants from Haiti.

On this anniversary, you will read many stories about the medical research on AIDS which—however remarkable in itself—has failed to produce an effective vaccine, let alone cure for the disease. This failure

---

This article appeared on Salon.com, June 12, 2001. Other writings on this subject include, "A Radical Holocaust" in *The Politics of Bad Faith*, and *Radical Son*, pp. 337-349. See also "AIDS: The Political Origins of an Epidemic," chapter 31 above, in this volume.

was predicted at the very outset by experts who warned that the only way to stem the tide of infection was through public health methods.

You will read many stories about the heroic efforts of activists in the gay community to lobby the government for more AIDS money, and to care for the sick and dying. None of these efforts should be confused with public health methods for combating epidemics, however. What you will not read is a single story about those methods, or how epidemics were combated, often successfully, for a hundred years prior to 1981—before gay activists inserted themselves into the public health system. What you will not read is how proven public health methods were opposed by AIDS activists, how public health officials surrendered to the activists' demands for veto-control over which methods were acceptable, or how these officials then colluded in subverting the system that had proved so successful in the past.

What you will not read is any evaluation of AIDS campaigns— mainly the "education" campaign—that activists demanded in place of proven methods. Yet the harrowing figures released on this anniversary show these billion-dollar, politically correct campaigns have failed miserably to contain the epidemic and to prevent it from spreading to other communities, particularly the African-American and Hispanic communities.

In the first five years of the epidemic, sexually transmitted AIDS was virtually confined to the white gay communities in three cities— New York, Los Angeles, and San Francisco. As a result of the obstruction of testing, reporting, contact-tracing, and infection-site closing by gay leaders and their allies in the Democratic parties controlling the administrations in these cities, public health officials could not warn communities in the path of the epidemic of the danger approaching them. In fact, as a result of the political restrictions imposed on them, they were not able to find out what that path was. As a result, by the end of the first decade of AIDS, Hispanics were 14 percent of those infected and blacks were 26 percent. A decade later, Hispanics were 19 percent of those infected and blacks an astounding 45 percent.

What you will not read in the twentieth anniversary coverage of the epidemic is any story reporting that today—as we move into the third decade of the epidemic with half a million dead and infection rates rising—the subverted public health system still does not require reporting of individual cases, testing of at-risk communities, contact tracing to warn individuals of possible infection, or the closing of sex clubs and other potential sites of infection.

Thus in addition to being a grim anniversary from the vantage of the dead and those who loved them, this is a disheartening occasion for those of us who followed the course of this contagion and have watched in disbelief the criminally ineffectual efforts that have been deployed in the name of political correctness to contain it. This anniversary also makes clear that as a nation we have learned nothing from the follies of the past and are headed into the next decade still prisoners of orchestrated ignorance and still relying on the politically shaped remedies that failed.

The following paragraph is taken from a lead story in the Health Section of the *Los Angeles Times*, the paper of record in one of the three epicenters of the epidemic. It was written by "*Times* health writer" Linda Marsa and rehashes the party line on AIDS, conveying "information" that is as brazenly ignorant as it is false. In perfect self-parody, the article is titled "A Legacy of Change": "It was a sheer accident that AIDS first struck a relatively cohesive group: young homosexuals in cities such as New York, Los Angeles and San Francisco, many of whom had honed their organizational and political skills during the gay rights movements of the 1970s. This was extraordinary: terminal illnesses don't discriminate, hitting rich and poor alike without regard to ethnicity, geography or sexual orientation."

In fact, far from being incidently related to gays and the gay rights movement of the 1970s, the AIDS epidemic is more accurately described as a *product* of the gay liberation of the 1970s and as inevitably concentrated in the very centers of gay life in America—San Francisco, New York, and Los Angeles. The AIDS epidemic is, in fact, impossible to imagine without the agitations and agendas of the radical gay movements that directly preceded it. It was the gay radical left that defined promiscuous anal sex with strangers in public urban environments—the primary cause of the epidemic—as "gay liberation."

It was this agenda of sexual liberation that caused the gay movement to think nothing of the massive epidemics of amoebiasis, rectal gonorrhea, syphilis, and hepatitis B that swept through gay communities in the decade preceding AIDS, producing astronomical infection rates and depleted immune systems along the way. It was the gay movement that regarded any intrusion by public health authorities to close the public sexual gymnasia called "bathhouses"—the primary sites of infection—as a "threat" to gay liberation (both before and after the onset of AIDS).

It was the gay left that successfully subverted the proven public health methods—reporting, testing, and contact-tracing—that had been proven effective in combating epidemic diseases in the past. It was the gay left that blocked government prevention programs from targeting at-risk communities (using the same fiction as the *Times* writer—that "AIDS is an equal opportunity disease"), and that persuaded government officials to put all the anti-AIDS eggs in the basket of incredibly expensive and—as everyone can now see—completely ineffective "education" campaigns instead. These campaigns were ineffective, first, because they did not specify anal sex as the primary sexual transmission route and, second, because they were not addressed to those who were specifically at risk, but to "everyone," and thus in effect to no one.

The late Michael Callen, creator of the organization "People with AIDS," and a pioneer of candor in the midst of these politically required lies, described how he came to New York as a young man from rural Iowa and heard gay radicals like the writer Edmund White address audiences in the gay community on the subject of sexual liberation. White told one such audience that "gay men should wear their sexually transmitted diseases like red badges of courage in a war against a sex-negative society." As a young romantic listening to this siren song of the left, Callen's natural response was to think: "Every time I get the clap I'm striking a blow for the sexual revolution." The ever-courageous Camille Paglia pointed out some years ago the obvious truth: "Everyone who preached free love in the 1960s is responsible for AIDS. This idea that it was somehow an accident, a microbe that sort of fell from heaven—absurd. We must face what we did."

Michael Callen explained exactly what "we" did: "Some of us believed we could change the world through sexual liberation and that we were taking part in a noble experiment. Unfortunately as a function of a microbiological . . . certainty, this level of sexual activity resulted in concurrent epidemics of syphilis, gonorrhea, hepatitis, amoebiasis, venereal warts and, we discovered too late, other pathogens. Unwittingly, and with the best of revolutionary intentions, a small subset of gay men managed to create disease settings equivalent to those of poor Third World nations in one of the richest nations on earth."

The gay community tragedy lay in the fact that those who pioneered in the establishment of gay rights had become seduced by the radical illusion that they could also change the world—including the laws of nature. These gay radicals exercised a controlling influence on the battle against AIDS, sabotaging public health science, and imposing their own politically acceptable approach to the epidemic which has resulted in the killing fields we now see.

Their responsibility includes especially the spread of AIDS into the black and Hispanic communities, which would have been prevented had traditional public health methods been aggressively deployed in the early years of the epidemic. The Hispanic and black communities are for the most part geographically separated from the gay communities where the epidemic first took hold. If there had been testing and tracing of those infected, focused warnings to those in their path, and a closing of the public infection sites, who knows how many lives could have been saved in the gay community itself, but especially in communities that lay outside the zones of the initial infection?

I offer these observations with no hope that they will have any effect. I have written about this radical holocaust (as I described it in *The Politics of Bad Faith*) for nearly the entire duration of the epidemic itself. Many others have raised their voices as well. Michael Fumento's *The Myth of Heterosexual AIDS*, and Gabriel Rotello's *Sexual Ecology* have made the case for ending the political control of the war against AIDS in a more scientific manner. Early Act-Up radicals like Larry Kramer, Michaelangelo Signorille, and Gabriel Rotello have had second thoughts about their former attitudes, faced what they did, and worked to change others' minds. They have established organizations dedicated to turning the tide. But to no avail.

The chief obstacle to any change in this unhappy tale is the media. AIDS is without question the worst reported story in the history of American journalism. From the press coverage of this twentieth anniversary, no one can take any hope that, absent a scientific breakthrough in preventions or cures, the next ten years will show any improvement in the toll.

33

The Meaning of Left and Right

AFTER THE FALL OF COMMUNISM, what remains of the division between left and right that has so defined our political lives? The terms are more than just a vestigial homage to 1789. They identify historical attitudes and traditions, the parties that have contended over the fate of modernity ever since. They recall the scars of battles won and lost, of aspirations realized and deferred. It is through them that we locate our historical forebears in the struggles for justice and human freedom, and it is through their causes that we assess our humanity and measure who we are.

Or have, until now. For with the fall of communism, we have reached a turning point in our collective lives. The history of revolutionary modernity—this narrative through which we have traditionally located our social selves—has finally come to a close. The tearing down of the Berlin Wall marked the end of the modern epoch as surely as the fall of the Bastille marked its beginning two centuries ago. Like all endings, this changes our understanding of what went before.

It is now impossible to console ourselves any longer with the illusion that socialism might have worked if only this path or that panacea had been tried. In our lifetime, the revolutions of the left have created despotisms and oppressions that dwarf all others on human record.

From *The Politics of Bad Faith* (1998).

Nonetheless, to the diehards of the radical culture, "left" still evokes the idealism of a "progressive" cause, while "right" remains synonymous with social reaction. It is time for a change in our understanding of the terms themselves.

In what sense can a bankrupt idea be called "progressive"? For two centuries, the socialist idea—the future promise that justifies the present sacrifice—has functioned as a blank check for the violence and injustice associated with efforts to achieve it. If the "experiments" have failed—so go the apologies for the left—the intentions that launched them were idealistic and noble. But it is no longer really possible to invoke the socialist fantasy to justify the assaults on societies that, whatever their faults, were less oppressive than the revolutionary "solutions" that followed their demise. The divisive crusades of the left and its failed "experiments" must be seen now for what they are: bloody exercises in civil nihilism; violent pursuits of empty hopes; revolutionary *actes gratuites* that were doomed to fail from the start.

Historical perspective imposes on us a new standard of judgment. Because they were doomed from their origin and destructive by design, these revolutionary gestures now stand condemned by morality and justice in their conception and not merely in their result. If there was a "party of humanity" in the civil wars that the left's ambitions provoked in the past, it was on the other side of the political barricades. In these battles, the enlightened parties were those who defended democratic process and civil order against the greater barbarism that we now know for certain the radical future entailed.

The difficulty which leftists have in digesting the term "counterrevolutionary" is really a litmus of their failure to understand the history they have lived. In our time, one hundred million people have been slaughtered in the revolutions of the left with no positive result, while millions more have been buried alive. Beyond the iron curtains of the socialist empires, whole cultures were desecrated, civilizations destroyed, and generations deprived of the barest essentials of a tolerable life. Yet the epithet "counterrevolutionary" still strikes progressives, who supported these empires, as a term of opprobrium and moral disgrace. What this record shows, on the contrary, is that "counterrevolution" is a name for moral sanity and human decency, a term for resistance to the epic depredations of dreamers like them.

—

To be a leftist is to be at war with the two most profoundly liberating achievements of modern history: the liberal state and the liberal economy. These are the twin pillars of what Hayek called the Great Society, which he described as a spontaneous, "extended order of human cooperation."[1] Such a society is not the product of vanguard schemes like the socialist design, but of a long process of adjustments to reality that eventually lead to more productive and humane institutions and rules. Capitalist democracy (a system as flawed as humanity is flawed) is, in this view, the highest stage of social evolution.

In contrast, socialism belongs to the dark, prehistory of mankind. In the words of Hayek, it is "a reassertion of that tribal ethics whose gradual weakening made an approach to [civilized market societies] possible."[2] Socialism belongs to a social stage based on the simple economy of small groups, a stage that had to be overcome in order to realize the great wealth-making potential of the market system. Far from being a progressive conception, the socialist ethic is atavistic and represents the primitive morality of preindustrial formations: the clan and the tribe. This is why its current incarnation takes the form of "identity politics," the latest revolt against bourgeois individualism and freedom.

Modern radicalism is the return of the repressed. Its values—equality, cooperation, unity—are the survival codes of small, vulnerable groups with knowable goals and shared interests. But the morality of tribal communities is self-defeating and disastrous when applied to complex economies, dependent on factors of production that are geographically dispersed and on trade exchanges that are transnational in scope. In the context of a modern extended economic order, where goals are not shared, where market prices encapsulate knowledge beyond the capacity of a central authority, and in situations so complex that no planner can rationally allocate economic tasks, the socialist agenda and its tribal ethos produce social atavisms—the paternalistic politics, fratricidal nationalism, and economic despotism characteristic of socialist states.

Socialist morality is a seductive illusion. Because it does not rest on real-world assumptions, the socialist ethic, if put into practice, would threaten to undermine the life basis of vast communities of present-day humanity and to impoverish much of the rest.

Far from being progressive, the left's demands for "social justice," if realized, would destroy the very basis of social wealth (as it already has in the former regions of the Soviet bloc). In the modern world, competition is not the contrary of cooperation, but the form that co-operation must take in order to coordinate the activities of millions of people unknown to each other, pursuing goals that are not common and cannot be shared. The profit motive is the engine of wealth not only for the rich but for the poor as well. In the real world, the attempt to plan economic systems produces inefficiency and waste; the attempt to redistribute wealth diminishes well-being and individual liberty; the attempt to unify society crushes its freedom; the ambition to make people equal establishes new forms of tyranny and submerges human individuality in totalitarian designs.

For a long time, the tribal ethos of socialism was concealed in the universalist membrane of the marxist movement and the liberationist impulse of its proletarian myth. But the collapse of communism has disintegrated the marxist idea and fragmented the culture of the international left. The result is a proliferation of post-marxian theories and identity politics that no longer base themselves on the universalist category of economic class but on the particularist identities of gender, ethnicity, and race. The class struggle has been replaced by status conflict, the universalist idea by quasi-fascist doctrines of racial solidarity, group rights, and antiliberal political agendas.

These agendas are still inspired by the essential radical theme. They share the Rousseauian desire to redefine and repossess the world in terms of a collective idea of self, to regenerate the lost paradise of human beginnings, and to unify alienated society under the redemptive aegis of a tribal will. "An atavistic longing after the life of the noble savage," as Hayek has written, "is the main source of the collectivist tradition."

Thus, the post-marxian left has begun its career by launching an all-out assault on the third great achievement of modern history, the liberal community itself. This community, whose paradigm is America, is founded in a universal compact that transcends tribal identities and the multicultural particularisms of blood and soil. "No nation before ever made diversity itself a source of national identity and unity," an historian has written, "a nation created by people of all classes and ethnicities, immigrating from all over the world."[3] America is the unique crystallization of an idea of nationality residing in a shared commitment to universal principles and pluralistic values. This creed is the culmination of an evolution that extends backward in time to Jerusalem, and Athens, and Rome. It encapsulates lessons that were accumulated through practice and acquired by faith, that are inscribed in the teachings of sacred tradition and the institutions of secular law. These traditions (as it happens, Judaeo-Christian traditions) and these institutions (in fact, bourgeois-democratic institutions) have led us to the truths that are self-evident, and on which our freedom finally depends.

VIII

THE ART OF POLITICAL WAR

34

The Art of Political War

THE REPUBLICAN PARTY claims to be the party of personal responsibility, yet it has become a party that takes no responsibility for the predicaments in which it finds itself. Instead, Republicans blame bias in the media, the liar in the White House, or their unprincipled opponents, or even the immorality of the American people to explain their defeats.

How can a party win in American politics if it has contempt for the judgment of the American people? It can't.

The greatest political deficiency of the Republican Party today is lack of respect for the common sense of the American people. "Respect" in this context does not mean following polls or focus groups or putting one's finger slavishly to the winds. It means that what is right politically (within a constitutional framework and consistent with deeply held principles) produces electoral majorities.

Liberals also fail to understand this. But they have been fortunate to have had in Bill Clinton a leader who does, who disregards their advice, and who uses his power as the head of their party to force them to pay heed to the voice of the people. The reason Bill Clinton survived his impeachment, riding high in the polls, is that he understood

From *The Art of Political War and Other Radical Pursuits* (2000). This essay was originally published as a pamphlet by the Committee for a Non-Left Majority in 1998.

what the electorate wanted and gave it to them (or at least made them think he had).

Despite the most flawed presidency in the twentieth century and the worst White House scandal since Watergate, Clinton was able to sustain his popularity by remaking the Democratic Party both tactically and ideologically, much against its will. While the liberal majority in his party dug in their heels and opposed free trade, welfare reform, balanced budgets, and a tough stance on crime, Clinton pursued a "triangulation" strategy with Republicans to do just the opposite.

As a result, in the mind of the public, Clinton Democrats appear to be the party of economic vibrancy, anticrime laws, welfare reform laws, budget surpluses, and free trade. That is what the American people want, and that is what they believe Clinton has delivered. Unless Republicans change their strategy and tactics to adapt to this reality, they are destined for political irrelevance. They cannot fight past wars and expect to win present battles.

Republicans will ask how can we in good conscience respect the judgment of the American people when they failed to support the impeachment and removal of a corrupt president? The question, of course, is rhetorical. The only possible answer is: Blame the people. But if conservatives really believe in America's constitutional order, their first political article of faith surely must be this: The people are sovereign.

Where complex issues of government, society, and law are concerned, truth is elusive. Conservatives ought to know that no one has a monopoly on truth, least of all politicians in government. Should the president be impeached? Is the minimum wage a boon to workers, or does it eliminate jobs? We think we know what is true, but we also know that we may be wrong. This humility is what makes conservatives, or should make them, democrats (lower case). We do not believe in rule by the anointed or in the divine right of the infallible.

Democracy arbitrates life's uncertainties through electoral pluralities. In America, nobody gets to decide what is true and what is false, what is right and what is wrong without the consent—or at least the tolerance—of a plurality of the American electorate. If the electorate is wrong, only the electorate can remedy its error. Hence, appropriate respect for the people's judgment is a moral imperative as well as a political necessity. If you do not have faith in the long-term good sense of the American public, then you do not really have faith in the system the Founders established. If the Founders had not had that original faith in the ultimate good sense of the American people, they would never have adopted a Constitution resting on the idea that sovereignty resides in its will.

IT'S THE POLITICS, STUPID

During the impeachment debate, the American people knew that Bill Clinton was corrupt and despised him as a person even as they did not want him removed from office. Most Americans knew he was guilty of perjury, but they were reluctant to see him impeached. Clinton escaped judgment because he based his defense on conservative principles and because Republicans were silent for eight crucial months and allowed him to define the issues. When Republicans finally found their collective voice, they talked past the immediate concerns of the American electorate and based their prosecution on issues that were too complex for the public to digest.

It's the politics, stupid.

For eight months between the time that Monica Lewinsky surfaced and President Clinton admitted their relationship, Republicans said nothing about the developing sex scandal. Meanwhile, the White House launched its own national campaign to define the issues for the American public. Republican silence was based on the hope that Clinton Democrats would self-destruct and the fear that Republicans could not handle the issue without shooting themselves in the foot. The two sentiments had the same reasoning behind them: Republicans were afraid to fight the political battle. It was because Republicans did not trust themselves to frame the scandal to their advantage that they hoped for a Democratic implosion.

In political warfare, if only one side is shooting, the other side will soon be dead. While Republicans vacated the battlefield from January to August 1999, the president's allies portrayed him as a victim of government abuse. They defined the issues surrounding the investigation as government invasion of privacy (a conservative principle) and government prosecutors out of control (a conservative concern). That Americans responded to this appeal should have been cause for conservative satisfaction, not dismay. It is not the American people that Republicans should blame for their failure to remove the president. They should blame their own political ineptitude.

When Republicans finally did make their case, they built their arguments on legalistic grounds that were either unintelligible to the majority of the electorate or were based on liberal principles they had themselves previously opposed—and which the public rejected.

Although impeachment is a political process conducted by the legislative branch, Republicans notably failed to focus on the *political* case for the removal of the president (the China foreign policy scandal would have been the obvious issue). Instead, Republicans relied on interpretations of the law and on legal arguments arising from the failed Paula Jones suit to make their case for removal.

A sexual harassment statute allowing the court to investigate the personal sexual histories of defendants in sexual harassment cases led to the discovery of Monica Lewinsky. This was actually a radical law that departs from the norms of American justice, which previously enshrined the principle that a defendant is presumed innocent until proven guilty. Even accused killers have the right to be tried on the charges at hand rather than for what they may have been convicted of doing in the past. But radical sexual harassment law allows courts to dredge up not only past convictions (of which Clinton had none), but past alleged crimes as well. Once allegations are part of the record and a "pattern" is established, the presumption of guilt can become overwhelming—which is why American law, before it was traduced by feminist theories, ruled out such practices.

"Sexual McCarthyism"—a charge that Democrats successfully used against the Republican prosecutors—was an invention of the radical left. Sexual harassment laws were designed by radical feminists, while conservatives opposed them. As a consequence of Republicans' folly in embracing their enemies' philosophy, the entire impeachment debate was framed by sexual harassment laws.

Furthermore, the impeachment debate revolved around questions only constitutional experts and trial lawyers could properly discuss with any claim to authority (Was the president's testimony in a sexual harassment case material or not? Was testimony in that same case about matters that should be private? What constitutes perjury? Are civil cases of perjury normally prosecuted? What is obstruction? What are impeachable offenses? Has the bar for an impeachable offense been set high enough in this case?). Because the debate was legalistic, many thought it was just plain irrelevant, particularly since Republicans constantly reminded them that impeachment is a political process and that political jurors render the verdict.

In other words, Republicans chose to fight on grounds where the public could not (or would not) follow them. Because the *legalistic* arguments of the Republicans failed to gain traction with a majority of the public, the Democrats' *political* arguments prevailed. The president's privacy had been invaded; government prosecutors had abused their power; a sex act was not a reason to remove a president the people had elected. A skeptical public was readily persuaded that the president was a victim of partisan attacks. In political terms, "victims" are underdogs, little guys, that is, the people themselves. In a democratic political contest, the winner is the one who persuades the people to identify with him. In a democracy, this is the first—and perhaps only—principle of political war: The side of the underdog, which is the side of the people, wins.

In the impeachment conflict, sound Democratic political strategy was reinforced by a full-employment economy, a soaring Dow, positive social trends (declining crime rates, increasing morality indices), and no clear political framing of the case for removal. In these circumstances, the public's (conservative) response of sticking with a twice-elected sitting president was perfectly understandable, even reassuring.

Of course, the Democratic campaign in defense of the president was a remarkable display of hypocrisy and double-talk, which is to say it was a virtuoso demonstration of how a purely political strategy was able to serve a political party in grave difficulty. Thanks to a superior grasp of political strategy, the actual inventors of sexual McCarthyism (remember the hounding of Justice Clarence Thomas?) were able to pin the same charge on Republicans. Liberals who had spent four decades rewriting the Constitution suddenly emerged as the champions of original intent ("the Constitutional bar for high crimes has not been met"). The veterans of half a century of antiwar crusades against the American military became overnight enthusiasts of wag-the-dog missile strikes in the Sudan, Afghanistan, and Iraq. The creators of the special prosecutor's office, who had ruthlessly used its powers to persecute three Republican presidents, became instant critics of prosecutorial excess and the loudest proponents of reform.

As the party of bankrupt principles, discredited policies, and two-faced political arguments, the Democrats have dramatically demonstrated how effective the art of political war can be in the hands of a party that understands its principles. An illustration of Republicans' idea of political warfare is the following slogan posted on a closed-circuit television program which the Republican Policy Committee produces for House members: "Republicans target the problems; Democrats target the politics."

There could hardly be a more succinct explanation of why Republicans are so regularly routed by their Democratic adversaries in battles like the impeachment process. It's the politics, stupid. If you do not focus on winning the political battle, you do not get to target the problems.

Before Republicans can begin to change this situation, they need to stop whining that life is unfair, that Bill Clinton "stole" their programs, and that Democrats do not play by the rules. They need to stop complaining that Democrats are unprincipled or that they follow a party line. (Of course they do. It's the politics, stupid.) They need to accept that Democrats are going to practice the politics of personal destruction and attribute to Republicans the sins they themselves have committed. They do it because that is the way they win.

When Republicans complain about forces they cannot control, they behave like victims and give up the power to determine their fate.

Democrats will be Democrats. They will be unprincipled and lie. Republicans can hope Democrats will behave better than this, but if Republicans go into battle expecting Democrats to be better than they are, they will only set themselves up for political ambush. Instead of complaining about others, Republicans should be asking themselves: How do they do it? How do they get away with it? What do they know that makes them able to package a bankrupt political agenda and sell it successfully to the American voter?

THE PRINCIPLES

Here are the principles of political war that the left understands, but conservatives do not:

1. Politics is war conducted by other means.
2. Politics is a war of position.
3. In political warfare, the aggressor usually prevails.
4. Position is defined by fear and hope.
5. The weapons of politics are symbols evoking fear and hope.
6. Victory lies on the side of the people.

First, a caveat. Politics is contextual: rules cannot be applied rigidly and succeed. If it is true that the aggressor usually prevails, there are times when he will not, and it is absolutely crucial to recognize them. If politics is war, it is also true that a war mentality produces sanctimony and self-serious moralizing, which can be deadly. To be effective, you need to get serious and lighten up at the same time. If politics is war, it is also a combination of blackjack, craps, and poker. Politically, it is better to be seen as a peacemaker than as a warmonger. But it is not always possible. If forced to fight, then fight to win.

1. *Politics is war conducted by other means.*

In political warfare you do not fight just to prevail in an argument, but rather to destroy the enemy's fighting ability. Republicans often seem to regard political combats as they would a debate before the Oxford Political Union, as though winning depended on rational arguments and carefully articulated principles. But the audience of politics is not made up of Oxford dons, and the rules are entirely different.

You have only thirty seconds to make your point. Even if you had time to develop an argument, the audience you need to reach (the undecided and those in the middle who are not paying much attention) would not get it. Your words would go over some of their heads and the rest would not even hear them (or quickly forget) amidst the bustle and pressure of daily life. Worse, while you have been making your argument the other side has already painted you as a mean-spirited, borderline racist controlled by religious zealots, securely in the pockets of the rich. Nobody who sees you this way is going to listen to you in any case. You are politically dead.

Politics is war. Don't forget it.

2. *Politics is a war of position.*

In war there are two sides: friends and enemies. Your task is to define yourself as the friend of as large a constituency as possible compatible with your principles, while defining your opponent as the enemy whenever you can. The act of defining combatants is analogous to the military concept of choosing the terrain of battle. Choose the terrain that makes the fight as easy for you as possible. But be careful. American politics takes place in a pluralistic framework, where constituencies are diverse and often in conflict. "Fairness" and "tolerance" are the formal rules of democratic engagement. If you appear mean-spirited or too judgmental, your opponent will more easily define you as a threat, and therefore as "the enemy" (see principle 4).

3. *In political warfare, the aggressor usually prevails.*

Republicans often pursue a conservative strategy of waiting for the other side to attack. In football, this is known as a "prevent defense." In politics it is the strategy of losers.

Aggression is advantageous because politics is a war of position, which is defined by images that stick. By striking first, you can define the issues as well as your adversary. Defining the opposition is the decisive move in all political war. Other things being equal, whoever is on the defensive generally loses.

In attacking your opponent, take care to do it effectively. "Going negative" increases the risk of being defined as an enemy. Therefore, it can be counterproductive. Ruling out the negative, however, can incur an even greater risk. In the last California senatorial election, Barbara Boxer—one of the most left-wing Democrats (in fact, the number one spender in the entire Congress)—crushed a bland, moderate Republican. Matt Fong was so moderate he was able to get the endorsement of the leading liberal papers—the *Los Angeles Times* and the *San Francisco Chronicle* (the first time they had endorsed a statewide Republican candidate since the 1960s)—and was running ahead in the polls. But Boxer went negative and Fong did not. As a result, Boxer was able to define herself as the moderate and Fong as the extremist. The American public favors the center. The decision to avoid the negative did not save Matt Fong from being defined by his opponent as mean-spirited. But it did cost him the election. Never say "never" in political battles. It is an art, not a science.

4. Position is defined by fear and hope.

The twin emotions of politics are fear and hope. Those who provide people with hope become their friends; those who inspire fear become enemies. Of the two, hope is the better choice. By offering people hope and yourself as its provider, you show your better side and maximize your potential support. But fear is a powerful and indispensable weapon. If your opponent defines you negatively enough, he will diminish your ability to offer hope. This is why Democrats are so determined to portray Republicans as mean-spirited and hostile to minorities, the middle class, and the poor.

The smear campaign against Clarence Thomas, for example, was designed to taint all black Republicans. It was a warning to other blacks who might stray from the Democratic fold. Without their captive black constituency—the most powerful symbol of their concern for the victimized—Democrats would be dead at the polls. They would lose every major urban center and become a permanent political minority. Democrats exploit their image as the party of blacks to stigmatize Republicans as the party of racists. The success of these tactics means that as a Republican you may have a lot to offer African Americans and other minorities, but you will have to work extraordinarily hard to get anyone to listen.

Democrats have successfully associated the Religious Right with moralistic intolerance. They have been helped by intolerant pronouncements from religious leaders and by political groups with politically toxic names like the "Moral Majority" and the "Christian Coalition." As a result, it is easy for liberals to portray them as a threat to any constituency that does not share their values: "They will impose their morals on you." It does not matter whether this is true or not. Once a negative image has taken hold, the target is wounded—often mortally—in the political battle.

To combat this form of attack, it is important to work away from the negative image your opponent wants to pin on you. If you know you are going to be attacked as morally imperious, it is a good idea to lead with a position that is inclusive and tolerant. If you are going to be framed as mean-spirited and ungenerous, it is a good idea to put on a smile and lead with acts of generosity and charity. This will provide a shield from attack. When Clinton signed the welfare reform bill he made sure he was flanked by two welfare mothers.

Symbols are so powerful that if you manipulate them cleverly, as Democrats do, you can even launch mean-spirited attacks on your opponents and pretend to be compassionate while doing it. Democrats understand, for example, that positioning themselves as victims gives them a license to attack. A gay politician like Barney Frank can assault an opponent and call it self-defense. The president's wife can issue McCarthy-like proclamations about a "vast right-wing conspiracy" and get away with it because she is a woman and the First Lady and has allies like James Carville and Sidney Blumenthal who will make her aggression look like self-defense. Likewise, Democrats rely on black extremists like Maxine Waters to slander Republicans as racists.

But remember this: using fear as a weapon can be dangerous. Enemies inspire fear; friends do not. That is why Clinton lets his surrogates do the dirty work. When and how to use fear is a political art. If you are a white male in a culture whose symbols have been defined by liberals, be careful when you go on the offensive and be sure to surround yourself with allies who are neither male nor white.

5. *The weapons of politics are symbols evoking fear and hope.*

The most important symbol is the candidate. Does the candidate, in his own person, inspire fear or hope? Voters want to know: Is the candidate someone who cares about people like me? Do I feel good about him, or does he put me on guard? Would I want to sit next to him at dinner? Style, especially for high public office, is as important as any issue or strategy. Jack Kennedy—a relatively inexperienced, do-nothing congressman and senator—was able to win a national election merely by reciting problems and then repeating the litany "we can do bettah." Why? In part it was because he was handsome, witty, young, and charming—and was not a zealot.

Republicans lose a lot of political battles because they come across as hard-edged, scolding, scowling, and sanctimonious. A good rule of thumb is to be just the opposite. You must convince people you care about them before they will care about what you have to say. When you speak, do not forget that a sound bite is all you have. Whatever you have to say, make sure to say it loud and clear. Keep it simple and keep it short—a slogan is always better. Repeat it often. Put it on television. Radio is good, but with few exceptions, only television reaches a public that is electorally significant. In politics, television is reality.

Of course, you have a base of supporters who will listen for hours to what you have to say if that is what you want. In the battles facing you, they will play an important role. Therefore, what you say to them is also important. But it is not going to decide elections. The audiences that will determine your fate are audiences that you will first have to persuade. You will have to find a way to reach them, get them to listen, and then to support you. With these audiences, you will never have time for real arguments or proper analyses. Images—symbols and sound bites—will always prevail. Therefore, it is absolutely essential to focus your message and repeat it over and over again. For a candidate this means the strictest discipline. Lack of focus will derail your message. If you make too many points, your message will be diffused and nothing will get through. The result will be the same as if you had made no point at all.

The same is true for the party as a whole. Democrats have a party line. When they are fighting an issue they focus their agenda. Every time a Democrat steps in front of the cameras, there is at least one line in his speech that is shared with his colleagues. "Tax breaks for the wealthy at the expense of the poor" is one example. Repetition insures that the message will get through. When Republicans speak, they all march to a different drummer. There are many messages instead of one. One message is a sound bite. Many messages are a confusing noise.

Symbols and sound bites determine the vote. These are what hit people in the gut before they have time to think. And these are what people remember. Symbols are the impressions that last, and therefore that ultimately define you. Carefully chosen words and phrases are more important than paragraphs, speeches, party platforms, and manifestos. What you project through images is what you are.

The faces that represent Republicans are also images. In a pluralistic community, diversity is important. Currently, too many Republican faces (what you see on your television screen) are southern white men.

America is based on the idea that individual merit is what counts. As conservators of the American principle, we reject artificial diversity and racial quotas. But this is political warfare. Images are what count. The image is the medium, and the medium is the message. Therefore, diversity is more than important. It is crucial to becoming a national majority. It is also crucial because it is just. As conservatives, as defenders of America's democratic principle, we want every constituency to feel included.

6. *Victory lies on the side of the people.*

This is the bottom line for each of the principles and for all of the principles. You must define yourself in ways that people understand. You must give people hope in your victory, and make them fear the victory of your opponent. You can accomplish both by identifying yourself and your issues with the underdog and the victim, with minorities and the disadvantaged, with the ordinary Janes and Joes.

This is what Democrats do best, and Republicans often neglect to do at all. Every political statement by a Democrat is an effort to say: "Democrats care about women, children, minorities, working Americans, and the poor; Republicans are mean-spirited, serve the rich, and don't care about you." This is the Democrats' strategy. If Republicans are to win the political war and become a national majority they have to turn these images around.

They also have to make their campaigns a cause. During the Cold War, Republicans had a cause. They were saving the country from Communism and—in the Cold War's later decades—leftist appeasers. The cause resonated at every level with the American people. Even the poorest citizens understood that their freedom was at stake in electing Republicans to conduct the nation's defense.

In a democracy, the cause that fires up passions is the cause of the people. That is why politicians like to run "against Washington" and against anything that represents the "powers that be." As the left has shown, the idea of justice is a powerful motivator. It will energize the troops and fuel the campaigns that are necessary to win the political war. Republicans believe in economic opportunity and individual freedom. The core of their ideas is justice for all. If they could make this intelligible to the American electorate, they would make themselves the party of the American people.

35

How to Beat the Democrats

D EMOCRATS WIN ELECTIONS because they understand a simple
fact: the key to American politics is the romance of the underdog. Americans like the story of the little guy who goes up
against the system and triumphs, a story about opportunity and fairness. To win the hearts and minds of the American voter, you have to
tap the emotions the story of the underdog evokes.

America's heroes are all cut from this common cloth. Whether it's
George Washington, Abraham Lincoln, Davy Crockett, Thomas
Edison, Henry Ford, Amelia Earhart, Jackie Robinson, Ronald Reagan,
or Colin Powell, the theme is always the same: the common man against
the odds. America's political romance is *Mr. Smith Goes to Washington*
to make things right. It is *Meet John Doe* who speaks for the voiceless.
It is Luke Skywalker who saves the planet by using the good side of
the Force to defeat the Empire. It is the odyssey of individuals who
challenge power, overcome adversity, and rise to the top. Everyone in
America thinks of himself as an underdog and a hero. Just ask Bill
Gates.

The cause of the underdog wins American hearts because it resonates with our deepest religious and moral convictions of doing good

From *How to Beat the Democrats and Other Subversive Ideas* (2000). This essay was
originally published as a pamphlet by Politicalwar.com in 2000.

and helping others. And because it is America's own story. We began as a small nation standing up to the world's most powerful empire. We dedicated ourselves to the idea that all men are created equal. We are a nation of immigrants who arrived with nothing and made fortunes in a new world. This is the American Dream. It's a story that will get you every time. But at election time, Democrats know how to wield it as a political weapon, and Republicans generally don't.

In deploying this weapon, Democrats use a version of the story that has a partisan edge. Through their grip on the media and academic culture, leftists have rewritten America's past. They have transformed it from an epic of freedom into a tale of racism, exploitation, and oppression. In their version, the American narrative is no longer a story of expanding opportunity, in which men and women succeed against the odds. They have turned it, instead, into a marxist morality play about the powerful and their victims.

During the presidential election campaign, that's what the "hate crimes" issue was really about. It was not about punishing hate crimes, but about setting the stage for a morality play in which Republicans would be cast as the devil.

In staging their political dramas, Democrats invariably claim to speak in the name of America's "victims." Every Democratic policy is presented as a program to help these "victims"—women, children, minorities, and the poor. Simultaneously, Democrats describe Republican policies as programs that will injure the weak, ignore the vulnerable, and keep the powerless down.

Republicans play right into the Democrats' trap because they approach politics as a problem of management. To Republicans, every issue is a management issue—the utility of a tax, the efficiency of a program, the optimal method for running an enterprise. Republicans talk like businessmen who want a chance to govern the country so that it will turn a profit.

There is nothing wrong with instituting good policies and running things efficiently. But while Republicans are performing these Gold Star tasks, Democrats are busy attacking Republicans as servants of the rich, oppressors of the weak, and defenders of the strong.

Listen to Mario Cuomo describing Republicans at the 1996 Democratic National Convention: "We need to work as we have never done before between now and November 5th to take the Congress back from Newt Gingrich and the Republicans, because ladies and gentlemen, brothers and sisters, the Republicans are the real threat. They are the real threat to our women. They are the real threat to our children. They are the real threat to clean water, clean air and the rich landscape of America." Mario Cuomo knows the language of political war.

Democrats connect emotionally with people's fears and concerns. They do so, because they directly engage the myth of the underdog: "I will fight for you, against the powerful" is the populist mantra Al Gore used in the presidential race to good effect. Although Gore is himself part of the power elite, a *Business Week*-Harris poll taken right after the Democratic convention showed that three-quarters of the public agreed with his attacks on Big Oil, pharmaceutical companies, and HMOs.[1]

The appeal to help the underdog and defend the victim resonates with all Americans, not just Democrats. This is because Americans are a fair-minded people. Most successful Americans came from humble origins themselves. They want to help others. They want everyone to have the chance to succeed.

So do Republicans. But Republicans rarely connect their policies and principles to this political romance.

There's a good reason for this. Republicans are busy defending the real America against the left's attacks and the caricature they have constructed. Republicans know that America is still a land of opportunity and freedom, and that nobody in America is really "oppressed." (Otherwise, why would poor, black, Hispanic, and Asian minorities be desperately seeking to come here? Why wouldn't they be leaving instead?)

But politics isn't just about reality. (If it were, good principles and good policies would win every time.) It's about images and symbols, and the emotions they evoke. This is a battle that Republicans almost invariably lose.

In the romance of the victim, as Democrats stage it, Republicans are always on the side of the bad guys—the powerful, the male, the white, and the wealthy. It's easy to see how Republican patriotism plays into this trap. Defending America is readily misrepresented as an attitude that says: "I'm all right, Jack, so you should be too." Democrats relish the opportunity to smear Republicans as the selfish party. "You say that African-American voters in Florida who punched their ballots twice should have read the instructions? So, you think there's *no* racism in America?"

Democrats attack instinctively because they think of Republicans as mean-spirited and intolerant, in the pockets of the rich, looking for a way to pay no taxes. In each presidential debate, Al Gore said something like this: "The problem is that under Governor Bush's plan [for a] 1.6 trillion dollar tax cut, mostly to the wealthy, under his own budget numbers, he proposes spending more money for a tax cut just for the wealthiest one percent than all the new money he budgets for education, health care, and national defense combined."

It does not really matter whether Gore's description of the Bush tax plan is accurate or not (and a lot of it is not). The *appearance* of the plan (and of all Republican tax plans) is that Republicans are the party of the wealthy who care more about themselves than those left behind. This is true even though George Bush labored hard, in his own plan, to provide greater percentage cuts to Americans with lower incomes.

The reason, of course, is that Democrats have rigged the game before it starts. Through their control of Congress, Democrats designed the tax code to make it an unfair system of economic plunder. Under their code, the harder you work and the more jobs you create, the more you are taxed. Under their code, the bottom 50 percent pay only 5 percent of the government bill for services they are more likely to use. Therefore, *every* fair refund of a tax surplus can be maliciously portrayed as a tax cut for the wealthy at the expense of the poor. And that's the way Democrats portray Republican tax plans.

The reality is that a tax refund to the very rich does not affect lives of the rich at all. George Bush's tax refund would not enable one member of the super-rich to buy the yacht he couldn't afford, take the vacation he couldn't plan, or pay for the education he thought was too expensive. He can already pay for all that *without* the refund. Think about it—he's *rich*.

What a tax cut really affects is the investment capital of the rich— their ability to create jobs and wealth for other Americans. (Or did you think it was government that created those?) As Republicans know—but seldom say—the Democrats' progressive tax code actually works *against* poor and working Americans. Unfortunately, to appreciate this fact requires an understanding of the economic system that most Americans (and apparently all Democrats) lack.

Politics is about perception. The perception an across-the-board tax cut creates is of an unfair "giveaway" to the "haves," as opposed to the "have nots."[2] This may not fool all of the people all of the time, or even most of the people some of the time. But it does create a pool of resentment and envy—powerful emotions—that Democrats convert into a political *force*.

It is true that an increasing number of Americans are now stockholders in the corporate economy and, as a result, Democratic populism has built-in limits. But the political energies that class envy generates are still more potent in a campaign than the satisfactions of fairness and economic good sense, which Republicans defend.

For the Democrats, the romance of the victim stirs the souls of their supporters and energizes their base. Equally important, it provides the nuclear warhead of their political attack, which is even greater when the combustible elements of gender and race are added. Responding to this attack must become a Republican priority. Learning how to do this will turn the political war around.

GOING ON THE ATTACK

As I pointed out in *The Art of Political War*, in political combat the aggressor usually prevails. Aggression is advantageous because politics is a war of position. Position is defined by images that stick. By striking first, you can define the issues and can define your adversary. Definition is the decisive move in all political wars. Other things being equal, whoever winds up on the defensive will generally be on the losing side.

Fortunately, Republicans can use the left-wing slant of the Democrats' attack against them. Contrary to the left's view, America is not a land of victims. It is a highly mobile society, with a mainly self-reliant citizenry that aspires upwards *through* the system, not against it. Republicans can also turn the Democrats' oppression myth around and aim its guns at *them*. In fact, using the romance of the underdog against the Democrats is the best way to neutralize their marxist attack, for the most powerful forces obstructing opportunity for poor and minority Americans, the most powerful forces oppressing them, are the Democratic Party and its political creation, the welfare state.

There is really nothing new in this idea. Republicans already oppose the policies of the Democrats as obstacles to the production of wealth and barriers to opportunity for all Americans. What is new is the idea of connecting this analysis to a political strategy that will give Republicans a decisive edge—that will neutralize the class, race, and gender warfare attacks of the Democratic left. Here are two examples.

Welfare. Democrats view taxes as contributions to charity. (Seriously. You should talk to a few Democrats if you doubt it.) Consequently, when Democrats designed a welfare system that cost taxpayers trillions, they considered it a double good deed. Welfare taxes benefited the poor and forced Americans to do the right thing.[3] Over the years, however, it became clear that government "charity" dollars were actually producing a social disaster—driving fathers from their children, bribing teenage girls to have children out of wedlock, subsidizing drug abuse, and destroying the work ethic of entire inner-city communities.

To address the problem, Republicans proposed welfare reforms that would put recipients to work and get others off the rolls. Democrats said "No," and dug in their heels. They had to defend the vast patronage system that welfare created for government bureaucrats, social workers, and other beneficiaries who could be counted on to vote for the Democratic Party.

But Democrats also knew that the romance of the victim would work in their favor. When Republicans proposed welfare reform, Democrats attacked them as mean-spirited and heartless. They said Republicans lacked compassion. They said Republicans were attacking the poor. They were *Nazis*.

Powerful moral images like this don't go away. They linger beyond the battle and resonate through future conflicts. In 1996, when Dick

Morris persuaded Bill Clinton to sign the Republican welfare bill "or lose the election," the images of Republicans—anti-poor and uncharitable—stuck. Clinton won the election and presided over a Republican welfare reform, claiming it as his own. It is now part of his "legacy," while Republicans are still seen as mean-spirited and uncaring.

Republicans assisted in their own political undoing when they put the arguments for welfare reform in management terms. In proposing reform, Republicans did not call welfare mothers to Washington to testify against a system that was breaking up their families, destroying their children, and blighting their communities. They did not call Democrats "racists" for not caring about the destructive impact the welfare system had on inner-city populations. They did not call them "Nazis." Instead, Republicans argued that the welfare system was "wasteful" and "inefficient," that it "wasn't working" and that it was an impediment to balancing the federal budget.

But welfare is a human problem. It isn't about economic budgets. It is about the destruction of human beings. Republicans were not oblivious to the human reality of the Democrats' welfare nightmare. They spoke about it. But they did not attempt to speak in the name of the underclass, as the champions of the underclass, or to frame a moral indictment of the Democrats as the focus of their campaign. They did not invoke the romance of the underdog or use the language of victimization and oppression. They did not portray the Democrats as the enemies and oppressors of the poor.

As a result, the debate about welfare took place on Democratic turf, in Democratic terms. It became an argument about whether the government should spend more or less on the poor—on "charity." Republicans allowed themselves to be put in the position of arguing that government should spend less. Democrats inevitably wanted to spend more. When the debate was framed in these terms, it was easy for Democrats to portray Republicans as stingy, mean-spirited, heartless, and uncaring. Republicans did it to themselves.

If it is an argument about budgets, more money for welfare appears to be greater generosity to the poor. In fact it was just the opposite. The Democrats' welfare programs were destructive to the poor.

More money spent on welfare was more money spent on a system that was blighting the lives of families and children.

Republicans should not have allowed the debate to be about government waste, about "welfare queens" rifling the public purse. They should have made it about government *harm*. They should have made it about government programs that *destroyed* the lives of poor and minority people (while allowing some to benefit unjustly). If Republicans had insisted on *those* terms, Democrats would be bearing the stigma today, and Newt Gingrich and the Republican congress would be seen as the heroes of minorities and the poor.[4]

Instead, the welfare system has been reformed and millions of poor people have been liberated from the chains Democrats forged. But because Republicans failed to stick the Democrats with responsibility for the suffering their policies caused, Bill Clinton and Al Gore have been able to claim credit for a welfare reform they resisted and that half their party opposed. And Republicans have lost a political issue.

Education. Another issue even more powerful than welfare is education. Democrats are regularly billed as the "education party." How is that possible? There is a human tragedy enveloping America's inner cities. Twelve million poor children, mainly black and Hispanic, are trapped in failing government schools that are teaching them nothing. As a result, they will never get a shot at the American Dream.

Virtually every school board and every administration in inner-city districts is controlled by Democrats, and has been controlled by Democrats for over fifty years. Everything that is wrong with inner-city schools that policy can fix, Democrats are responsible for. Democrats and their allies run the public school system for the benefit of adults at the expense of children. Put in the language of political war: *Democrats have their boot heels on the necks of poor, black, and Hispanic children.* But Republicans are too polite to mention it.

How bad *is* the inner-city school crisis? The Los Angeles school district recently defined the problem. Officials had declared their intention to end the practice of "social promotion," which lets students who have failed move on to the next grade.[5] But in January 2000, the school district announced it would have to postpone the plan. The reason? A feasibility study showed that if the plan were instituted, officials would have to hold back 350,000 students—*half* the entire school population.[6]

Half the school population is learning nothing! This is an atrocity. It is no secret that these children are poor, Hispanic, and black, and that for them an education is the only chance they will ever have for a better life. But Democrat-controlled schools are teaching them nothing! They will never be part of the information economy. They will never get decent paying jobs. And the Democrats—who oppose the opportunity scholarships and school vouchers that would rescue them from this disaster—are doing everything in their power to keep poor children trapped in the very schools that are failing them.

It gets worse. Shortly after the school district announcement, the Los Angeles Teachers Union demanded a 21 percent pay raise for its members. The union leader announced that his members would strike if bonuses were given as rewards to individual teachers who actually raised their students' grades. That would be setting "teacher against teacher." That would be competition.

Democratic legislators fully supported the socialist union and its selfish demands. Once again, Democratic leaders pledged to fight to keep poor, black, and Hispanic children trapped in the failing schools. At the same time, they send their own children to expensive private ones. When Al Gore was asked why he opposed school vouchers for black children while sending his own son to a private school, he said: "If I had a child in an inner city school, I would probably be for vouchers too." He said, "Leave my children out of it."[7]

Where is the Republican outrage? Where are the Republican voices exposing this hypocrisy and holding the Democrats to account? Where is the Republican plan to liberate these children and get them an education?

In fact, Republicans do have such a plan. For years, conservatives have been building a movement to reform education and provide adequate schools to poor and minority children. Instead of running the schools on bankrupt socialist principles, these reformers propose to reward teachers and schools that do their job, and hold the others accountable. The main mechanism they propose for school reform is economic choice—putting the education dollar directly in the hands of poor parents. This will force inner-city schools to serve their constituents instead of merely exploiting them. It will establish a connection between performance and reward without which no reform can succeed.

But instead of rushing to the barricades with moral indictments of the Democrats who defend the existing system, instead of stigmatizing them as enemies of reform and of the poor, black, and Hispanic children who are languishing in them, Republicans do what? They approach the problem timidly and discreetly. They distance themselves from conservative voucher movements and instead make legislative proposals that are modest and "reasonable." They put forward bills that are designed to win over members of the opposition.

But this ignores the reality of the system the Democrats have created, which provides billions of federal dollars to enrich adults and to secure their political loyalty at the expense of the children. Democrats will not become "reasonable" until the American people understand what they are doing! The only way this will happen is if Republicans make the Democrats' oppression of poor and minority children the focus of their political attack.

If Republicans do not frame the indictment of Democrats, no one is going to do it for them. They cannot depend on the media to do it. The media is in the hands of the cultural left. This is the principal reason Republicans are perceived as lacking compassion (and Democrats are not) and as the party of the rich (while Democrats are not).

Democrats are both well-heeled and mean-spirited. Their programs oppress the poor. They have used their power to create public housing slums that are breeding grounds for drugs and crime. They have weakened the criminal justice system, allowing predators to make war on the vulnerable and the poor. And they have broken the bottom rungs of the ladder of success for poor, black, and Hispanic children.

But don't expect the media to tell this story. The successes of the school choice programs that conservatives have created are not going to be trumpeted by left-wing editors and journalists. Instead, they will be spun as failures whenever possible. There will be no press crusades to document the depredations that Democrats have committed on the lives of poor children. No Pulitzer prizes will be awarded for exposing their crimes.

Consequently, Republicans must do their own work in indicting the oppressors and promoting an agenda that will liberate the oppressed. To do this, Republicans must come up with a program that is so big that it dramatizes the issues all at once, and the press cannot ignore it.

Last year, Congressman Jim Rogan did just that. He devised a plan to spend one hundred billion dollars over ten years on scholarships for the twelve million poor, black, and Hispanic children in Title 1 schools. The bill would provide a $6,800 scholarship (the average public school tuition) for each of these children to enable them to find a school that would teach them. The scholarships would be granted under a formula that restricts them to one-quarter of the students in a given school in any one year. In this way, classroom size would be reduced and spending per pupil increased.

If Republicans were to support such a bill, they would frame the issue as it should be framed, change their public image overnight, cast the Democrats as heartless reactionaries, ram them up against the education unions, and drive a wedge the size of Texas through their urban-minority base. They probably won't. But whatever they do, Republicans must remember to:

- Think politics along with policy.
- Speak the language of moral indictment.
- Frame Democrats as oppressors of minorities and the poor.
- Use the romance of the underdog to win the American heart.

IX

THE WAR ON TERROR

36

Know Your Enemy

THE WAR THAT WAS JOINED ON SEPTEMBER 11, 2001, is defined by three simple but brutal facts. Our enemy is able to penetrate our borders and strike us in our homes; he can strike us with weapons of mass destruction; and he has made clear that his intention is not to change our policies, but to obliterate us and destroy our civilization itself. Because of these facts, the imperative of defending ourselves as quickly and effectively as possible is greater in this war than in any we have ever fought.

In all wars, the first essential is to know your enemy. Everything you can do to thwart his objectives or to protect your life and the lives of your countrymen depends on this knowledge.

Who, then, is the enemy that threatens our destruction? Officially he has been defined in terms of "terror" and "evil," which are generic terms that describe the means by which he has chosen to fight the war, rather than why he is fighting or how we have become his target. They do not tell us who he is. The failure to name our enemy precisely is a source of weakness in erecting our defenses. In attempting to establish security at our borders, and in our airports and harbors, we have denied ourselves the ability to target those who have targeted us. The policy

---

This article first appeared on FrontPageMagazine.com on July 24, 2002, under the title "Know Your Enemy and What He Believes."

that refuses to identify the enemy by name is a policy that asks us to fight in the dark. Yet every terrorist who slips through our security net is capable of killing tens of thousands of innocent civilians.

But we know who our enemy is, no matter that he or anyone else chooses to deny it. We have seen his face, even if we are still reluctant to give him a name. We are at war with radical Islam and with those who offer radical Islam aid and comfort, and this means we are at war with the international radical left. Both see America as the "Great Satan," embodying the twin evils of capitalist oppression and western domination. The attacks on the Twin Towers and the Pentagon were attacks on the twin symbols of American wealth and power, as defined both by the Islamists and the left.

An al-Qaeda manifesto published six months after 9/11 makes the agendas of the Islamic radicals abundantly clear. "Why We Fight America," issued by al-Qaeda spokesman Suleiman Abu Gheith, recently appeared on an al-Qaeda website hosted by the Center for Islamic Research and Studies.[1]

The statement asks why the world is surprised by what happened on 9/11—pretty much the same question asked within weeks of the horrific attack by radicals Noam Chomsky, Tariq Ali, Edward Said, Barbara Kingsolver, Arundhati Roy, and sundry professors at anti-American rallies on college campuses across the nation. And the answer is pretty much the same as well: "What happened to America [on 9/11] is something natural, an expected event for a country that uses terror, arrogant policy, and suppression against the nations and the peoples, and imposes a single method, thought, and way of life, as if the people of the entire world are clerks in its government offices and employed by its commercial companies and institutions."

Anyone who was surprised by 9/11, the al-Qaeda statement continues, does not understand the root causes of the attack, and in particular "the effects of oppression and tyranny on [the victims'] emotions and feelings." Instead, such people must think "that oppression begets surrender, that repression begets silence, that tyranny leaves only humiliation."

In fact, according to al-Qaeda, humiliation, deprivation and oppression inspire rage against the oppressor. And this righteous indignation—indistinguishable from that of the radical left—is what al-Qaeda's anti-American war is about. Unlike the western left, however, al-Qaeda does not wage its war in the name of an international proletariat or the "dispossessed," and its goal is not some kind of secular socialist utopia. Al-Qaeda's war is about the future world reign of Islam. The al-Qaeda manifesto asks how can a Muslim accept humiliation and inferiority, "when he knows that his nation was created to stand at the center of leadership, at the center of hegemony and rule, at the center of ability and sacrifice? . . . When he knows that the [divine] rule is that the entire earth must be subject to the religion of Allah— not to the East, not to the West—to no ideology and to no path except the path of Allah?"

Credulous advocates of appeasement in the west like Ted Turner and the wife of the British Prime Minister Tony Blair are in their own minds so superior to the Muslims who hate them that they don't consider the possibility that the Islamic faithful could actually mean what they say. Justifying Arafat's suicide brigades, Cherie Blair commented, "As long as young people feel they have got no hope but to blow themselves up, you are never going to make progress." This is an inanity heard nightly on cable talk shows from spokesmen for the political left. But the Middle East Research Institute has translated an interview in the Arab press with the mother of a suicide bomber, who has nothing to say about her lack of hope or about root causes like poverty, thwarted national desires, and social injustice. What she says is this:

> I am a compassionate mother to my children....Because I love my
> son, I encouraged him to die a martyr's death for the sake of
> Allah...*Jihad* is a religious obligation incumbent upon us, and we
> must carry it out. I sacrificed [my son] Muhammad as part of my
> obligation. This is an easy thing. There is no disagreement [among
> scholars] on such matters. The happiness in this world is an in
> complete happiness; eternal happiness is life in the world to come,

through martyrdom. Allah be praised, my son has attained this happiness . . . . I prayed from the depths of my heart that Allah would cause the success of his operation. I asked Allah to give me 10 [Israelis] for Muhammad, and Allah granted my request and Muhammad made his dream come true, killing 10 Israeli settlers and soldiers. Our God honored him even more, in that there were many Israelis wounded. When the operation was over, the media broadcast the news. Then Muhammad's brother came to me and informed me of his martyrdom. I began to cry, "Allah is the greatest," and prayed and thanked Allah for the success of the operation. I began to utter cries of joy and we declared that we were happy. The young people began to fire into the air out of joy over the success of the operation, as this is what we had hoped for him.

This is not a voice of despair, but hope for homicide and life everlasting. Nor is the will to commit genocide confined to the martyrs who actually blow up little children, but is shared by the entire community of radical Islam. It comes not from despair, but from a hope for heaven—a desire to serve the expansion of territorial Islam and to do God's will. Nothing could be more obvious except to those overcome by liberal arrogance that denies what it sees in order to explain it away, in order to "understand" it, and thereby to surrender to it.

The hope for heaven is the same fanatical inspiration that caused believers in socialism to kill tens of millions of innocent unbelievers over the course of the twentieth century.

The present war against America may be about humiliation and a sense of inferiority stemming from Islam's centuries of eclipse, but it is not about despair. The al-Qaeda manifesto is not addressed to people who have nothing. Quite the opposite. The al-Qaeda manifesto is an appeal to people who have something—and in whom it is a form of religious nobility to give up what they have, to sacrifice life itself for the glory of Islam: "As long as the Muslim knows and believes . . . he will not—even for a single moment—stop trying to achieve [the universal triumph of Islam], even if it costs him his soul . . . his time, his property and his son."

This is not a war about land in the Middle East or the structure of a Palestinian state, or a U.S. military presence in the Arabian peninsula. It is a war about redemption. In this way it exactly parallels the communist crusade that dominated the last century. In the eyes of the communists, America stood in the way of heaven—a socialist paradise on earth where "social injustice" would no longer exist. In the eyes of radical Islam, America—the Great Satan—stands in the way of Islam's rule, and thus of human redemption, and it is for this reason America must be destroyed.

Thus, the al-Qaeda proclamation: "America is the head of heresy in our modern world, and it leads an infidel democratic regime that is based upon separation of religion and state and on ruling the people by the people via legislating laws that contradict the way of Allah and permit what Allah has prohibited. This compels the other countries to act in accordance with the same laws in the same ways…and punishes any country [that rebels against these laws] by besieging it, and then by boycotting it. By so doing [America] seeks to impose on the world a religion that is not Allah's."

Americans, wake up! Your enemies hate you not for what you have done, but for who you are. You are infidels. They hate you because you are democratic and tolerant and unbelieving. They hate you because you are Christians ("America's standing with the Christians of the world against the Muslims has stripped the camouflage from its face"), and they hate you because you are Hindus and Buddhists, secularists and Jews.

This war is not a war that awaits us. It is a war we are in. Americans have hardly begun to understand this, but the enemy is already keeping score: "We have not reached parity [with America's alleged attacks on Muslims. Therefore], we have the right to kill four million Americans—two million of them children—and to exile twice as many and wound and cripple hundreds of thousands. Furthermore, it is our right to fight them with chemical and biological weapons, so as to afflict them with the fatal maladies that have afflicted Muslims because of the [Americans'] chemical and biological weapons."

Americans have also hardly begun to understand that if radical Islam is one face of our enemy, the other is the radical left. For two hundred years, the radical left has believed in a religion promising a heaven on earth whose end justifies any means. That is why progressives like Lenin, Stalin, and Pol Pot killed so many innocent people. That is why radical leftists in America and other European countries have joined in denouncing America's war of self-defense and in abetting the Arab crusade to obliterate Israel and (in the process) exterminate the Jews of the Middle East.

How serious are some American leftists about supporting the war to destroy their own country? Attorney Lynn Stewart is a veteran of the radical left going back to the 1960s and is the lawyer for the "blind sheik," who led the first terrorist attack on the World Trade Center in 1993. Six people were killed in the attack and one thousand injured. Stewart is associated with the Center for Constitutional Rights—a leftist group committed to anti-American radical causes. Its agenda is to dismantle the Constitution in a revolutionary future but also to use it in the present as a radical weapon to weaken the American state. Stewart has been a supporter of communist causes and Arab terrorists for her entire professional life. Recently, the Attorney General indicted Stewart for helping the sheik, who is now in prison, to communicate with his terrorist followers in the Middle East and further his bloody agendas.

A chorus of the usual suspects from the left has rallied to her defense and attacked U.S. Attorney General Ashcroft for allegedly infringing on the civil liberties of the imprisoned terrorist and his lawyer. The National Lawyers Guild, the ACLU, the *Nation,* and other "progressive" institutions of the left support Stewart as a "persecuted" civil libertarian.

In 1995, the *New York Times* interviewed Stewart and reported the following: "Ms. Stewart suggested that violence and revolution were sometimes necessary to right the economic and racial wrongs of America's capitalist system." Stewart said this: "I don't believe in anarchistic violence, but in directed violence. That would be violence directed at the institutions which perpetuate capitalism, racism, and sexism, and the people who are the appointed guardians of those institutions, and accompanied by popular support."

The World Trade Center is an institution which perpetuates capitalism and—in the eyes of the left—racism and sexism as well. According to every leftist—from the *Nation* magazine to the Chomsky fifth column—America is a land of capitalism, racism, and sexism, and the enforcer of this unholy trinity on a global scale. This is the world that the Islamic radicals call *Dar Al-Harb*: the world of darkness, the world that is not socialist and that is not Islam. According to Lynn Stewart and the al-Qaeda faithful, the people who dwell in *Dar Al-Harb* and support its profane agendas deserve to die. This is what the present Islamic holy war is about, and Americans better understand it sooner rather than later.

37

Port Huron and the War on Terror

FORTY YEARS AGO, I wrote the first book about the New Left,[1] which was also a kind of manifesto of our publicly proposed agendas for a more democratic and racially equal America. I say "publicly proposed" because as leftists we knew we could not announce what we really intended, which was a socialist revolution in America. As "new" leftists, we retained the illusion that socialism was a workable future, and that we could avoid the "mistakes" the Soviets had made, which had tarnished and compromised the socialist agenda. We also told ourselves that we could not be candid about what we intended because of America's repressive political atmosphere at the time. But, in fact, McCarthyism was already dead, and the real reason it was so difficult for us to articulate our socialist intentions was because they had been so thoroughly discredited by the historical record.

In the same year, a much more famous (and equally disingenuous) document appeared, called "The Port Huron Statement," which was the founding manifesto of the Students for a Democratic Society (SDS). The Port Huron Statement did not admit to its socialist agendas, but called instead for "participatory democracy," by which it meant a direct democracy (or "people's democracy")—a democracy that would

---

This article first appeared on *Salon.com* July 29, 2002, under the title "Forty Years after Port Huron," and has been edited for this book.

embrace the economic order as well. This was exactly how Marx had described the communist future, but the Port Huron statement prudently refrained from acknowledging that fact.

SDS quickly became the largest organization of the New Left, enrolling close to one hundred thousand members at its peak, and spearheaded the movement against America's anti-communist war in Vietnam. But a movement that had begun with slogans about "democracy" emblazoned on its banners, ended up—a bare seven years later—embracing totalitarian police states like Cuba and North Vietnam and genocidal communist movements like the Cambodian Khmer Rouge. In its final spasms of revolutionary fervor, SDS spawned leaders like Bernardine Dohrn and Bill Ayers who called for actual war against "Amerikkka" and went "underground" to lead the first political terrorist cult in this country.

As it happens, Tom Hayden, who was the most famous of the authors of the Port Huron statement, was also one of the loudest voices calling for a "war of liberation" in "Amerikkka" and the creation of armed "zones of liberation" in American college towns. Although he didn't go underground with the Weathermen, Hayden gave their cause his moral and political support. Hayden even formed his own guerrilla *foco* (a term lifted from Che Guevara's strategist, Regis Debray) called the "Red Family," whose members trained at local firing ranges for the battles to come.

Not surprisingly, in the years that have passed, Hayden has not cared to recall the details of these episodes or explain how this political degeneration might be connected to the principles he helped to draft at Port Huron. Nor have any of the New Left historians of this period. This failure is all the more striking because the disastrous direction in which he and others led the New Left was actually predicted at the moment of its founding by dissenters from the Port Huron consensus. These were notably the late Irving Howe and his disciple, Michael Harrington. Even in 1962, Harrington and Howe saw that Hayden and his comrades were totalitarians in the making.

These thoughts are provoked by a feature story in the August 5, 2002, issue of the *Nation*, titled "The Port Huron Statement at 40," and co-authored by Hayden and another sDs founder, Dick Flacks—now a professor at uc Santa Barbara. In their article, Hayden and Flacks celebrate the longevity and influence of their manifesto, and particularly its central organizing concept, "participatory democracy." In doing so, they write as though the seeds of malevolence they sowed (and which the nation reaped) were something of which to be proud. But their rosy nostalgia is made possible only by a selective forgetting of the sort Milan Kundera has explored so eloquently in his writings about the totalitarian delusion. It is, in fact, their own romance with totalitarianism that Hayden and Flacks have conveniently forgotten.

Thus Hayden describes himself in those early days as a "a Midwestern populist by nature, rebelling apolitically against the boring hypocrisy of suburban life—until the Southern black student sit-in movement showed that a committed life was possible." This is beyond disingenuous. How did such a political innocent find himself in the *leadership* of a socialist organization (sDs was an offshoot of the League for Industrial Democracy) surrounded by marxists—including his co-author, Dick Flacks—who were self-consciously attempting to escape the *cul de sac* in which they had been put by the calamities and crimes of the Stalin era? Hayden and Flacks are typical of the left in their self-conscious effort to distort the meaning of their own history. The only way to understand the "Port Huron Statement" is as a document that attempts to preserve the marxist vision without its guilty association with communism (which is what they hope to achieve by their current mendacity as well). About this there really are no grounds for dispute.

The key battle at Port Huron, recounted in many histories of the events but not addressed in the Hayden-Flacks reminiscence, was whether to include members of the Communist Party in the coalition that would be sDs.[2] This battle provides the key to understanding what transpired afterwards. Harrington, who was present at the sDs founding, wanted the new organization to make a clear and principled break with the communist past—a past shared by most at the founding. Hayden and Flacks (a scion of communists himself) did not want to make so dramatic a break. They were both "anti-anti-communists" in the political vernacular of choice. They were critical of Stalinism, but they still wanted a socialist revolution in America and, despite their criticism of what Stalin had done, they refused to support—and in fact opposed—America's Cold War against the Soviet bloc.

Hayden and Flacks describe the dispute in the following terms: "While the draft Port Huron Statement included a strong denunciation of the Soviet Union, it wasn't enough for LID[3] leaders like Michael Harrington. They wanted absolute clarity, for example, that the United States was blameless for the nuclear arms race . . . In truth, they seemed threatened by the independence of the new wave of student activism."

This is a serious distortion of the facts. In the first place, denouncing abuses of power in the Soviet Union in 1962 was not only easy for leftists who were not actually members of the Communist Party, but absolutely necessary. It was easy because the head of the Soviet Communist Party himself, Nikita Khrushchev, had denounced "Stalinism" and its crimes six years before. It was necessary because no leftist movement would have any credibility with Americans if it did not denounce Stalinism or the abuses of power that persisted in the Soviet Union. This admission that communism had indeed committed monstrous injustices had no consequences for socialist belief because most leftists passed off the blame for the crimes to America and the West, and their Cold War against communism. To be anti-anti communist was in effect to blame America and the West for what had gone wrong in the Soviet Union and its satellite states.

Contrary to Hayden and Flacks's claim, what Harrington and Howe actually felt threatened by was the lack of absolute clarity on the issue of communist totalitarianism by SDSers like Hayden and Flacks. Harrington and Howe saw the failure of SDS to exclude communists as an expression of political blindness that would determine the future course of the New Left itself. Anti-anti-communism betokened the unwillingness of SDS to make a principled break with communist ideas, communist states and communist causes.

History has proved Harrington and Howe right. The first step down this fatal path was the inclusion of communists in the new radical organization. The next steps were to support the communist gulag in Cuba and the communist war in Vietnam.[4] It was another logical step to embrace communist ideas and to emulate communist practices, which is what eventually led to the spectacle of the SDS election of 1968 in which two factions of Maoists vied with the pro-communist revolutionaries of Weathermen for the leadership of what had become the New Left's largest organization. This political slide was greatly encouraged by the anti-American agenda of the Port Huron Statement—an agenda which has shaped the left's antagonisms and sympathies ever since.

None of this history is mentioned or addressed in the Hayden-Flacks nostalgia piece. To be fair, they do quote a critic or two, one of whom happens to be me, but only in passing and without further comment. "The former radical David Horowitz reads the [Port Huron] statement as encoding a 'self-conscious effort to rescue the communist project from its Soviet fate.'" This is a quotation from my autobiography, *Radical Son*, where I describe the New Left as an attempt to get rid of the Stalinist bathwater without throwing out the socialist baby. The illusion that we could do that was, in my retrospective view, our fatal flaw. *Radical Son* is an account of how the commitment to a socialist agenda and the unwillingness to be identified with the anti-communist cause inexorably led New Leftists to embrace totalitarian agendas and causes, including the bloody wars of Ho Chi Minh and Pol Pot.

Tom Hayden is one of the few New Leftists who has given even a moment's thought in print to the millions of peasants in Southeast Asia we helped to slaughter by backing the communists and their "wars of liberation." Unfortunately, Hayden's moment of clarity—recorded in his memoir, *Reunion*—proved to be both half-hearted and brief, and he seems to have forgotten it altogether. He is currently too busy embracing the terrorist agendas of the IRA to reflect seriously on the tragedies of the past.

Reading Hayden and Flacks's *Nation* article, one would never know that these issues—momentous as they were—existed at all. In their account, the New Left was not really related to the Old Left but was born out of a generalized apathy of the 1950s generation, oblivious to the possibility that any problems might exist in society at large. Thus, "on some campuses, professors and students were questioning the Cold War arms race"—as though the rest of the nation had failed to notice it or were too stupid to give it any thought. "There were stirrings on the fringe, too, where students were listening to Bob Dylan and rock and roll. SDS represented the first defections from the mainstream."

In fact, SDS didn't represent defections from anything, nor were its members "mainstream." Defections from the mainstream happened later, as a result of the military draft, when college students reluctant to risk their lives in war came scurrying into its ranks. In 1962, SDS was pretty much a collection of red diaper babies and political fellow travelers trying to jumpstart a moribund left, whose support for the communist gulags had brought their ideas into disrepute and decimated their ranks. That is why the pivotal concept of the manifesto they adopted—and the idea that Hayden and Flacks are most eager to celebrate—was not socialism but "participatory democracy." It was a term that could not be found in any existing socialist texts or associated with any actual communist regimes. It thus promised freedom from the stigma that had become attached to these schemes. The same motivation had previously caused communists to call themselves "progressives" and later inspired leftists to call themselves "liberals."

Even now Hayden and Flacks want readers to take the term at face value: "'Participatory democracy' sought to expand the sphere of public decisions from the mere election of representatives to the deeper role of 'bringing people out of isolation and into community' in decentralized forms of decision-making. The same democratic humanism was applied to the economy in calls for 'incentives worthier than money,' and for work to be 'self-directed, not manipulated.'"

Who do these authors think they're fooling at so late a date? What economy do the authors have in mind that is based on "incentives worthier than money"—*Cuba*? The phrase "participatory democracy" may be fresh, but the concept is stale and utterly discredited by the economic and political miseries it produced on an epic scale.

The idea of participatory democracy is a venerable socialist concept, whose roots lie in anarchist dogmas and in Marx's celebration of the Paris Commune. Anarchists called the political instruments of participatory democracy "workers councils;" the Bolsheviks called them "soviets." The names may be different, but the idea is the same: an egalitarian economy and society—the political enforcement of an equality of condition through the social ownership of the economic order; the destruction of due process and hierarchy—professional, scientific, meritocratic, or traditional in the name of "social justice," which is itself a name for totalitarian rule. (Why totalitarian? Because the implementation of the left's idea of social justice requires the elimination of the private sphere and the state control of every aspect of social life that might produce unequal or "unjust" outcomes.)

"It was no wonder," write Hayden and Flacks, "that the [Port Huron] statement was inspired by participatory democracy. Participation is what we were denied, and what we hungered for. Without it, there was no dignity. Parents and professors lectured us, administrators ordered us, draft boards conscripted us, the whole system channeled us, all to please authority and take our place in line." Reading these words one wonders what it must be like to have lived as long as Hayden and Flacks and to have forgotten so much, or learned so little. Still no appreciation of all that parents and professors and authority have brought them, or of what life would be like in their absence.

So it is no accident (as we used to say) that this old pair of unreconstructed "revolutionaries" should, forty years later, have no wiser view of the world. It is also no accident that (worse yet) they should take specific pleasure in the influence they have had in encouraging the most destructive elements in contemporary culture—the hate-America, corporation-phobic urban guerillas of the next left. As Hayden and Flacks write:

> There is a new movement astir in the world, against the inherent violence of globalization, corporate rule and fundamentalism that reminds us strongly of the early 1960s. . . . The war on terrorism has revived the Cold War framework. An escalating national security state attempts to rivet our attention and invest our resources on fighting an elusive, undefined enemy for years to come, at the

inevitable price of our civil liberties and continued neglect of social justice. To challenge the framework of the war on terrorism, to demand a search for real peace with justice, is as difficult today as challenging the Cold War was at Port Huron.

What was difficult for Hayden, Flacks and the New Left about "challenging the Cold War," was that it was their country's war against socialists like themselves and on behalf of human freedom. One-and-a-half billion people liberated from the chains of Soviet imperialism testify to that, even if Hayden and Flacks have failed to understand it yet. What is difficult for Hayden, Flacks, and their leftist friends about challenging the war on terror is really no different. In opposing the war on terror, they are pitting themselves against America's efforts to make the world safe for its system—for tolerance, for political liberty and free economies, and for life itself. What is interesting is that Hayden and Flacks, and their editors at the *Nation*, should be so forthright in declaring their intention to weaken and undermine America's defense against terror and to use disingenuous crusades for "civil liberties" and "social justice" as the instruments for accomplishing their destructive agendas. Let's hope the American people are taking note of these adversaries within, and preparing an appropriate response.

38

Clinton's Pardoned Bombers

URING THE SUMMER DAYS, the Santa Monica promenade is a mecca for pleasure seekers and the curious. Its bricked sidewalks are crowded with Angelenos gawking at the antics of mimes, jugglers, and break-dancers who put on a good show that is also free. In August 2001, just before the World Trade Center bombing, I was taking a Saturday evening stroll with my wife past these sights, when I was given the opportunity to see one of Bill Clinton's infamous pardons in action—out of prison and back on the streets.

The last time I saw Linda Evans was thirty-two years before, in Berkeley, speaking to a packed hall of student radicals at the university. Evans was one of the leaders of the Weathermen, then a new radical sect that had taken over the national student organization SDS and destroyed it because it wasn't revolutionary enough. She had come to the university with fellow militant Ted Gold to recruit troops for the global race war the Weathermen believed had already begun. The only role white radicals could play in this war, they said, was to serve as a Fifth Column of saboteurs and terrorists inside the "belly of the beast," which is the way the left referred (and still refers) to America. White radicals were needed to blow things up, sow social chaos, and hasten "Amerikkka's" destruction (which is the way they spelled their country's

From *How to Beat the Democrats and Other Subversive Ideas* (2002).

name). "Vietnam is burning," Evans screamed at the audience. "It's only white skin privilege that prevents American cities from being burned too." Everyone present knew what this meant. Berkeley deserved to be put to the torch. Only our own racism stopped us from lighting the match.

The year was 1969. A few months later, Evans and Gold disappeared from sight and into what the "communiqués" issued by their leader Bernardine Dohrn identified as the Weather Underground. The first of these communiqués was a formal declaration of war against the United States. Shortly thereafter, three of the Weathermen were blown up in a Greenwich Village townhouse while making a bomb filled with roofing nails which they intended to detonate at a dance at nearby Fort Dix. Ted Gold was one of the three. Months later, Linda Evans was arrested for transporting weapons and explosives in Detroit, and for crossing state lines to incite a riot. The charges were eventually thrown out on a technicality: the wiretaps that identified her had been unauthorized.

On her release, Evans resumed her anti-American activities as a self-styled fighter against "racism/white supremacy and Zionism" and as a supporter of communist movements in Central America. In a profile on a "political prisoners" support website, her activities in these years are described as "working to develop clandestine resistance, capable of conducting armed struggle as part of a multi-level overall revolutionary strategy." On May 11, 1985, she was arrested again, charged, and then convicted for acquiring weapons, fake IDs, and safe houses, and of terrorist actions. Her targets included the U.S. Capitol Building, the National War College, the Navy Yard Computer Center, the Navy Yard Officers' Club, Israeli Aircraft Industries, the FBI, and the New York Patrolman's Benevolent Association. In her possession were 740 pounds of dynamite. Evans was sentenced to forty years in prison.

But then her Clinton patrons intervened. The agent of her mercy was the blimpish New York congressman Jerry Nadler, one of President Clinton's staunchest defenders during the impeachment process and one of Senator Clinton's chief supporters during her election bid. Nadler appealed to Clinton, and the President responded. As the last hours of the Clinton era expired, Linda Evans was freed. It was twenty-four years shy of her full sentence.

The serendipity that brought me into Linda Evans's presence a second time was a glance into the window display of the Midnight Special Bookstore, a radical haunt on the Santa Monica promenade, which featured anti-Bush posters and Noam Chomsky tracts, along with choice events on the progressive calendar. In the window display, I noticed an announcement that Evans would be presenting a film and talk that evening about "political prisoners."

When my wife and I entered the store, we saw that about thirty people had seated themselves on folding chairs in the back to watch the film, which was almost over. We sat through a sequence that featured Laura Whitehorn, a member of Evans's radical network who had been released on parole. At the conclusion of the film, which scrolled a long list of "political prisoners" still in jail, Evans herself appeared and asked the audience to form a circle around her. I had remembered her as a small, fiery, blond woman, with a pretty face hardened and flushed by revolutionary fervor. She was softer now, actually teary-eyed from watching the film of her comrades (as she referred to them) who were still in prison.

As she wiped her tears and apologized for the show of emotion, I noticed that the years had piled flesh on her petite frame, giving her a roly-poly look and making her seem softer still. There was no hard edge to her voice as she began to explain how people were oppressed in prison and oppressed in America, and how their oppressors were white racism and imperialism. I wondered to myself how the other listeners squared this dark picture of things with the carnival of Saturday night revelers on the promenade. But Evans gave no thought to this cognitive dissonance at all. Instead, she pursued her tales of social woe, focusing on one of her comrades who had been denied even the ability to attend her prison pottery classes because of "the arthritis in her hands," as if this were yet another injustice inflicted by the System with which she was still obviously at war.

Her very solicitousness suggested the leader of a help group for the victims of unspeakable crimes who were ignored or forgotten by everybody else. In addition to cop-killer Mumia Abu Jamal, the most famous "political prisoner" on the list at the end of the film, Evans mentioned three comrades, in particular, who were in need of support. These were Sara Jane Olson, Jamil Al-Amin, and Kathy Boudin.

The very first questioner from the audience asked Evans what it was that these individuals had done to be singled out for such punishment. Evans seemed a little uncomfortable with the question from such an audience. In her answer, she singled out Olson and Brown because both had trials scheduled for the fall. Olson, she said, was accused of attempting to "fire bomb" a police car, hesitating over the words "fire" and "bomb" as though it was still an effort for her to lie about such things. In fact it was pipe bombs that Olson had randomly planted under *two* police cars, which would have killed the occupants if they hadn't malfunctioned first. "It didn't even go off," Evans griped, as though the failure to succeed in murdering one's victim absolved one for the criminal intent.

She proceeded then to the next level of excuse. After failing at this final revolutionary mission twenty-five years before, Olson had changed her name, which was really Kathy Soliah, and had lived as the wife of a doctor in Minnesota and raised three children. This fact was then used to underscore the sinister character of the state, which was so determined to prosecute her that it was charging her with complicity in *all* the crimes of the Symbionese Liberation Army, whose soldier she had once been. Sara Olson's attorney, Shawn Chapman, who was in the audience, rose to second these observations. Neither she nor Evans ever got around to explaining, however, that this "liberation army" had assassinated the first black superintendent of Oakland's public schools with cyanide-tipped bullets and had murdered a female bystander in the course of a bank robbery, or that Sara Olson had publicly championed the crimes of the organization as acts of "social justice" at the time. If prosecutors had evidence linking her to the conspiratorial organization that planned such acts, it was perfectly legitimate for them to charge her for their consequences.

Evans then talked about Jamil Al-Amin, who had been known in the 1960s as H. Rap Brown. When arrested for killing a policeman,

Brown, she pointed out, was an "imam" in a Moslem temple in Atlanta, a community worker who helped the drug addicted and the
poor. She indicated that this was the reason the police had targeted
him. "There was a shootout," she said, introducing the events that led
to his arrest. Two police officers had gone to Brown's home at night
with a warrant for traffic tickets. "Who arrests people at night for traffic
tickets?" Evans asked in the most suspicious tone she could muster.
One of the officers was killed in the "shootout" that followed. The
surviving officer had reported that the fleeing gunman had been
wounded and was bleeding. But when police tracked Brown three days
later to another state, Evans said, he had no wound. Key facts that
Evans omitted were that both officers were black, that they had not
anticipated trouble and consequently were not wearing vests, and had
been ambushed with a firearm that Brown owned and that was found
in his possession. Evans did not attempt to explain why an innocent
man should flee for three days until a massive manhunt tracked him
down, or why the Atlanta police force, whose chief was a black woman
in a liberal city whose mayor was also black, would want to murder or
falsely imprison a community holy man whose name was H. Rap Brown.

When an elderly gentleman in a straw hat sitting near me asked
Evans how she defined "political prisoners," she answered, "every prisoner in American jails is a victim of political circumstance." It was a
common theme of the 1960s that divided the delusional world of radicals from everyone else's. Almost defensively, as though to maintain
my own sanity, I thought first of the Night Stalker, a psychopath who
had raped and murdered forty men, women, and children, and then of
the recent front page saga of a fugitive who had been captured after
killing his whole family with a knife. In Linda Evans's eyes, evil was a
political circumstance called Amerikkka; and, more specifically, the
"white" corporate power structure.

The separate reality of radicals, which made them unable to comprehend their own deeds, was made vivid for me in a *New York Times*
story I read later about the parole appeal of Evans's third political
prisoner, Kathy Boudin. The *Times* had run a series of stories on Boudin,
doing everything possible to create sympathy for her as her appeal date

approached. Like Sara Jane Olson, Boudin proposed herself as a "changed woman," who had been incarcerated almost as a matter of mistaken identity: "Today, her supporters say, Ms. Boudin is a different woman. During her 20 years in prison she has helped to create several innovative programs for AIDS victims, incarcerated mothers and inmates seeking to take college courses."[1] As part of its promotional effort on Boudin's behalf, the *Times* even ran a three-thousand-word feature on her graduation from the college program she had created, which was funded by actress Glenn Close and *Vagina Monologues* author Eve Ensler among others. Boudin's boosters included the *Nation* magazine, numerous organizations advocating "prisoner rights" and "social justice" and, in general, the socially prominent and influential mandarins of the "progressive" elite.

Like her comrades, Kathy Boudin is—despite all these cosmetics of social uplift—a lifelong enemy of American democracy and a committed terrorist. She was part of the Weathermen team constructing the anti-personnel bomb whose explosion in the New York townhouse killed three of the guilty and prevented the loss of innocent lives. Far from renouncing her communist and terrorist past, Boudin is part of the same radical network that fuels Linda Evans's seditious projects and remains an integral part of the permanent revolution both signed on to in the 1960s. In the following decade, when Jimmy Carter was in the White House, Kathy Boudin joined a gang of black criminals calling themselves the May Nineteenth Communist Movement and became part of the getaway team in a $1.6 million robbery of a Brink's armored vehicle. The funds would have financed a revolution to carve a "New Afrika" out of the United States.[2]

In the botched robbery attempt, an innocent Brinks guard and two Nanuet police officers were killed. Nine children ranging in age from two months to twenty-one years were left without fathers and with permanent wounds that are beyond the powers of the courts or Kathy Boudin to heal. One of the murdered officers was Waverly Brown, the first black policeman on the Nanuet force, whose hiring was the result of a lengthy civil rights struggle undertaken by blacks and whites in the Nanuet community. Yet here is how Kathy Boudin explained to the *New York Times* her collusion in the cold-blooded killings of these men: "I went out that day with a lot of denial. I didn't think anything would happen; in my mind, I was going back to pick up my child at the baby-sitter's."

Susan Rosenberg was a comrade of Kathy Boudin and Linda Evans, a former Weather Underground bomber, a member of the May Nineteenth Communist Movement, and a participant in the Brinks robbery. Like Boudin, Rosenberg went to fancy private institutions, the Walden School and Barnard College, and—as a 1960s radical—became part of a terrorist network called "The Family," which included the above organizations as well as the Black Liberation Army and the Red Guerrilla Resistance. On November 7, 1983, "The Family" bombed the U.S. Capitol in a blast that "ripped through a conference room near the Senate offices of then minority leader Robert C. Byrd." The bombers issued a war communiqué, explaining that "we purposely aimed our attack at the institutions of imperialist rule rather than at individual members of the ruling class and government. We did not choose to kill any of them this time. But their lives are not sacred."[3]

Susan Rosenberg also participated in making possible the escape to Cuba of Joanne Chesimard, aka Assata Shakur, wanted in connection with the ambush assassination of a New Jersey state trooper. Shakur was convicted of the murder and was serving a life sentence when Rosenberg helped her escape. In 1984, Rosenberg was captured with Evans at a New Jersey warehouse where they were unloading the 740 pounds of explosives. She also was in possession of fourteen weapons including an Uzi submachine gun. As in the case of other left-wing murderers for political causes, Rosenberg became a progressive hero, supported by celebrity defenders of political criminals like Noam Chomsky and William Kunstler, both of whom actively lobbied for her release. Since she had been sentenced to fifty-eight years for her crimes, prosecutors decided not to pursue murder charges in connection with the killing of the three officers in the Nanuet robbery.

This proved to be a mistake. Like Evans, she gained the support of Congressman Nadler and, along with Evans, was pardoned by Clinton on his last day in office.

Linda Evans, Susan Rosenberg, Sara Olson, and Kathy Boudin are, in fact, part of the ongoing terrorist "Family," a community of political monsters who have regrouped—at least publicly—as an amnesty organization for "political prisoners." Although the *New York Times* and other left-leaning media are ready to portray them as idealists (*60 Minutes* performed the service for Rosenberg), these are not prisoners of conscience. They are prisoners without conscience, incapable of even a minimal accounting of what they willed and did fifteen or thirty years ago, or what—given the right circumstances—they would be willing to attempt in the future. The threat they represent lies not just in their monstrous deeds. It lies in the fact that their evil is protected by the mask of left-wing "idealism" they have adopted and that the left-wing media obligingly preserves for them. By consciously concealing their agenda in a aura of vulnerability and innocence and a desire for "social justice," they are able to manipulate institutions of power in American society, and in particular in the Democratic Party, making the unsuspecting (but also the fellow-traveling) abettors of their malign intent.

For forty years, Linda Evans and a network of political comrades have inhabited an alternative reality that makes innocence seem criminal and their own criminality like nobility itself. They are supported in their delusions by an academic industry in anti-white, anti-capitalist, anti-male, anti-American ideologies and screeds. As in the days of the Weathermen, the supporters of their unholy war are recruited from college campuses. Three thousand benighted activists attended a conference this year at the University of California to protest the "prison-industrial complex." The event was organized by an academic hero, Angela Davis, a lifelong servant of communist police states while they existed, and a comrade of revolutionary criminals. In New York, a similar rally demanding the right of felons to vote was organized by the misnamed Center for Constitutional Rights and was addressed by such speakers as Democratic gubernatorial candidate Andrew Cuomo and television pundit Arianna Huffington.

The ideas behind this movement are the ideas of the anti-American, anti-globalization left. Their agenda is to attack legitimate law

enforcement and to defame American justice as a system of racial oppression and—though they do not reveal this aspect to outsiders—to
enlist the antisocial and the violent as a military vanguard. "Like the
military/industrial complex, the prison industrial complex is an inter-
weaving of private business and government interests. Its twofold purpose is profit and social control. . . . This monumental commitment to
lock up a sizeable percentage of the population is an integral part of
the globalization of capital." These sentences are taken from a pamphlet written by Linda Evans and her lover, Eve Goldberg, under the
title *The Prison Industrial Complex and the Global Economy.*

As their pamphlet makes clear, the new radicalism is the old Weatherman race war brought up to date. Globalization is depicted as the
white man's aggression against the non-white races of the world. It is
American capitalism versus Third World victims. The prison networks,
the "social justice" organizations, the anti-globalist protesters are the
fifth column vanguards envisaged by the Weathermen, declaring war
on the Empire and plotting to tear down its walls from within. "Tear
Down the Walls" is actually the name of the next big mobilization of
Linda Evans's army, an "International Human Rights Conference on
Winning Amnesty for U.S Political Prisoners and Prisoners of War"—
Mumia Abu Jamal, Kathy Boudin, and H. Rap Brown among them.
The majority of the "political prisoners of war," the conference bro-
chure explains, "are Black/New Afrikans . . . .These political prisoners
of war are women and men incarcerated because of their involvement
in political activities which challenged the unjust nature of the U.S.
socioeconomic system and its hegemonic policies around the world."

The conference was to be held seven months later at the end of
March 2002, in the mecca of the revolutionary faith, Fidel Castro's
Cuba, one of the last surviving communist police states. It is entirely
fitting that the sadistic tyrant was himself to be the conference host
having turned his unhappy nation into the world's oldest island prison.

39

Why Israel Is the Victim:
A Brief History of the Middle East Conflict

ZIONISM IS A NATIONAL LIBERATION MOVEMENT, identical in most ways to other liberation movements that leftists and progressives the world over—and in virtually every case but this one—fervently support. This exceptionalism is also visible at the other end of the political spectrum: in every other instance, right-wingers oppose national liberation movements that are under the spell of marxist delusions and committed to violent means. But some on the extreme right make an exception for the movement that Palestinians have aimed at the Jews. The opposition to a Jewish homeland at both ends of the political spectrum identifies the problem that Zionism was created to solve.

The "Jewish problem" is just another name for the fact that Jews are the most universally hated and persecuted ethnic group in history. The Zionist founders believed that hatred of Jews was a direct consequence of their stateless condition. As long as Jews were aliens in every society they found themselves in, they would always be seen as interlopers, their loyalties would be suspect, and persecution would follow. This was what happened to Captain Alfred Dreyfus, whom French

---

This article first appeared on FrontPageMagazine.com on January 17, 2002. It has been edited for this book.

anti-Semites falsely accused of spying and who was put on trial for treason by the French government in the nineteenth century. Theodore Herzl was an assimilated, westernized Jew, who witnessed the Dreyfus frame-up in Paris and went on to lead the Zionist movement.

Herzl and other Zionist founders believed that if Jews had a nation of their own, the very fact would "normalize" their condition in the community of nations. Jews had been without a state since the beginning of the Diaspora, when the Romans expelled them from Judea on the west bank of the Jordan River, some two thousand years before. Once the Jews obtained a homeland—Judea itself seemed a logical site—and were again like other peoples, the Zionists believed anti-Semitism would wither on its poisonous vine and the Jewish problem would disappear. Here is what happened instead.[1]

THE BEGINNINGS

In the 1920s, among their final acts as victors in World War I, the British and French created, out of the ashes of the empire of their defeated Turkish adversary, the states that now define the Middle East. In a region that the Ottoman Turks had controlled for four hundred years, Britain and France drew the boundaries of the new states, Syria Lebanon, and Iraq. Previously, the British had promised the Jewish Zionists that they could establish a "national home" in a portion of what remained of the area, which was known as the Palestine Mandate. But in 1921 the British separated 80 percent of the Mandate, east of the Jordan, created the Arab kingdom of "Transjordan," and barred Jews from settling there. It was created for the Arabian monarch, King Abdullah, who had been defeated in tribal warfare in the Arabian peninsula and lacked a seat of power. Abdullah's tribe was Hashemite, while the vast majority of his subjects were "Palestinian" Arabs.

What was left of the original Palestine Mandate—between the west bank of the Jordan and the Mediterranean sea—had been settled by Arabs and Jews. Jews, in fact, had lived in the area continuously for 3,700 years, even after the Romans destroyed their state in Judea in 70 AD. Arabs became the dominant local population for the first time in the seventh century AD, as a result of the Muslim invasions. These Arabs were largely nomads who had no distinctive language or culture to separate them from other Arabs. In all the time since, they had made no attempt to create an independent Palestinian state west or east of the Jordan, and none was ever established.

The pressure for a Jewish homeland was dramatically increased of course by the Nazi Holocaust which targeted the Jews for extermination and succeeded in killing six million, in part because no country—not even England or the United States—would open their borders and allow Jews fleeing death to enter. In 1948, the United Nations voted to partition the remaining portion of the original Mandate that had not been given to Jordan, to make a Jewish homeland possible.

Under the partition plan, the Arabs were assigned the Jews' ancient home in Judea and Samaria—now known as the West Bank and the Gaza Strip on the border with Egypt. The Jews were allotted three slivers of disconnected land along the Mediterranean and the Sinai desert. They were also given access to their holy city of Jerusalem, but as an island cut off from the slivers, surrounded by Arab land and under international control. Sixty percent of the land allotted to the Jews was the Negev desert. The entire portion represented only about 10 percent of the original Palestine Mandate. Out of these unpromising parts, the Jews created a new state, Israel, in 1948. The idea of a Palestinian nation, or a movement to create one, did not even exist.

Thus, at the moment of Israel's birth, Palestinian Arabs lived on roughly 90 percent of the original Palestine Mandate—in Transjordan and in the UN partition area, but also in the new state of Israel itself. There were eight hundred thousand Arabs living in Israel alongside 650,000 Jews (a figure that would increase rapidly as a result of the influx of refugees from Europe and the Middle East). At the same time, Jews were legally barred from settling in the thirty-five thousand square miles of Palestinian Transjordan, which eventually was renamed simply "Jordan."

The Arab population in the slivers called Israel had actually more than tripled since the Zionists began settling the region in significant numbers in the 1880s. The reason for this increase was that the Jewish settlers had brought industrial and agricultural development with them, which attracted Arab immigrants to what had previously been a sparsely settled and economically destitute area.

If the Palestinian Arabs had been willing to accept this arrangement, in which they received 90 percent of the land in the Palestine Mandate, and under which they benefited from the industry, enterprise, and political democracy the Jews brought to the region, there would have been no Middle East conflict. But they were not.

Instead, the Arab League—representing five neighboring Arab states—declared war on Israel on the day of its creation, and five Arab armies invaded the slivers with the aim of destroying the infant Jewish state. During the fighting, according to the UN mediator on the scene, an estimated 472,000 Arabs fled their homes and left the infant state. Some fled to escape the dangers, others were driven out in the heat of war. They planned on returning after an Arab victory and the destruction of the Jewish state—the outcome their leaders promised.

But the Jews—many of them recent Holocaust survivors—refused to be defeated. Instead, the five Arab armies that had invaded their slivers were repelled. Yet there was no peace. Even though their armies were beaten, the Arab states were determined to carry on their campaign of destruction, and to remain formally at war with the Israeli state. After the defeat of the Arab armies, the Palestinians who lived in the Arab area of the UN partition did not attempt to create a state of their own. Instead, in 1950, Jordan annexed the entire West Bank and Egypt annexed the Gaza Strip. There were no Arab protests.

REFUGEES: JEWISH AND ARAB

As a result of the annexation and the continuing state of war, the Arab refugees who had fled the Israeli slivers did not return. There was a refugee flow into Israel, but it was a flow of Jews who had been expelled from Arab countries. All over the Middle East, Jews were forced to leave lands they had lived on for centuries. Although Israel was a tiny geographical area and a fledgling state, its government welcomed and resettled six hundred thousand Jewish refugees from the Arab countries. No Arab country welcomed Palestinian refugees or allowed them to become citizens.

At the same time, the Jews resumed their work of creating a new nation in what was now a single sliver of land. Israel had annexed a small amount of territory to make their state defensible, including a land bridge that linked them to Jerusalem.

In the years that followed, the Israelis made their desert bloom. They built the only industrialized economy in the entire Middle East. They built the only liberal democracy in the Middle East. They treated the Arabs who remained in Israel well. To this day the very large Arab minority, which lives inside the state of Israel, has more rights and privileges than any other Arab population in the entire Middle East. There is no Arab country in the Middle East, for example, whose Arab citizens can vote.

This is especially true of the Arabs living under Yasser Arafat's corrupt dictatorship, the Palestine Authority, which today administers the West Bank and the Gaza Strip, and whose Arab subjects have no rights. In 1997, in a fit of pique against the Oslo accords, Palestinian spokesman Edward Said himself blurted this out, calling Arafat "our Papa Doc," after the sadistic dictator of Haiti, and complaining that there was "a total absence of law or the rule of law in the Palestinian autonomy areas."

The present Middle East conflict is said to be about the "occupied territories"—the West Bank of the Jordan and the Gaza strip—and about Israel's refusal to "give them up." But during the first twenty years of the Arab-Israeli conflict, Israel did not control the West Bank or the Gaza Strip. When Jordan annexed the West Bank and Egypt annexed the Gaza strip after the 1948 war, there was no Arab outrage. But the war against Israel continued.

One reason there was no Arab outrage over the annexation of the West Bank was because Jordan is a state whose ethnic majority is Palestinian Arabs. On the other hand, the Palestinians of Jordan are disenfranchised by the ruling Hashemite minority. Despite this fact, in the years following Jordan's annexation of the West Bank, the Palestinians displayed no interest in achieving "self-determination" in

Hashemite Jordan. It is only the presence of Jews, apparently, that incites this claim. The idea that the current conflict is about "illegally occupied territories" is only one of the many Arab deceits—now widely accepted—that have distorted the history of the Middle East wars.

THE ARAB WARS AGAINST ISRAEL

In 1967, Egypt, Syria, and Jordan—whose leaders had never ceased to call for the destruction of Israel—massed hundreds of thousands of troops on Israel's borders and blockaded the Straits of Tiran, closing the Port of Eilat, Israel's only opening to the East. This was an act of war. Because Israel had no landmass to defend itself from being overrun, and to avoid destruction, Israel struck the Arab armies first and defeated them for a second time. It was in repelling these armies that Israel came to control the West Bank and the Gaza strip, as well as the oil-rich Sinai desert. Israel had every right to annex these territories captured from the aggressors—a time-honored ritual among nations, and in fact the precise way that Syria, Lebanon, Iraq, and Jordan had come into existence themselves. But Israel did not do so. On the other hand, neither did it withdraw its armies or relinquish its control.

The reason was that the defeated Arab aggressors once again refused to make peace. Instead, they declared themselves still at war with Israel, a threat no Israeli government could afford to ignore. By this time, Israel was a country of two to three million surrounded by declared enemies whose combined populations numbered over one hundred million. Geographically, Israel was so small that at one point it was less than ten miles across. No responsible Israeli government could relinquish a territorial buffer while its hostile neighbors were still formally at war. This is the reality that frames the Middle East conflict.

In 1973, six years after the second Arab war, the Arab armies again attacked Israel. The attack was led by Syria and Egypt, abetted by Iraq, Libya, Saudi Arabia, Kuwait, and five other countries who gave military support to the aggressors that included an Iraqi division of eighteen thousand men. Israel again defeated the Arab forces. Egypt—and Egypt alone—agreed to make a formal peace.

The peace was signed by Egyptian president Anwar Sadat, who was subsequently assassinated by Islamic radicals, paying for his statesmanship with his life. Sadat is one of three Arab leaders assassinated by other Arabs for making peace with the Jews.

Under the Camp David accords that Sadat signed, Israel returned the entire Sinai with all its oil riches. This act demonstrated once and for all that the solution to the Middle East conflict was ready at hand. It only required the willingness of the Arabs to agree.

Even to this day, the Arabs claim that Jewish settlements in the West Bank are the obstacle to peace. But the Arab settlements in Israel—they are actually called "cities"—are not a problem for Israel, so why should Jewish settlements be a problem for the Arabs? The claim that Jewish settlements in the West Bank are an obstacle to peace appears to be based on the assumption that the Jews will never relinquish any of their settlements. But the Camp David accords prove this false. In fact, the claim is really based on the assumption that Jewish settlements will not be allowed in a Palestinian state, an Arab decision that is the essence of the entire problem: the unwillingness of the Arabs to live side by side with "infidel" Jews.

The Middle East conflict is not about Israel's occupation of the territories; it is about the refusal of the Arabs to make peace with Israel, which is an inevitable by-product of their desire to destroy it. This desire is encapsulated in the word all Palestinians—"moderates" and extremists—use to describe the creation of Israel. They call the birth of Israel the "Nakhba," the catastrophe.

SELF-DETERMINATION IS NOT THE AGENDA

The Palestinians and their supporters also claim that the Middle East conflict is about the Palestinians' yearning for a state and the refusal of Israel to accept their aspiration. This claim is also false. The 1948 UN partition created a Palestinian state. The Jews accepted it, but the Arabs did not. The Palestine Liberation Organization was created in 1964, sixteen years after the establishment of Israel and the first anti-Israel war. The PLO was created at a time the West Bank was not under Israeli

control but was part of Jordan. The PLO, however, was not created so
that the Palestinians could achieve self-determination in Jordan, which
at the time comprised 90 percent of the original Palestine Mandate,
including the West Bank. The PLO's express purpose, in the words of
its own leaders, was to "push the Jews into the sea."

The official "covenant" of the new Palestine Liberation Organization referred to the "Zionist invasion," declared that Israel's Jews were
"not an independent nationality," described Zionism as "racist" and
"fascist," called for "the liquidation of the Zionist presence," and specified
that, "armed struggle is the only way to liberate Palestine." In short,
"liberation" required the destruction of the Jewish state. The PLO was
not even created by Palestinians but by the Arab League, the corrupt
dictators who ruled the Middle East and had attempted to destroy
Israel by military force in 1948, in 1967, and again in 1973.

For thirty years, the PLO covenant remained unchanged in its call
for Israel's destruction. Then in the mid-1990s, under enormous international pressure following the 1993 Oslo accords, PLO leader Yasser
Arafat agreed to revise the covenant. But no new covenant was drafted
or ratified. Moreover, Arafat assured Palestinians that the proposed
revision was purely tactical and did not alter the movement's ultimate
goals. He did this explicitly in a speech given to the Palestine Legislative Council, in which he called on Palestinians to remember the
Prophet Muhammad's Treaty of Hudaybiyah. Muhammad had entered into a ten-year peace with the Koresh tribe back in the seventh
century, known as the Hudaybiyah Treaty. The treaty was born of
necessity. Two years later, when he had sufficient military strength,
Muhammad attacked and conquered the Koresh, who surrendered
without a fight. So much for peace treaties.

THE STRUGGLE TO DESTROY ISRAEL

The Middle East struggle is not about right against right. It is about a
fifty-year effort by the Arabs to destroy the Jewish state, and the refusal of the Arab states in general and the Palestinian Arabs in particular to accept Israel's existence. If the Arabs were willing to do this,

there would be no occupied territories, and there would be a Palestinian state.

Even during the "Oslo" peace process—when the Palestine Liberation Organization pretended to recognize the existence of Israel, and the Jews therefore allowed the creation of a "Palestine Authority"—it was clear that the PLO's goal was Israel's destruction, and not just because its leader invoked the Prophet Muhammad's own deception. The Palestinians' determination to destroy Israel is abundantly clear in their newly created demand of a "right of return" to Israel for "five million" Arab refugees. The figure of five million refugees who must be returned to Israel is more than ten times the number of Arabs who actually left the Jewish slivers of the British Mandate in 1948.

In addition to its absurdity, this new demand has several aspects that reveal the Palestinians' genocidal agenda for the Jews. The first is that the "right of return" is itself a calculated mockery of the primary reason for Israel's existence—the fact that no country would provide a refuge for Jews fleeing Hitler's extermination program during World War II. It is only because the world turned its back on the Jews when their survival was at stake that the state of Israel grants a "right of return" to every Jew who asks for it.

But there is no genocidal threat to Arabs, no lack of international support militarily and economically, and no Palestinian "Diaspora" (although the Palestinians have cynically appropriated the very term to describe their self-inflicted quandary). The fact that many Arabs, including the Palestinian spiritual leader—the Grand Mufti of Jerusalem—supported Hitler's "Final Solution," only serves to compound the insult. It is even further compounded by the fact that more than 90 percent of the Palestinians now in the West Bank and Gaza have never lived a day of their lives in territorial Israel. The claim of a "right of return" is thus little more than a brazen expression of contempt for the Jews, and for their historic suffering.

More importantly, it is an expression of contempt for the very idea of a Jewish state. The incorporation of five million Arabs into Israel would render the Jews a permanent minority in their own country, and would thus spell the end of Israel. The Arabs fully understand this, and that is why they have made it a fundamental demand. It is just one more instance of the bad faith the Arab side has manifested through every chapter of these tragic events.

Possibly the most glaring expression of the Arabs' bad faith is their deplorable treatment of the Palestinian refugees and refusal for half a century to relocate them, or to alleviate their condition, even during the years they were under Jordanian rule. While Israel was making the desert bloom, and relocating six hundred thousand Jewish refugees from Arab states, and building a thriving industrial democracy in its allotted sliver of land, the Arabs were busy making sure that their refugees remained in squalid camps in the West Bank and Gaza, where they were powerless, without rights, and economically destitute.

Today, fifty years after the first Arab war against Israel, there are fifty-nine such refugee camps and 3.7 million "refugees" registered with the UN. Despite economic aid from the UN and Israel itself, despite the oil wealth of the Arab kingdoms, the Arab leaders have refused to undertake the efforts that would liberate the refugees from their miserable camps, or to make the economic investment that would alleviate their condition. There are now twenty-two Arab states providing homes for the same ethnic population, speaking a common Arabic language. But the only one that will allow Palestinian Arabs to become citizens is Jordan. And the only state the Palestinians covet is Israel.

THE POLICY OF RESENTMENT AND HATE

The refusal to address the condition of the Palestinian refugee population is—and has always been—a calculated Arab policy, intended to keep the Palestinians in a state of desperation in order to incite their hatred of Israel for the wars to come. Not to leave anything to chance, the mosques and schools of the Arabs generally—and the Palestinians in particular—preach and teach Jew-hatred every day. Elementary school children in Palestinian Arab schools are even taught to chant "Death to the heathen Jews" in their classrooms as they are learning to read. It should not be overlooked that these twin policies of deprivation (of the Palestinian Arabs) and hatred (of the Jews) are carried out without protest from any sector of Palestinian or Arab society. That in itself speaks volumes about the nature of the Middle East conflict.

All wars—especially wars that have gone on for fifty years—produce victims with just grievances on both sides. And that is true in this case. There are plenty of individual Palestinian victims, as there are Jewish victims, familiar from the nightly news. But the collective Palestinian grievance is without justice. It is a self-inflicted wound, the product of the Arabs' xenophobia, bigotry, exploitation of their own people, and apparent inability to be generous towards those who are not Arabs. While Israel is an open, democratic, multi-ethnic, multicultural society that includes a large enfranchised Arab minority, the Palestine Authority is an intolerant, undemocratic, monolithic police state with one dictatorial leader, whose ruinous career has run now for thirty-seven years.

As the repellent attitudes, criminal methods, and dishonest goals of the Palestine liberation movement should make clear to any reasonable observer, its present cause is based on Jew-hatred, and on resentment of the modern, democratic West, and little else. Since there was no Palestinian nation before the creation of Israel, and since Palestinians regarded themselves simply as Arabs and their land as part of Syria, it is not surprising that many of the chief creators of the Palestine Liberation Organization did not even live in the Palestine Mandate before the creation of Israel, let alone in the sliver of mostly desert that was allotted to the Jews. Edward Said, the leading intellectual mouthpiece for the Palestinian cause, grew up in a family that chose to live in Egypt and the United States. Yasser Arafat was born in Egypt.

While the same Arab states that claim to be outraged by the Jews' treatment of Palestinians treat their own Arab populations far worse than Arabs are treated in Israel, they are also silent about the disenfranchised Palestinian majority that lives in Jordan. In 1970, Jordan's King Hussein massacred thousands of PLO militants. But the PLO does not call for the overthrow of Hashemite rule in Jordan and does not hate the Hashemite monarchy. Only Jews are hated.

It is a hatred, moreover, that is increasingly lethal. Today, 70 percent of the Arabs in the West Bank and Gaza approve the suicide bombing of women and children if the targets are Jews. There is no Arab "Peace Now" movement, not even a small one, whereas in Israel the movement demanding concessions to Arabs in the name of peace is a formidable political force. There is no Arab spokesman who will speak for the rights and sufferings of Jews, but there are hundreds of thousands of Jews in Israel—and all over the world—who will speak for "justice" for the Palestinians. How can Jews expect fair treatment from a people that collectively does not recognize their humanity?

A PHONY PEACE

The Oslo peace process begun in 1993 was based on the pledge of both parties to renounce violence as a means of settling their dispute. But the Palestinians never renounced violence, and in the year 2000, they officially launched a new intifada against Israel, effectively terminating the peace process.

In fact, during the peace process—between 1993 and 1999—there were over four thousand terrorist incidents committed by Palestinians against Israelis, and more than one thousand Israelis killed as a result of Palestinian attacks—more than had been killed in the previous twenty-five years. By contrast, during the same period, 1993 to 1999, Israelis were so desperate for peace that they reciprocated these acts of murder by giving the Palestinians in the West Bank and Gaza a self-governing authority, a forty-thousand-man armed "police force," and 95 percent of the territory their negotiators demanded. This Israeli generosity was rewarded by a rejection of peace, suicide bombings of crowded discos and shopping malls, an outpouring of ethnic hatred, and a renewed declaration of war.

In fact, the Palestinians broke the Oslo accords precisely because of Israeli generosity, because the government of Ehud Barak offered to meet 95 percent of their demands, including turning over parts of Jerusalem to their control—a possibility once considered unthinkable. These concessions confronted Arafat with the one outcome he did not want: peace with Israel. Peace without the destruction of the "Jewish Entity."

Arafat rejected these Israeli concessions, accompanying his rejection with a new explosion of anti-Jewish violence. He named this violence—deviously—"The Al-Aksa Intifada," after the mosque on the Temple Mount. His new jihad was given the name of a Muslim shrine to create the illusion that the Intifada was provoked not by his unilateral destruction of the Oslo peace process, but by Ariel Sharon's visit to the site. Months after the Intifada began, the Palestine Authority itself admitted this was just another Arafat lie.

In fact, the Intifada had been planned months before Sharon's visit as a follow-up to the rejection of the Oslo accords. In the words of Imad Faluji, the Palestine Authority's communications minister, "[The uprising] had been planned since Chairman Arafat's return from Camp David, when he turned the tables on the former U.S. president [Clinton] and rejected the American conditions." The same conclusion was reached by the Mitchell Commission headed by former U.S. Senator George Mitchell to investigate the events: "The Sharon visit did not cause the Al-Aksa Intifada."

In an interview he gave after the new Intifada began, Faisal Husseini—a well-known "moderate" in the PLO leadership, compared the Oslo "peace process" to a "Trojan horse" designed to fool the Israelis into letting the Palestinians arm themselves inside the Jewish citadel in order to destroy it. "If you are asking me as a Pan-Arab nationalist what are the Palestinian borders according to the higher strategy, I will immediately reply: 'From the river to the sea'"—in other words, from the Jordan to the Mediterranean, with not even the original slivers left for Israel. Note too, Husseini's self-identification as a "Pan-Arab nationalist." Just as there is no Palestinian desire for peace with Israel, there are no "Palestinian" Arabs.[2]

MORAL DISTINCTIONS

In assessing the reasons for the Middle East impasse, one must also pay attention to the moral distinction between the two combatants as revealed in their actions. When a deranged Jew goes into an Arab mosque and kills the worshippers (which happened once), he is acting alone and is universally condemned by the Israeli government and the Jews in Israel and everywhere. But when an Arab suicide bomber wades into a crowd of families with baby strollers leaving evening worship, or enters a disco filled with teenagers or a shopping mall crowded with women and children, and blows them up (which happens frequently), he is someone who has been trained and sent by a component of the PLO or the Palestine Authority. He has been told by his religious leaders that his crime will get him into heaven where he will feast and have seventy-two virgins, his praises will be officially sung by Yasser Arafat, his mother will be given money by the Palestine Authority, and his Arab neighbors will come to pay honor to the household for having produced a "martyr for Allah." The Palestinian liberation movement is the first such cause to elevate the killing of children—both the enemy's and its own—to a religious calling. Even Hitler didn't think of this.

It is not only the methods of the Palestine liberation movement that are morally repellent. The Palestinian cause is itself corrupt. The "Palestinian problem" is a problem created by the Arabs themselves, and can only be solved by them. The reason there are Palestinian "refugees" is that no Arab state, except Jordan, will allow them to become citizens. The organs of the PLO and the Palestine Authority, despite billions in revenues, have deliberately left them to stew in refugee camps for fifty years. In contrast, Israel has been steadily absorbing and settling Jewish refugees. In Jordan, Palestinians already have a state in which they are a majority, but which denies them self-determination. Why is Jordan not the object of the Palestinian "liberation" struggle? The only possible answer is because it is not ruled by Jews.

There is a famous "green line" marking the boundary between Israel and its Arab neighbors. That green line is also the bottom line for what is the real problem in the Middle East. It is green because plants are growing in the desert on the Israeli side but not on the Arab side. The Jews got a sliver of land without oil and created abundant wealth and life in all its rich and diverse forms. The Arabs got nine times the acreage, but all they have done with it is to nurture the poverty, resentments, and hatreds of its inhabitants. Their oil wealth has been invested in guns and explosives. Out of these dark elements they have created and perfected the most vile anti-human terrorism the world has ever seen: suicide bombing of civilians. In fact, the Palestinians are a community of suicide bombers: they want the destruction of Israel more than they want a better life.

If a nation state is all the Palestinians desire, Jordan would be the obvious solution. (So would settling for 95 percent of the land one is demanding—the Barak offer rejected by Arafat.) But the Palestinians also want to destroy Israel. This is morally hateful. It is the Nazi virus revived. Despite this, the Palestinian cause is generally supported by the international community with the singular exception of the United States (and to a far lesser degree Great Britain). It is precisely because the Palestinians want to destroy a state that Jews have created—and because they are killing Jews—that they enjoy international credibility and otherwise inexplicable support.

THE JEWISH PROBLEM ONCE MORE

It is this international resistance to the cause of Jewish survival, the persistence of global Jew-hatred that, in the end, proves false the Zionist hope of a solution to the "Jewish problem." The creation of Israel is an awe-inspiring human success story. But the permanent war to destroy it undermines the original Zionist idea.

More than fifty years after the creation of Israel, the Jews are still the most hated ethnic group in the world. Islamic radicals want to destroy Israel, but so do Islamic moderates. Hatred of Jews is taught in Islam's mosques, in Egypt and in other Arab countries *Mein Kampf* is a bestseller, and the anti-Semitic forgery, *The Protocols of the Elders of Zion*, is promoted by the government press throughout the Arab Middle East. Jewish conspiracy theories abound, as in the following statement from a sermon given by the Mufti of Jerusalem, the spiritual leader of the Palestinian Arabs, in the Al-Aksa mosque on July 11, 1997: "Oh Allah, destroy America, for she is ruled by Zionist Jews."

For the Jews in the Middle East, the present conflict is a life and death struggle, yet every government in the UN with the exception of the United States and sometimes Britain regularly votes against Israel in the face of a terrorist enemy, who has no respect for the rights or lives of Jews. After the al-Qaeda attack on the World Trade Center, the French ambassador to England complained that the whole world was endangered because of "that shitty little country," Israel. This caused a scandal in England, but nowhere else. All that stands between the Jews of the Middle East and another Holocaust is their own military prowess and the generous, humanitarian support of the United States.

Even in the United States, however, one can now turn the television to channels like MSNBC and CNN to see the elected Prime Minister of a democracy equated politically and morally with Yasser Arafat who is a dictator, a terrorist, and an enemy of the United States. One can see the same equivalence drawn between Israel's democracy and the Palestine Authority, which is a terrorist entity and an ally of America's enemies al-Qaeda and Iraq.

During the Gulf War, Israel was America's firm ally while Arafat and the Palestinians were Saddam Hussein's staunchest Arab supporters. Yet the next two U.S. Governments—Republican and Democrat alike—strove for even-handed "neutrality" in the conflict in the Middle East, and pressured Israel into a suicidal "peace process" with a foe dedicated to its destruction. It is only since September 11 that the United States has been willing to recognize Arafat as an enemy of peace and not a viable negotiating partner.

The Zionists' efforts created a thriving democracy for the Jews of Israel (and also for the million Arabs who live in Israel), but failed to normalize the Jewish people or make them safe in a world that hates them. In terms of the "Jewish problem" that Herzl and the Zionist founders set out to solve, it is safer today to be a Jew in America than a Jew in Israel. This is one reason why I, a Jew, am an unambivalent, passionate American patriot. America is good for the Jews as it is good for every other minority who embraces its social contract. But this history of the attempt to establish a Jewish state in the Middle East is also why I am a fierce supporter of Israel's survival, and have no sympathy for the Palestinian side in this conflict. Nor will I have such sympathy until the day comes when I can look into the Palestinians' eyes and see something other than death desired for Jews like me.

40

Can There Be a Decent Left?

FIFTEEN YEARS AGO, Peter Collier and I assembled a group of disillusioned New Leftists for a conference in Washington we called "Second Thoughts." These thoughts had been provoked by many factors and events, but most instrumental among them was the wholesale slaughter of innocents in "liberated" Cambodia and Vietnam by political forces that had been supported by the left. It was not the first sprouting of such radical second thoughts. Generations of leftists before us had been repelled by the similar crimes of Stalin and Mao and Castro, and had shed their progressive worldviews for more sober and conservative values. Indeed, Irving Kristol, who was on a panel of elders we invited to our conference, observed that second thoughts had begun with the creation of the modern left during the French Revolution and had been repeated many times since. Our second thoughts he said, somewhat sardonically, were in fact a Yogi Berra moment of déjà vu all over again.

And now it is déjà vu once more. The events of 9-11 and their aftermath have produced a whole new generation of second thoughters in various stages of reassessment. These include such luminaries of the literary left as Salman Rushdie, Martin Amis, and Christopher

---

This article first appeared on *Salon.com*, April 1, 2002, and has been edited for this book.

Hitchens, who this fall joined with their sometime opponents to defend America—the arch "imperial" power of the age—against a radical Islamic enemy, which they previously might have regarded as representative of the oppressed Third World. Now the editor of *Dissent*, Michael Walzer, has come forward with an articulate posing of the same questions and an understanding of how far to push them. A philosopher, social critic, and life-long democratic socialist, Walzer has pointedly entitled his article, "Can There Be a Decent Left?"

Others can measure the seriousness of this question in the fact that insofar as there is a "decent left," Michael Walzer has been an exemplary member of it throughout his political career. I should interject here that I crossed political swords with Walzer nearly forty years ago, when I was a young and combative marxist in England. I do not remember the substance of our disagreements, and I cannot locate my copy of *Views*, the obscure left-wing magazine that printed them. But I am as certain that he was the more civil of the two of us as I am that he was the more correct on the issues.

There is a sense, moreover, in which the faction of the left that *Dissent* represents is itself the decent faction. During the 1960s, *Dissent*'s founder, Irving Howe, symbolized the resistance within the left to the totalitarian elements that came to dominate it. Although in the 1980s its editors were seduced into a "critical" defense of the Nicaraguan regime, they have an otherwise honorable record of having opposed communism throughout the Cold War, even if they only grudgingly supported or—worse—were often excessively critical of America's efforts to contain the communist threat.

Yet there is a sense, also, in which "decency" describes Walzer's own temperament more than it does the politics of the *Dissent* community. One obvious manifestation of decency is to respect those you disagree with if they deserve it. I must interject here that *Dissent* was hostile to our own second thoughts, and *Dissent* editor Paul Berman once described me as a "demented lunatic"—as though the redundancy were necessary to establish the scale of my political sins. *Dissent*'s other philosophical figure, Richard Rorty, has defined *his* left as a movement "against cruelty," while his own writings have featured crude demonizations of his conservative opponents, whose ideas a civilized progressive would be bound to dismiss. He has even celebrated the left's political domination of the universities, the result of an ideological cleansing of conservatives that he would certainly deplore if the roles were reversed.

In eras gone by, political second thoughts tended to focus on the left's active support for nightmare regimes, which it mistakenly took to be the embodiment of its utopian dreams. By contrast, Walzer's doubts originate in his observations of the left's passivity in regard to the defense of America against a nightmare threat. This is not wholly different from the past, but it is different enough to warrant attention.

"Many left intellectuals live in America like internal aliens, refusing to identify with their fellow citizens, regarding any hint of patriot feeling as politically incorrect," Walzer writes. "That's why they had such difficulty responding emotionally to the attacks of September 11 or joining in the expression of solidarity that followed." In their first responses, he notes, leftists failed "to register the horror of the attack or to acknowledge the human pain it caused." Instead, they felt *schadenfreude*, a German word meaning joy at another's misfortunes, a "barely concealed glee that the imperial state had finally gotten what it deserved."

Even though some of these leftists regained their "moral balance" (for many it was more likely a sense of political self-preservation), they still exhibited a myopic attitude when addressing the problem of what should be done. Their sense of being internal exiles in America was again at the root of the symptom: "That's why their participation in the policy debate after the attacks was so odd; their proposals (turn to the UN, collect evidence against bin Laden, and so on) seem to have been developed with no concern for effectiveness and no sense of urgency. They talked and wrote as if they could not imagine themselves responsible for the lives of their fellow-citizens. That was someone else's business; the business of the left was . . . what? To oppose the authorities, whatever they did."

As a result, the left put its energies into defending the civil liberties of . . . suspected terrorists. Walzer is himself still unwilling to address such facts so bluntly. This would mean finally stepping away from the left, which he is evidently unready to do. So he applauds the exaggerated concern of the left for, say, the prisoners of Camp X-Ray, calling it "a spirited defense of civil liberties" and a "good result." But this is a minor hesitation in the face of the large question he has raised about the way the left sees and feels itself to be an alien force in its own country. For this is a classic second thought.

In my own passage out of the left, nearly twenty years ago, it occurred to me that my revolutionary comrades never thought to address the obvious questions for social reformers: "What makes a society work? What will make *this* society work?" In all the socialist literature I had read, there was not a chapter devoted to the problem of how wealth is created. Socialist theory was exclusively addressed to the conquest of power and the division of wealth that someone else had created. Was it any surprise that the socialist societies they created broke records in making their inhabitants poor?

Michael Walzer puzzles at length over the failure of the left to understand the religious nature of the al-Qaeda enemy: "Whenever writers on the left say that the root cause of terror is global inequality or human poverty, the assertion is in fact a denial that religious motives really count. Theology, on this view, is just the temporary, colloquial idiom in which the legitimate rage of oppressed men and women is expressed." He notes that "a few brave leftists" like Christopher Hitchens have described the al-Qaeda movement as a "clerical fascism." (Actually this is a lingering political correctness in Walzer. Hitchens described al-Qaeda as "Islamo-fascists," which is quite different from those Catholic clerics who supported Franco in Spain.) But he does not seem to grasp the religious roots of radicalism generally, and therefore fails to understand the affinity of American radicals for al-Qaeda and its Palestinian kin.

The indecent left reacted badly to 9/11, concludes Walzer, because ideologically it is still under the spell of the marxist schema. These "ideologically primed leftists were likely to think that they already understood whatever needed to be understood. Any group that attacks the imperial power must be a representative of the oppressed, and its agenda must be the agenda of the left. It isn't necessary to listen to its spokesmen. What else can they want except . . . the redistribution of resources across the globe, the withdrawal of American soldiers from wherever they are, the closing down of aid programs for repressive governments, the end of the blockade of Iraq, and the establishment of a Palestinian state alongside Israel?"

This is an excellent reading of the political left. But Walzer is still puzzled: "I don't doubt that there is some overlap between this program and the dreams of al-Qaeda leaders—though al-Qaeda is not an egalitarian movement, and the idea that it supports a two-state solution to the Israeli-Palestinian conflict is crazy. The overlap is circumstantial and convenient, nothing more. A holy war against infidels is not, even unintentionally, unconsciously, or 'objectively,' a left politics. But how many leftists can even imagine a holy war against infidels?"

This question reveals a gap in Walzer's perception of the left that has its roots in his own decency and in the fact that, after all is said and done, he is a moralist and reformer, not a revolutionary. There is, in fact, a large literature examining the religious character of the modern revolutionary left written by authors as different as Berdyaev, Talmon, Voegelin, Niemeyer, Furet, and Kolakowski.[1] If one looks, it is not hard to see how the left's social melodrama fits neatly the traditional Judeo-Christian eschatologies, from which its key texts were derived (Marx, after all, came from a long line of rabbis). There is the Fall from an idyllic communal state, the travail through a vale of suffering and tears, and then, through adherence to the doctrine of the faith, a social redemption. In this radical Passion, there is also the quest for moral purity and the purges—witch-hunts in fact—that result. The redemption, of course, comes not through the agency of a divine Messiah but through the actions of a political vanguard and its power in the revolutionary state.

In the last thirty years, but particularly in the last dozen, it has been impossible for leftists to visualize the utopian redemption that once motivated their (mis-labeled) "idealism." The catastrophe of every socialist scheme of the twentieth century has had a devastating effect on left-wing optimism and replaced it with a corrosive nihilism that makes it impossible for most leftists to defend a country which compared to its enemy might actually be described as a heaven on earth. All that remains of the revolutionary project is the bitter hatred of the society its exponents inhabit, and their destructive will to bring it down. This answers Walzer's question as to how self-styled progressives could be either so unwilling or so slow to defend their own country—a tolerant, secular democracy—in the face of evil and its terrorist attacks.

Peter Collier and I drew attention to this nihilism more than a decade ago in a book we wrote about our own second thoughts. We, too, pointed out the sense of alienation as the defining element of the "progressive" left. As editors of *Ramparts* magazine, we had ordered a cover that featured a seven year old—the son of our art director Dugald Stermer—holding the flag of the Vietcong, America's communist enemy in Vietnam. The cover line said, "Alienation is when your country is at war, and you want the other side to win."

Oddly enough, in our second thoughts book, *Destructive Generation*, we offered as an exemplary statement of this alienation a quote from Michael Walzer: "It is still true," Walzer had written, "that only when I go to Washington to demonstrate do I feel at home there." The statement made more than a decade ago measures Walzer's present second thoughts. Like Christopher Hitchens, who published a beautiful tableau of his own transition for *Vanity Fair* after 9/11, Michael Walzer has come home.

Walzer's second thoughts are not really different from the second thoughts of others before him, despite his stubborn unwillingness to let go of the alienating force. As presently stated they are a revulsion at the nihilism of the left, rather than a rejection of the left's visionary goals. In the end, Walzer does not actually answer the title question of his article with a "no." But he comes very close. "I would once have said that we [the left] were well along: the American left has an honorable history, and we have certainly gotten some things right, above all, our opposition to domestic and global inequalities. But what the aftermath of September 11 suggests is that we have not advanced very far—and not always in the right direction. The left needs to begin again."

Those of us who have gone farther than Walzer in these reppraisals are naturally skeptical of this optimism. The left has been beginning again since the French Revolution—and over and over again. The question is mis-posed by Walzer. Can there be decent leftists? Yes. But can a decent left be reincarnated from the dark history of the last two hundred years? Probably not. And if it has to begin once more after all this tragedy—if it is to be déjà vu all over again—why not give it up and save the world another century of grief?

41

Alienation in a Time of War

WHEN PETER COLLIER AND I PUBLISHED *Destructive Generation* more than a decade ago, it provoked—among other responses—one of the most savage attacks on us that anyone has written before or since. The author of this hit, Rick Hertzberg, is now a senior editor at *The New Yorker.* I mention this in the interest of disclosure, since I am about to address an article of his, which is an attack on the Constitution and eerily related to the original assault on Collier and myself.

That assault was inspired by a reference we made in our book to Hertzberg's friend, Michael Walzer, editor of the socialist magazine *Dissent.* In *Destructive Generation,* Collier and I suggested that a key to understanding the radical agendas of 1960s leftists could be found in the alienation they felt from their own heritage. We offered as an example a statement that Walzer had made. The only time he felt at home in Washington, he had said, was when he went there to protest.

This was the trigger of Hertzberg's attack. In his view, we had conflated Walzer—and by implication himself—with the hate-America, Vietcong-loving radicals of the New Left. In his eyes, this was unfair, and even outrageous. Not only did he and Walzer not share the pro-

---

This article first appeared on FrontPageMagazine.com on August 6, 2002. It has been edited for this book.

communist allegiances of these radicals, they had fought them in ideological combat. As socialists, Hertzberg and his friends identified with the left and often fiercely rejected American capitalism and its political governors. But it was also true that they were willing to make a separate peace when the occasion presented itself. After the 1960s, Hertzberg had even gone to Washington to write speeches for Jimmy Carter.

Hertzberg's sensitivity to any link with a left that had slipped its patriotic moorings was a product of the select political space he had chosen as his own. As a "democratic socialist," he belonged to a progressive elite, carrying the torch of the true socialist faith against reactionaries on both sides of the political barricades. At a May Day gathering of Socialist Party veterans held in Washington this year, he unveiled this conceit at the core of his faith: "I still believe that the anti-communism of the socialist was a superior kind of anti-communism. A lot of people here are all too familiar with the old, long noble struggle for the good name of socialism: the endless explanations that no, socialism isn't the same as communism, and no, socialism isn't some milder form of communism, and yes, socialism is in fact the very opposite of communism. That struggle . . . forced you to think clearly. . . just what it was you were against and just what it was you were for."

Those outside Hertzberg's faith, might not be so easily convinced that what he and his vanguard were for was "the very opposite of communism," but his presentation was nothing if not forceful: "You weren't against communism because communism had aspirations of equality. You weren't against communism because communism wanted free medical care for everybody. You were against it because it crushed democracy and terrorized people and ruled by violence and fear, and systematically destroyed the most elementary and indispensable liberties, like freedom of speech."

In other words, being a democratic socialist made you an avatar of the best of all possible worlds—both socialist and free. It was obviously unforgivable that anyone should attempt to sully your reputation with guilty associations and improper conflations, as Peter Collier and I had done.

But fate intervened, and the terrorist attack on America had recently caused Hertzberg's idol, Michael Walzer, to make the same conflation and the same association. Reflecting on 9/11 in a spring editorial for *Dissent*, Walzer came remarkably close to the very perception that Collier and I shared that provoked Hertzberg's wrath a decade before.

In his editorial, Walzer asked whether there could be a "decent left"—a question provoked by the spectacle of his progressive comrades rushing to judgment against their own country in the wake of 9-11. Walzer wondered about the depths of an alienation that could cause people to refuse to come to the defense of their country even when it was attacked. "Wasn't America a beacon of light to the old world, a city on a hill, an unprecedented experiment in democratic politics?"

Two months after Walzer posed these questions, Hertzberg responded with an article in the July 29 issue of the *New Yorker*. It was billed by the editors as "Hendrik Hertzberg on Our Flawed Constitution." According to Hertzberg, while America's democratic values may have been inspirational, America's institutions did not merit such respect, nor did they provide a democratic model of governance others should follow. Once again Hertzberg was laying down a marker that separated him from the crowd. To provide a foil for his argument, Hertzberg referred to a book by Robert Dahl that asked the question, *How Democratic Is Our Constitution?* The answer: not nearly enough.

Challenging America's founding principles is fair enough, even perhaps at an hour in which both the nation and its ideals are under ferocious attack. But Hertzberg's authorial voice betrays a hostility that goes beyond fair comment. From Dahl, for example, he cites a negative summary of America's performance in respect to economic inequality, energy efficiency, and social expenditures. For good measure, he adds, "although Dahl doesn't mention this, we seem to be getting straight A's in world domination."

Defending his assault, Hertzberg notes that he is not the first to strike at the Founding: "Treating the Constitution as imperfect is not new. The angrier abolitionists saw it, in William Lloyd Garrison's words, as a 'covenant with death and an agreement with hell.' . . . Academic paint balls have splattered the parchment with some regularity." According to Hertzberg, however, this critical facility is confined to intellectual and political elites. For the unwashed mass, questioning the Constitution remains unthinkable: "But in the public square the Constitution is beyond criticism. The American civic religion affords it Biblical or Koranic status, even to the point of seeing it as divinely inspired. It's the flag in prose." This makes the terrain dangerous for vanguard reformers like himself, particularly now: "The Constitution of the United States is emphatically not something to be debunked, especially in the afterglow of sole-superpower triumphalism."

But can Hertzberg really be referring to this country when he claims the Constitution cannot be challenged? Did he miss the feminist clamor over the Constitution's failure to protect women or the movement for an Equal Rights Amendment that this sentiment spawned? Is he oblivious to the complaint from the right that the Framers failed to provide a defense clause for the unborn? Was he comatose in the aftermath of the last presidential election when agitated Democrats, including United States senators and the former First Lady, called on the nation to scrap the Electoral College and alter the way the Constitution has mandated our choice of presidents for over two hundred years?

What really upsets Hertzberg is not any superstitious attachment Americans may have to a constitutional sacred cow, but his own isolation from the conviction of ordinary Americans that the system has worked; and that it has worked pretty well—enough to make America a "beacon of light" to the rest of the world.

Hertzberg's perverse distance from his countrymen is also manifest in his opening remarks about the Founding itself: "The most blatantly undemocratic feature of the document that the framers adopted in Philadelphia in 1787 was its acceptance—indeed, its enshrinement—of slavery, which in its American form was as vicious and repugnant as any institution ever devised by man."

Ever devised by man? What about Auschwitz? The Soviet gulag? How about the slavery in Egypt that built the pyramids? How about the institution of virgin sacrifice among the Incas? How about black slavery in Cuba or Brazil? Perhaps Hertzberg is unaware that in Carribbean slave societies the mortality rates for slaves exceeded the birth rates. Perhaps he is ignorant of the fact that slavery in the United States was the only slavery in the West whose environment encouraged the natural generation of the slave population so that, between the signing of the Constitution and the Civil War, the slave census in the United States increased more than five-fold. Everywhere else in the hemisphere, slaves had to be imported to make up the manpower deficit caused by attrition.[1]

To write, as Hertzberg does, that the Constitution *enshrined* slavery is misleading at best. Far from glorifying the institution, the framers avoided even using the words "slave" or "slavery" because most of them abhorred the institution, were determined to end it, and were convinced that it would shortly die of its own reactionary weight.

Hertzberg's distortion of the intentions of the founders does not end here. Listing the constitutional compromises they made with slavery, he writes, "Most notoriously, under Article I, Section 2, a state's allotment of seats in the House of Representatives (and, by extension, its Presidential electors) was determined by counting not only 'free Persons' but also 'three-fifths of all other Persons.' This is simply diabolical, because to the insult of defining a person held in bondage as three-fifths of a human being it added the injury of using that definition to augment the political power of that person's oppressors."

This is simply false. Far from being either an insult or an injury, the three-fifths compromise actually *weakened* the power of the Southern slaveholders who had demanded, "slaves should stand on equality with whites." Both the injury *and* the insult were inflicted by those who demanded that slaves be counted as *five* fifths of a person. Had the Constitution counted slaves as full persons for purposes of allotting congressional seats, it would have maximized the voting power of the slave states.

Hertzberg's distortion of this history is even worse than it appears, because it is based on the suppression of a more basic fact. All the constitutional compromises with slavery were necessary in order to achieve a union which, within twenty years, abolished the slave trade and within a single generation freed the slaves themselves. The only real moral issue involved in the constitutional arrangement was whether the framers should have made *any* compromise with the slave-holding South. Should there have been a union at all? On this question the final word belongs to Frederick Douglass, the most important free black person in the republic, and a former slave himself: "My argument against the dissolution of the American Union is this: It would place the slave system more exclusively under the control of the slaveholding states, and withdraw it from the power in the Northern states which is opposed to slavery.... *I am, therefore, for drawing the bond of the Union more closely, and bringing the Slave States more completely under the power of the Free States.*"[2]

While Douglass's statement underscores the injustice of Hertzberg's attack, it may also be said to understate it. In 1787, the American founders had just completed the only successful colonial rebellion in human history, defeating the greatest empire of the age. If the northern states had rejected a compromise with the South, it is perfectly reasonable to imagine that the British imperialists (who burned the White House in 1812) would have forged an alliance with the southern slave states and crushed the North. Then slavery would have been institutionalized throughout the continent. There would have been no Civil War, and it is anyone's guess when the slaves might eventually have been freed.

Hertzberg acknowledges the amendments outlawing slavery and guaranteeing equal rights that were incorporated into the Constitution after the South's defeat. "But nothing was done to alter the political institutions that in 1860 had held four million people—one American in eight—in bondage and that, for the next century and, arguably, more, denied millions of their 'free' descendants both equal protection and the franchise."

So stated, this is another incomprehensible charge. The enslavement of four million people was not the result of American political institutions but a legacy of the British Empire and the necessity of compromise to hold that empire at bay. But as Hertzberg continues his attack, his logic is revealed. Because of America's flawed political institutions—Hertzberg has in mind the "undemocratic" Senate and judiciary—"even so grotesque and obvious an injustice as apartheid in the public schools[3] was beyond the ability of the national government to correct. And when, after ninety years, formal, official school segregation was outlawed the deed was done through the exercise of un-elected, unaccountable, unchecked, quasi-legislative judicial power."

In short, Hertzberg's disenchantment with the American system is that it is not "majoritarian." In pursuing social justice, the federal government is unable to ignore state's rights, judicial precedents, and pretty much all the checks and balances that have made America's political history different from, say, that of revolutionary France. Like other socialists, Hertzberg yearns for a government that can enforce the General Will and secure social justice through a popular assembly, directly elected by the people—one man, one vote.

In addition to the American judiciary, the United States Senate is the institution that currently thwarts this General Will. "Once slavery was removed, the most undemocratic remaining provision of the Constitution was, and is, the composition of the Senate—its so-called equality of representation, whereby each state gets two senators, regardless of population." Hertzberg may regard this representation as unfair (he would also not like the Electoral College) but the founders devised it specifically to provide a check on the will of the people, which they famously distrusted. The other chamber is known as the "People's" House because it is elected once every two years instead of six and is composed of members who represent equal portions of the electorate. The Senate was the framers' device to slow the machinery of popular justice because they recognized that popular injustice—the tyranny of the majority—was an equally likely result of democratic power unchecked.

Summing up his argument, Hertzberg cites Dahl: "Compared with the political systems of other advanced democratic countries, ours is among the most opaque, complex, confusing, and difficult to understand." On the other hand, along with England's equally complex constitutional monarchy, it is the most stable democracy that history records.

By contrast the advanced democratic countries that Dahl has in mind include France—with its bloody revolutions and five Republics—and Germany, of which no more need be said.

Ignoring these unpleasant realities, Hertzberg insists on a "true" democracy whose government could ride roughshod over communities that don't agree with his political agendas. Consider the argument he makes against senatorial privilege: "The rejection of the Versailles Treaty and the League of Nations after the First World War and then of preparedness on the eve of the Second are only the best known of the Senate's many acts of foreign policy sabotage, which have continued down to the present, with its refusal to ratify international instruments on genocide, nuclear testing and human rights."

Hertzberg concedes that, "some will take all this as proof that the system has worked exactly as the framers planned," but adds: "To believe that, one must believe that the framers were heartless, brainless reactionaries."

So Americans who disagree with Hertzberg are heartless and brainless and reactionary. It is narcissism and arrogance like this, not unusual for social reformers, that made the framers fearful of democratic majorities in the first place and determined to provide restraints that might prevent majorities from tyrannizing everyone else.

The founders were not radical democrats or socialists like Hertzberg, but conservatives who had a healthy distrust of political passions and who devised a complex system designed to frustrate the schemes of social redeemers and others convinced of their own invincible virtue. If it were not for the undemocratic power vested in the Supreme Court, schools might still be legally segregated. If it were not for rights granted to the states, slavery might have spread throughout the nation. If it were not for the confusing, opaque, and difficult-to-understand American framework, the descendants of Africans who were dragged to this country in English chains might not today be the freest and richest blacks in the world.

What makes these historical issues important now is that our nation is under attack. It must confront its enemies, moreover, in a state weakened by thirty years of cultural assaults from the left that have

made many Americans ambivalent about their heritage. Moral ambivalence about one's country can lead to a lack of resolve in defending
it. But there is really no historical justification for Americans to be
ambivalent about their history or heritage. As Michael Walzer and
President Bush have both pointed out, this nation is still a beacon of
freedom to the rest of the world, and its defense is important not only
to us, but to them as well.

42

Neo-Communism

HOW TO IDENTIFY THE CONTEMPORARY POLITICAL LEFT? Current usage refers to everyone left of center as "liberal." Yet what are currently identified liberals *liberal* about? In many areas they are determined to intervene, regulate, and control people's lives, or redistribute their income. Obviously, when radicals like Ramsey Clark and communists like Angela Davis are referred to as "liberals"—as they routinely are—the obfuscation works to their advantage and against the interests of veracity and democracy. The term "liberal" should be reserved for those who occupy the center of the political spectrum; those to the left are better referred to as leftists, which is what they are.

This is the easy part of rectifying the political lexicon. There is another more difficult aspect, however, which is how to identify the "hard" left, namely, those who are dedicated enemies of America. In practice, it is easy to identify such leftists and not difficult to describe them. They are people who support hostile regimes like North Korea, Cuba, and China, or—more commonly—believe the United States to be the imperialist guardian of a world system that radicals must defeat before they can establish "social justice."

This article first appeared on FrontPageMagazine.com on May 1 and 2, 2003, under the title "Taking on the Neo-Coms," parts 1 and 11. It has been edited for this book.

Adherents of this anti-American creed variously describe themselves as "marxists," "anti-globalists," "anti-war activists" or, more generally, "progressives." Their secular worldview holds that America is responsible for reaction, oppression, and exploitation across the globe and causes them to regard this country as the moral equivalent of militant Islam's "Great Satan." This explains the otherwise incomprehensible practical alliances that individuals who claim to be avatars of social justice make with Islamofascists like Saddam Hussein.

Among the intellectual leaders of this left are Noam Chomsky, Howard Zinn, Gore Vidal, Edward Said, and Cornel West; among its figureheads, Angela Davis and Ramsey Clark; among its cultural icons, Tim Robbins, Barbara Kingsolver, Arundhahti Roy, and Michael Moore; among its political leaders, Ralph Nader and the heads of the three major "peace" organizations (Leslie Cagan, Brian Becker, and Clark Kissinger); among its electoral organizations, the Green Party and the Peace and Freedom Party; among its elected officials, Congresswoman Barbara Lee (D-CA) and Congressman Dennis Kucinch (D-OH); among its organizations, the misnamed Center for Constitutional Rights and the National Lawyers Guild; among its publications and media institutions, the *Nation, Z Magazine,* the *Progressive, Counterpunch,* Pacifica radio, Indymedia.org, and commondreams.org. Like the Communist Party in the heyday of the Soviet empire, the influence of the hard left —intellectually and organizationally—extends far beyond the institutions, organizations, and publications it controls.

Yet what to call them? One of this left's survival secrets has been its ability to embargo attempts to identify it by labeling those who do "red-baiters" and "witch-hunters," as though even to name it is to persecute it. These same people, on the other hand, think nothing of labeling *their* opponents "racists" and "fascists," or calling the president of the United States a "Nazi" puppet of the oil cartel. Yet their defense strategy is highly effective in the tolerant democracy they are determined to destroy. I myself have been called a "red-baiter" and "McCarthyite" for pointing out that the current "peace" organizations like International ANSWER and Not In Our Name are fronts for the Workers World Party—a marxist-Leninist vanguard that identifies with

North Korea—and the Revolutionary Communist Party, a Maoist sect. The facts are obvious, unarguable, and proudly acknowledged by the principals, but their implications are unpleasant and therefore suspect.

Nothwithstanding this difficulty, a more significant concern is that the term "communist" in the context of the contemporary left can be misleading. While the Communist Party still exists and is even growing, it is a minor player and enjoys nothing approaching its former influence or power in the left. Even in the hard left, the Communist Party USA is only a constituent part of the whole whereas once, along with its front groups, it dominated progressive politics.

In these circumstances, for reasons I will make clear, the best term to describe this left is "neo-communist," or "neo-coms" for short.

The place to begin in understanding the neo-coms is the period following 1956, when the left sloughed off its communist shell and became first a "new left" and then what might be called a "post-new left." In my own writings, particularly *Radical Son* and *The Politics of Bad Faith*, I have shown that the "new left" was in reality no such thing. Beginning as a rejection of Stalinism, by the end of the 1960s the New Left had become virtually indistinguishable from the communist predecessor it claimed to reject. This was as true of its marxist underpinnings as of its anti-Americanism or indiscriminate embrace of totalitarian revolutions and revolutionaries abroad.

An example of the New Left's degeneration into old left communism at the end of the 1960s is provided in a formal declaration by a "solidarity" delegation to Kim Il Sung's dictatorship in North Korea, led by Black Panther leader Eldridge Cleaver. The invitation was extended by the "Committee for the Peaceful Unification of the Fatherland." *Los Angeles Times* columnist, Robert Scheer, a spokesman for the current anti-war left, was one of the signers of the declaration. The statement read: "Since the peoples of the world have a common enemy, we must begin to think of revolution as an international struggle against U.S. imperialism. Our struggle in the U.S. is a genuine part of the total revolutionary assault on this enemy."[1]

The New Left imploded at the end of the 1960s, a victim of its own revolutionary enthusiasm, which led it to pursue a violent politics it could not sustain. America's withdrawal from Vietnam in the early 1970s deprived the left of the immediate pretext for its radical agendas. Many of its cadre retired from the "revolution in the streets" they had tried to launch and entered the Democratic Party. Others turned to careers in journalism and teaching, the professions of choice for secular missionaries. Still others took up local agitations and discrete campaigns in behalf of the environment, feminism, and gay rights—without giving up their radical illusions. In the 1980s, spurred by the Soviet-sponsored "nuclear freeze" campaign and by the "solidarity" movements for communist forces in Central America, the left began to regroup without formally announcing its re-emergence or proclaiming a new collective identity as its 1960s predecessor had done.

At the end of the decade, the collapse of the Soviet empire ushered in an interregnum of confusion for the left, calling a temporary halt to this radical progress. In the Soviet debacle, "revolutionary" leftists confronted the catastrophic failure of everything they had believed and fought for during the previous seventy years. Even those radicals who recognized the political failures of the Soviet regime believed in what Trotsky had called "the gains of October"—the superior forces of socialist production. But the leftist faith proved impervious to this rebuttal by historical events. Insulated by its religious devotion to the progressive idea, the left survived the refutation of its socialist dreams. Instead of acknowledging their wrongheaded commitment to the socialist cause, they looked on the demise of what they had once hailed as "the first socialist state," as no more than an albatross that providence had lifted from their shoulders.

In short, having defended the indefensible for seventy years, they were suddenly relieved that they would no longer have to. Turning their backs on their own past, they pretended it was someone else's. They said, "The collapse of socialism doesn't prove anything because it wasn't real socialism. Real socialism hasn't been tried." This subterfuge rescued them from having to make apologies for abetting regimes that had killed tens of millions and enslaved tens of millions more. Broken eggs with no omelet to show for it—not a workable socialist result. Better yet, there was no need to acknowledge that the country whose efforts they had opposed and whose actions they had condemned had liberated a billion people from the most oppressive empire the world had ever seen. They had no need for second thoughts about what they had done. They just went on to the next destruction, the newest incarnation of the radical cause.

This act of historic bad faith was the foundation of the left's revival in the decade that followed. It was the necessary premise of its reemergence as the leader of the anti-globalization and "antiwar" movements that came at the end of the 1990s and the beginning of the millennium. The hard left was now ready to resurrect its internal war against America at home and abroad.

If one looks at almost any aspect of this left—its self-identified intellectual lineage (Hegel, Nietzsche, Marx, Heidegger, Fanon, Gramsci—in sum, the totalitarian tradition), its analytic model (hierarchy and oppression), its redemptive agenda (social justice as state-enforced leveling) and its enemies (imperialist America and the American "ruling class") one would be hard put to find a scintilla of difference with the communist past. Of course leftists themselves will have none of this. Most of them will proclaim their anti-Stalinism (even as they embrace its practices); and will not defend the communist systems that have in any case collapsed. But so what? The Soviet rulers denounced Stalin. Were they any less communists for that?

It seems appropriate, therefore, to call the unreconstructed hardliners, "neo-communists"—a term that accurately identifies their negative assaults on American capitalism and their anti-American "internationalist" agendas. It may be objected that the term "neo-communist" does not describe a group which itself identifies with the term, but then neither does "neoconservative." There is no current movement calling itself "neoconservative," nor do the individuals so designated refer to their own ideas as "neoconservative." "Neoconservative" is, in fact, a label that was imposed by the left on a group of former Democrats, loosely grouped around Senator "Scoop" Jackson who left the party fold at the end of the 1970s to join and support the Reagan Administration. It was accepted out of necessity for a while, because the left so dominates the political culture that resisting it was futile.

But it is no longer used by neoconservatives because, as Norman Podhoretz long ago observed, "neoconservatism" is indistinguishable from conservatism itself. No "neoconservative" that I am aware of has challenged Podhoretz's conclusion. Yet others insist on describing conservatives—particularly those whom they regard as "hard-line" conservatives—with this label. If the "neo" shoe can be made to fit conservatives, why not the hard-line left?

"Neo-communism," then is a term to identify the contemporary left, which opposed the American war and opposes the America peace, which denounces American corporations and the global capitalist system; it is a term to describe anti-American leftists who demonize the American economic system and identify it as a "root cause" of global problems. An objection to this usage might be that some members of this left—perhaps many—no longer advocate a communist future in the strict sense. Many in fact call themselves anarchists and would be eager to denounce (costless as that might be now) the late Soviet state.

I have already provided one answer to this objection. There is no group that identifies its politics as "neoconservative," either. There are no "neoconservative" organizations (official or unofficial) and there is no "neoconservative" policy or plan. Yet there is little objection to the use of "neoconservative" to describe what others consider a readily identifiable political position.

The resistance to the term "neo-communist," derives from a misunderstanding of the nature of a political left that is proud of its communist heritage—gulags aside—(as this left mainly is) and still clings to socialist "solutions" and the revolutionary idea (as this left mainly does). There are always (and inevitably) two sides to the revolutionary coin. The first is negative and destructive, since it is necessary first to undermine the beliefs, values, and institutions of the old order which must be destroyed before a new one can be established. The second is positive and utopian, a vision of the future that condemns the present.

For half a century now, ever since Khrushchev's revelations about the crimes of Stalin, the left has been exclusively driven by its negative agendas. (This has become even more the case since the pathetic implosion of the socialist system.) Leaders of the contemporary left have put forward no serious plans for the post-capitalist future. More importantly, none of the energies that drive them are inspired by such plans. The left's inspirations are mainly negative and nihilistic, and have been so for nearly fifty years.

For even in its innocent beginnings, the New Left defined itself by negatives, as "anti-anti-communist." It was a "new" left because it did not want to identify with communism. But it also did not want to oppose communism either, because then it would have had to support America's Cold War. "Anti-anti-communism" was the code for anti-Americanism. What the left wanted was to oppose America and its "sham democracy."

There is a sense, of course, in which the left has always been defined by its destructive agendas. Its utopian vision was just that—*utopian*, a vision of nowhere. In practice, socialism didn't work. But socialism could never have worked because it is based on false premises about human psychology and society, and a gross ignorance of human economy. In the vast library of socialist theory (and in all of Marx's works), there is hardly a chapter devoted to the creation of wealth—to what will cause human beings to work and to innovate, and to what will make their efforts efficient. Socialism is a plan of morally sanctioned theft. It is about dividing up what others have created. Consequently, socialist economies don't work: they create poverty instead of wealth. That this is unarguable historical fact now has not prompted the left to have second thoughts. Because its positive agendas are unworkable, to characterize the left by its negative critiques and destructive agendas is perfectly appropriate; everything else, everything it claims to intend, everything it does in fact intend, is so much utopian air.

In an article written at the end of the war on Iraq,[2] I identified several exemplars of the neo-communist left, one of whom sent me a response. Maurice Zeitlin is a professor of sociology at the University of California, Los Angeles, and the co-author of a faculty resolution condemning the United States' "invasion" of Iraq—after the fact. Because the resolution was drafted and passed after the liberation of Baghdad, its agendas are clearly aimed at America and not the reality in Iraq.

I have known Maurice Zeitlin for more than forty years, since we were both New Left radicals in the 1960s. In my article, I pointed out that Zeitlin, speaking at an academic conference, had recently hailed the late Cuban communist, Che Guevara, as "a leader of the first socialist revolution in this hemisphere." He had also said, "[Guevara's] legacy is embodied in the fact that Cuban revolution is alive today despite the collapse of the Soviet bloc," and also that, "No social justice is possible without a vision like Che's."[3] I concluded that it was Zeitlin's neo-communist agenda, and not any specifics of the war, that had inspired the post-hoc UCLA faculty resolution against the U.S. action.

Zeitlin's response to this article took the form of a terse and angry e-mail, which he sent to my assistant, Elizabeth Ruiz, referring to me in the third person. This e-mail affords a further look into the mind of the neo-communist left.

In my article I had mentioned that Zeitlin and Robert Scheer had written one of the first books celebrating the communist revolution in Cuba. Zeitlin was irritated because I didn't mention in my article that I had edited this book. ("You can tell Davey for me that he might have mentioned in this column that he edited the book by myself and Scheer on Cuba—and we thanked him in the acknowledgments.") Zeitlin appeared to think that this fact implicated me in his radical politics in a way I had not already written about in my autobiography, *Radical Son*. He continued: "To think that I saved him from an enraged audience and protected his right to speak at the *Los Angeles Times* Festival of Books a few years ago."[4] I have also written about this incident. "Saved" is a little over-the-top for the remarks Zeitlin made in defense of my right to express myself. Book readers are not the most violent of audiences and in any case the event was being televised on C-SPAN. The point Zeitlin seems to want to make is that since he defended my free speech at UCLA, he cannot be called a neo-communist.

Why not? Didn't communists defend the principle of free speech in America when they stood up to Senator McCarthy? Communists are great defenders of freedom in the democracies they want to overthrow. It enhances their power to subvert the system. Didn't Lenin himself defend the right to vote in democratic Russia—before abolishing it as soon as he took power?

In the second brief paragraph of his e-mail, Zeitlin makes his objection clearer, and makes explicit the defense of good intentions: "[David] knows damn well that I have long opposed execrable regimes like Hussein's, years before, indeed, Bush even knew who Hussein was. He also knows that I wrote severe criticisms of the restrictions on rights in revolutionary Cuba in *Ramparts*, when he was its very editor and still gung ho for Fidel."

This cri de coeur begs the most important question: What does it mean to oppose Saddam Hussein's "execrable regime" and at the same time oppose the effort to change it? Or to condemn the regime change *after* the fact when Iraqis are rejoicing in the streets? What are intentions worth when actions contradict them? Are Zeitlin's critiques of Castro harsher than Khrushchev's criticisms of Stalin? Did Khrushchev cease to be a Communist because he criticized Stalin? Zeitlin's attempt at self-exculpation does not provide answers.

Zeitlin was indeed critical of the Cuban revolutionary regime, and was critical even earlier than he indicates. He is correct as well that as a fellow leftist I did not want to see such criticisms aired. (However, I would not describe myself at the time as exactly "gung ho for Fidel.) But the fact is that I published his critique. As it happens, Zeitlin could have cited a much more impressive instance of his New Left independence from the communist past.

In 1960, before the creation of *Ramparts*, Zeitlin had visited Cuba and interviewed Che Guevara, who was then the second most powerful man in the dictatorship. We published the interview in the first issue of our Berkeley magazine, *Root and Branch*, which was one of the political journals that launched the New Left (Robert Scheer was also an editor). The rest of us were both shocked and impressed when we read the interview and realized what Maurice had done.

He had not just interviewed Guevara, already a radical legend. He had challenged Guevara's policies and in effect called into question his revolutionary credentials. Maurice had asked Guevara about the role he thought trade unions should play in a socialist country, specifically Cuba. Should they be independent—as New Left socialists like us wanted—or should they be appendages of the state, as Lenin and Stalin had made them? Maurice reminded Guevara that the elimination of independent unions, the organizations of the revolutionary class, had paved the way for the Soviet gulag. Guevara, angered by the question and by Maurice's temerity in raising it, would not criticize the Soviets and abruptly changed the subject.

Zeitlin had put Guevara to the test and Guevara had failed. The interview revealed that Guevara was a Stalinist himself. We all recognized the significance of what he had said. Yet to our shame, we continued to support the Cuban regime anyway, knowing that it was destined to be a totalitarian gulag—because that was the *intention* of its creators. Maurice did write a subsequent critique of the Cuban regime for *Ramparts*. But like us, he continued to support the regime and to attack the United States and its efforts to restore freedom to Cuba. Later, when I had second thoughts about my political commitments and parted with comrades like Maurice Zeitlin, I wrote about my regrets for defending a regime that has become the most sadistic dictatorship in Latin American history. Except for Ronald Radosh and other "second thoughters" who have also turned their backs on the left, I don't know of any New Left radicals who have done the same.

The left's silence over these unforeseen consequences of its political commitments underscores the pitiful impotence and ultimate irrelevance of good intentions, however good they may be. What does it matter that we *wanted* to create a "new" left or a "*democratic* socialism," if we did not put our actions behind these desires, if we did not apply the same standards of judgment (and action) for socialist tyrannies as we did for others? What were our "critiques" worth if we were prepared to continue our support for such regimes, or to remain part of a movement that actually defended them? What are Zeitlin's critiques worth if he preserves the myth of Che's leadership and the viability of the socialist idea?

Forty years later, the results of our defense of the Cuban revolution are indisputable. Cuba is an island prison, a land of regime-in-

duced poverty, misery, and human oppression greater by far than under the old regime it replaced. Yet despite his criticisms, Maurice Zeitlin
is still defending the Cuban "revolution"—along with its patron saint,
Che Guevara. As a UCLA professor, he is now teaching a new generation of college students who have no memory of this past to idolize the
communist predator he criticized forty years before, calling him an
inspiration for the future! ("No social justice is possible without a vision like Che's.") In view of this record, what do Zeitlin's parenthetical
condemnations and critical asides matter?

Zeitlin's political career reminds me of a short story by Irwin Shaw,
"The Ninety-Yard Run," about a college football star who makes a
ninety-yard run in his senior college year, which turns out to be the
high point of his life. It's downhill all the way for him after that. In
defining the term "neo-communist" as applied to leftists like Zeitlin, I
was careful to be specific. I defined a neo-communist as "a political
radical and a determined opponent of America and its capitalist democracy." What I had in mind in this description was not just a political outlook, but an outlook reflecting a profound feeling of alienation
from America and a hostility towards it that only someone who is or
had been a radical himself could really understand.

In the 1980s, I was given a personal insight into Maurice Zeitlin's
own profound alienation from his country—a country that had provided him intellectual freedom, a six-figure income, and opportunities
to travel all over the world doing research and writing marxist tracts at
American taxpayers' expense. When the incident in question occurred,
I had not seen Maurice nor heard from him in more than twenty years.
I had no idea whether he had had second thoughts like mine or whether
he was still on the left. Our paths crossed, so to speak, because of a
newspaper report about another 1960s radical named Margaret Randall,
who was applying for the reinstatement of her American citizenship.
She was supported by a chorus of radicals, who claimed that in resisting her request, the State Department was trampling on her civil rights.

This news item so outraged me that I promptly wrote a letter to
the *Los Angeles Times* urging the authorities to deny her request. The
reason Randall no longer had her citizenship was that she had joined a

movement of local terrorists in Mexico City who were attempting to obstruct the 1968 Olympic games. When the street battles were over and many lay dead, she publicly renounced her American citizenship and attacked her homeland as a "fascist" state. She then went to live in communist Cuba and work as a teacher, indoctrinating Cuban school-children in the communist creed. In my letter to the *Times*, I urged officials to demand that Randall apologize to her country before re-turning the citizenship she had renounced. Being an American, in my view, meant accepting a social contract that included a commitment to democracy and individual freedom. I thought Randall should be treated like a new citizen-applicant and required to make a formal commit-ment to her country and its principles before receiving her citizenship back. What is America if it is not a nation of citizens committed to these common ends?

Maurice read my letter to the *Los Angeles Times*. His reaction, which I learned about through a mutual friend, was, "I wonder how low Horowitz will sink next?" This came as a shock to me, because I re-membered Maurice's bold defense of freedom to Che Guevara years before and was unaware of his political evolution since. This remark told me more about Maurice's political commitments than I wanted to know.

The purpose of the term "neo-communist" is to identify a segment of the left that regards the United States as the root cause of interna-tional evil because it is the guardian of the international property sys-tem. In the eyes of such radicals, this makes America the bulwark of the prevailing system of "social injustice" in the world. These proposi-tions have profound implications for one's political loyalties and com-mitments and explain how individuals who claim to honor peace, justice, equality, and freedom, can interpose themselves between America and a political monster like Saddam Hussein.

At a anti-war teach-in at Columbia College during the war, an-thropology professor Nicholas DeGenova made himself notorious by wishing for "a million Mogadishus"—a million American military de-feats. The public outrage at his remarks was a response to the idea that anyone could wish for American troop casualties. But this was to miss the forest for the trees. As DeGenova himself explained in defending his remarks, what he meant was not that a lot of Americans should be killed (the left imagines it can separate support for America's troops from support for America's wars), but that a defeat for America would be a victory for humanity. This is the way DeGenova put it: "What I was really emphasizing in the larger context of my comments was the question of Vietnam and *that* historical lesson. . . . What I was intent to emphasize was that the importance of Vietnam is that it was a defeat for the U.S. war machine and a victory for the cause of human self-determination."[5] DeGenova might have added, "for social justice."

This is the essence of the neo-communist vision. It explains how leftists like Maurice Zeitlin can condemn America's liberation of Iraq, despite the fact that they recognize that Iraq's regime is "execrable" and that the Iraqi people have been freed from tyranny. "The analogy between Mogadishu and Vietnam," DeGenova elaborates, "is that they were defeats for U.S. imperialism. . . . The analogy between Mogadishu and Iraq is simply that there was an invasion of Somalia and there was an invasion of Iraq."[6]

A key to the mentality of the left is that it judges itself by its best intentions, and judges its opponents—America chief among them—by their worst deeds. Or by the fantasies of what their worst deeds might be. By imagining a perfect world of social justice that leftists, unopposed, will create, even America's most positive achievements can be made to look bad. If a world can be created in which everyone will be fed and have shelter and medical attention, then the fact that it isn't can be attributed to America, because America is the guardian of the international "status quo."

Therefore, every good that America has achieved can be seen in its reality—from the point of view of social justice—as a negative instead. It may be the case, for example, that America has raised unprecedented millions out of the ranks of poverty into a comfortable middle-class existence. But a neo-communist sees this achievement as one that is realized at the expense of a million greater achievements. A historical good that America has accomplished is thus turned into a malevolent result. By extension, when the left acts to weaken America or defend

America's enemies, it is really advancing the cause of social progress. This is the neo-communist creed.

Therefore, let us call such radicals neo-communists, or neo-coms (or small "c" communists) for short. They are *neo*-communist because in the past the communist left was driven by the illusion that the Soviet Union was actually a "workers paradise" and that true socialism had been achieved. Communists who defended Stalin's oppressive state believed that Russia was really a paradigm of human freedom. Consequently, they experienced none of the problems of cognitive dissonance such as their political heirs do today. Neo-communists know the execrable nature of regimes like Iraq's, but defend them against American arms nonetheless. Yet, unlike Moscow, Baghdad is not their socialist mecca. In order to sustain their antagonism to America's intervention to liberate Iraq, they must disconnect their intentions from their actions and their actions from the results.

Neo-communists survive on bad faith. In the past, communists believed in what they did; today, neo-communists justify their deeds by invoking the excuse of good intentions. But isn't this just what all utopians do? If you believe in a future that will redeem mankind, what lie will you not tell, and what crime will you not commit, to make the future happen? This is why progressives have committed every crime in the last half century and lied to all, especially themselves. The communist mantra that "the ends justify the means" is exactly the rationalization that neo-communists use to defend their alliances with reactionary Islamic radicals and fascist regimes. Using good intentions to justify evil deeds is the first requirement of a utopian bad faith.

X

ENVOI

43

Roads Not Taken

SOME TIME AGO, a stranger sent an e-mail to my website that posed two questions I had been thinking about for some time, and seemed therefore uncannily personal. "I was curious," the correspondent said, "if you have ever looked at your political 'apostasy' and wondered whether, if circumstances had been different—if you had not been involved with the Panthers or if your friend had not been murdered by them—you would still be a marxist today. Was your apostasy a result of an inexorable intellectual development, or were you forced into your second thoughts?"

It is a question that everyone gets around to asking himself. If this circumstance had been otherwise, if I had made this choice instead of that one, would my life have been different? It is a question as old as philosophy—the mystery of free will.

Not everyone, of course, experiences such a dramatic turning in his life as I did when the Black Panthers murdered my friend Betty Van Patter twenty-five years ago. But we all have them: roads taken and not taken, decisions that changed our lives, and perhaps ourselves as well. Such changes can be personal as well as intellectual, but each time they occur we face the question once again: Are they essential or only secondary to who and what we are?

From *The Art of Political War and Other Radical Pursuits* (2000). It has been edited for this book.

In my own case, I find it easier to answer this question when it is about my intellectual development, the change in my perception of the political world. I do not know whether the intensity of my ideological transformation or the tone of my politics would have been different if they had not been provoked by an act of brute criminality committed by my political allies. But I am confident that the change would have come. I have many friends and acquaintances who had "second thoughts" similar to mine and found themselves rejecting the ideas and understandings that motivated them when they were young. I have no reason to suppose it would have been different for me.

One of the first pieces I wrote about the episode that changed my political life was an article called, "Why I Am No Longer a Leftist," which appeared in 1986 in the *Village Voice*. It drew explicit parallels between the crime the Panthers had committed and the much larger and more famous crimes for which the left as a whole was responsible that had caused others like me to reconsider their beliefs. As a leftist I had developed habits of mind that caused me to look at "classes" rather than individuals and to be wary of the merely incidental or contingent. Many leftists have written to dismiss my second thoughts, saying, "Why should one mistake matter?" suggesting that what the Panthers did was aberrant and not characteristic of progressives.

This was an attitude that I once would have shared. It was important for me, therefore, to analyze my own case to decide whether it was indeed unique, and therefore whether it should affect my outlook as a whole. In the brief article I wrote for the *Village Voice*, and in much greater detail in my memoir, *Radical Son*, I did just that.

The personal question is not so easy to resolve. There are ingrained patterns to our lives, grooves we move in, which were as evident in mine before the tragedy as they are now. Yet I have indeed changed, and nobody who knew me before this happened has failed to note the difference. I wouldn't want to exaggerate these changes—the gravities of one's character are powerful indeed—but they have occurred. The trauma of this murder and of the betrayals that followed had a profound impact on me. If you ask me about this change, I will tell you that it was the pain that caused it. Pain can force us out of our groove.

Every day following Betty's murder, the pain stabbed at my heart, until eventually it broke me. One day it said: "You cannot stay in this place. If you do, you will die."

The most powerful inertia in our lives is fear. It is what restrains us from acting differently than we have and keeps us in grooves that are familiar and seem safe. When I was caught between the fear and the pain, it was the pain that proved the greater force and conquered my inertia. It was the need to escape spiritual death that caused me to alter my course.

My correspondent's second question was an unexpected one, more perplexing than the first: "Do you ever feel that you are wasting your breath? Do you think that truth will ever matter? No matter what you prove or disprove, in the end the truth will remain in the shadows of what people want to hear and want to believe."

I agree more with this thought than I care to. It is the human wish to be told lies that keeps us where we are. A stoic realism lies at the heart of the conservative viewpoint. It is about accepting limits that are absolute, which the human condition places on human hope.

One could define the left as just the opposite: the inability to come to terms with who we are; the obstinate, compulsive, destructive belief in the fantasy of transformation, in the desperate hope of an earthly redemption.

I have watched my friends, whose ideas created an empire of inhumanity, survive the catastrophe of their schemes and go on to unexpected triumph in the ashes of their defeat. Forced to witness the collapse of everything they once had dreamed and worked to achieve, they have emerged unchastened by their illusions to renew their destructive utopian crusades. The society they declared war on has even rewarded them. Today they are cultural navigators in the nation most responsible for the worldwide collapse of their ideology. I cannot explain this dystopian paradox other than to agree that politics is indeed irrational and socialism a wish as deep as any religious faith. I do not know that the truth must necessarily remain in the shadows. But I am persuaded that a lie grounded in human desire is too powerful for reason to kill.

Notes

Preface

1 Paul Berman, "The Intellectual Life and the Renegade Horowitz," *Village Voice*, August 1986.
2 Jay Nordlinger, *National Review*, April 3, 2002.
3 Salon.com, August 26, 1999.

Introduction

1 *Radical Son*, x.
2 Horowitz interview, April 16, 2002.
3 The other two were *New University Thought* and *Studies on the Left*.
4 An excerpt from the opening chapter is reprinted in "A Generation of Silence," chapter 4.
5 See "New Politics," chapter 5.
6 *Shakespeare: An Existential View*. The chapter on *Much Ado About Nothing* was anthologized in a twentieth century critics series. An excerpt is reprinted in "Skepticism and Romance," chapter 3.
7 See Chapter 4 below.
8 *The Free World Colossus: A Critique of American Foreign Policy in the Cold War*. Under the title, *From Yalta To Vietnam*, it was translated into French, German, Dutch, Swedish, Norwegian, Spanish, Japanese and Hebrew.
9 Berman, op cit. "[Horowitz was] the author of some of [the Left's] best thumbed pages."

10   *Empire & Revolution: A Radical Interpretation of Contemporary History.*
     Published in England under its original title, *Imperialism and Revolution.*

11   *The Fate of Midas and Other Essays.* An excerpt from the essay "Hand-
     Me-Down Marxism and the New Left," his critique of SDS, is reprinted in
     Chapter 6 below.

12   A reprint of Horowitz's introduction to *Isaac Deutscher: The Man and His
     Work.* This was a *festschrift* Horowitz edited after Deutscher's death.

13   Horowitz interview, July 3, 2002.

14   These events are described in the sectons of *Radical Son* called "Panthers"
     and "Private Investigations." See also "Black Murder Inc.," in *Hating Whitey
     & Other Progressive Causes.* An excerpt from Radical Son concerning these
     events is printed in "Questions," Chapter 10 below.

15   *Radical Son,* 271.

16   "A Political Romance," in *Hating Whitey & Other Progressive Causes.* The
     piece was written on request for the "Life" feature of the *New York Times
     Sunday Magazine* and rejected by editor Eric Copage as not being suitable
     to the feature. Shortly thereafter, a similar "second thoughts" piece by an-
     other author, but with the politics reversed appeared in the "Life" section.
     Horowitz had written about leaving the left, the piece the *Times* chose to
     print was about remaining in the left despite its "mistakes."

17   "A Political Romance," in *Hating Whitey & Other Progressive Causes,* 284
     ff.

18   *Radical Son,* 308.

19   Kate Coleman, "The Party's Over," *New Times,* July 10, 1978.

20   "Better Ron Than Red," *Village Voice,* September 30, 1986.

21   Dan Flynn, "Panther Leader Seale Confesses," *FrontPageMage.com,* April
     23, 2002 (http://www.frontpagemag.com/guestcolumnists2002/flynn04-23-
     02.htm).

22   Todd Gitlin, *The Sixties: Years of Hope Days of Rage* (New York: Bantam
     Books, 1993).

23   Kenneth O'Reilly, *Racial Matters: The FBI's Secret File on Black America,
     1960-1972* (New York: Free Press 1991).

24   "Still No Regrets" in *How To Beat the Democrats.*

25   Crossman, Richard, ed. *The God That Failed* (Harper & Row, 1950).

26   This refers only to the fact that Horowitz grew up in a Communist house-
     hold and absorbed its political views. Horowitz was never actually a mem-
     ber of the Communist Party and after the 1956 Khrushchev Report was a
     New Leftist.

27 One of the exceptions is Horowitz's swan song to the past, "Left Illusions," which appeared in *The Nation* in 1979, and is reprinted in this volume as Chapter 11 below. The other exception, an article on foreign relations, appeared in *Mother Jones* in 1980.

28 Despite the dual-authorship attribution—required for contractual reasons—Peter Collier was the author of the Roosevelt volume.

29 *The First Frontier. The Indian Wars & America's Origins: 1607-1776.* The original title, *Promised Land*, was rejected by the publisher, though it more accurately describes the subject of the book.

30 For a comprehensive account of the bloodbath that occurred in Indochina after the Communist takeovers in Indochina, see Stephane Courtois, Nicolas Werth, et al., eds., *The Black Book of Communism: Crimes, Terror, Repression* (Cambridge: Harvard University Press, 1999).

31 "An Open Letter to the 'Anti-War' Demonstrators: Think Twice Before You Bring The War Home," in *How to Beat the Democrats and Other Subversive Ideas*, 157-59.

32 *Radical Son*, 337

33 Ibid.

34 "A Radical's Disenchantment," *The Nation*, December 8, 1979. Reprinted with its original title, "Left Illusions," in chapter 11.

35 Reprinted with its original title, "Goodbye To All That," in *Deconstructing the Left*, available from the Center for the Study of Popular Culture, Los Angeles.

36 Horowitz interview, June 2, 2002.

37 *Destructive Generation*, op. cit.

38 Horowitz interview, June 7, 2002.

39 Norman Podhoretz interview, May 26, 2002.

40 *The Politics of Bad Faith: The Radical Assault on America's Future.*

41 Ibid., 43.

42 An excerpt from "The Road To Nowhere," is reprinted as chapter 14.

43 Ibid., 51

44 Ibid., 56

45 Ibid., 114

46 "The Meaning of Left and Right," *The Politics of Bad Faith*, 139. An excerpt is reprinted in chapter 33.

47 See chapter 31.

48 Horowitz interview, June 10, 2002.

49 Ibid, June 10, 2002.

50   *Hating Whitey: And Other Progressive Causes.*

51   The original title for the book was "Hating White People Is A Politically Correct Idea." It was changed at the request of the publisher.

52   Ibid., 90.

53   Horowitz, "V-Day, 2001," see chapter 30.

54   "Up From Multiculturalism," in *Sex, Lies & Vast Conspiracies*, 1995.

55   *The Art of Political War and Other Radical Pursuits.*

56   *Uncivil Wars: The Controversy Over Reparations for Slavery*, 7. See "Racism and Free Speech," in chapter 18, which is excerpted from the book.

57   The managing editor, Walter Isaacson, took the view that White had only expressed an "opinion," and that he was bound to defend his columnists' freedom of expression even if the opinion was wrong about the facts. This incident is described in detail in the chapter titled "Racial Dialogue" in *The Art of Political War and Other Radical Pursuits*, 93ff.

58   Horowitz did reply in his own publication www.frontpagemag.com in an article titled "Ordeal By Slander," reprinted in *The Art of Political War & Other Radical Pursuits.*

59   "The Ayatollah of Anti-American Hate" in *How to Beat the Democrats and other Subversive Ideas.*

60   "Sinews of Power," *Ramparts*, October 1969, 32-42.

61   Noam Chomsky, *Problems of Knowledge and Freedom* (New York: Pantheon Books), 71

62   Horowitz interview, June 28, 2002. The article is reprinted in this volume, see "Left Illusions," chapter 11.

63   *The Nation*, November 16, 1998.

64   Berman, *Dissent*, Winter 1998, p. 119; Horowitz reply, *Dissent*, Spring 1998, p. 122. Berman was irate because Horowitz had used the passage praising his work from Berman's *Village Voice* attack in an advertisement for *Radical Son.*

65   Norman Podhoretz interview, June 17, 2002.

66   Richard Pipes interview, June 21, 2002.

67   Ramesh Ponnuru, "Radical Son: A Generational Odyssey," *First Things* (August/September 1997): 61-66.

68   Paul Hollander interview, May 13, 2002.

69   David Horowitz, private communication with the author.

70   Hank Holzer interview, July 15, 2002.

Author's Note

1   Richard Posner, *Public Intellectuals* (Cambridge, Mass.: Harvard University Press, 2002). By Posner's standard, I rank number seventy-four among the leading one hundred public intellectuals in America. I am not especially impressed by the methodology behind this conclusion, but it does provide a measure by which to judge the disinterest of politicized "scholars" in the work of conservatives generally and mine in particular.

4 *A Generation of Silence*

1   A twelve-year-old black youth murdered in Mississippi in 1955 for allegedly whistling at a white woman.

2   A reference to the Bay of Pigs invasion and the attempt by the Kennedy Administration to free Cuba from Fidel Castro's rule.

3   This comment was translated into the slogans of the 1964 Free Speech Movement ("Do Not Spindle Or Fold" and "I am not an IBM card)." The book itself, directly influenced Mario Savio, the leader of the "Free Speech Movement" who decided to come to Berkeley after reading it. Cf. *Radical Son*, 113.

4   In San Francisco. The demonstration was broken up, and when the Committee produced a film called "Operation Abolition" attacking the demonstrators and the student left organized a response, these events became one of the seminal moments in the creation of the New Left.

5 *New Politics*

1   This passage was a New Leftist declaration of independence from the albatross of Stalinism. It caused *Student* to be attacked in the Communist Party's newspaper *People's World* by journalist Carl Bloice. Communist Party leader Dorothy Healey wrote me a private letter of support after this attack. Family friends and other members of our Communist community also took a negative view of what I had written. See *Radical Son*, 16-17.

2   Christopher Caudwell, *Studies In A Dying Culture*. Caudwell was an English Stalinist who was killed in the Spanish Civil War. I wrote papers in my courses at Columbia using his Marxist texts.

7   *Solzehnitsyn and the Radical Cause*

1   The writer was Saul Landau.

2   This preposterous view of Soviet achievements was one of the principal delusions of anti-stalinist radicals like myself, including my mentor Isaac Deutscher. See my discussion of this in "The Road to Nowhere" in *The Poliltics of Bad Faith*, included in this volume, chapter 14 below.

8   *The Passion of the Jews*

1   Exodus 23:9.

2   Since the Jews purchased the land, often at exhorbitant prices my description of what took place as "dispossession" is misplaced.

3   For my present views on the Vietnam War, see "My Vietnam Lessons," chapter 12 below.

4   This is an example of how far ideological thinking through abstractions can lead one away from the practical realities of a situation. Israel, a modern liberal democracy obviously is not at all like the regimes in the named countries.

5   This is also far from the reality. The Arabs living in Israel have more rights than the Arabs of any other country in the Middle East.

6   On the other hand, Jews are forbidden even to settle in every Arab state.

7   From the vantage of 2002, in contrast to what I said at the time, this identification of the leftwing sources of a new anti-Semitism looks prescient.

8   This refers to "progressive" currents in the mainline churches.

9   This was disingenuous of me. I wrote the "Black Panther position paper," which was published in *The Black Panther* newspaper (May 25, 1974). In retrospect, although Newton was interested in political ideas, I think he accepted the position paper and had the article published mainly to flatter and thereby control me. For my involvement with Newton and my later views of the Panthers see *Radical Son*, and "Black Murder Inc. in *Hating Whitey & Other Progressive Causes*.

10   Shortly after this was written I discovered through painful experience that the radical's "community of faith" is a fantasy, and a destructive one at that. (See "Questions," chapter 11, and *Radical Son*, 276.) In this way, the essay identifies a pivotal second thought in my ideological odyssey.

9   *Telling It Like It Wasn't*

1   Gitlin, *The Sixties: Years of Hope, Days of Rage.*
2   In the perverse rewriting of the history of this decade, even this slogan has been bowdlerized to "democracy is in the streets," a slogan that I for one never encountered at the time.
3   In the last year of his life and isolation, King surrendered to the pressures of the left and spoke out against the Vietnam War in the hope of recapturing his leftwing constituencies. But he never did.
4   I have described the cynical planning of the riot in *Radical Son*, 165-68.
5   Paul Berman, *A Tale of Two Utopias, The Polticial Journey of the Generation of 1968*, 1996.

10   *Questions*

1   Betty Van Patter was a bookkeeper at the magazine I edited, *Ramparts*, whom I recruited to do the bookkeeping for a Black Panther elementary school I had helped to create. Her murder by the Panthers in December 1974 marked the turning point in my political life. I have described the circumstances of this murder in *Radical Son* and in "Black Murder Inc.," *Hating Whitey and Other Progressive Causes.*
2   Huey Newton, "Minister of Defense" and leader of the Black Panther Party.
3   Chairman of the Black Panther Party.
4   The Panther's K-6 school for their children. I had raised funds to purchase a Baptist Church in East Oakland and turn it into the Oakland Community Learning Center, a tax-exempt institution. I recruited Betty Van Patter to keep the accounts of the school.
5   *A Taste of Power*, 1993. In 1974, at the time of Betty's murder, Elaine Brown was the leader of the Black Panther Party in Oakland, a position she assumed after Huey Newton fled to Cuba to avoid prosecution on a murder charge.
6   This was the name the Panthers gave their enforcers. Cf. *Radical Son*. Also Hugh Pearson, *The Shadow of the Panther*, 1993
7   This is the pseudonym for a Black Panther I worked with, who provided me with information after Betty's murder.
8   A famous Yiddish poet and leftist, liquidated by Stalin.

9   Currently editor of *Tikkun* magazine.

10 Ellen Sparer, a childhood friend had been sodomized and strangled by a black teenager she had befriended. The story of this tragedy and its impact on me is told in "Unnecessary Losses," *The Politics of Bad Faith* and in *Radical Son*.

11 Reprinted in this volume, chapter 8 above.

12 I worked at the Bertrand Russell Peace Foundation in London from 1963 to 1967.

11   *Left Illusions*

1   Baez had written an "Appeal to the Conscience of North Vietnam," to protest the post-peace repression in Vietnam. Even though the ad blamed the United States for its role in the war, she was denounced as a CIA agent by Tom Hayden and Jane Fonda for her efforts (*Radical Son*, 302-03). Later I appeared on a television talk show with Baez to discuss the Vietnam War. During the discussion she peremptorily dismissed my views saying, "I don't trust someone who's had second thoughts." Stern and Radosh had published an article based on FBI files released under the Freedom of Information Act suggesting that Julius Rosenberg was indeed a Soviet spy. There was an uproar in the left and the two of them came under vitriolic attack from their (now) ex-friends. My role in the genesis of this article and the subsequent book by Radosh and Joyce Milton (The Rosenberg File) is described in *Radical Son*, 300-02.

2   *The Nation*'s Richard Falk was one of the outspoken promoters of the idea that the Ayatollah's revolution would be a "liberation" for Iran.

3   This was wishful thinking.

4   Chomsky's extreme adverse reaction to this reference, which is described in *Radical Son* (he wrote me two six-page single-spaced, vituperative and personally abusive letters in response), caused me to begin a reassessment of his character. For my second thoughts on Chomsky, see, "The Ayatollah of Anti-American Hate" in *How To Beat The Democrats & Other Subversive Ideas*.

5   Chomsky of course ignored this obvious criticism and went on to elaborate the same preposterous thesis in his most famous book, *Manufactured Consent*, co-authored with Edward S. Herman.

6   This refers to the Carter Administration's response to the Soviet invasion of Afghanistan.

7　Another, by Gareth Porter, however, did admirably deal with Vietnam's invasion of Cambodia.

8　It never *has* managed to establish this grip.

12　*My Vietnam Lessons*

1　See Chapters 4 and 5 for excerpts from *Student*.

2　That is, until the Gulf War of 1991.

13　*Semper Fidel*

1　The anti-Communist peasant army in Nicaragua.

2　Carlos Franqui, *Family Portrait With Fidel: A Memoir*, 1984.

14　*The Road to Nowhere*

1　This was originally written as a letter to Ralph Miliband, an English Marxist and author of *Parliamentary Socialism* and other works, who was my mentor during the years I was in England, 1963-67.

2　Lee Baxandall.

3　Isaac Deutscher, "The Meaning of De-Stalinization," in *Ironies of History* (Oxford, 1966), 21. Cf. Deutscher, *The Prophet Outcast*, 521: "Through the forcible modernization of the structure of society Stalinism had worked towards its own undoing and had prepared the ground for the return of classical Marxism."

4　Deutscher, "The Meaning of De-Stalinization," 58.

5　Deutscher, "Four Decades of the Revolution," in *Ironies of History*, 58.

6　Ibid.

7　Deutscher, "The Irony of History in Stalinism," in *Ironies of History*.

8　Deutscher, "Problems of Socialist Renewal: East and West," in *Socialist Register*, 1988.

9　Kolakowski, *Main Currents of Marxism*, vol. 1, *The Founders*, chap. 1, "Origins of the Dialectic."

10　Miliband, "Kolakowski's Anti-Marx," op. cit.

11　Zbigniew Brzezinski, *The Grand Failure* (New York, 1989), 237. For facts about Soviet society cited below, see also "Social and Economic Rights in the Soviet Bloc," special issue of *Survey*, August 1987; Richard Pipes, "Gorbachev's Russia: Breakdown or Crackdown?" *Commentary*, March

1990; Walter Laqueur, *The Long Road to Freedom: Russia and Glasnost* (New York, 1989); and *Wall Street Journal*, June 28, 1989.

12   Robert Heilbroner, "After Communism," *The New Yorker*, September 10, 1990.

13   Murray Feshbach and Alfred Friendly, Jr., *Ecocide in the USSR* (New York, 1993).

14   The USSR in *Figures for 1987* (Washington, D.C., 1988), 254.

15   Figures from Brzezinski, op. cit., 36, and George Gilder, "The American 80s," *Commentary*, September 1990. Gorbachev cited by Gilder.

16   Z (Martin Malia), "To the Stalin Mausoleum," *Daedalus*, Winter 1990.

17   A good post-communist example of this perverse mentality is on display in Benjamin Barber's jeremiad *Jihad vs. McWorld* (New York, 1966).

18   Robert Conquest, *The Harvest of Sorrow* (New York, 1986); Mikhail Heller and Aleksandr Nekrich, *Utopia in Power* (New York, 1986).

19   John Gray, "Totalitarianism, Reform and Civil Society," in *Totalitarianism at the Crossroads*, (Bowling Green, Kentucky, 1990).

20   Heller and Nekrich, op. cit., pp. 15-17

21   Isaac Deutscher, *The Prophet Unarmed: Trotsky 1921-1929* (New York, 1965), 1-2. The internal quote refers to a passage from Machiavelli that Deutscher had used as an epigraph to *The Prophet Armed*: "The nature of the people is variable, and whilst it is easy to persuade them, it is difficult to fix them in that persuasion. And thus it is necessary to take such measures that, when they believe no longer, it may be possible to make them believe by force."

22   Aleksandr Solzhenitsyn, *The Gulag Archipelago*, vol. 1, 433ff.

23   Ibid, 435n.

24   Sam Dolgoff, ed., *Bakunin on Anarchy* (New York, 1971), 319; emphasis in original.

25   Ludwig von Mises, *Socialism*.

26   John Gray, op. cit.; Friedrich Hayek, *The Constitution of Liberty; Law, Legislation and Liberty*; and other works. Hayek's discussion of the calculation problem is included in vol. 1 of his collected works: *Socialism and War* (Chicago, 1997).

27   E. P. Thompson, *The Poverty of Theory*.

28   Karl Marx, *Capital* (Moscow, 1961), 80.

29   Ibid., 72.

30   Isaac Deutscher, *The Prophet Outcast*, 510-11.

15 *Memories in Memphis*

1 Jim Sleeper, *Liberal Racism*, New York, 1997; cf. also Shelby Steele, *A Dream Deferred*, NY, 1999.
2 See Noel Ignatiev and John Garvey, *Race Traitor*, NY 1996 "Abolish the White Race By Any Means Necessary,", 90-114; "Aux Armes!", 93-95
3 Ibid., 80
4 The *Chronicle of Higher Education*, April 5, 1999, reported that enrolment of blacks on all the University of California campuses was only twenty-seven students less than in 1997.
5 This is a standard charge made against anyone who challenges the leftwing orthodoxy on race. In fact, only a modest proportion of my writings are about race, and these are the expression of a lifelong interest in civil rights.

16 *Liberals and Race*

1 I use the term "liberal" in its current usage as a matter of convenience. The terms "liberal" and "conservative" like other terms of our political discourse have been imposed on us by the long-running cultural hegemony of the left. This cultural dominance was first established during the Enlightenment, an era that saw the emergence of a modern left. Even the "father of modern conservatism," Edmund Burke, for example, was in fact a political liberal, but has been labeled a conservative. What passes for liberalism in our time, on the other hand, is more often than not a species of leftism or social radicalism. Chris Matthews is not a radical but his liberalism has been significantly affected by radicalism. I have written about this issue in the introduction to *The Politics of Bad Faith*, 1998
2 William Julius Wilson, *The Declining Significance of Race: Blacks and Changing American Institutions*, Chicago 1980.
3 Diane McWhorter, *New York Times*, July 29, 2001.
4 These statistics and the opinion surveys can be found in Abigail and Stephan Thernstroms' *America in Black and White*, 1997.
5 *San Francisco Chronicle*, July 16, 2001.
6 See, for example, John McWhorter, *Losing the Race*, 2000.
7 www.census.gov/hhes/poverty/histpov/hst-pov4.html.
8 Thernstroms, op.cit. p. 233.
9 Stephan and Abigail Thernstrom, op.cit., 226

10   Janet Vandenabelee and Jodi Upton, "Colleges' Retention of Blacks Dis-
     mal," *Detroit News*, July 15, 2001.

17   Ten Reasons Why Reparations Are a Bad Idea

1   That is, after substracting the tax contribution of the African American
     community. The figure for welfare payments alone of somewhere between
     $1.3 trillion and $1.8 trillion in *net* income transfers was calculated for me
     by Robert Rector of the Heritage Foundation.
2   When Lyndon Johnson launched the War on Poverty, he made a speech at
     Howard University, June 4, 1965, explicitly identifying the special burdens
     of black Americans because of the legacies of slavery and segregation. See
     Uncivil Wars: The Controversy Over Reparatons For Slavery, 2001, 122-24.
3   What has been established is that Heming's child was fathered by a Jefferson
     male. Another suspect is Jefferson's brother Randolph. Cf. "The Jefferson-
     Hemings Scholars Commission Report," April 12, 2001. http://
     www.mindspring.com/-tjshcommission/. The commission exonerated
     Jefferson.

18   Racism and Free Speech

1   Hentoff, op.cit.
2   Harvey Silverglate and Alan Kors, *The Shadow University*, op. cit pp. 20-21
3
4   www.IWF.org. Mason Stockstill, "Students Protest Publication of Ad In
     Newspaper. *Daily Bruin Online*, May 21, 2001.
5   Scott B. Wong, "Women's Groups Demand Apology From Bruin For Ad,"
     Daily Bruin Online, May 17, 2001.
6   *Daily Bruin Online*, May 17, 2001.
7   Ibid.
     Hentoff, "Ruffian Fake Radicals," *The Village Voice*, April 24, 2001; cf.
     Michael Kent Curtis, *Free Speech*, University of Kentucky, 2001.
9   The *Spectator* had rejected the reparations ad. Like many such papers, how-
     ever, it had assigned its reporters to cover the story of the controversy,
     while ready access to the Internet allowed anyone interested on campus to
     see the ad itself. The *Spectator*'s refusal to run the ad was ostensibly based
     on a policy of not printing any political ads and after some negotiation it

finally did agree to open the pages of its summer edition to an op-ed column I wrote on the controversy.

10 This aspect of the controversy was covered by the Internet journal *DiversityInc.com*. Candice Choi, "Anti-Reparations Ads Protected Under First Amendment Author Argues," April 6, 2001.

11 In fact, the ad was never submitted to the *Voice*.

12 Jonathan Alter, "Where PC Meets Free Speech," *Newsweek*, April 2, 2001.

13 The woman carrying the sign, along with most of the Spartacists, was white.

14 I have written about the plight of inner city schools and urged Republicans to take up this cause in particular in *The Art of Political War*, Dallas 2000, 52ff. In my plan to "reshape the Republican Party" in the same volume, point 2 of a recommended Republican agenda is: "Give minorities and the poor a shot at the American Dream" (35).

15 Richard Cohen, "Specious Speech," *The Washington Post*, March 22, 2001

16 Thomas Sowell "Reparatons For Slavery?" July 14, 2000 (Creators syndicate) www.townhall.com and Walter Williams "Reparations For Slavery ," July 12, 2000   (Creators syndicate) www.townhall.com. Walter Williams, "Does America Owe Reparations," February 7, 2001. The idea that blacks alive today owed a debt to America was suggested by Sowell years ago.

17 Dorothy Benton-Lewis, MIT debate, April 7, 2001. http://video.C-Span.org:8080/ramgen/ndrive/e040701_slavery.rm.

18 Randall Robinson, *The Debt*, 52.

19 Ibid., 208.

20 Randall Robinson, *Defending The Spirit: A Black Life In America*, 1998, xiii.

21 Ibid., 1

22 *Houston Chronicle*, front papers to *Defending The Sprit*.

23 *Raleigh News and Observer*, ibid.

24 *Booklist*, ibid.

25 Robinson, *Defending The Spirit*, 3.

26 Ibid., 53.

27 Ibid.

28 Op. cit., xiv.

29 *New York Times*, January 22, 1998

30 Robinson, Op. cit. p.3

31 *The World Tomorrow*, May, 1928, in *Zora Neale Hurston*, The Library of America, 1995, 829.
32 Ibid., 827-8.

19   *Conservatives and Race*

1   www.frontpagemag.com
2   There are indeed "Whiteness Studies" curricula in the contemporary academy, but they are predictably about white racism and oppression of blacks.
3   For a more formal argument of this view of American conservatism, see "A Conservative Hope," in *The Politics of Bad Faith*.
4   For a discussion of this, see *The Politics of Bad Faith*, 1998.
5   See chapter 8.

20   *The Intellectual Class War*

1   Peter Berger, *The Capitalist Revolution*, 1986.

21   *Missing Diversity*

1   I was present at the meeting.
2   Cited in Peter Collier and David Horowitz, eds., *Surviving the PC University*, 1993.
3   See chapter 22, "Wake Up America."

22   *Wake Up America*

1   www.Denison.edu/mlk/mlk2002.htm.
2   The speech is available on videotape at C-Span.org. The subject of the talk is also the subject of the first section of *How To Beat The Democrats & Other Subversive Ideas*.
3   *How To Beat The Democrats & Other Subversive Ideas*.
4   A quotation from Euripides.

23   *The Era of Progressive Witch-Hunts*

1   *Portland Oregonian*, November 1, 1992.
2   See "AIDS: Political Origins of An Epidemic," chapter 31. See also "An

American Killing Fields," chapter 32 and "A Radical Holocaust," in *The Politics of Bad Faith*.

3   Harvey Silverglate and Alan Kors, *The Shadow University: The Betrayal of Liberty on America's Campuses*, 1998.

4   I have described some of these experiences in "Visit to a Small College," in *Hating Whitey & Other Radical Pursuits*, 142ff. See also chapters 22 . Further documentation is available from organizations like the National Association of Scholars (www.nas.org) and The Foundation for Individual Rights in Education (www.thefire.org)

5   January 6, 1993. The show was called "Second Thoughts."

6   Tape available through the Center for the Study of Popular Culture, Los Angeles.

7   *The Diversity Hoax*, David Wiener and Marc Berley, eds., The Foundation for Academic Standards and Tradition, 1999. Cf. also the discussion of the politics of the California Civil Rights Initiative and its opposition in *The Politics of Bad Faith*, 8ff.

8   For an account of this campaign, see Ward Connerly, *Creating Equal* (San Francisco: Encounter Books, 2000).

9   Ibid., 63.

10 Ibid., 64.

11 This is really the analog of the charge made by Stalinist prosecutors in the 1930s that any dissent from the party line was "anti-Soviet"—i.e., tantamount to joining the class enemy.

12 Larry Elder, "Campus Gulag," www.frontpagemagazine.com, October 2, 2000.   See Harvey Silverglate and Alan Kors, *The Shadow University*, 1998.

13 Alan Kors, "Thought Reform 101," *Reason*, March 2000.

14 Kors and Silverglate, *The Shadow University*, 194.

15 See my essays on McCarthyism, "McCarthy's Ghost" (with Peter Collier), *Destructive Generation*, 1989 and "Ordeal By Slander," in *The Art of Political War*, 2000. Also "Carl Bernstein's Communist Problem and Mine" in this volume, chapter 24.

16 Among the apologetics for American Communists, the works of Professor Ellen Schrecker stand out for their unrelenting subservience to the party's own line at the time on the issues relevant to the investigations.

17 As someone who attended a university in the 1950s and held the very opinions (Marxist and Communist) that were then under attack, I can attest that the atmosphere was entirely different. Faculties in the McCarthy Era

were generally either hostile to the investigations or uncomfortable with them in a campus setting. Students with views like mine were protected not persecuted by faculty.

18   Silverglate and Kors, especially Part II: "The Assault on Free Speech."

24   Carl Bernstein's Communist Problem

1   In the original article, I used a pseudonym.
2   Cf. the writings of academic historians (and communist apologists) Ellen Schrecker and Robin D.G. Kelley.
3   The best account of the mental world of American Communists is Aileen Kraditor, "*Jimmy Higgins*"—*The Mental World of the American Rank-and-File Communists, 1930-1958*, 1988.
4   Details of this incident are recounted in John Haynes and Harvey Klehr, *Venona: Decoding Soviet Espionage in America*, 1999, 279-80. In the first version of *Radical Son*, I remembered this incident incorrectly. I corrected the details in the paperback version.
5   Carl Bernstein, *Loyalties*, 1991.
6   Emphasis in original.
7   Emphasis in original.
8   These examples are taken from Lewis Coser and Irving Howe, *The American Communist Party: A Critical History*, 1974.
9   *Scoundrel Time*, 1976.

25   Et Tu, John?

1   Haynes and Klehr.
2   For example, Ellen Schrecker, *No Ivory Tower: McCarthyism and the Universities*, 1986 and *Many Are The Crimes*, 1999. The self—identification of the majority of academic historians of Communism with the Communist left is described in John Earl Haynes, "The Cold War Debate Continues "in the *Journal of Cold War Studies*, 2:1 (Winter 2000). Available at www.johnearlhaynes.org.
3   I have written about McCarthyism in the following texts: "The Ghost of McCarthy," in *Destructive Generation*; "Carl Bernstein's Communist Problem and Ours," in *Deconstructing the Left*; and "Ordeal By Slander," in *The Art of Political War and Other Radical Pursuits*, as well as in my autobiography, *Radical Son*.

4 November 11, 1997

5 Drudge had a $10,000 contract with AOL. The judge eventually severed AOL from the case.

6 Mike Kelly was, at the time, editor of *The New Republic*.

7 Huey Newton, the leader of the Black Panthers was tried and convicted of killing a California Highway patrolman. He was released after three and a half years on a technicality. Los Siete was a group of Hispanic gang bangers who had killed a policeman in San Francisco. When Peter Collier and I were editors of *Ramparts* magazine we ran a cover story defending them. They were acquitted but several were later convicted of other violent crimes.

8 February 14, 1998.

9 February 14, 1998.

10 These attacks are described in *Radical Son*, 1997.

11 The "Second Thoughts Conference" was held in Washington, DC, in October 1987. Peter and I had organized a gathering of ex-New Left radicals, including several who were now Democrats and who had been disenchanted with the destructive activities and anti-American passions of our former comrades. It was our first public "coming out" as a group, and we were apprehensive about having our ideas and reflections misrepresented. These concerns proved accurate. After interviewing us on the eve of the conference, Blumenthal filed a malicious and error-filled account of our agendas, which effectively shut us off from the mainstream of the political culture for more than a decade. Blumenthal allowed none of the complexity of our thoughts or our event to filter through his partisanship.

Blumenthal was not alone. There were parallel and even more overtly partisan attacks by Christopher Hitchens, Eric Alterman, Alexander Cockburn, and Todd Gitlin, who attended the event. These gentlemen—along with Blumenthal—had gathered at a dinner party at Hitchens's house prior to the event to plot their journalistic sabotage of our conference. I learned this final detail from Hitchens sixteen years later, in May 2003.

12 Rick Hertzberg, now an editor at *The New Yorker*, and the writer Paul Berman, a professor at the New School for Social Research.

13 Unlike Blumenthal, Sipple lost his job over the accusation.

26 *Michael Lind and the Right-Wing Cabal*

1 In 2001, Steel became chairman.

27 *Defending Christopher Hitchens*

1   I spoke—or wrote—too soon. Following the attack on the World Trade Center on September 11, 2001, Christopher began a political odyssey that did resemble those of second thoughts before him.

29 *From Red to Green*

1   Gerhart Niemeyer, *Between Nothingness and Paradise*, 1998.

30 *V-Day, 2001*

1   *USA Today*, Feburary 8, 2001.

33 *The Meaning of Left and Right*

1   F.A. Hayek, *The Fatal Conceit: The Errors of Socialism*, Chicago, 1988, 6.
2   Hayek, *The Mirage of Social Justice*, 133-34; cf. Hayek, *The Fatal Conceit*, chap.1.
3   Lawrence Fuchs, cited in Arthur M. Schlesinger Jr., *The Disuniting of America*, Tennessee., 1991, 79.

35 *How to Beat the Democrats*

1   "The VNS exit poll showed Gore winning majorities of the vote on all the issues he emphasized as part of his populist approach; indeed, among voters who said issues, rather than 'qualities,' mattered most, Gore ran up a healthy lead of 55 to 40 percent." Ruy Teixeira, "Lessons for Next Time," *The American Prospect*, December 18, 2000.
2   Even speaking about the "haves" and the "have nots" provides a good example of how the left rigs the game through its control of the language we use. Seventy percent of American millionaires are self-made. It would be more accurate to speak of "the "dos" and the "do nots", the "cans" and the "cannots," the "wills" and the "will nots." But that would be blaming the "victims."
3   It was the same with their lawsuits against tobacco companies that lined the pockets of the trial lawyers but failed to reduce teenage smoking. In the eyes of Democrats it was a good faith effort to get Americans to do the

right thing, and it filled the coffers of the forces that do good (the Demo-crats).

4 Remember Reagan. Reagan resisted the Soviet Union and called it an "evil empire"—to liberals' everlasting consternation and dismay—and became a hero to the Soviet people when the Wall finally came down.

5 "Social promotion" is a scheme invented by progressives, in the name of "self-esteem," to deceive students—mainly poor, black and Hispanic—into believing that they are learning something when they are not. Instead of giving them "F's" and holding them back, progressive "educators" all over the country promote failing students until they graduate. It's only after graduation, when they go into the economy to look for a job and start a life that they discover they are functional illiterates and have been cheated of their opportunity.

6 *Los Angeles Times*, January 20, 2000.

7 "Democratic Presidential Candidates Debate at Harlem's Apollo Theater," CNN, February, 21, 2000.

36 *Know Your Enemy*

1 www.memri.org, Special Dispatch No. 388. June 12, 2002.

37 *Port Huron and the War on Terror*

1 *Student*, 1962. See chapters 4 and 5 in this volume.

2 E.g., James E. Miller, *Democracy Is In The Streets*, 1988.

3 The League for Industrial Democracy, which was the parent organization of SDS.

4 Of course, sophisticated New Leftists told themselves that this was "criti-cal" support, meaning that they understood that Cuba and North Viet-nam were repressive dictatorships. They justified this support by ascribing the repression to a "necessity" imposed by the anti-communism of the West.

38 *Clinton's Pardonned Bombers*

1 *NewYork Times*, April 20, 2001

2 This story has been ably told in John Castellucci, *The Big Dance: The Un-told Story of Kathy Boudin and the Terrorist Family that Committed the Brinks' Robbery Murders*, 1986.

3   This and other details in Barbara Olson, *The Final Days, The Last, Desper-
     ate Abuses of Power by the Clinton White House*, 2001, 21-23.

39   *Why Israel Is the Victim*

1   These and most of the other facts in this article are available in Mitchell
     G. Bard, *Myths and Facts: A Guide to the Arab-Israeli Conflict* which is
     online at www.JewishVirtualLibrary.org
2   David Remnick, "In A Dark Time," *New Yorker*, March 18, 2002, 51; *The
     Case Against Arafat: The Campaign By Yasir Arafat and the Palestinian Au-
     thority to Destroy Israel*, introduction by Ambassador Jeanne Kirkpatrick,
     published by the Zionist Organization of America, 2002, 5

40   *Can There Be a Decent Left?*

1   I have, of course, written extensively about this myself in *Radical Son* and
     The Politics of Bad Faith.

41   *Alienation in a Time of War*

1   Robert Fogel and Stanley Engerman, *Time On The Cross: The Economics of
     American Negro Slavery*, Boston 1974, 20ff.
2   Frederick Douglass, "The Constitution of the United States: Is It Pro-
     Slavery or Anti-Slavery?", 1860. Emphasis added.
3   Hertzberg means—but does not say—in the South.

42   *Neo-Communism*

1   *The Black Panther* August 8, 1970:19. The declaration is dated July 14, 1970.
2   "Neo-Communism: The Forty Years War," frontpagemag.com, April 22,
     2003.
3   Argiris Malapanis, UCLA Symposium, "LA Symposium Debates Che and
     the Cuban Revolution," *The Militant*, November 24, 1997.
4   From: Maurice Zeitlin Sent: Tuesday, April 22, 2003 9:41 PM. To: Eliza-
     beth Ruiz. Subject: David Horowitz
5   Thomas Bartlett, "The Most Hated Professor in America," *Chronicle of
     Higher Education*, April 18, 2003. http://chronicle.com/weekly/v49/i32/
     32a05601.htm.
6   Ibid.

Bibliography

BOOKS

Student: The Political Activities of the Berkeley Students, Ballantine, 1962
The Free World Colossus, Hill & Wang, 1965
Shakespeare: An Existential View, Hill & Wang, 1965
Empire and Revolution: A Radical Interpretation of Contemporary History, Random House, 1969
The Fate of Midas and Other Essays, Ramparts Press, 1973
The First Frontier: The Indian Wars and America's Origins, 1607-1776, Simon & Schuster, 1978
Radical Son: A Generational Odyssey, Free Press, 1997
The Politics of Bad Faith: The Radical Assault On America's Future, Free Press, 1998
Sex, Lies Vast Conspiracies, Second Thoughts Books, 1998
Hating Whitey: And Other Progressive Causes, Spence, 1999
The Art of Political War And Other Radical Pursuits, Spence, 2000
Uncivil Wars: The Controversy Over Reparations for Slavery, Encounter, 2001
How to Beat the Democrats and Other Subversive Ideas, Spence, 2002

WITH PETER COLLIER

The Rockefellers: An American Dynasty, Holt, Rinehart and Wilson, 1976
The Kennedys: An American Drama, Summit Books, 1984
The Fords: An American Epic, Summit Books, 1987

Destructive Generation: Second Thoughts about the Sixties, Summit Books, 1989
Deconstructing the Left: From Vietnam to the Persian Gulf, Second Thoughts Books 1991

EDITED COLLECTIONS

Containment and Revolution, Beacon Press, 1967
Marx and Modern Economics, Monthly Review Press, 1968
Corporations and the Cold War, Monthly Review Press, 1969
Isaac Deutscher: The Man and His Work, Macdonald & Co., 1971
Radical Sociology: An Introduction, Canfield Press, 1971
Counterculture and Revolution, Random House, (with Craig Pyes), 1972
Second Thoughts: Former Radicals Look Back at the Sixties, Madison Books, (with Peter Collier) 1989
Second Thoughts about Race in America, Madison Books, (with Peter Collier), 1991
Surviving the PC University: the Best of Heterodoxy, (with Peter Collier) Second Thoughts Books, 1993
The Heterodoxy Handbook: How to Survive the PC Campus, Regnery, (with Peter Collier), 1994
Public Broadcasting and the Public Trust, (with Laurence Jarvik) Center for the Study of Popular Culture, 1995
The Race Card: White Guilt, Black Resentment, and the Assault on Truth and Justice, Prima Publications, (with Peter Collier), 1997
Immigration National Security Post 9-11, Center for the Study of Popular Culture, 2002
The Hate-America Left, Center for the Study of Popular Culture, 2003

PAMPHLETS

The Universities and the Ruling Class: How Wealth Puts Knowledge in Its Pocket, Bay Area Radical Education Project, 1969
Sinews of Empire, New England Free Press, 1970
My Vietnam Lessons, Accuracy in Media, 1985
The "Peace" Movement, Second Thoughts Project, 1991
The Feminist Assault on the Military, Center for the Study of Popular Culture, 1992
Queer Revolution: The Last Stage Of Radicalism, Center for the Study of Popular Culture, 1992

Liberal Racism: The College Student's Common-Sense Guide to Radical Ideology and How to Fight It, Center for the Study of Popular Culture, 1994

It's A War, Stupid! (with Peter Collier) Center for the Study of Popular Culture, 1996

Marx's Manifesto: 150 Years of Evil, Center for the Study of Popular Culture, 1998

Why I'm Not A Liberal, Center for the Study of Popular Culture, 1998

The Art of Political War: How Republicans Can Fight to Win, Committee for a Non-Left Majority, 1999

Who's Responsible for America's Security Crisis? Center for the Study of Popular Culture, 1999

The Death of the Civil Rights Movement, Center for the Study of Popular Culture, 2000

Hillary Clinton And The Racial Left, Center for the Study of Popular Culture, 2000

The War Room: A Pocket Guide to Victory, PoliticalWar.com 2000

Progressive Crime Wave, Center for the Study of Popular Culture, 2001

The Ayatollah of Anti-American Hate, Center for the Study of Popular Culture, 2001

How the Left Undermined America's Security, Center for the Study of Popular Culture, 2002

How To Beat The Democrats: A Primer For Republicans, PoliticalWar.com, 2001

Noam Chomsky's Jihad Against America (with Ronald Radosh), Center for the Study of Popular Culture, 2001

Progressive Crime Wave, Center for the Study of Popular Culture, 2001

Think Twice… Before You Bring the War Home, Center for the Study of Popular Culture, 2001

Know Your Enemy: America's War Against Radical Islam At Home And Abroad, Center for the Study of Popular Culture, 2002

Political Bias In America's Universities, Center for the Study of Popular Culture, 2002

Reparations and Racial Double Standards, Center for the Study of Popular Culture, 2002

Why Israel Is The Victim In The Middle East, Center for the Study of Popular Culture, 2002

Who Is the "Peace Movement," Center for the Study of Popular Culture, 2003

MAGAZINE ARTICLES 1962–2003

1962–1965

"The Question About Meaning," *Root and Branch*, Winter 1962

"La Dolce Vita," *Root and Branch*, Winter 1962

Correspondence: Reply to Mr. Kofsky, *Monthly Review*, December 1962

"The Roots of Alienation—A Critique of the Soviet Draft Program," *Root and Branch*, Spring 1963

"Bob Dylan—Commodity or Genius," *Peace News* (date unknown)

"The Alliance for Progress" *The Socialist Register*, Monthly Review Press, 1964

"Victims of Anomie," *The Nation*, June 15, 1964

"Pursuit of Victory," *Views*, Autumn 1964

"Review: The Technological Society," *Monthly Review*, June 1965

"Hiroshima and the Cold War," *Liberation*, September 1965

"Monopoly Capital," *Liberation*, November 1966

"Fifty Years of Cold War," *Liberation*, December 1966

"Revisionist Tales of Negotiations With the Communists," *Ramparts Magazine*, June 29, 1968

"Big Brother as a Holding Company," (with David Kolodny), *Ramparts Magazine*, November 30, 1968

"Proving Poverty Pays," (with David Kolodny) *Ramparts Magazine*, December 14, 1968

"Foundations: Charity Begins at Home," *Ramparts Magazine*, April 1969

"Billion Dollar Brains: How Wealth Puts Knowledge in Its Pocket," *Ramparts Magazine*, May 1969

"Behind the Sino/Soviet Dispute," *Ramparts Magazine*, June 1969

"Rocky Takes a Trip," *Ramparts Magazine*, August 1969

"Hand-me-down Marxism and the New Left," *Ramparts Magazine*, September 1969

"Sinews of Empire," *Ramparts Magazine*, October 1969

1970–1979

"Bertrand Russell: The Final Passion," *Ramparts Magazine*, April 1970

"Social Science or Ideology?" *Social Policy*, September/October 1970

"Marxism and Its Place in Economic Science," *Berkeley Journal of Sociology*, 1971/1972,

"Revolutionary Karma vs. Revolutionary Politics," *Ramparts Magazine*, March 1971

"Politics and Knowledge: An Unorthodox History of Modern China Studies," *Bulletin of Concerned Asian Scholars*, Summer-Fall 1971

"The Making of America's China Policy," *Ramparts Magazine*, October 1971

"The China Scholars and U.S. Intelligence," *Ramparts Magazine*, February 1972

"Asian Tragedy; Purge in China," *Ramparts Magazine*, March 1972

"The China Question and the American Left," *Ramparts Magazine*, July 1972

"Nixon's Vietnam Strategy," *Ramparts Magazine*, August 1972

"Cruel Reconciliation," *Ramparts Magazine*, November 1972

"U.S. Foreign Policy 1957-1970" *Encyclopedia Britannica*, 1972

"Historians and the Cold War: The Battle Over America's Image," *Ramparts Magazine*, August-September 1973

"Triumph of Arrogance," *The Center Magazine*, Center for the Study of Democratic Institutions, Vol VII, No. 1, January/February 1974

"Solzhenitsyn and the Radical Cause," *Ramparts Magazine*, June 1974

"Fascism and Other Nightmares," *Ramparts Magazine*, September 1974

"The Passion of the Jews," *Ramparts Magazine*, October 1974

"To Be Young, Rich and Unhappy in America," *Esquire*, February 1976

"A Radical's Disenchantment," *The Nation*, December 8, 1979

1980-1989

"The 1980 Guide to Both Cold Wars," *Mother Jones*, May 1980

"Doing It: The inside Story of the Rise and Fall of the Weather Underground," (with Peter Collier) *Rolling Stone*, September 30, 1982

"The First Hollywood President," (with Peter Collier) *California Magazine*, June 1984

"Why the Pain Hasn't Ended for Ethel's Family," (with Peter Collier), *Ladies' Home Journal*, September 1984

"Nicaragua: A Speech to My Former Comrades on the Left," *Commentary*, June 1986

"Another 'Low Dishonest Decade' on the Left, *Commentary*, January 1987

Letters, *Commentary*, May 1987

Letters, *Commentary*, July 1987

"Cristina," (with Peter Collier) *Good Housekeeping*, October 1987

"McCarthyism: The Last Refuge of the Left," *Commentary*, January 1988

Letters, *Commentary*, April 1988

"Dartmouth Dignifies the Hate-Filled Angela Davis," *Human Events*, March 1989

'Panthers, Contras, and Other Wars: 'Destructive Generation': an exchange," *New Republic*, June 26, 1989

"Still Taking the Fifth," *Commentary*, July 1989

"Noam Chomsky's Paranoid Polemics Fuel Political Left," *Human Events*, July 1989

"Slouching Towards Berkeley: Socialism In One City," (with Peter Collier) *Public Interest*, Winter 1989

"The Devastating Legacy Of America's Liberal-Left," *Human Events*, December 1989

1990-1999

"Making the Green One Red: Environmental Politics," *National Review*, March 19, 1990

"Responses," *Tikkun*, November-December 1990

"The Radical Paradigm and the New Racism," *First Things*, November 1990

"Socialism: Guilty as Charged," *Commentary*, December 1990

Correspondence, *First Things*, February 1991

"Coalition Against the U.S.," *National Review*, February 25, 1991

"Review: Encyclopedia of the American Left," *First Things*, March 1991

"Conservative Questions," *National Review*, May 13, 1991

"Back to Our Roots," *National Review*, May 13, 1991

"The Politics of Public Television," *Commentary*, December 1991

"Utopian Passions," *First Things*, April 1992

"PC Cover-Up," (with Peter Collier), *Heterodoxy*, April 1992

"First Homo-eroticism, Then Homo-phobia, and Now...Homo-McCarthyism," *Heterodoxy*, April 1992

"The Ten Worst College Administrators," (with Peter Collier), *Heterodoxy*, April 1992

"Socialism by Any Other Name," *National Review*, April 13, 1992

"PC Riot," (with Peter Collier), *Heterodoxy*, May 1992

"The Ten Wackiest Feminists On Campus," (with Peter Collier), *Heterodoxy*, May 1992

"Anglophobia," *National Review*, July 20, 1992

"Shaping America's Values Debate," *Heritage Foundation Reports*, September 15, 1992,

"Ms. America Goes to Battle," *National Review*, October 5, 1992

"Are We Conservatives? The Paradox of American Conservatism," *Heritage Foundation Reports*, December 15, 1992

"The Queer Fellows," *The American Spectator*, January 1993

"The Liberal Inheritance," *Heterodoxy*, January 1993

"Gays March On Pentagon," *Heterodoxy*, February 1993

"Tailhook Witch-Hunt," *Heterodoxy*, October 1993

"MacKinnon Lunacy," *Heterodoxy*, November 1993

"The Decline of Academic Discourse: The MLA Fiasco," *Heterodoxy*, January 1994

"Interview with Michael Moriarty," *The Defender*, July 1994

"Treason of the Clerks," (with Peter Collier), *Heterodoxy*, September 1994

"Funding the Left," in Jarvik, London, Cooper (eds): *The National Endowments: A Critical Symposium*, Second Thoughts Books, 1995

"Panther Movie Glamorizes Violent Black Militants," *Human Events*, June 2, 1995

"The Race Card," (with Peter Collier) *Heterodoxy*, October 1995

"Leftwing Fascism and the American Dream," *William Mitchell Law Review*, Vol 22, No. 2, 1996

"Hooked on Institutional Racism," *Heterodoxy*, April 1996

"Clarence Page's Race Problem, And Mine," *Heterodoxy*, May/June 1996

"Today's Culture Wars: A Message to Our Friends," *Center News*, Summer 1996

"Political Cross-Dresser," *Heterodoxy*, September 1996

"Queer Revolution," *The Material Queer: a LesBiGay Cultural Studies Reader*, Westview Press, (Contributor), 1996

"It's a War, Stupid!" *Heterodoxy*, November 1996

"Treason of the Heart,' *Heterodoxy*, January/February 1997

"Why I'm Not a Liberal," Center News, Spring 1997

"Scenes from the '60s: One Radical's Story, *American Enterprise*, May-June, 1997

"Many Thousands Gone," *Heterodoxy*, June 1997

"Johnnie's Other O.J.," *Heterodoxy*, September 1997

"Up from Multiculturalism," *Heterodoxy*, January 1998

"Karl Marx at the L.A. Times," *Heterodoxy*, March 1998

"150 Years of Evil," *Heterodoxy*, April 1998

"The Clinton Scandal: A Feminist Titanic," *Center News*, Winter 1998

"An Intellectual Omerta: Marginalizing Conservative Ideas," *Heterodoxy*, November 1998

"I, Rigoberta Menchu, Liar," *Heterodoxy*, December 1998/January 1999

"Telling the Republican Story," *Rising Tide*, Spring 1999

"The Last Survivor of Camelot," *Redbook*, October 1999

"What Would They Think of the 90s?" *American Enterprise*, November 1999

2000–2003

Newspaper and Internet articles through 2003 are archived at www.frontpagemag.com

Index

473

A NOTE ON THE AUTHORS

DAVID HOROWITZ, a founder of the New Left move-
ment in the 1960s, is the nationally known author of
Radical Son and *Hating Whitey*. He is president of the
Center for the Study of Popular Culture.

JAMIE GLAZOV is the managing editor of *FrontPage*
magazine. He holds a PH.D. in history with a specialty
in Soviet Studies and is the author of *Canadian Policy
Toward Khrushchev's Soviet Union* (McGill-Queens
University Press, 2002).

This book was designed and set into type
by Mitchell S. Muncy,
with cover art by Stephen J. Ott,
and printed and bound
by Bang Printing,
Brainerd, Minnesota.

The text face is Adobe Caslon,
designed by Carol Twombly,
based on faces cut by William Caslon, London, in the 1730s,
and issued in digital form by Adobe Systems,
Mountain View, California, in 1989.

The index is by IndExpert,
Fort Worth, Texas.

The paper is acid-free and is of archival quality.

35